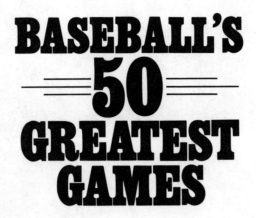

BASEBALL'S
50
GREATEST
GAMES

Hank Aaron hits #714 on the way to record-breaking #715.

BASEBALL'S 50 GREATEST GAMES

Bert Randolph Sugar

Exeter Books

NEW YORK

TO MY WIFE, SUZY, WITHOUT WHOSE HELP THIS BOOK
WOULD HAVE BEEN FINISHED FOUR MONTHS EARLIER

Produced by Wieser & Wieser, Inc.,
118 East 25th Street, New York, NY 10010

Copyright © 1986 by Bert Randolph Sugar
All rights reserved.

First published in the U.S.A., 1986
by Exeter Books.
Distributed by Bookthrift

Exeter is a trademark of Bookthrift
Marketing, Inc.
Bookthrift is a registered trade mark of
Bookthrift Marketing, Inc.
New York, New York.

ISBN 0-671-08346-5

Designed by Combined Books.
Printed in the United States of America.

PHOTO CREDITS:
Focus on Sports, 222 East 46th Street, NY 10017
T.C.M.A. Ltd., 220 12th Avenue, NY 10001
Worldwide Photos, Inc., 50 Rockefeller Plaza, NY 10020

Contents

Introduction

The scene is a familiar one: There, seated at the bar of their favorite watering hole, are several scholars of the religion known as baseball, all arguing, like contemplatives of olde, the mysteries of their cult. Only, whereas religious contemplatives of yore argued over minor points of esoterica, like the number of angels on the heads of pins and other such wonderfulnesses, these modern day disturbers of the peace are throwing around words like "Great"— as in "Greatest Game," "Greatest Moment," "Greatest Performance" and all manner of "Great," large and small—and then hurrying to support their contention with mental crayon portraits, the bar not allowing anything sharper to be used on the premises.

It was one night earlier this year when, in search of the similarly sick and afflicted, I found myself standing at just such a bar crooking my elbow in the companionship of three believers of the first water. And scotch as well. One of the three, a devout Philadelphia Phillies' phanatic, employed the ism "Great" to describe anything and everything his idols had ever done, including merely taking the field to do battle. The second, his temple of worship Fenway Park, began to read off his doctrines of faith, holding that the only games that could truly be judged worthy of the word "Great" *had* to be those, and only those, that concerned the Boston Red Sox. And the Third, a New York Yankee zealot, down to his Yankee-yuppie pinstripes, started Godding it up, sermonizing that the two beliefs, "Great" and "Yankees," were one and the same, no imitators need apply.

By now I had begun to feel like a fly in a scotch and soda: Attracting attention and comment, but not enjoying it. And figuring I had little to contribute to the babel then going on 'round my hat— after all, as a lifelong Washington Senators' fan, how could I in good conscience offer up anything in the name of "Greatness" that had to do with a team whose double-play combination of my youth had been Cass Michaels-to-Sam Dente-to the parking lot?— I asked permission to be excused from the goings-on. Permission granted, not that they'd miss me anyway. As I took the most circuitous route home, I let their words slowly marinate, along with everything else. What exactly, I wondered, was "Greatness"? How did one define it? And what made a game "Great"?

After sleeping on the problems at hand and head, I decided to pursue my objectives the next morn. First I took Noah Webster's imposing tome off my shelves, blew the accumulated dust of several years off its jacket and looked up the word "Great." There it was, defined as an adjective meaning such things as "Significant," "Important," "Remarkable," "Outstanding," and other such things that all sounded better in advertisements than in helping me with my problem. No help there.

A few days later I chanced to find myself in the company of a number of sportswriters who had seen thousands of games between them, many of them as undistinguished as indistinguishable. In the hopes that some might have shone through in the record books of their minds, I asked them: What would you consider to be five of the "Greatest" games in baseball history?

The four elder phrase-distillers I inveigled into sharing my company and my quandry were Maury Allen, Bob Creamer, Keith Morris and Harold Rosenthal, a foursome who between them had seen as many games as the grass at Yankee Stadium, but who were far less greener. Now, normally, whenever I hear someone utter those magic words, "I remember . . . ," I reach for my coat. However, these four, dropping the phrase into their conversation as one would an olive into a martini, garnished their "Great" games list with reminiscences that were both pleasing to the ear and to the memory. The games they mentioned went back as far as 1941 (Owen's dropped third strike) through 1947 (Lavagetto's break-up of Bevens' no-hitter) and 1951 (Thomson's "Shot Heard 'Round the World") and up through 1956 (Larsen's Perfect Game), with a couple of more current games mentioned like Fisk's Home Run (1975) and Bucky Dent's Home Run (1978). But, with rare exceptions—such as Creamer's naming the last game of the 1912 Series and the first of the '23 Series—most of the games contributed to the list were directly attributable to memory.

I had the beginning of an idea for a book and the bare-bones beginning of a menu of "Greatest" games as well. But that was all. Still no definition. Oh sure, some people had given meaning to the word "Greatest," including my friend Thomas Hauser who had written a column in which he called the July 31, 1953, game between the New York Yankees and the St. Louis Browns quote The Greatest Game Ever Played unquote. The reason being, as Hauser wrote: "It was the first Major League Baseball game I ever attended." That was somewhat similar to a concert audience which breaks into applause when a performer who has nothing to do with a song introduces it from the stage, applauding themselves for recognizing the song, nothing more. And most, Hauser included, tend to applaud those games they recognize more than those they don't.

For millions like Hauser, who have become fans of the National Pastime over the past thirty years or less, those ancients who played before their memory are somewhat discredited: Ruth becomes boiler-plate, Cobb totters, and the deeds of Mathewson and Johnson have been copyrighted by tens of thousands of lesser lights. But they are no more guilty of filing "Great" games under "M" for memory or "S" for sentiment than those graybeards who have propped themselves up with the yellowing newsclips of their youth and face the frightening specter of falling out of their chairs whenever they hear that anything "Great" happened after 1930.

Having now listened to men of old talk about the good ol' days as if the clock had never moved and younger men whose world started but a few years ago—and to whom this era will be their "good ol' days" in just a decade—reminisce about the day before yesterday, it became apparent that whatever the age of the fan, he was forever entombed in a prolonged boyhood, all games, great and small, their link with youth. I therefore found myself cherishing the memories of all, young and old alike, without actually embracing them; Applauding their recognition of "Great" games of their generation, but accepting them along generational fault lines.

Burdened with both schools of thought and carrying their

perceptions as carefully on my shoulders as I would twin buckets of scotch and soda, I hunkered down at O'Reilly's Pub, where baseball is spoken fluently, even if the patrons who speak it don't. And there, amidst a barful of napkins with something that resembled writing on them, it hit me what both had been saying: A "Great" Game was one they had either been at or wished they had been at!

Who amongst us, courtesy of a time warp, would not have liked to have been in attendance at the game where Ruth either did or did not "Call" his shot? Merkle miss his base? Aaron hit his homer? Rose make his hit? Larsen pitch his Perfect Game? Etc., etc., etc.

And so I started scribbling down those games, less under the amorphous and misleading title "Greatest," than those games I wished I had been at when something-or-other occurred that lifted the game out of the ordinary context of happenings by one magic moment of drama. Not games picked on the basis of nostalgia—which is a strong stream of water which turned on us through our mental hose tends to disturb our present and drown out our perceptive—or on the basis of regional loutishness. But games that I wished I were at, pure and simply, games indelibly imprinted in a sort of mental Hall of Fame.

As my pile of O'Reilly's bar napkins grew, containing "Great" games I wish I could have attended—Vander Meer's second no-hitter here, Ted Williams' home run in the 1941 All-Star Game there, and seventh games of World Series everywhere—thoughts, like little sprigs of mistletoe on a dead tree, began to decorate my mind. Had anyone ever put together such a list before?, I wondered. And then it occurred to me, in 1976, for the One Hudredth Anniversary—not to be confused with the 100th Anniversary in 1939 nor the 100th Anniversary in 1969—baseball had honored its five "Most Memorable Moments" in a vote by 2391 writers from amongst 72 nominees. And that very same year, the Society for American Baseball Research had also put together a grouping, calling theirs the "Outstanding Game," and voted on by 108 members of SABR. Why not peek at them and see what they came up with?, I muttered aloud, to no one in particular.

For those who like comparing lists, here are those two polls:

"Baseball's Most Memorable Moments"—1976 Poll Conducted by Baseball

1. Hank Aaron's 715th Home Run, 1974
2. Bobby Thomson's "Shot Heard Round the World," 1951
3. Don Larsen's Perfect Game, 1956
4. Babe Ruth's "Called Shot," 1932 World Series
5. Joe DiMaggio's Hit Streak Stopped, 1941

"Outstanding Game"
Society for American Baseball Research, 1976 Poll

1. Bobby Thomson's "Shot Heard Round the World"
2. Don Larsen's Perfect Game
3. Double No-Hit Game, 1917
4. 26-Inning Game, 1920
5. Bill Mazeroski's Home Run, 1960 World Series
6. Harvey Haddix's "Perfect Game"
7. 1934 All-Star Game, Hubbell's Five-Straight Strike Outs
8. Carlton Fisk's Home, 1975
9. 1929 A's-Cubs World Series, 10-Run Inning
10. Addie Joss' Perfect Game, 1908
11. Play-Off of Merkel "Boner" Game, 1908
12. Bill Wambsganss' Unassisted Triple Play, 1920 World Series
13. Gabby Hartnett's "Home in the Gloaming", 1938
14. Ted Williams' Home Run, 1941 All-Star Game
15. (Tie)
    Detroit's 1–0 Win, August 17, 1882, in 18-Inning Game
    7th Game, 1924 World Series, Winning Run Scored on Ball Hitting Peeble Marichal-Spahn, 16-Inning Pitching Duel, July 2, 1963
18. Cleveland-Boston Play-Off Game, 1948
19. Jack Chesbro's Wild Pitch, Boston vs. New York, 1904
20. Last Game, 1950 Season, Brooklyn vs. Phillies
21. Jackie Robinson's Catch, 14-Inning Game, September 30, 1951
22. 7th Game, 1912 World Series, Boston vs. New York Giants, Snodgrass Muff
23. Bob Gibson's 17 Strike-Out Game, 1968 World Series
24. (Tie)
    First Perfect Game, Lee Richmond, June 12, 1880
    Johnny Vander Meer's Second No-Hitter, 1938
    Jackie Robinson's First Major League Game, 1947

What they and other lists put together by experts and so-called experts proved was that no two experts have ever or will ever see eye-to-eye on such a subjective rating as "Greatest Games." However, I decided now to put my finger in the already overflowing pot and begin ascribing varying degrees of greatness to those games I had already identified as belonging to the specie "Greatest Games." It became a problem articulated best by the late sportswriter Al Buck, who asked, "If you grow a near-perfect peach, then produce a similar fruit, can you honestly say one is better than the other?" But, searching both my memory and the bottom of my glass, I began compiling what I came to call my "Rubiyat of the Scotch-and-Soda," a list of games in descending order of "Greatness" that was to change as often as my drink.

Next there was research to do for each of the 50 on the list. For no game ever happened in a vacuum, baseball being a continuum, a constant greening of itself, if you will. And every one of my "50 Greatest Games" possessed not only an undercurrent of drama and an unfolding of personalities that began well before the game—and in some instances continued after the game—but had something to recommend it, to distinguish it.

If, has been said, a writer is only as important as the story he has to tell, then the stories behind these "50 Greatest Games" have been told by some of the most important writers in the history of sportswriting, all of whom gave great story. And like Dimitri Tiomkin, who accepted the Academy Award for his film score of the movie High Noon in 1952 by giving "Thanks to Tchaikovsky, Shostakovich, and Prokofiev," his cultural forebears, I would like to give "Thanks" to mine, whose works I read twice in the name of research rather than once in the name of plagarism:

Franklin P. Adams, Nelson Algren, Lee Allen, Maury Allen, Dave Anderson, Roger Angell, Bugs Baer, Bob Broeg, Heywood Broun, Warren Brown, Jimmy Cannon, John P. Carmichael, Raymond Chandler, Murray Chass, Ellery Clerk, Jr., Bill Corum, Peter Coutros, Robert Creamer, Harry Cross, Arthur Caley, Dan Daniel, James P. Dawson, Jordan Deutsch, Dave Distel, John Drebinger, Charles Dryden, Charles Einstein, James T. Farrell, Stanley Frank, Peter Golenbock, Frank Graham, Milton Gross, Arnold Hano, James R. Harrison, Bob Hertzel, Don Honig, Bill James, Harold (Speed) Johnson, Harold Kaese, Roger Kahn, John Kiernan, Leonard Koppett, John Lardner, Ring Lardner, Fred Lieb, Ed Linn, Arthur Mann, W. O. McGeehan, Roscoe McGowen, Tom Meany, Larry Merchant, Ogden Nash, Daniel Okrent, Dan Parker, Shirley Povich, Joe Reichler, Quentin Reynolds, Grantland Rice, Robert Riger, Larry Ritter, Harold Rosenthal, Emil Rothe, Damon Runyon, Art Rust, Jr., H. G. Salsinger, Al Silverman, Herbert Simons, Marshall Smelser, H. Allen Smith, Ken Smith, Red Smith, Robert Smith, Wendell Smith, Al Spink, J. G. Taylor Spink, Al Stump, Bill Veeck, Joe Villa, Joe Williams, and Dick Young.

Before I release you to start your own arguments with the man bellying up to to the bar next to you, I wish to make two final points: One, in considering "Great" games, the game itself and its importance took precedence over a performance, no matter how great. For that reason, a game like the sixth game of the 1975 World Series is rated higher as a "Great Game" in my estimation than Don Larsen's performance, a "Great" performance only. Secondly, this list is not meant to convince you, which would weaken you, but merely to stimulate you, for that is the nature of what basically is a Bar-bet book.

That's all there is . . . So when the guy next to you starts any statement with the words "What was the Greatest . . . ," and then launches into a series of memories posing as "Great Games," remember!, you too can play the game. For in the final analysis, your assessment is as valid as his. Or mine, for that matter.

Bert Randolph Sugar
Chappaqua, New York
June 7, 1986

1 Bobby Thomson's "Shot Heard 'Round the World"

New York Giants vs. Brooklyn Dodgers, Play-Off Game, October 1, 1951

A S WE DEAL IN THAT LIMBO OF MEMORIES THAT COMPRISES the whole of baseball, there are very few moments that stay with us. But there is one. It was an instant when time was separated and unified at one and the same moment; one everyone this side of a hundred remembers, and can tell you exactly where they were when they heard of it; one magnificent moment pressed between the pages of time: Bobby Thomson's "Shot Heard 'Round the World" in the 1951 National League Play-Offs.

On the off-chance you might be one of those few living baseball fans who cannot sort through the other minutiae beclouding your mind's-eye in order to envision that moment in time, a thought as unbelievable as Santa Claus suffering from terminal vertigo, let us try to help you out a little. The 1951 National League Play-Offs were a three-game set-to between baseball's version of the feuding Hatfields and McCoys, the New York Giants and the Brooklyn Dodgers before those two franchises had hibernational ambitions for west coast locations.

Their rivalry was such that it formed an institution, one of the most enduring in the whole of sports and one which dated back to the days when baseball was in knickers in the old, old National League before the turn of the century. By the second decade of the Twentieth Century, the rivalry began to take on a more defined look in the persons of John J. McGraw of the proud Giants and Wilbert Robinson of the tatterdemalion Dodgers—then called the "Robins," both in honor and dishonor of his name. They were former teammates and now blood enemies who led their troops into battle in what can best be characterized as New York's mini-civil war.

Throughout the years the disgust these two teams brought to the followers of the other was constantly refreshed by the presence of men like the Giants' Bill Terry who had the *chutzpah* to derisively ask "Is Brooklyn still in the League?," only to find they were indeed, sweeping the final two games of the 1934 season to deprive his Giants of the pennant. For the next decade or so, while the two teams battled for bragging rights to both sides of the East River, the implacable hatred subsided somewhat, although never enough for the two sides to exchange pleasantries at Christmastime. Then, on July 16, 1948, the long-festering hatred flared anew. For that was the day that Leo Durocher jumped ship, deserting Brooklyn to replace Mel Ott—the man Durocher had used as the brunt of his "Nice guys finish last" quote—as manager of the detested Giants. Suddenly, the civil war was on again, reaching, if possible, new levels.

Inheriting a team of heavy hitters with all the speed of sack race losers, Durocher determined to build a club in his own image: Scrappy, hungry, talented and mean. By 1950 he had the nucleus of "his" team, trading Sid Gordon, Buddy Kerr and Willard Marshall to the Braves for Eddie Stanky and Alvin Dark, two proven winners and, more important, genetic links to his "Gashouse Gangs" of yore. Making a late-season run, the Giants finished the '50 campaign just five games behind the front-limping Phillies, the closest the Giants had been to the top since Bill Terry's

1938 edition. Going into the 1951 season, Durocher's team was picked by most of those with delphic designs to hit paydirt where he had only prospected the previous year, and to edge out their traditional rivals, the Dodgers, for the pennant.

For their part, the party of the second part, the Dodgers, had made a managerial change of their own going into the 1951 season. During the winter Branch Rickey had sold his interest in "The Bums" to Walter O'Malley and, following Horace Greeley's advice, gone west to become General Manager of the Pittsburgh Pirates. O'Malley, now boss of all he surveyed, was hardly bound in his detailed inspection by the geographic bounds of the stadium, and started the scrutinization of "his" team with the front office. Wanting to rid himself of all vestigial reminders of Rickey, he now fired the man who had been manager of the Dodgers since Durocher's departure, Burt Shotton—an associate of Rickey's, off and on, since their days with the St. Louis Browns back in 19-aught-14—and replaced him with Durocher's old Brooklyn coach, Chuck Dressen.

But Dressen had come encumbered with a mortgage, the mortgage of having once been Durocher's first lieutenant. Carl Erskine, one of those who witnessed first-hand Dressen's ascendancy to the Brooklyn throne, told writer Peter Golenbock of Dressen's "Obsession to prove to the world that he had been the brains, that it hadn't been Durocher who had called the shots, but rather that he substantially helped Leo gain his managing reputation in Brooklyn." And so Dressen went into 1951 on a crusade with what bargain-basement psychiatrists would call a burning desire to prove he had been more than a spearcarrier to Durocher's greatness and a driving need to make his mark on the baseball world. Together Durocher and Dressen would become the lightning conductors of the renewed Giant-Dodger rivalry.

However, the season started less as a rivalry than a runaway. With the Dodgers winning eight of their first 12 and the Giants losing 12 of their first 14—11 of those in a row, including five to Brooklyn—the rivalry began to take on the look of a promise unkept as the Giants fell a fast seven games behind the Dodgers. Their feet caught in quicksand and as bereft of motion as a sail without wind, the Giants finally broke their streak on the last day of what T. S. Eliot called "the cruelest month," by beating, appropriately enough, the Dodgers on April 30th. With some minor tacking, the Giants went on to win 14 of their next 21 games to raise their record to 17-and-19 by May 25th. That was the day they were to get the strong tail wind they so desperately needed; for that was the day they called up a young 20-year-old outfielder from Minneapolis named Willie Mays.

Mays, who in Minneapolis had been hitting .477, non-Celsius, came freighted with the hopes and expectations of Durocher and the millions of Giant fans everywhere. But truth to tell, in his first three games the cup bearer of the Giants' future went hitless. Nevertheless, proving that no tonic, however popular or widely-advertised, could have so instantly a reviving effect as a win, Mays' presence in the line-up was enough for the Giants to win all three games over the Phillies to go over .500 for the first time all season.

Mays was to get his first hit his first time up in the Polo Grounds, a mammoth home run over the left-field roof on the first pitch served up to him by Boston's Warren Spahn, the Giants' only run in a 4-1 loss as they fell back to .500. Finishing the month of May at the break-even mark, the Giants finally went over .500 early in June, and by July 1st were six games over .500 and five-and-a-half behind the front-running Dodgers.

Had there but been an investiture, the Dodgers would have been universally crowned as National League champs on July 4th. Not only was that the magic day when teams in first place are conceded the pennant by the amateur handicappers at papers throughout the land, but it was also the day the Dodgers bet the Giants in the first of a three-game series; a series Brooklyn would go on to sweep as the starter kit of an eight-game winning streak to go nine-and-a-half up on the Giants. Dressen, who after a three-game sweep of New York earlier in the year had told those in charge of the deathless phrase department "The Giants is dead"—only to be ridiculed by purists and supported by a professor at Columbia who claimed "is" is right—now made no mistakes about it, bellowing out to one and all the unambiguous, "We knocked them out; they'll never bother us again."

Indeed, as the Dodgers went on yet another tear at the end of the month, it began to look like the pennant race could be called off on account of lack of interest. Winners of 10 straight and seventeen out of twenty through the first half of an August 11th double-header versus the Braves—the first baseball game ever to be televised in color—the Dodgers had a 70-35 won-lost record and, more importantly, a 13½-game lead over the Giants.

However, that first-game victory would serve as Brooklyn's high-water mark. Or, as sportswriter Harold Rosenthal wrote, "Just as you mark a child's height on the wall, this would have been a good place for Charlie Dressen to have made that pencil mark." With a little bit more than two-thirds of the season gone, Dressen's operatives seemed to have everything well in control: Preacher Roe was 15-2; Don Newcombe, 15-5; Ralph Branca, 9-3; Clyde King, 13-4; and Duke Snider was flirting with Babe Ruth's record. Not even Brooklyn's loss of the twin bill's nightcap to the Braves, reducing their lead to a "mere" 13 games by nightfall, was enough to cause even the most ardent Giant rooter to crook an elbow in a hopeful toast to his team's chances.

But hopeful toasts were to become the order of the day starting the very next day, August 12th, when the Giants rekindled the dying embers of hope with a winning streak of 16 in a row, all but three at their home Polo Grounds. Beginning what Red Smith called "the greatest reversal since Serutan," the scales suddenly fell from their eyes and the Giants came alive, beating the Phillies in a Sunday double-header and then sweeping the Dodgers in a three-game series with George Spencer, Jim Hearn and Sal Maglie combining to hold the Dodgers to a total of just four runs.

The hero of the sweep, however, was not Spencer, nor Hearn, nor even Maglie, but the newcomer, Willie Mays, who, in the middle game of the set made what *Time* Magazine called "The Throw." Tied 1-1 with Billy Cox at third and one out in the eighth, Mays, flowing against the current and charted by his unerring instinct, caught Carl Furillo's looping fly ball going to his left and then, instead of stopping to set and throw, spun completely around in a balletic pirouette and "just threw the twine off the ball" on a direct line to catcher Wes Westrum in plenty of time to retire the speedy and speechless Cox. Another who was rendered equally speechless was Dressen who could only mutter, "He'll have to do that again before I believe it!"

Mays, after going one-homer-for-his-first-26-times-at-bat, had suddenly given lie to the slander he couldn't hit Major League pitching, wielding his bat as if it were a toothpick. During his first Western swing, Mays went on a ten-game hitting streak with four home runs and 16 RBI's. But more than occasionally the youngster with all the paraphenalia of a great would betray his promise with a rookie's mistake, such as the time he failed to touch third after hitting an inside-the-park homer or when, on another occasion, he ran across the pitcher's mound on his way back to first from third in an effort to beat a throw after a catch in the deepest regions of the Polo Grounds. Still, as the Giants' win streak mounted to 16 and the Dodgers' lead dwindled to five, Durocher would be quoted as saying, "The spark was Mays."

Mays gave Durocher something else besides "spark": he also gave him a chance to put together the type of club he had always wanted. With Mays now a fixture in center, Durocher first moved his former center fielder Bobby Thomson over to left, and then, when his regular third baseman, Hank Thompson, with a "P," suffered a spike wound in July, Durocher moved Thomson, without a "P," in at third, putting Monte Irvin in left to give him an outfield alignment of Irvin in left field, Mays in center and Don Mueller in right. With an infield of Whitey Lockman at first, Stanky at second, Dark at short and Thomson at third, Wes Westrum catching and a starting pitching staff of Sal Maglie, Larry Jansen, Jim Hearn, Dave Koslo and George Spencer, Durocher had finally disposed of the unfair advantage the Dodgers had over the Giants at the beginning of the year. Now his only problem was in minimizing their fair advantage in the standings.

Meanwhile, over on the Brooklyn side of the East River, while the Dodgers had seen their once-invincible lead gradually melt to just five games, the League-leading team was hardly falling apart. However, there was some indication their manager was, acting for all the world like a slide rule extending his guesswork to a second place. Where in his salad days Dressen could be counted on for all the answers, now he could be heard hollering from the bench, "Hold 'em fellas, I'll think of something." And then, with the Giant steps getting ever closer, Dressen publicly berated Erv Palica, his young right hander, who only the previous year had won 13 games and now was laboring with a terrible two-and-six record, intimating Palica lacked courage.

Salvation for the Dodgers hardly lay in that direction. Nor did it lay in the direction of the Polo Grounds where, on the first two days of September, the Dodgers lost two more to the Giants, Don Mueller getting five homers and driving in a total of ten runs in the two-game series. Beginning to feel their pennant slip away from them, the Dodgers stabilized somewhat and by the time the two teams embarked on their last Western trip of the year had actually increased their lead one-half game to five-and-a-half. The Giants won six of their nine road games, but only had a one-game gain in the standings to show for it when they returned home on September 20th. As the days dwindled down to a precious few, it began to look like the pennant would be a hollow formality, the Dodgers four-and-a-half ahead with only ten games to play.

But the Giants could no more be melted than ice welded nor iron melted and won their next three against the Braves while the Dodgers were losing two-out-of-three to the Phillies. Now the incredible shrinking lead was down to two-and-a-half with but four games to go for the Giants and seven for the Brooks. And counting. On September 25th the Giants gave new meaning to the word "comeback," beating the Phillies 5-1 for their 34th win in their last 41 games while the Dodgers were losing a double-header to the Braves. The lead rabbit's margin was suddenly only one game and it began to look like it would fail a hare short of the finish line.

The Dodgers were now, not unlike Humpty Dumpty, trying to put back together their crumbling hopes. Their pitching staff was in disarray, Palica humiliated and then drafted; Clyde King, virtually useless after having come down with tendonitis; and Clem Labine, brought up in late July, the winner of his first four starts, now in Dressen's doghouse and relegated to the bench where he was of no use to the team polishing the seat of his pants. Their hitting, also, was in trouble, with early-season batting stars Gil Hodges and Duke Snider experiencing slumps down the stretch. It seemed nothing more could happen to the Dodgers.

But that was before September 27th, a day when baseball trivia history was made. At the expense of the Dodgers. Playing the final game of the three-game series against the Braves in Boston, the Dodgers went into the bottom of the eighth tied with the Braves at three. With the potential winning run on third, Jackie Robinson cleanly fielded a ground ball hit to him and fired it home to catcher Roy Campanella in an attempt to get the onrushing Brave baserunner, Bob Addis. Plate umpire Frank Dascoli called Addis "safe" with the Braves' fourth—and, as it turned out, winning—run. An argument ensued as the Dodgers took more than minor issue with the call, explaining their position to Dascoli in two languages, English and profanity. As Campanella, then coach Cookie Lavagetto and finally the entire Dodger bench joined in, Dascoli decided he had brooked enough of their insults and, in the order of their appearance, began ejecting those who had a hand in his discomfiture out of the game, starting with Campanella and then Lavagetto. Unable to find the ringleaders of the uprising on the bench, he ordered a mass evacuation, throwing out the entire Dodger bench. One of those cleared off the Dodgers' bench by Dascoli was a young outfielder named Bill Sharman, just called up by the Dodgers. Sharman, who would never play a Major League game, would go down in history as being the only player ever to be thrown out of a Major League game without ever having played in one.

The Dodgers, who had just seen their lead shrink to just one-half game over the idle Giants, carried on their dispute after the game, taking out their anger and frustration on the umpires' dressing room door which had remained discreetly shuttered against any such disturbances. Finally, after exhausting all of the known obscenities then in use, and a few new ones unknown even to baseballkind, all pointing out defects in the umpires' spiritual make-ups, some of the Dodgers—led by Preacher Roe, who had just lost his third game of the year on the disputed call against 22 wins—took out their remaining frustration by kicking at the offending door, shattering it in their best imitation of Lou Groza.

The next day the Dodgers booted another, this time a game, as they continued their long trip down the shadow of life. It was almost as if there were footnotes to the plot and all one had to add was Ibid. Up 3-0 in the sixth, Dodger starter Carl Erskine gave up

one run in the sixth, two in the eighth on Andy Seminick's homer and lost it in the ninth on two walks and two singles. Suddenly there was no margin for safety, the Giants had pulled even to the Dodgers with a 93-58 record. Or vice versa, if you're keeping track.

With two games left in the season, both teams sent forth their mound aces to do battle in "must"-win situations. The Giants won their ninth game in their last ten behind Sal Maglie as he beat Boston 3-0 for his twenty-third win; down in Philadelphia Don Newcombe beat the Phillies 5-0 for his 20th win and only the Dodgers' second in their last eight. Now only one game remained for each team.

Up in Boston the Giants closed out their triumphant road show on a winning note, beating the Braves on Larry Jansen's five-hitter, 3-2, for his 22nd win and the team's 10th in their last 11 games. Playing the game with split vision—one eye on the scoreboard, the other on the game—the Giants knew by the time their game was over at 3:35 that the Dodgers, playing down in Philadelphia, were losing 8-5 in the sixth. And that pitchers Preacher Roe, Ralph Branca and Clyde King had all been dispatched early to sample of the Shibe Park waters.

Assured that the Dodgers had emotionally packed it in, the Giants dressed hurriedly in order to make the five o'clock train back to New York, a victorious train trip at that. Hurrying onto the train, Durocher, growling and sounding like he had half swallowed something or other, scornfully barked to no one in particular, "Turn on the damn radio and let's see how badly they beat those bastards." But there wasn't a single radio in the carload. Unable to make a call before the train stopped in New Haven, Durocher finally directed one of his go-fers to get off the train and find out how "those bastards" had done.

What he would find out was that the Dodgers, down 5-8, had rallied in the eighth on four hits to tie the score. Pulling out all stops, and anyone out of the bullpen, all applications begrudgingly accepted, Dressen now called on his stopper, Don Newcombe, to hold the Phillies; a move matched by Phillies' manager Eddie Sawyer, who brought in his stopper, Robin Roberts. Together the two brought the game under control, throwing donuts for the next few innings as the game moved past the union limit and on into extra innings tied at eight.

In the bottom of the twelfth, the Phillies loaded the bases with two outs, bringing to bat first baseman Eddie Waitkus, a left-handed hitter. Catching one of Newk's fastballs, Waitkus slashed a grass-scorching liner to the right-side of second base for an apparent game-winner. But quicker than any observer could say "Jack Robinson," the Brooklyn second baseman leaped to his right, his body extended full-length, and backhanded the ball, failing to the ground in a cloud of dust. Some of those in the press box, peering through the gathering dusk, swore that Robinson had trapped the ball on a skidding bounce and, in the words of one of those who observed the play, "when he saw he had no chance for a play at the plate, faked the umpires out of their shoes with a dramatic fall." But umpire Lon Warneke, dramatic fall or no, punched the air with his hand to signal that, at least in his humble estimation, it had been a fair catch and the third out. Robinson was to follow up his incomparable catch with an even more improbable home run two innings later to give the Dodgers a 9-8, 14-inning victory. And a stirring come-from-behind win that put them into a tie for the pennant and into the Play-Offs against the Giants.

On the train back to New York, Durocher, his teeth bared in that mirthless smile that usually accompanied his displeasure, heard out all the details of the Dodgers' miraculous win. Then, with the realization that there would be yet another day, or days, he announced loudly, "All right everybody, we're working tomorrow. It'll be Hearn pitching for us." Meanwhile, down in Philly, after celebrating the homer by Robinson that had prevented the greatest collapse in baseball history, Dressen got down to business: deciding on his starter for the next day's Play-Off game. Having pawned not only all his promises, but his future as well going with seven pitchers in the finale, Dressen now had to recycle one of them. After some consideration, he selected the second of the seven, Ralph Branca, to carry the Dodger Blue in the opening game.

A coin toss dictated that the first game of the three-game moveable feast would be played at Ebbets Field. And almost before Jackie Robinson had won Sunday's game with his late-inning heroics, the fans had started lining up for the historic first game of the Play-Offs, both sides more than adequately represented, and all trading abuse and insults tinged with a so's-your-old-man inflection with those identified as being loyal members of the opposition. At the head of the ever-multiplying line sat a devoted Brooklyn fan who had camped out earlier in the week wanting to be the first customer through the gates for what he believed would be a Dodger-Yankee Series game. Now as the gates finally opened to admit the teeming masses, he took a deep breath and shouted to all behind him, "To hell with this. I'm not going in there. I hate the Giants!"

Ebbets Field, with its scalloped stands hanging out over the field like rows of buck teeth, rocked with the roars of patriotism and chauvinism as 30,751 paying inmates posing as fans jammed the old park to the gunwales on a beautiful Indian summer day when absolutely nothing else seemed to be going on in the borough of Brooklyn. And when Andy Pafko—the same Andy Pafko acquired in a mid-season trade called by reporter Arch Murray "the most barefaced baseball swindle of recent years," and one which everyone who bled Dodger blue was convinced meant the pennant—smote a homer in the second off Hearn, it seemed as if the whole of Brooklyn exploded into one wild scream. But that was to be their only chance to scream as Hearn limited Dodger bats to four other meaningless singles all day. On the other glove, the Dodger starter, Ralph Branca, pitched almost as effectively, giving up just six hits. Unfortunately, while four were inside the park, the other two were outside, including a two-run shot by Bobby Thomson in the fourth and a solo shot by Monte Irvin in the eighth, accounting for all the Giants' runs in their 3-1 win.

With Dame Fortune now about to hang a funeral blanket over the Dodgers' chances equal to the weather blanket shrouding the Polo Grounds for Game Two, Dodger manager Dressen, with the tacit and tactical understanding that there was no tomorrow, grasped at any straw in the storm to stay the inevitable. After a large amount of weeping and gnashing of teeth, the straw he finally selected from his severely pruned pitching staff was rookie Clem Labine—who hadn't pitched since he ran afoul of Dressen 11 days earlier and gotten in Dutch with the Dutchman. Working his breaking stuff beautifully, Labine proved Dressen's right to be wrong about him, giving up five hits in the first four innings and—after a 41-minute rain delay—giving up only one more in the final five as the Dodger bats came alive to even the play-off with a 10-0 win.

As the drama unfolded in three movements, like the puzzle of the carpenter's rule, all the chips were now piled on Game Three. Past glories and glamours no longer mattered; this was the game for all the marbles. And, as it turned out, for all time.

Durocher, following his credo that "You don't save a pitcher for

tomorrow; tomorrow it may rain," selected his two fair-weather pitchers, Sal Maglie as his starter and Larry Jansen, on the oftchance he may be needed, in the bullpen for relief purposes. Dressen had toyed with the idea of starting his skinny left hander, Preacher Roe. But the Preach's frail frame had taken one beating too many down the stretch, and Dressen had to come back with Newcombe, who already had put in 14²/₃ innings, hard, in the last two games of the season. It was strength-against-strength, hope-against-hope and thrill-atop-thrill.

Maglie had the reputation, well-deserved, of being "The Barber." Some of the more charitable attributed his nickname to his continual five-o'clock shadow. Others, particularly those who had faced him in the batter's box, more cynically chalked up his label to his razor-sharp control and, not incidentally, to his ability to shave a little off opposing batsmen who stood a little too close to the plate. Whatever its origin, the name obscured an appreciation of the pitcher with the perpetual malevolent scowl who could throw three kinds of curves, had won five "Must" games against the Dodgers during the regular season, and had led the National League in wins and fewest hits rendered per game during the season.

But almost before you could rattle off his credentials, Maglie was in trouble in the very first inning, walking Pee Wee Reese and Duke Snider, Snider on four straight serves, and then giving up a single to Robinson for a 1-0 Dodger lead—the third straight game in which the Dodgers had scored first.

Maglie now returned to advertised form and for the next five innings held the Dodgers in check. But the score still stood 1-0 after six, thanks in large part to "Newk's" three-hit pitching. And also the heads-down baserunning of Bobby Thomson, who, in the second, with Whitey Lockman on first, had blasted a drive down the left-field line and, running like a truant schoolboy out on a romp, had sauntered into second only to find it already occupied by the aforementioned Mr. Lockman. After standing around second for a second, his mouth opening and shutting like a goldfish's, Thomson tried to follow the bread crumbs back to first but was run down and tagged out, effectively ending any thoughts the Giants might have harbored of a comeback rally. Up in the press box, the press was being advised by an impersonal voice dripping with more than a smidgen of irony: "Thomson has hit safely in fifteen consecutive games."

As the gloom on the Giants' bench matched that of the pea-soup enveloping the field, the flood lights were turned on at that very instant, all the better, as Red Smith said, for "the Giants to see and count their runners on each base."

Finally, after waiting six innings for the wheel to turn, the Giants dented home plate in the seventh on a double by Irvin, a sacrifice by Lockman on which the Dodgers retired nobody and a long sacrifice fly by the one and same Thomson who had already been charged with a debt he was now repaying. The score was now tied at one. But not for long.

The Dodgers, having once been so close to the Promised Land they could touch it, now made one more grab at it. Trying to turn back both "The Miracle of Coogan's Bluff" and the calendar to those happier days when they owned the National League, they rallied in the eighth with two singles by Reese and Snider, a wild pitch by the once-magnificent Maglie, a single by Pafko past Thomson at third and another single by Cox getting through the now-porous Thomson who played like he was merely baby-sitting the glove for a friend. All told, four hits and three runs and a 4-1 lead for the Dodgers.

But where once Newcombe had run on a high octane content, he was beginning to wind down from his "Iron Man" performance of 21²/₃ innings over the last five days, his personal gas tank now all but dry. After the Dodgers had taken their 4-1 lead, Newk began to use words like "tired" to anyone in the dugout who could hear him. His pleas, however, fell on deaf ears, particularly those of the Dodgers' spiritual leader, Jackie Robinson, who just looked at Newcombe and shouted in disbelief: "Don't give me that shit. Go out there and pitch!" And pitch Newk did in the bottom of the eighth, polishing off the stunned Giants one-two-three. Now there were only three outs to go.

With the game going into the last inning of the 157th game of the season, the majority of those in the stands, diehard Giant fans all, sat less mutinous than sullen, almost tearful in their indignation that their team had come so close and yet remained so far. The only noise in the stands seemed to come from those who identified themselves readily as Dodger fans, their voices now acting as a countdown to the Giants' chances of pulling off their well-advertised "Miracle," chanting "Three more outs" and anything else that came to their collective minds. With the two camps treating each other with all the deference of lepers, hardly anyone seemed to notice, or care, that Larry Jansen had retired the Dodgers in order in the top of the ninth. The only thing that mattered now was the bottom of the ninth, the Giants' last turn at bat.

As the Giants prepared for their final chance at the brass ring, Leo Durocher, still lighthearted, still hopeful, and still not accepting the situation as unalterable, addressed his operatives in a voice that had to be modified to keep from breaking dishes two blocks away. "All right," he screamed to one and all, "We've come this God-damn far already and we've still got a God-damn chance to hit." And so saying, moved out to his third-base coaching position as if he had just solved all the problems that beset the world, starting with those now facing the Giants.

Lead-off hitter Alvin Dark, hitless for the last two games, apparently took Durocher's pep talk to heart, slapping at one of Newk's fastballs and driving it to the right-side of the infield. As first baseman Gil Hodges and second baseman Jackie Robinson, in the words of writer Charles Einstein, "crossed each other's paths like the blades of a scissors coming together," the ball somehow, someway escaped their grasping gloves, ticking off Hodges' mitt for a seeing-eye single.

The Unlucky Number 13: Ralph Branca

With Dark on first, manager Dressen now directed Hodges to hold the runner on the bag, something as unexplainable as the Biblical word "Selah," Dark's run a meaningless one in the total scheme of things. And with Hodges enchained to first, compliments of Dressen's directive, the next hitter, Don Mueller—called "Mandrake the Magician" for the good and sufficient reason he wielded his bat like a wand—magically singled through the man-made hole, Hodges barely missing his little bouncing hopper on a lunging back-handed stab, the ball leaking through for another single, just far enough to send Dark to second.

Suddenly, with men on first and second and the tying run at the plate in the person of Monte Irvin, Giant fans erupted in screams born of hope and fancied piety, invoking the help of any and all divinities who could come to their aid. But it was almost as if they had been made mad by the gods who were now about to destroy them as Irvin hit a high foul pop-up to Hodges for the first out and, as if to emphasize the Giants' frustration, slammed his bat to the ground, breaking it cleanly.

Now it was the turn of the Flatbush Faithful to whoop it up, to wave their banners and to renew their chant, reducing it by one to "Two more outs, two more outs, two more outs . . ." But it was not to happen. For the next man up, Whitey Lockman, drove one of Newcombe's fastballs on a line to the opposite field, the ball, slicing into the gap in left-center for a double scoring Dark with the Giants' second run. Mueller, off and running with the hit, slid hard into third, spraining his left ankle on impact. After attending to the fallen Mueller for several minutes, the Giant trainer called for the paramedics to bear Mueller's body to the clubhouse thus providing Red Smith with a chance to call it "the corniest possible sort of Hollywood smaltz—stretcher-bearers plodding away with an injured Mueller between them, symbolic of the Giants themselves."

During the time it took to administer to Mueller, there were other doings that would bear out Smith's characterization of the goings-on as "the corniest possible sort of Hollywood smaltz." For now Dressen, who had had Ralph Branca and Carl Erskine warming up in the bullpen from the seventh inning on, had finally come to share Newcombe's diagnosis and determined to remove his tiring pitcher. Having called the bullpen several times and talked to his coach, Clyde Sukeforth, he called down one last time and asked his trusted aide, "You got him ready? Are you ready down there?" Sukeforth, who only had once choice, Branca, Erskine nursing a sore arm, replied, "Hell, yes. He's ready. He's *been* ready." And with that, Dressen called in Branca to relieve Newcombe and pitch to the next batter, Bobby Thomson.

As Branca finally reached the mound, he was met by a group of well-wishers: Pitcher emeritus Don Newcombe, who had waited for him and solemnly shook his hand before leaving; Manager Chuck Dressen, who gave him the obligatory changing-of-the-guard litany, ending with a "Get him out!," no instructions, merely a "Get him out?", and Rube Walker, the catcher-pro-tem, filling in for the injured Roy Campanella, who went over the signs with Branca and then the strategy, get ahead of Thomson and then waste one. And with that, the most historic moment in all of baseball was about to come front and center as Bobby Thomson stepped into the box.

But even while Thomson was taking his place in the batter's box, there were those in the stands already indulging in the National Pastime's own national pastime: Second-guessing. With pinch-runner Clint Hartung on third and Whitey Lockman on second, first base is open; why not walk Thomson? Especially since Thomson has fed off Dodger pitching, and Branca especially, almost as if they were his personal nose-bag, hitting seven of his 31 home runs off Dodger pitching, two of them off Branca, including one in the first game of the Play-Offs. Moreover, Thomson is hot, the man on deck, Willie Mays, is not. Why bother pitching to a man who has raised his average in the last two months from .222 to .292 and has two hits and one sacrifice fly in his three at-bats today? But almost before those arguing this thesis could get the words out of their mouths, they were met by the purists who answered baseball's most important commandment that thou shalt not put the winning run on base. And Thomson represented both that winning run and that shalt not.

But all the suppositions came to a stop when it became evident Branca had no intention whatsoever of walking Thomson. Eschewing the blindfold, he fired his first pitch, one he later described as having "mustard on it," a fastball right down the middle. Strike One. Now, as Branca studied Thomson the way a scientist studies a specimen, Rube Walker held up his glove for the agreed-upon waste pitch inside. Branca tried probing, Thomson again, dealing up a fastball up and in, but not inside enough. Thomson swung in an uppercutting motion, the ball soaring off his bat with overspin. Into the air and into the record books at one and the same second.

As the ball took off down the left-field line heading straight toward the stands, Branca turned to watch the lethal drive, hoping against hope it would sink and saying to himself over and over again, "Sink, sink, sink . . ." The ball began its downward arc and left fielder Andy Pafko retreated as far as he could go, his stern pressing against the left-field wall at approximately the 315-foot mark, and then just dropped his arms in futility as the ball went over his head and into the stands, clearing the fence by no more than six inches.

The fans erupted in blasts, making an Aeolian trombone of the stands, while down on the field Thomson, by now halfway to first, stopped running and started jumping straight up and down, his kangaroo leaps taking him around the basepaths. Up in the broadcast booth, Giant broadcaster Russ Hodges, left with powers barely those of respiration, cried into the microphone, ". . . it's gonna be . . . I believe . . . The Giants win the pennant!. . . the Giants win the pennant!. . . the Giants win the pennant!. . . Bobby hit into the lower deck of the left field stands . . . The Giants win the pennant and they're going crazy . . . I don't believe it . . . I don't believe it . . . I will NOT believe it!. . ."

Meanwhile, down on the field, Thomson's home run had loosed the tiger, fans and action spilling out onto the field in a celebration of gaiety as fans and players alike all began screaming with something of the wild joy which prisoners feel at the announcement of their release. Eddie Stanky came tearing out of the Giant dugout faster than anyone ever remembered him running, and grabbed Durocher in his third-base coaching box, the two clinging together like two ship-wrecked survivors coming together on a wave-swept beach as they fell to the ground. Others raced to home plate to greet Thomson in a mob scene that would have done justice to a V-E Day welcoming crowd. And there, on the periphery of the crowd at home, was umpire Lou Jorda, positioning himself as best he could to make sure the triumphant hero stepped on home plate.

Thomson finally made his leisurely way around the basepaths, bounding atop home plate with one last mighty kangaroo leap. And, as he did so, only two non-Giant fans remained to witness the culmination of the most melodramatic moment in baseball's history: Jackie Robinson, who had been following Thomson's triumphant trot all the way around the basepaths to make sure he touched each and every base, and Ralph Branca, destined forevermore to wear the can tied to his tail as the pitcher who served up

"The Shot Heard Round the World" and lost the third game to the Giants by a 5-4 score. With Thomson's journey at a conclusion, Branca turned as slowly as a door to walk the last mile or so to the faraway centerfield clubhouse. And the last thing anyone noticed was the number on the back of his uniform: Number 13.

Call it "The Miracle of Coogan's Bluff," call it "The Shot Heard Round the World," or even "The Scot Heard Round the World," in honor of Thomson. But also call it the greatest moment in baseball.

GIANTS CAPTURE PENNANT, BEATING DODGERS 5-4 IN 9TH

The Box Score

BROOKLYN DODGERS

	AB.	R.	H.	PO.	A.
Furillo, rf.	5	0	0	0	0
Reese, ss.	4	2	1	2	5
Snider, cf.	3	1	2	3	0
Robinson, 2b.	2	1	1	3	2
Pafko, lf.	4	0	1	4	1
Hodges, 1b.	4	0	0	11	1
Cox, 3b.	4	0	2	1	3
Walker, c.	4	0	1	1	1
Newcombe, p.	4	0	0	1	1
Branca, p.	0	0	0	0	0
Total	34	4	8	*25	13

NEW YORK GIANTS

	AB.	R.	H.	PO.	A.
Stanky, 2b.	4	0	0	0	0
Dark, ss.	4	1	1	2	2
Mueller, rf.	4	0	1	0	0
cHartung	0	1	0	0	0
Irvin, lf.	4	1	1	1	0
Lockman, 1b.	3	1	2	11	1
Thomson, 3b.	4	1	3	4	1
Mays, cf.	3	0	0	1	0
Westrum, c.	0	0	0	7	1
aRigney	1	0	0	0	0
Noble, c.	0	0	0	0	0
Maglie, p.	2	0	0	1	2
bThompson	1	0	0	0	0
Jansen, p.	0	0	0	0	0
Total	30	5	8	27	11

*One out when winning run scored
aStruck out for Westrum in eighth
bGrounded out for Maglie in eighth
cRan for Mueller in ninth.

Brooklyn .... 1 0 0 0 0 0 0 3 0—
New York .... 0 0 0 0 0 0 1 0 4—

Thomson forces his way through the crowd at home.

2 The Pebble that Broke the Giant's Back

Washington Senators vs. New York Giants, 7th Game, 1924 World Series, October 10, 1924

THE 1924 WORLD SERIES HAS BECOME ONE OF THOSE TWICE-told tales that will be told and retold until one day the person who challenges its authority will be labeled an iconoclast. Or worse. It all begins with a bad break, which oftimes, far from being a disaster, can be the very best thing that could have happened. And, in the case of the 1924 Series, was.

The story starts, oddly enough, in 1907, with a little-known catcher named Cliff Blankenship, who played for an even lesser-known group of athletes called the Washington Senators. Blankenship broke his finger 37 games into the '07 season; a season that was to see the Senators go down to defeat with such a dismal monotony and startling variety that they would lose a total of 102 games and finish 43-and-a-half games behind the pennant-winning Detroit Tigers and a mere 11 out of seventh.

All season long Washington manager Pongo Joe Cantillon had been bombarded with letters from a traveling salesman from the D.C. area extolling the virtues of a semi-pro pitcher from "Idaho's Snake River Valley League." Most of the missives from the self-appointed scout contained rosy write-ups of the prospect's prowess, containing florid phrases like: "This boy throws so fast you can't see them;" Or, "He knows where he is throwing the ball because if he didn't there would be dead bodies strewn all over Idaho;" And even, "This boy has a pitch that is faster than Amos Rusie's and control that's better than Mathewson." Most of these calling cards of hope found their way into Cantillon's round filing cabinet-hyphen-waste receptacle.

Now, however, with Blankenship sitting around watching his bones mend, Cantillon pressed his disabled catcher into duty, making him an extra-curricular scout. Giving Blankenship his marching orders, the Washington manager sent him first to Wichita to "look in on" a young outfielder then leading the Western Association in batting and to sign him "if he doesn't come too high." And then, so the scouting expedition shouldn't be a total waste, Cantillon gave his catcher-cum-scout further instructions to continue his odyssey on to Idaho to take a "look-see" at the young pitching phenom, adding "Take a bat and if you can get one foul off him, forget it!"

Blankenship made his pit stop at Wichita and signed up the outfield prospect, one Clyde Milan—who would go on to hit .285 in 16 years for the Senators—and then entrained for Weiser, Idaho, telling one and all that he was on his way "to look over some palooka who they say is striking out everybody. Probably isn't worth a dime, and I'm on a wild-goose chase for Cantillon."

Arriving in the small burg of Weiser, the Washington catcher was told by the townsfolk that the youngster he was about to see was no rhinestone in the rough, but the real goods, one who had theretofore pitched 85 scoreless innings and struck out 188 opposing batsmen in his 12 appearances. But Blankenship had heard such tall tales before and was prepared to sell them short. What he wasn't prepared for, however, was the sight of a gangly, six-foot-and-change pitcher who looked like one of nature's irregularities. With long and stringy arms which flowed out of his uniform at odd

angles and long wrists as loose as a man shaking them out, the youngster threw in a ropelike, somewhat whiplike motion, coming three-quarters overhand, almost sidearm by way of third base. Blankenship's eyes enlarged to the dimensions of saucers, the tip of his nose quivered like a rabbit's and unseen hands began to pour ice water down his spine as he witnessed the youth throwing the ball as effortlessly as a man throwing his hat on the bed.

Even though the 19-year-old lost the game 1-0 in 12 innings on two infield bobbles, Blankenship had seen enough to sign the "Palooka" on the spot. Thus began the legend of Walter Johnson, the greatest pitcher in the history of baseball.

Johnson's first start came on August 2, 1907, when he was simultaneously thrown to the wolves and the Tigers, that fearsome crew of Cobb, Crawford & Co. For three innings the raw-boned rookie, working easily and effortlessly, if gracelessly, kept the Tigers from fattening their League-leading batting averages. Finally, impressed with the futility of taking their regular cuts against Johnson, Detroit took to bunting their way on base, beating them out and beating Johnson in the process on just six hits, three of which were bunts.

In his next outing Johnson would win his first game, the first of 416 during his career. But he had already begun to make an impression even before he had made a mark. Davy Jones, Detroit's lead-off batter, and the first to face him in the Majors, said of Johnson, "He had those long arms, absolutely the longest arms I ever saw. They were like whips, that's what they were. He'd just *whip* that ball in there . . ." Sam Crawford, who also faced Johnson in that first game, said that Johnson "reminded me of one of those compressed-air machines . . . comes in so fast when it goes by it swooshes. You hardly see the ball at all. But you hear it, swoosh . . ."

Johnson continued to swoosh his pitches past batters, pitches that begot two whistles, one coming in and the other of the appreciative batter as he admired it. It was this pitch with the sound of a train's yowl that inspired Grantland Rice to call him "The Big Train;" and then to add, "How do you know what Johnson's got?/ Nobody's seen it yet." Damon Runyon would later comment, "He's got a gun concealed up his person and he shoots 'em up there." With no curve to speak of and no change of pace to speak of—something catcher Gabby Street discovered when he called for a curve and got a "Swoosh" and stopped bothering—Johnson continued to shoot them by batters while playing with the most pitiful and pitiable group of athletes ever to wear Big League uniforms, a team immortalized in Charles Dryden's "First in War, First in Peace and Last in the American League" line. Throwing a ball that almost assumed a funnel shape and mowed down a path nine miles through the batter's box, this native of Kansas "swooshed" his way to 82 wins in his first five years—always ranking amongst the pitching leaders in complete games, strikeouts and ERA—for a team that never vacated the depths of the second division.

By 1912 Johnson had established his credentials, his molten

15

JOHNSON BATTLES TO HIS GOAL AT END

fastball moving the New York *Times* to call him "The greatest pitcher of modern days, undoubtedly the greatest the game has produced." That was the year Johnson won 32 games, 16 of them in a row to set the American League record, and led the League in strikeouts and ERA. In 1913, Johnson had the greatest year any pitcher ever had: He won 36 games, the most in the League, led the League in winning percentage, complete games, innings pitched, strikeouts, and shutouts and gave up only 38 bases on balls in 346 innings, less than one a game.

Throwing a ball that was both an aspirin and a headache—and described always in onamatophoeic terms, as in Lefty Grove's characterization of "That fast ball down around the knees . . . Whoosh!"—Johnson set records wholesale: Most strikeouts, 3,508; Most innings pitched, 5,923.2; Most shutouts, 110; Most complete games, 531; Most consecutive scoreless innings, 56, etc., etc., etc. And even though many of his records have fallen by the wayside, the black type in the record book can never capture the greatness of the man who was such that the second-best man in his class is not considered to be in his class at all.

Johnson was so overpowering that Cleveland shortstop Ray Chapman once took two blurred streaks that swooshed by and threw away his bat, no longer wanting to argue with his desperate fate. Umpire Billy Evans called to Chapman, then disappearing in the direction of the dugout, "Hey, that's only strike two." Without turning around, Chapman shouted over his shoulder, "I know. You can have the next one, it won't do me any good." George Pipgras, who only saw Johnson at the tail-end of his journey, once took two called strikes and stepped out of the box, nettled and at sea, muttering at Washington catcher Muddy Ruel, "Muddy, I never saw those pitches." Ruel, grinning through the bars of his mask, accompanied his throwing the ball back to Johnson with a "Don't let it worry you, he's thrown a few Cobb and Speaker are still looking for."

Others were left as collectively bereft of locomotion as a sail without wind at the near sight of the "Big Train's" fast ball, unable to tell Johnson's baseball from his elbow as it honed in on them from ground-top level, his knuckles almost scrapping the ground. Such were the wonders of Johnson's fast ball that all were forced to agree with poet Ogden Nash: "The Big Train in his prime/Was so fast he could throw/Three strikes at a time."

The only players who ever had anything resembling a remote chance against Johnson's offerings were those he was disposed to

be lenient to—like rookies he wanted to make look good or an occasional friend, like Sam Crawford, when the game had long been decided; Joe Jackson, who did what was natural in the face of a typhoon, taking a well-timed half-swing; and Ty Cobb, who dug in ever so close to the plate, playing on Johnson's fear of hitting a batter—and still, despite the homesteading rights he established with his toehold, Cobb could only hit Johnson at a .233 clip, far below his record .367 average.

As the '20s dawned, the premier pitcher in all of baseball, with 10 straight 20-game seasons behind him, was still far from his one dream: A World Series win. With the sand in his hourglass beginning to sift down—his 1920 record his worst since his rookie season, an 8-10 sore-armed season punctuated by his only no-hitter—it seemed he might never see that dream come true. His team, the Washington Senators, albeit no longer "Last in the American League"—thanks to the Philadelphia Athletics who had taken a permanent lease on the cellar dwellings—were still sixth-class citizens. And with managers changing with all the frequency of Roman emperors after Nero, enthroned and dethroned by owner Clark Griffith, it looked like the team would never gel into anything more than a fourth or fifth place club, at best.

But then, in 1924, everything came together. After years of frustration and worse, both Washington and Johnson were to rise to the top of baseball's mountain in one of the greatest games ever.

1924 started out no different than any other year for Washington, with Griffith naming his fifth manager in five years. But this time his selection *was* different, it was Bucky Harris, the 27-year-old second baseman. Harris immediately made himself popular with his teammates by asking them to "Go out and make me look good." And they did, with Sam Rice leading the League in hits, Goose Goslin in runs batted in, and a 36-year-old pitcher named Walter Johnson, the essence that vivified him suddenly restored, leading the League in wins, winning percentage, ERA, games started, and strikeouts and, not incidentally, winning the Most Valuable Player Award. Together the team hit .294, won 92 games and won the pennant, their first ever, by two games over the heavily-favored New York Yankees.

Over in the National League the Giants had repeated for the fourth time in four years, edging out the Brooklyn Dodgers by one-and-a-half games and the Pittsburgh Pirates by three. But there was a tarnish to their crown, and worse, a stink, that threatened the World Series. For, during the last week of the season, New York utility outfielder Jimmy O'Connell had approached Phillies' short-shop Heinie Sand before a crucial game and said, in an undertone, "It'll be worth $500 to you if you don't bear down too hard against us today." Sand reported the "proposition" to his manager, Art Fletcher, who in turn reported it to the National League president and he to Judge Kenesaw Mountain Landis, the Commissioner of Baseball who had been brought into the game to clean up just such treacherous acts. Acting as both proposer and seconder, Landis held a series of meetings with those named, including O'Connell, coach Cozy Dolan, and three of the Giants' biggest stars; second baseman Frankie Frisch, rightfielder Ross Youngs and first baseman George Kelly. After hearing them all, Landis suspended supernumeraries O'Connell and Doland for life and cleared the three superstars. Still, there was an outcry, with American League president Ban Johnson demanding that Brooklyn be substituted for New York and Pittsburgh president Barney Dreyfuss urging that the entire Series be called off. Despite the uproar, the autocratic Landis ordered that the Series "Go on as planned."

Even with the controversy the Giants were a team of giants in deed as well as name, their roster containing seven future Hall of

Freddy Lindstrom awaits the ball that never comes.

OF EIGHTEEN-YEAR TRAIL

"The Big Train" that could, Walter Johnson, delivers in relief in the 7th Game of the '24 Series.

Famers and their bench harboring enough ambitions, past, present and future to form a second unit. It was, therefore, no surprise that the sporting fraternity installed them as solid betting favorites. But the country, which followed its heart not its pocketbook, had its own favorites: Washington and Walter Johnson, who had finally made it into the World Series in the eighteenth year of his fabled career.

Johnson, as soft of character as he was hard of pitch, was besieged by well-wishers. And ticket-seekers. As opposed to Shakespeare's maids in modesty who said "No," Johnson couldn't quite bring himself to turn down anyone and went out-of-pocket $1,000 to buy tickets for those who asked—leading one observer to note, "It's a good thing Walter isn't a female, otherwise he'd always be in the family way." Some of the tickets Johnson bought were claimed, but almost as many went unclaimed, and by the time he took the mound for the opening game of the Series he had over $350 worth of tickets left in his pocket.

Distracted by the demands, awed by the attention and un-nerved by the pressure, Johnson was actually shaking before Game One when asked to pose with President Coolidge who had become less a Senator fan than a Walter Johnson fan. So, too, were almost every one of the 35,760 crammed into tiny Griffith Stadium and its temporary seats as the "Big Train" took the mound for his long-delayed World Series start.

Once on the mound—or, to be exact, no mound, leveled to the ground as it was, in order to maximize his side-arm slings and arrows—Johnson settled down. Throwing the ball straight as a plumb-line, he retired the Giants one-two-three in the first inning. But in the second, with two strikes on him, "Long" George Kelly, the National League's RBI leader, blooped a ball over the temporary barrier in left field for a home run and a 1-0 Giants' lead. And when Bill Terry, again with two strikes, hit a wrong-way homer of somewhat less-than-Chinese proportions into the same "temps," in the fourth, the score stood at 2-0, Giants. Washington got one back in the sixth on a double by Earl McNeely and tied the score in the bottom of the ninth on a Roger Peckinpaugh double. So the game went into extra innings. It was the first time an opening game of a Series had gone beyond nine innings and an omen of things to come.

Tiring from his ordeal, the ample ghost that was once Johnson continued to stand and deliver. But his efforts were matched by Giant pitcher Art Nehf, who shut down the Senators. Then, in the 12th, no longer able to rekindle the embers that once were, Johnson gave up two walks, sandwiched around a hit, to load up the bases and then gave up hits numbered 13 and 14 to Youngs and Terry for two runs and a 4-3 Giant win.

With the Nation's Idol beaten, it looked like those with Delphic franchises had been right. But behind old Tom Zachary, throwing something that resembled a one-fingered knuckleball and making the Giants wave their wands in the wind, Washington came back to win Game Two by an identical 4-3 score and even up the Series. Game Three saw the Giants, led by young Bill Terry, pummell four Washington pitchers for 12 hits and a 6-4 win. However, the Senators, with "The Wild Goose of the Potomac," Goose Goslin, hitting a three-run homer, beat the Giants 7-4 win in Game Four to again even the Series at two apiece and bring on Johnson for Game Five.

Johnson, waiting to hear the echoes of an earlier day, went to the mound for the Senators in Game Five. But he was merely a memory of his greatness now, striking out only three Giants and giving up 13 hits—four by second-year third baseman Freddie Lindstrom and another by rookie Bill Terry, who now had four hits

in seven at bats against the once-great—as Johnson went down to his second defeat, 6-2. Now it appeared that those echoes of greatness would never be heard again.

But when Tom Zachary won Game Six to once again even the count, the stage was set for echoes. And more. Much more.

Game Seven was a game ripe for strategems. And spoils. Normally there was no one better in the managerial dodge at such maneuvering than John J. McGraw, a master strategist who believed that the secret of all successful operations consisted in the overlooking of no eventuality. A good challenge always stimulated McGraw's reflexes; almost causing him, like Pavlov's dog, to salivate. But this time it was not McGraw who salivated, but McGraw who instead got salivated on, caught in the switches as it were. For before the deciding game, Bucky Harris went to his owner, Clark Griffith, with a benevolent little ruse. Noticing that McGraw platooned his troops—batting left-handed Terry against right handers and right-handed Irish Meusel against lefties—Harris came up with a plan to get the bothersome Terry out of the game as soon as possible: He would start right-hander Curly Ogden and then bring in lefty George Mogridge after just one batter. Realizing

Game 7 October 10 at Washington									N.Y.	000 003 000 000						
New York	Pos	AB	R	H	RBI	PO	A	E	Was.	000 100 020 001						
Lindstrom	3b	5	0	1	0	0	3	0	Washington	Pos	AB	R	H	RBI	PO	A	E
Frisch	2b	5	0	2	0	3	4	0	McNeely	cf	6	0	1	1	0	0	0
Youngs	rf-lf	2	1	0	0	2	0	0	Harris	2b	5	1	3	3	4	1	0
Kelly	cf-1b	6	1	1	0	8	1	0	Rice	rf	5	0	0	0	2	0	0
Terry	1b	2	0	0	0	6	1	0	Goslin	lf	5	0	2	0	3	0	0
a Meusel	lf-rf	3	0	1	1	1	0	0	Judge	1b	4	0	1	0	11	1	1
Wilson	lf-cf	5	1	1	0	4	0	0	Bluege	ss	5	0	0	0	1	7	2
Jackson	ss	6	0	0	0	1	4	2	Taylor	3b	2	0	0	0	3	1	
Gowdy	c	6	0	1	0	8	0	1	b Leibold		1	1	1	0	0	0	0
Barnes	p	4	0	0	0	1	2	0	Miller	3b	2	0	0	0	1	1	0
Nehf	p	0	0	0	0	0	0	0	Ruel	c	5	2	2	0	13	0	0
McQuillan	p	0	0	0	0	0	0	0	Ogden	p	0	0	0	0	0	0	0
e Groh		1	0	1	0	0	0	0	Mogridge	p	1	0	0	0	0	0	0
f Southworth		0	0	0	0	0	0	0	Marberry	p	1	0	0	0	1	0	0
Bentley	p	0	0	0	0	0	0	0	c Tate		0	0	0	0	0	0	0
									d Shirley		0	0	0	0	0	0	0
									Johnson	p	2	0	0	0	0	1	0
Totals		45	3	8	1	x34	15	3	Totals		44	4	10	4	36	14	4

Pitching	IP	H	R	ER	BB	SO
New York						
Barnes	7⅔	6	3	3	1	6
Nehf	⅓	1	0	0	0	0
McQuillan	1⅓	0	0	0	0	1
Bentley (L)	1⅓	3	1	1	1	0
Washington						
Ogden	⅓	0	0	0	1	1
Mogridge	*4⅓	4	2	1	1	3
Marberry	3	1	1	0	1	3
Johnson (W)	4	3	0	0	3	5

*Pitched to two batters in 6th.

x One out when winning run scored.
a Flied out for Terry in 6th.
b Doubled for Taylor in 8th.
c Walked for Marberry in 8th.
d Ran for Tate in 8th.
e Singled for McQuillan in 11th.
f Ran for Groh in 11th.

Doubles—Goslin, Leibold, Lindstrom, McNeely, Ruel. Triple—Frisch. Home Run—Harris. Stolen Base—Youngs. Sacrifice Hits—Lindstrom, Meusel. Double Plays—Kelly to Jackson, Jackson to Frisch to Kelly, Johnson to Bluege to Judge. Left on Bases—New York 10, Washington 8. Umpires—Dinneen, Quigley, Connolly, Klem. Attendance—31,667. Time of Game—3:00.

that this was a battle plan that would have brought tears of joy to the eyes of Robert E. Lee, Griff seconded Harris' emotion.

So Curly Ogden, the most improbable starter in the history of the World Series—with just four starts and a 3-1 record—took the mound for the all-important seventh game of the Series. McGraw, of course, started Bill Terry at first and penciled in the name of Long George Kelly in the outfield. Ogden struck out the first man he faced, Lindstrom, on just three pitches. Harris, riding his hunch, decided to let Ogden stay around a little while longer, but when he walked the second man, Frankie Frisch, Harris pulled him and inserted his left hander, Mogridge. Now McGraw could shift his forces to meet the new challenge, but once having done so could not shift back again. So he stayed with his starting line-up as Mogridge, not quite the dish McGraw had ordered, set down the Giants on two hits for the first four innings.

In the Washington fourth, Bucky Harris hit his second Series homer—one more than he had hit all season—to give the Senators a 1-0 lead. But then, in the sixth, the Giants' bats, which had shown patience and forebearance for the previous five innings, came to life. The first man up, Ross Youngs, walked. Then Kelly singled, sending Youngs to third. It was at this point that the two managers began jockeying for position, with McGraw, looking for an edge, actually at a disadvantage. Calling back Terry, who was the Series' leading hitter with six hits in 14 at bats, he inserted the right-handed hitting Meusel to face the left-handed Mogridge. Harris, now rid of Terry, pulled Mogridge and replaced him with his ace reliever, right-hander Firpo Marberry. For the moment it looked like McGraw had won the one-upsmanship contest, with Meusel flying out deep to Sam Rice in right to drive in Youngs with the tying run. And when, one single and two errors later, the Giants scored two more runs of the tainted variety, the Little Napoleon had a 3-1 lead. But he had also exhausted his options, something he would come to regret later.

With Giant starter Virgil Barnes pitching a masterful three-hitter, the game went into the bottom of the eighth, the Senators down by two runs and time running out on them. But then, with one out, pinch-hitter Nemo Leibold, batting for a poor player who fretted and strutted upon the stage and then was heard from no more named Tommy Taylor, doubled down the third-base line. And Muddy Ruel, who had theretofore gone for the Series collar, got his first hit, a single off Kelly's glove, to put the tying runs aboard. Bennie Tate, pinch-hitting for pitcher Marberry, walked to load the bases. After Earl McNeeley lined out for the second out, it brought up to the plate Bucky Harris, the man who had asked his troops at the beginning of the year to "Make me look good." Now Harris was the one who made his operatives "look good" by bouncing a sharp chopper down the third-base line. Just as Lindstrom reached for the ball with all the delicious expectation of a clerk grabbing at his weekly pay envelope, the ball hit a pebble and bounced over his head, two runs scoring and the score suddenly knotted at three all.

The game now went into the top of the ninth. Suddenly the stands at old Griffith Stadium rocked with the din and roar of patriotism, as the fans began chanting "We want Johnson," almost dreaming out loud. The chants soon became a bellows as the Washington faithful screamed with a maltreatment of lungs unheard of in Washington baseball history. And then, there he was, shuffling out in his familiar, behind-the-plow gait, arms dangling at his side, eyes staring straight ahead. As he neared Harris, the second baseman-manager asked him, "Well, what do you think?" Johnson only answered, "Gimme the ball," and continued on to the mound in an almost matter-of-fact approach.

For the next four innings Johnson retired the Giants more by force of his reputation than by his skill, getting into trouble in every inning. In the ninth, Frisch tripled to deep center with one out and was left stranded when Johnson struck out Kelly on three pitches and induced the man McGraw had substituted for Terry, Meusel, to ground out to third. In the tenth he walked the lead-off batter and then retired Travis Jackson on strikes and got catcher Hank Gowdy to bounce into a double-play. In the 11th he gave up a hit to the oddly-shaped bottle bat of Heinie Groh, walked Youngs and then struck out Kelly again to get out of the inning. In the twelfth he gave up a lead-off single and, with his heart in his glove, worked his way out of the jam by striking out Hack Wilson.

As Johnson ambled off the field after the top of the twelfth, long past the normal game limit, the Washington fans gave him a roar of appreciation, hoping against hope that he would not have to go back into the crucible for an unlucky thirteenth. But when lead-off batter Ralph Miller grounded out, their excitement lessened and fears increased. And when the next batter up, Muddy Ruel, lifted a fast ball from Giant relief pitcher Jack Bentley behind the plate for a loud foul, they fell into total silence.

But something was happening to the ball, now being wafted around on a prankish flurry of air over the head of catcher Hank Gowdy. Below it, Gowdy was giving his own imitation of a vaudeville juggling act: First he threw his mask down and stepped on it; then he kicked it away, all the while circling under the descending ball; then he stepped on his mask again, almost as if it had jumped up and bit him; and then he tripped on the offending mask and staggered forward in a move that looked like he was dancing at his own wake as the ball fell into his mitt and just as quickly fell to the ground. Ruel, as saved as a martyr at the stake, celebrated his reprieve by doubling down the third-base line for his second Series hit, in his last two at bats, raising his average from .050 to all of .095. The stands came to life again as up to the plate came Walter Johnson with a chance to win his own game. But the best Johnson, a good hitting pitcher, could do was slam a low-bouncing ball in the direction of Travis Jackson at short. Jackson managed to manhandle the ball and the Senators now had runners at first and second with only one out.

That brought up the man the press had dubbed "The Earl of California," young Earl McNeely, who earlier in the year had cost Griffith $50,000. Now he was to prove his worth, every penny of it, as he slashed a bouncing ball down the third-base line, almost a twin brother to Harris' in the eighth. As Ruel raced toward third, Lindstrom reached down to pick up the hopper, and then, suddenly!, the ball again struck a pebble—who knows if it was the same pebble in which the Senators had already established a proprietary interest—and bounded over the third baseman's head into left field. As Little Muddy from the Big Muddy continued churning his stubby legs with manifest gusto toward home with the winning run, it was only fitting that the man who picked up the seeing-eye ball in left field was Irish Meusel, the player McGraw had inserted into the line-up in place of Terry and who now stood as the symbol of the Little Napoleon's Waterloo. Accepting the Giants' fate as unalterable, Meusel merely put the ball in his pocket and headed with the rest of his teammates to the losers' locker-room.

Losing pitcher Jack Bentley was to sum up everyone's feelings when he told his crestfallen teammates, "Cheer up, fellers . . . I guess the Good Lord couldn't stand seeing Walter Johnson lose again." Indeed, as has been said, the mills of all higher authorities grind very slowly. But never as slowly as they had for Walter Johnson.

3 Bill Mazeroski's Home Run

Pittsburgh Pirates vs. New York Yankees, 7th Game, 1960 World Series, October 13, 1960

STORIES OF A WHITE HUE WOULD HAVE YOU BELIEVE THAT Abner Doubleday actually had a hand in founding baseball, even though the majority opinion holds that the founder of the National Pastime was a man named Alexander Cartwright. But no matter who founded the game, the World Series of 1960 confounded it.

For the 1960 Series was a war raged on the field and on the record books at one and the same time, so uncut to any pattern that it was, in reality, two Series: The three-game Series won by the New York Yankees and the four-game Series won by the Pittsburgh Pirates. It was the story of pop-gun versus howitzer, of a baseball David taking on a Goliath, and, in the end, of a man whose name was more easily pronounced than spelled, a man called "Maz." And therein lies the tale of one of the greatest games in baseball history, the seventh game of the 1960 World Series.

The Pittsburgh Pirates of 1960 were the lineal descendants of the old, old Pirates, the team that represented "The Iron City" in the National League when Pittsburg didn't even have an "H" to hiss in. Starting with the first year of the National League's eight-team alignment in 1900 through the first decade of the Twentieth Century, the Pirates were the National League's most successful club, winners of four of the League's first ten pennants, the team of Honus Wagner, Fred Clarke and Deacon Phillippe. However, beginning in 1911, the Pirates began a descent from the League's elite to its second-class powers, losing as many times as they won and falling into the basement in 1917. And then, with the infusion of such greats as Pie Traynor, Kiki Cuyler, Max Carey and the Waner Brothers, the Pirates once again rose to the top of the National League mountain in 1925 and in 1927.

But the 1927 pennant, punctuated by an humiliating four-game loss to the Yankees in the Series, was to serve as the Pirates' line of demarcation. For the next quarter of a century, while the Pirates would sometimes find themselves in the rarefied atmosphere of the first division, more oft than not they would succumb to gravity and fall into the lower strata. By 1952, after hitting every bump on the bottom of the road, they had become the most God-awful team in baseball. That was the year manager Billy Meyer, after another of his team's embarrassing 112 losses, told an assembled group that included Ralph Kiner and Joe Garagiola, but also included Murray Dickson, Howie Pollet, Catfish Metkovich, Bobby Del Greco and a host of others whose names have thankfully escaped memory: "You clowns could go on 'What's My Line' in full uniforms and stump the panel."

The very models of perseverance, the Pirates maintained their death grip on last place for the next three years. Finally, in 1956, they moved up, almost imperceptibly, to the heady level of seventh. But when the Pirates got off to their by-now traditional eighth-place start in '57, Danny Murtaugh was named as "stop-gap" manager. As interim manager, Murtaugh drove his thereto-fore uninspired troops to 26 wins in 51 games and finished the season in a flat-footed tie with the equally-dreary Cubs for seventh place. And then, in 1958, the man with the square chin and bulldog face took almost the exact group of athletes who had finished in last-cum-seventh the year before and finished second with them, deservedly winning the Manager of the Year title. In 1959, with many people riding the Pittsburgh bandwagon, Murtaugh's winningest pitcher, Bob Friend, wasn't, his .300 hitters didn't, and the Pirates finished fourth.

But 1960 was to be different: Friend came back with 18 wins; Bob Skinner got some key hits; Roberto Clemente and Dick Groat hit .300 again, Groat leading the League at .325; and Bill Mazeroski, the aforementioned "Maz," and Don Hoak proved to be the keys to the League's leading defense. Put them all together and they spelled P-E-N-N-A-N-T. The Pirate fans, who had suffered through more parlous times and a longer drought than the Pharoah's minions, suddenly had themselves a winner, their first since 1927.

The Pirates' opponents in the '60 Series were the New York Yankees who, since beating the Pirates lo those 33 years before, had appeared in 19 other Series, beating every other National League club in turn. This modern edition of the Yankees was a throwback to Yankee teams of yore, a window-breaking crew that hit a League-record 193 homers, 35 more than the '27 Yankees. Their two big guns, Mickey Mantle and Roger Maris—condensed by claustrophobic headline writers to plain ol' "M&M" in the name of space—led the American League in six offensive categories, usually finishing one-two.

But if M&M could make the ball melt into the stands, the Yankee's pitching staff could just as easily melt on the mound. To call them "mediocre" would be putting the best face on their arms, for never had a pennant winner's top victor had so few wins as the '60 Yankees—Art Ditmar leading the staff with but 15. This disarming group included an inelegant "Bulletless" Bob Turley, his fastball no more and reduced to confusing batters with his curve rather than convincing them with his fast one; an indifferent Whitey Ford, winner of only 12 of 21 decisions and able to complete just eight of 29 starts; and an ineffective Ryne Duren, pitching now with tasteless but painstaking devotion, and posting an ERA of stratospheric proportions, 4.96. In fact, with the notable exceptions of starter Jim Coates and reliever Bobby Shantz, the value of the package far exceeded its contents.

Yankee manager Casey Stengel, trying at one and the same time to win his record-breaking eighth World Series and to put to rest those persistent rumors of his imminent "retirement," now had to deal with selecting a starting pitcher for Game One of the Series from this group with their arms up for adoption.

After investigating all avenues open to him, Stengel found himself in a managerial cul-de-sac. His first choice for Game One at Forbes Field was Whitey Ford, a veteran Series performer with five career wins. But because all five had come at Yankee Stadium, Stengel decided to start him in Game Three, the first game back at Yankee Stadium. Reviewing the rest of his assembled troops, Stengel, with reasoning that was peculiar to him, dismissed those he called his "Green Peas"—translated: Those with no World

Series experience—in the belief that experience was the name ballplayers gave their mistakes and that possession of one minimized the other. But with a total of only 20 innings of Series experience among the rest, excluding Ford, and 10 of those belonging to Turley, Stengel was still stuck for a starting pitcher for Game One.

Pitching coach Eddie Lopat put forward the name of rookie Bill Stafford, winner of all of three games during the season, arguing that "This kid is the closest thing I've seen to Ford." But the rest of Stengel's braintrust, coaches Ralph Houk and Frankie Crosetti, were adamantly opposed to starting a rookie in Game One and, pulling apart the haystack, pulled out their needle: 15-game winner Art Ditmar. And so the Yankees' starting pitcher in Game One became Art Ditmar, the pitcher of least resistance.

Unfortunately, Ditmar also performed like the pitcher of least resistance. Staked to a one-run lead in the Yankees' first, courtesy of Roger Maris' homer off Pirate starter Vern Law, Ditmar took the mound in the Pittsburgh first. And that was about all he took. By the time Stengel had brought in Coates to pick up Ditmar's sputtering torch, he had pitched to six batters and retired just one, the other five reaching base through hit, walk and error, with a couple of stolen bases thrown in for good measure. Coates retired the last two Pirate batters in the first, but by that time the score was 3-1, Pirates. The Pirates went on to score two more in the fifth and another in the seventh as Law, with the able assistance of reliever ElRoy Face and his electric fork ball, held off the Yankees for a 6-4 opening game win.

Game Two saw Stengel come back with Turley. And for 8⅓ innings the man whose repertoire had once contained nothing but an unhittable fastball now kept the Pirates off-balance with an equally unhittable curve, his triumph of mind over batter such that for the first time in his career he registered no strike-outs. But the Yankee story wasn't Turley, but instead the Yankee bats which registered hit-after-hit with monotonous regularity and startling variety as they pummelled six Pirate pitchers for 19 hits and the second-highest number of runs in Series history in a 16-3 romp.

The Series now moved back to Yankee Stadium for Game Three with Whitey Ford trotted out for the ceremonial occasion, much like the Queen's jewels. Contradicting his pitches in mid-air, Ford was unbeatable, as advertised, holding the Pirates to but four hits—and beginning a streak that ultimately would break Babe Ruth's cherished scoreless-inning mark. Pirate manager Murtaugh saw his pitchers go through the rights and lefts of passage as the Yankees continued their fungo practice on six Pittsburgh pitchers, getting 16 hits and 10 runs—the majority of those coming on Bobby Richardson's grand-slam homer and record six runs-batted-in—as the Yankees went up in the Series two-games-to-one with a 10-0 massacre.

Game Four saw Murtaugh come back with his opening day winner, Vern Law, and Stengel go with Ralph Terry, another of his "green peas." Going into the top of the fifth, Terry had a no-hitter and a 1-0 lead on Skowron's fourth-inning home run. But in the fifth the Pirates tore up what Red Barber was wont to call "the pea patch," getting three hits and three runs, the big hit a blooping dying quail off the bat of Bill Virdon. The Yankees rallied in the bottom of the seventh, narrowing the gap to 3-2. With only one out, two on and Bob Cerv coming to bat, Pirate manager Murtaugh, who only the previous day had brought in reliever-after-reliever as fire-fighters only to get punching bags instead, now called on ElRoy to face Cerv. However, it wasn't to be Face's fork ball so much as Virdon's forked glove that preserved the Pirates' win.

Face, who described his patented fork ball as "a change of speed, thrown with the same motion as the fastball, one which sank," threw perhaps half a dozen fork balls a game, regardless of how many he was credited with by Pirate announcer Bob Prince. But its threatened presence made such demands on batters that it set up the rest of the pitches in his arsenal, including his fast ball. Now Cerv came to bat looking for the dreaded fork ball. And when Face came in with a slider was so relieved he less laced the ball gingerly than frescoed it fearlessly on a line to the furthest reaches of center field. But one who could, and did, reach it was Virdon, who had taken off with the crack of the bat and, crashing into the fence at the 400-foot mark, outleaped the ball as it descended into the seats, cradling it in his outstretched glove for a game-saving catch. That was it for the Yankees as Face went on to retire the last seven batters and wrap up the 3-2 win for the Pirates. Unbelievable as it sounded, the team that was down by 24 hits and 20 runs after four games had evened the Series at two games apiece.

Stengel had to go back to his pitching well for Game Five to fetch a starting pitcher. Again his choice came down to a choice between Stafford and Ditmar. And once again, he chose Ditmar and chose wrong. This time around Ditmar went all of one-and-a-third innings, giving up three hits and three runs. Stafford finally came into the game, pitching five innings of three-hit ball. But by that time, it was too late as Harvey Haddix, with Face again in relief, held the Yankees to five hits for a 5-2 Pirate win. Now the Series headed back to Pittsburgh with the Pirates in command, three games-to-two.

Even as the Series returned to a city now rocking with the din and roar of patriotism as all Pittsburghers merged in the premature celebration of their first World Series since 1925 and "Beat 'Em Bucs" signs and posters dotted the landscape like dandelions a lawn in spring, Pirate manager Murtaugh also faced a dilemma. However, his predicament didn't concern his pitching selection, as had Stengel's, but instead that of his first baseman.

For most of the season—and for four of the first five games of the Series—his starting first baseman had been Dick Stuart, the famed "Doctor Strangeglove," who performed less as the bedrock of the Pirates' infield than its rock. In fact, Stuart was so inartistic in his practice that the normally quiet Murtaugh, who went by the credo, "Better to say nothing," earlier in the year, when the public address system blared forth with the information that anyone caught interfering with a ball in play would be ejected from Forbes Field, was moved to wryly remark: "I hope Dick Stuart doesn't think that means him." Now with both his bat and his glove available to be rented out for advertising purposes for all the good they were doing, Murtaugh had been asked whether he would consider platooning the left-handed hitting Rocky Nelson for Stuart as he had in Game Two. Murtaugh had been emphatic in his response that regardless of Yankee pitching, the right-handed hitting Stuart would be his first baseman.

Bill Mazeroski, flanked by two other Series heroes, ElRoy Face (l) and Harvey Haddix (r)

The Team of Destiny: (l to r, front row) Gene Baker, Roberto Clemente, Batboy Recker, Joe Christopher, Tom Cheney, ElRoy Face, Rocky Nelson, Bill Mazeroski, Bob Oldis, (middle row) Danny Murtaugh, Coach Frank Oceak, Coach Sam Narron, Coach Bill Burwell, Coach Lenny Levy, Smoky Burgess, Dick Schfield, Gino Cimoli, Bob Skinner, Hal Smith, Bill Virdon, Don Hoak, (top row) Traveling Secretary Bob Rice, Harvey Haddix, Bob Friend, Coach Mickey Vernon, Dick Groat, Joe Gibbon, Dick Stuart, Earl Francis, George Witt, Vernon Law, Fred Green, Vinegar Ben Mizell, George Sisler, and Trainer Danny Whelan

So saying, Murtaugh started Stuart on first in Game Six, although truth to tell it wouldn't have made any difference if he had played *both* Stuart and Nelson at one and the same time. For Yankee pitcher Whitey Ford, like a vaudeville juggler who never varies his act, picked up right where he had left off in Game Three, shutting down the Pirates on seven meaningless singles. Meanwhile, Yankee bats, which had taken a two-day holiday, erupted again in a reign of terror, as starter Bob Friend and five other Pirate pitchers were all removed in caskets made by Hillerich & Bradsby. With Bobby Richardson driving in three runs to raise his Series total to a record-setting 12 and Yankee runners almost lapping each other on the basepaths, the Yankees got 17 hits and 12 runs to win 12-0 in a game that wasn't as close as the score indicated.

The Series now stood at three games apiece, with an important technical difference: The Yankees' three wins were fashioned on 52 hits and 38 runs; the Pirates' on 25 hits and 14 runs. To many of the phrase-distillers, the Series was all but over, the Pirates obviously inferior in station to the team that was rewriting the Yankee legend with their bats. The problem, according to many of those who had access to a typewriter, was that the Yankees hadn't taken the Pirates lightly enough. However, for particulars on what happened next, we refer you to Abraham Lincoln's sonnet about "fooling all the people," etc.

Proving there was nothing habitual about his indecision, Stengel approached Stafford the night before Game Seven and told the youngster he was his selection to be the starting pitcher for the deciding game of the Series. Stafford, who had won his spurs with five scoreless innings in relief in a losing cause in the fifth game, thanked his manager and confidently told him not to worry. But by the time Stengel had had a chance to drink on his decision, he began to treat his hunch like an idea he was afraid was wrong. And so, in a move that would qualify him either for a medal or for a urinanalysis, he changed his mind and went with the winner of Game Two, Bob Turley.

Turley lasted all of six batters. After retiring the first two Pirate batters in the bottom of the first, Turley walked left fielder Bob Skinner. That brought to bat Rocky Bridges, finally inserted at first by Murtaugh in lieu of the hopelessly polite Dick Stuart who had shown no malice aforethought at the plate, his Series stats reading three-singles-for-20-at-bats. Turley ran the count to two-and-one on Bridges and then came forward with a pitch down the middle. Before the ball had come to its final resting place it had traveled 350 feet from home and cleared the 30-foot screen in front of the lower right-field stands. The score was quickly 2-0, Pirates, as the fans rent the air with hosannahs. And then, in the second, when the Pirates began to work on Turley anew, with lead-off batter Smoky Burgess singling down the right-field line, Stengel finally decided that nothing would do Turley so well as his leave-taking and replaced him with the party of his first choice, Bill Stafford.

Stafford was to spare his manager immediate embarrassment over his decision to start Turley by taking over where his predecessor had left off, walking the first man to face him and then allowing Bill Mazeroski to outrun a bunt by making a hurried, off-balance throw to first. Suddenly, before you could say Turley-Stafford, the bases were loaded with none out. But Stafford brought the situation under momentary control by inducing Pirate pitcher Vern Law to bounce into a pitcher-to-home-to-first double play. Seconds later, however, Bill Virdon ignited the stands into explosions of glee by singling to right-center and driving home both remaining baserunners. The score stood 4-0, Pirates, at the end of two.

Bidding to become the 11th pitcher to win three games in a Series, Law went into the fifth with a one-hitter, his 4-0 lead seemingly safe. Even after Bill Skowron drove a wrong-field solo homer into the upper right-field deck in the fifth to make it 4-1, there seemed little for loyal Buc rooters to get excited about. But a lead against the Yankees was nothing you could either bank nor bank on. And in the sixth, the thunder that had taken so long to erupt finally came. Bobby Richardson, who already had enough

Series hits to last a lifetime, started the Yankees off with a single. After Law walked Tony Kubek, Murtaugh had seen enough and waved in his ace reliever, ElRoy Face, in an effort to reduce the Yankees' bats into plowshares.

Throughout the game, Yogi Berra, already famous for his line, "You're never out of it 'till you're out of it," had been saying, over and over, "If we can get Law out and Face in, we'll win!" Hardly as quotable, but as things turned out, far more prophetic. For, after Face had retired the first man he faced, Roger Maris, and then given up a run-producing single to Mickey Mantle, he came Face-to-face with the owner of the quote. Now Berra the seer hit a seeing-eye home run into the upper deck in right field, as close to the foul pole as one could get without going wrong. All of a sudden the game had turned over on its back and the Yankees had a 5-4 lead.

Two innings later the lead conclusively changed hands as the Yankees added two more runs off Face on a walk to Berra and hits by Skowron, substitute catcher Johnny Blanchard and third baseman Clete Boyer. The stands began to stir a little impatiently as the teams changed sides for the bottom of the eighth with the local heroes on the short end of a 7-4 score. More than a few local Starbucks and movers of dreams from somewhere under the slopes of the Monongahela raised their voices in supplication to Dame Fortune to help in their cause, in pursuit of which, only a few innings before, their team had come close enough to touch the hem of Fortune's skirt, but which now seemed doomed to failure.

Their entreaties were answered. Or perhaps unnecessary. For unbeknownst to even the most fervent believer, the Good Dame had already begun to point her gnarled finger. First she pointed it in the direction of shortstop Tony Kubek, who twice before in the Series had moved to left field in the later innings for defensive purposes, his place at short taken by Joe DeMaestri. But now, as Kubek started to run out to take Berra's place, Stengel decided not to make the switch, keeping Berra in the game for a possible at-bat in the ninth. And then, like the famed digit in Omar Khayyam's verse, her moving finger having pointed, it moved on, now directing its attention to the infield with potholes in its macadamized surface that would do credit to the streets of New York. Both player and playing surface so fingered would soon figure in one of the most memorable freak plays in World Series history.

Pittsburgh's eighth started with pinch-batter Gino Cimoli hitting a single off the left-handed offerings of Bobby Shantz, the diminutive reliever who had come on in the third and rendered the Pirates' bats harmless, retiring eleven straight batters at one point. Shantz, who had already worked his union maximum, five innings, longer than any appearance during the year, might well have made it more had it not been for the intervention of Fate at this point. For here was the moment she had been waiting for, the moment when she would step in; rather heavy-handedly, let it be known. Bill Virdon, the second Pirate batter in the inning, hit a hard, three-hopper in the direction of Tony Kubek, the kind of ball that is diagrammed in all instructional books as the ideal double-play ball. As Kubek reached for the ball with all the expectation of a tot on Christmas morn reaching for its presents, the ball hit a pock mark on the skin of the infield and, almost as if possessed, jumped up at Kubek, hitting him in the Adam's Apple. Kubek went down with all the force of a man shot, clutching at his throat and gasping for breath, the gypsy ball laying but a few feet away.

Now there were two men on and the only man out was Kubek, removed from the field with a severely bruised vocal chord and rushed to a local hospital for observation. Stengel sent in Joe DeMaestri to take Kubek's place but left in Shantz, the best-fielding

pitcher of his era, to pitch to Dick Groat in an obvious bunt situation. But Groat, a magician with the bat, singled past the pulled-in Boyer at third to bring home Cimoli with Pittsburgh's fifth run. That was all for Shantz. Now Stengel referred the matter to his bullpen, removing his ace lefty and bringing in Jim Coates, the lean right-hander who had a 13-3 record during the season. With the bunt still on, the next batter up, Bob Skinner, laid one down, advancing both runners into scoring position. And when the next batter, Rocky Nelson, flied out to right, Virdon chose to remain at third rather than challenge Roger Maris' rifle arm.

Now only one out away from getting out of the inning, Coates had only to dispose of Roberto Clemente, the Pirate great-to-be who had one hit in each of the previous six Series games, but none so far in the one game that made all the difference. That minor oversight was soon to be remedied, but only because of a major Yankee oversight. Clemente hit a chopper to the right side of the infield, scooped up by Skowron. But as Clemente tore down the line, determined on his immortality not to be thrown out, and Skowron pivoted to make the throw to Coates at first, the pitcher, studying Skowron's handiwork almost as if he were paid to watch, failed to get over to the bag in time. Clemente had his infield hit and Pittsburgh had its second run of the inning and sixth of the game.

That brought to the plate Hal Smith, the back-up catcher who had taken over in the top of the eighth for Smoky Burgess, removed the previous inning for a pinch-runner. With a sinking feeling that getting through the inning had become a survivor sport, Coates worked very carefully to Smith, the count going to three-and-two. Knowing that a pitcher cannot be too careful in his choice of pitches, Coates came in with his bread-and-butter pitch, a letter-high fastball. But Smith, feeding on it like catnip, reduced everything to its essentials with one swing of the bat, driving the ball to left field; not a parabolic blast, but an arrow-straight one that cleared the Forbes Field left-field wall with plenty to spare. As that fusion of souls known as Pittsburgh fans screamed in collective maltreatment of their vocal chords and threw paper and banners in the air, Coates stared at them as if they were personally responsible and then joined in, throwing his glove some ten feet into the air. Before it had come to earth, Stengel was on his way out to replace him with Ralph Terry, his fifth pitcher of what was becoming a very long afternoon.

Terry got the third out of the inning, finally!, but not before the Pirates had come back to score five runs, three on Smith's home run, and take a 9-7 lead into the top of the ninth. But with every play possessing the digitalis of excitement, the utterly improbable scenario hadn't yet played itself out. As Casey Stengel's clock was about to strike midnight in his last stand as manager of the Yankees, his team was about to come back with antidotes of their own.

Just when Pirate fans would have thought his bat had been worn thin with hits, Bobby Richardson continued to insert his oar in the most bothersome manner, getting his eleventh hit of the Series to start off the Yankee ninth. Adhering to that time-honored principal in the managerial dodge which holds that you throw in everything in the seventh game of a Series, deck chairs included, Pirate manager Murtaugh had brought in one of his front-line pitchers, Bob Friend, to pitch the ninth. But Friend proved to be as ineffectual now as he had in his two Series starts and gave up a second single to the second man to face him, Dale Long, pinch-hitting for DeMaestri. With that Murtaugh threw in another deck chair, calling in the winner of Game Five, Harvey Haddix.

Haddix promptly got the first man he faced, Roger Maris,

forcing him to foul to Smith back of the plate. But the next man up, Mickey Mantle, singled to right-center, scoring Richardson with the Yankees' eighth run and sending the tying run in Long over to third. Now as Pirate fans sat tense and giddy with emotions running the gamut from expectation to foreboding, Haddix came in with his offering to Yogi Berra. Berra slashed at the ball and sent a scorching one-hopper down the first-base line. Whereas the Pirates' normal starting first baseman, Dick Stuart—he of the "Doctor Strangeglove" notoriety—would have been handcuffed by the ball, Rocky Nelson instead handcuffed the shot and stepped on the bag to retire Berra for the second out. But Mantle, already the rightful occupant of the base, seeing he had no chance of making second, backslid into first, diving under Nelson's tag. That instinctive move, touched with more than a tinge of specialized intelligence, not only prevented the double play that would have ended the game, but also allowed Gil McDougald, pinch-running for Long, to score the tying run. And that was how the inning ended when Haddix forced Skowron to ground to Groat: Tied at 9-9.

The most two-sided game in baseball history now went into the bottom of the ninth. As Ralph Terry took the mound he looked in to see the first—and, as it turned out, only—man he would face: Bill Mazeroski, known to the baseball world as "Maz," and also known to the pitchers in that world as a fastball hitter. Now, as Maz bisected the plate with his bat, at one and the same time calling for a pitch right there in his wheelhouse and weaving sand castles in the air, Terry came plateward with his first pitch, a pitch described by Maz as "a fastball, high and inside."

Almost before he had received it, Yankee catcher Johnny Blanchard was calling time and hurrying out to the mound, there to tell Terry, "Come on . . . Get it down!" Terry nodded, and in an effort to take a little off the top, held the ball in his hand until he could almost feel its stitches, finally delivering it, getting it down a little. Ever so little. What happened next was that Maz swung and got it up, a lot, a rocket red glare, igniting the sky and the stands at the same time. As Yogi Berra stood at the base of the wall, stock still like a granite cliff above the canyon of the Ohio, watching the ball disappear from sight, Maz, who "didn't think I hit it hard enough to clear the wall," was then "busting my tail steaming toward second base." But as the noise made by 1,000 trucks going over a wooden bridge suddenly exploded in his ears, he looked up and saw the umpire making a circle in the air with his hand. Now, with the realization that he had hit the Series-winning home run, he ran around the basepaths, not so much in a home run trot as in an imitation of a kangaroo in heat, whirling his right arm madly in exhultation, his left clutching his hat.

Rounding third, Maz was almost carried home by the tidal wave of humanity which had now flooded the field, everyone wanting to pummel the man who symbolized the triumph of Everyman against the odds, the man whose home run had defeated a team that had outscored them by 28 runs, outhit them by 82 percentage points and 31 hits and whose pitching staff had a lower ERA by 3.54 runs. But what these refugees from the law of averages had was Bill Mazeroski. Plus a belief that life is never a mismatch. And that was enough to win, 10-9, in one of baseball's most exciting moments, ever.

'KNEW IT WAS GOING,' SAYS MAZEROSKI OF SERIES-WINNING HOMER

"Maz," the man whose bat won the kind of game the Yankees normally won

1960

Game 7 October 13 at Pittsburgh

	N.Y.	000 014 022
	Pit.	220 000 051

New York	Pos	AB	R	H	RBI	PO	A	E
Richardson	2b	5	2	2	0	2	5	0
Kubek	ss	3	1	0	0	3	2	0
DeMaestri	ss	0	0	0	0	0	0	0
d Long		1	0	1	0	0	0	0
e McDougald	3b	0	1	0	0	0	0	0
Maris	rf	5	0	0	0	2	0	1
Mantle	cf	5	1	3	2	0	0	0
Berra	lf	4	2	1	4	3	0	0
Skowron	1b	5	2	2	1	10	2	0
Blanchard	c	4	0	1	1	1	1	0
Boyer	3b-ss	4	0	1	1	0	3	0
Turley	p	0	0	0	0	0	0	0
Stafford	p	0	0	0	0	0	1	0
a Lopez		1	0	1	0	0	0	0
Shantz	p	3	0	1	0	3	1	0
Coates	p	0	0	0	0	0	0	0
Terry	p	0	0	0	0	0	0	0
Totals		40	9	13	9	x24	15	1

Pittsburgh	Pos	AB	R	H	RBI	PO	A	E
Virdon	cf	4	1	2	2	3	0	0
Groat	ss	4	1	1	1	3	2	0
Skinner	lf	2	1	0	0	1	0	0
Nelson	1b	3	1	1	2	7	0	0
Clemente	rf	4	1	1	1	4	0	0
Burgess	c	3	0	2	0	0	0	0
b Christopher		0	0	0	0	0	0	0
Smith	c	1	1	1	3	1	0	0
Hoak	3b	3	1	0	0	3	2	0
Mazeroski	2b	4	2	2	1	5	0	0
Law	p	2	0	0	0	0	1	0
Face	p	0	0	0	0	0	1	0
c Cimoli		1	1	1	0	0	0	0
Friend	p	0	0	0	0	0	0	0
Haddix	p	0	0	0	0	0	0	0
Totals		31	10	11	10	27	6	0

Pitching	IP	H	R	ER	BB	SO
New York						
Turley	*1	2	3	3	1	0
Stafford	1	2	1	1	1	0
Shantz	***5	4	3	3	1	0
Coates	‡	2	2	2	0	0
Terry (L)	*****‡	1	1	1	0	0
Pittsburgh						
Law	**5	4	3	3	1	0
Face	3	6	4	4	1	0
Friend	****0	2	2	2	0	0
Haddix (W)	1	1	0	0	0	0

a Singled for Stafford in 3rd.
b Ran for Burgess in 7th.
c Singled for Face in 8th.
d Singled for DeMaestri in 9th.
e Ran for Long in 9th.
x No outs when winning run scored.

Double—Boyer. Home Runs—Berra, Mazeroski, Nelson, Skowron, Smith. Sacrifice Hit—Skinner. Double Plays—Stafford to Blanchard to Skowron, Richardson to Kubek to Skowron, Kubek to Richardson to Skowron. Left on Bases—New York 6, Pittsburgh 1. Umpires—Jackowski, Chylak, Boggess, Stevens, Landes, Honochick. Attendance—36,683. Time of Game—2:36.

*Pitched to one batter in 2nd.
**Pitched to two batters in 6th.
***Pitched to three batters in 8th.
****Pitched to two batters in 9th.
*****Pitched to one batter in 9th.

4 Snodgrass' Muff

Boston Red Sox vs. New York Giants, 7th Game, 1912 World Series, October 16, 1912

BACK IN THE DAYS WHEN THE WORLD IN A GOLDEN AIRSHIP wafted on two wings, the press and baseball, the New York Giants ruled over both. The manager of the Giants was a rotund fire plug named John McGraw, a man so respected by his players that if he asked them to jump out of an 8th-story window, they would, secure in the knowledge that he would figure out a way to keep them from getting hurt before they hit the ground. So adored by the press they fashioned a special nimbus for him. And so revered and feared by the general public they ceded him special powers. It was believed by all that his lightest wish was law in everything but the laws of nature and God. In the 1912 World Series he was to run afoul of both.

Return with us now to those thrilling days of yesteryear, the year 1912, when George M. Cohan stood tall in his musical comedy, Forty-Five Minutes from Broadway, his fellow member of the Lambs John J. McGraw sat atop the National League and God was in His heaven and all seemed right with the world. At least that part of the world that called New York its home.

For the second year running the Giants had won the National League pennant, stealing 319 bases to go with their team .286 batting average and the most runs scored in National League history, 823. But it was more than their stolen bases and hitting that carried them to the top; it was their pitching. Led by Rube Marquard's 19 consecutive wins at the start of the year and 26 wins in all, Christy Mathewson's 23 wins and rookie spitballer Jeff Tesreau's 17, the Giants leaped off to a 14½ game lead by the halfway mark, July 4th, and continued on their merry, winning 103 games overall and outdistancing the pack by 10 full games at the wire.

Over in the American League, after many years of having taken byroads, side paths and detours since their last pennant back in 1904, the Boston Red Sox had finally found the Red Brick Road back to the top, coinciding with the opening of their new stadium, Fenway Park. These were the storied Red Sox of the famed Speaker-Hooper-Lewis outfield, a threesome which richly deserves the entitlement of the greatest outfield in baseball history. Connie Mack, manager of the 1911 World's Champion Athletics, had paid the trio with brio the ultimate compliment when he said, "A single that goes through to the outfield should score a man from second. But that doesn't go when we play Boston." Led by Tris Speaker, called "The grandest ballplayer in the country" in that quaint way the vital two-cent essays had of describing contemporaries, the Boston outfield had no less than 80 assists during the year, topped by Speaker's record 35.

With a fielding style that defied normal nomenclature, Speaker would play short center, close enough to be called a "Fifth infielder." Staking claim to more territory than an Alaskan Sourdough, "Spoke" could race in to engulf a ball hit to the shallow parts of the outfield or, if hit over his head like a smelly well-oiled hair tonic, take off ahead of the ball and the wind and outrun it for a graceful over-his-head catch. With Speaker patrolling center and everything that passed for same, left fielder Duffy Lewis could devote his attentions to the left-field foul line and the sloping eight-foot embankment in front of the wall in the newly-opened Fenway Park called, appropriately enough, "Duffy's Cliff." Over in right the estimable Harry Hooper held sway, innovating almost as he played and introducing such nuances to playing the outfield as sunglasses, the shoe-string catch and the rump-slide catch and even the practice of outdueling Fenway fans with outstretched hands for the ball.

However, three players do not a team make. And even though the Red Sox had the hitting to go with their airtight defense, the suspicion was that because this was the same exact unit that had finished fifth the year before—with the notable addition of first baseman-manager Jake Stahl—that the sturdy right arm of "Smokey" Joe Wood had carried Boston to the pennant, almost single-handed. For all Wood, called "Smoke" for good reason by his teammates, had done was to win 34 games, 16 of those in a row, complete 35 of his 43 starts and pitch 10 shutouts. On the day he was outdueled by Wood for Wood's 14th straight win, the man considered the fastest pitcher in baseball history, Walter Johnson, answered one of those improbable questions newsmen were fond of asking even back in the good ol' days with a "Can I throw harder than Joe Wood? Listen, mister, there's no man alive can throw harder than Smokey Joe Wood."

And so it came as no surprise that Stahl selected Joe Wood to start the first game of the 1912 Series for Boston. Nor that McGraw sacrificed young Tesreau, holding his two aces, Mathewson and Marquard, for Games Two and Three. Ahead 4-3 in the bottom of the ninth and with the tying and winning runs on second and third, Wood bore down and struck out shortstop Art Fletcher and pinch-hitter Otis Crandall. Wood recalled the moment later to social historian Larry Ritter: "They say that was the first time Crandall ever struck out at the Polo Grounds. The count was three and two . . . and I fanned him with a fast ball over the outside corner. I doubt if he ever saw it, even though he swung at it . . . that pitch was one of the fastest balls I ever threw in my life."

Game Two was played at Fenway Park in front of a fanatic band of Red Sox fans who called themselves the "Royal Rooters." Led by Boston mayor John "Honey Fitz" Fitzgerald and local clothing merchant "Nuf Sed" McGreevey—so named because any time there was an argument he became the supreme authority, ending any such shenanigans with his famous closing words, "Nuf Sed"—the "Royal Rooters" had disrupted the first World Series back in 1903 by constantly singing what Pittsburg Pirate third baseman Tommy Leach called "That damn 'Tessie' song." Substituting their own lyrics for the words of the currently popular "Tessie," the fans, in the words of Leach, "sort of got on your nerves after a while," and the Pirates went down to defeat, rabbit ears and all.

Now Fitzgerald, McGreevey and the rest of the "Royal Rooters" singled out Mathewson as their target to serenade. After about forty choruses of "Matty, why do you pitch so badly?," "plus seven Boston batters, the Red Sox had a 3-0 lead. But Boston

1912

Game 7 October 16 at Boston

New York	Pos	AB	R	H	RBI	PO	A	E
Devore	rf	3	1	1	0	3	1	0
Doyle	2b	5	0	0	0	1	5	1
Snodgrass	cf	4	0	1	0	4	1	1
Murray	lf	5	1	2	1	3	0	0
Merkle	1b	5	0	1	1	10	0	0
Herzog	3b	5	0	2	0	2	1	0
Meyers	c	3	0	0	0	4	1	0
Fletcher	ss	3	0	1	0	2	3	0
b McCormick		1	0	0	0	0	0	0
Shafer	ss	0	0	0	0	0	0	0
Mathewson	p	4	0	1	0	0	3	0
Totals		38	2	9	2	*29	15	2

Pitching	IP	H	R	ER	BB	SO
New York						
Mathewson (L)	9⅓	8	3	2	5	4
Boston						
Bedient	7	6	1	1	3	2
Wood (W)	3	3	1	1	1	2

N.Y.   0 0 1   0 0 0   0 0 0   1
Bos.   0 0 0   0 0 0   1 0 0   2

Boston	Pos	AB	R	H	RBI	PO	A	E
Hooper	rf	5	0	0	0	4	0	0
Yerkes	2b	4	1	1	0	0	3	0
Speaker	cf	4	0	2	1	2	0	1
Lewis	lf	4	0	0	0	0	0	0
Gardner	3b	3	0	1	1	1	4	2
Stahl	1b	4	1	2	0	15	0	1
Wagner	ss	3	0	1	0	3	5	1
Cady	c	4	0	0	0	5	3	0
Bedient	p	2	0	0	0	0	1	0
a Henriksen		1	0	1	1	0	0	0
Wood	p	0	0	0	0	0	2	0
c Engel		1	1	0	0	0	0	0
Totals		35	3	8	3	30	18	5

a Doubled for Bedient in 7th.
b Flied out for Fletcher in 9th.
c Reached on error for Wood in 10th.
* Two out when winning run scored.

Doubles—Gardner, Henriksen, Herzog, Murray 2, Stahl. Stolen Base—Devore. Sacrifice Hits—Gardner, Meyers. Left on Bases—New York 11, Boston 9. Umpires—O'Loughlin, Rigler, Klem, Evans. Attendance—17,034. Time of Game—2:37.

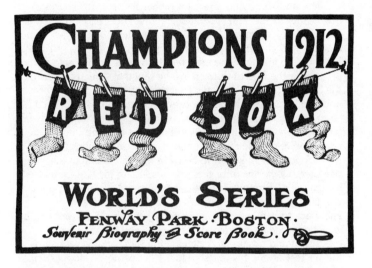

CHAMPIONS 1912 RED SOX

WORLD'S SERIES

FENWAY PARK · BOSTON ·

Souvenir Biography & Score Book.

DESPERATE FINISH WINS SERIES FOR RED SOX IN TENTH, 3 TO 2

Mathewson Weakens After Snodgrass Drops Engle's Easy Fly—Speaker's Single and Gardner's Sacrifice Fly Give Boston Two Runs and the Final Game—Errors Lost for New York

Hooper's Wonderful Catch Robs Doyle of Home Run—Wood Pitches Last Three Innings

How the Red Sox Won Game in Tenth Inning

starter Ray Collins had difficulty holding on to the lead, giving up single runs in the second and fourth. And after Lewis failed to negotiate the hazardous embankment in the eighth, dropping a fly ball which opened up the flood gates for a Giant three-run inning of their own, the two teams went into overtime tied at five. Each team tallied once in the tenth, and then, with the sun losing a game of hide-and-seek to the gathering clouds, the game was called at the bottom of the eleventh.

The rules of the time provided for an immediate replay of a tie game on the same field where the tie game took place. And so, the very next day, McGraw sent Marquard to the mound to duel Boston 20-game winner Buck O'Brien. Again the game was decided on the last out. With two men on and the Red Sox one run down in the bottom of the ninth, Boston catcher "Hick" Cady caught one of Marquard's offerings on the fat end of his bat and drove it to destinations unknown, somewhere in the vicinity of deep right-center. Fleet-footed Josh Devore took off after the arrow-straight drive with the crack of the bat and finally caught up to it, cradling the ball in his outstretched hands and continuing to the clubhouse on the dead run. With darkness and fog enveloping the field, few of the "Royal Rooters" could make out what had happened, and thought the Red Sox had won the game, cheering madly.

It was that kind of a Series; with all the thrills, spills and chills worthy of the name "Great Series." But when Wood beat Tesreau again in Game Four and rookie Hugh Bedient bested Mathewson in Game Five, it looked like the Red Sox, with a commanding 3-1 lead, would win a foreshortened "Great Series."

As the Red Sox entrained for New York already tasting victory, first-year owner James McAleer came through the Pullman housing his players. Searching out his manager, he asked Stahl, "Jake, who are you going to pitch tomorrow?" Stahl, who looked forward to dancing with the girl what brung him, answered "Wood," adding "Who else?" McAleer, undoubtedly thinking ahead to the potential big gate in Boston for Game Six, named that somebody "else": Bucky O'Brien, the loser of Game Three. And O'Brien, proving to be consistent if nothing else, did little else, giving up five Giant runs in the one and only inning he pitched, losing for the second time to Marquard.

Now the two teams shuttled back to Boston with the Red Sox still ahead three games-to-two and a chance to wrap it up with Wood to burn. But the game became secondary to the goings-on in the stands. Or rather, the goings-on *not* in the stands. For somehow, someway, somewhere someone in the front office, through a mux-ip, had sold the Royal Rooters' left-field pavilion seats on a first-come-first-served basis. The Royal Rooters, who had come to view their seats as sacred, found it sacrilegious that others could have taken their place in the pavilion. Trumpeting their fight song, they first marched through the aisles and then, when that brought them no closer to their announced aim, they waxed restive and, assaulting the pregnable barriers that separated field and stand, descended upon the greensward, singing, screaming and cursing in boyish whoops born of stress and frustration. For more than a half hour, while first security police and then mounted police pushed them this way and that, trying to corral them and move them back into the stands, the group of unruly taggers-after amputated the scenery and grubbed its roots. And, not incidental to our story, kept the unjacketed Wood standing around, his trusty right arm up to no good.

Wood, his arm deader than the proverbial twopenny, was cuffed about like a batting practice pitcher, the Giants getting seven hits and six runs off him before the first inning was through. So too

Giant Outfielder Fred Snodgrass, the unfortunate "goat" of the Series

Christy Mathewson, New York's "Big Six"

and out-for-out. Then, in the third, Red Murray, who had gone 0-for-the-Series the previous year, drove in Devore with a double that screamed just past Speaker, his fingers actually touching the ball, for a 1-0 Giants' lead.

The Giants came close to giving Matty a second run—and undoubtedly the game—in both the fourth and fifth innings. But in the fourth the laws of nature intervened and in the fifth Harry Hooper and some divine help made blank paper of the boxscore.

Four days earlier, during Game Five, McGraw had complained to the powers-that-be that a Boston triple which had gone into the blind alley off the left-field bleachers and given the Red Sox an all-important—and as it turned out, winning—run should thereafter be considered a ground-rule double. The officials, who knew that McGraw could make any act a scene, a function, a setting for an impromptu discourse, acceded to his request on the spot. The rule came back to haunt the Giants in the fourth when lead-off batter Buck Herzog drove one to the exact same spot in the passage between the stands and was given a ground-rule double instead of the triple his hustle had won him, there to perish on base three outs later.

Fate and some authority of a higher nature conspired against the Giants in the fifth, taking the human form of Boston right fielder Harry Hooper. Assuming his position before the game, Hooper had chanced upon a small piece of paper on the grass. Picking it up in one of the pre-prandial moves ballplayers so often do to clear the field of distractions, he saw that "it was a picture of the Sacred Heart of Jesus, with a little prayer." Reading the prayer and tucking it into his pant pocket, Hooper, in order to keep his lamp trimmed and burning to receive any blessing that might befall him, "Asked Jesus if it was His will to let us win and . . . I made a resolution to receive the Sacraments at the first opportunity."

Hooper's blessing was to come in the fifth inning in the shape of a Larry Doyle line drive that was headed for the temporary seats in right field. Turning his toes out to pasture, Hooper, in a move combining grace and genuflection, ran in a smooth and unbroken line, back to ball, toward the temporary stands. As he reached the wall, he turned his head to locate the ball and found he was "in the exact spot and position to catch it," the ball hanging weightless in the air just above his left shoulder. "It seemed," Hooper wrote years later to Red Sox historian Ellery Clark, Jr., "to be suspended in air. I reached up with my right hand and the ball settled in the palm of my hand without much impact . . . almost as if someone had placed it in my hand." After making the bare-handed catch, Hooper, without breaking stride, broke the barrier of the temporary stands in a leap of faith—and one into baseball history as well—his fall broken by joyous Bostonians who held him aloft whilst he held the ball aloft in his bare hand for all to see. Deprived of one, if not two, vital runs, Matty made the one he had go far indeed, reducing the Red Sox bats to matchwood as foreordained by dealing up great gobs of his famed Fadeaway. He even executed a cute maneuver—if such a diminutive adjective can be applied to such a great talent—by cutting off a Chief Meyers' throw to second on a double-steal and catching Sox baserunner Steve Yerkes with his sox down as he broke from third, thus ending an incipient Boston rally in the bottom of the sixth.

But in the seventh, that grappling hook known as fate finally got ahold of the Giants and separated them from their lead. The moment came with one out in the Boston seventh and nobody on. Manager Stahl, fighting off a Fadeaway, hit a blooper off his fists into short left-center. Shortstop Art Fletcher, backing up, called for the ball and then, like Balsaam's ass, dug in his heels, stopping stubbornly just short of where the ball landed, leaving Murray and

was Wood, who now went south to join his arm. The Red Sox's only memorable contribution to the game was an unassisted double-play by Tris Speaker who caught a line drive on the dead run and outraced the baserunner from second base to the bag. But that was hardly enough and suddenly the Series, which had once been 3-1 in Boston's favor, was deadlocked at three games apiece, with the Red Sox trying desperately to snatch defeat from the jaws of victory.

The deciding game was to be played in Fenway, courtesy of a coin toss used to decide such matters of state. With Wood and his arm dead to the world and O'Brien equally so, Stahl was forced to come back with the winner of Game Five, Hugh Bedient, to face the man McGraw and Giant fans everywhere wanted when the chips were down: Baseball's beau idol, Christy Mathewson.

With the Royal Rooters and their many supporters boycotting the game, only 17,000 fans showed up to see the seventh and deciding game. And what might arguably be called the most exciting game in baseball history.

For two-plus innings Bedient, who had outdueled Mathewson just four days before, matched the Pitcher-Prince pitch-for-pitch

Snodgrass short of breath and short of the ball as well. Mathewson, a perfectionist who was doomed forever to be unsatisfied, was so unnerved by the play that he served up four straight balls to the next batter, Heinie Wagner, to put men on first and second. He then retired Hick Cady for the second out.

Manager Stahl, waving frantically from second, now substituted pinch-hitter Olaf Hendriksen for pitcher Bedient. Hendriksen, who had not come to bat in the Series, stood in now to face the awesome Matty. Matty blazed a fast ball by Hendriksen for strike one and then got the man they called "Swede" to foul one off for strike two. Matty, trying to waste the cripple, came in high and outside with his third offering. Hendriksen, almost practicing pacifism, probed at the ball with a dull resignation to his fate. His late, left-handed swing caught the ball and sent it richocheting down the third-base line and off the bag into left field for a run-producing double to tie the score at New York 1, Fate 1.

"Smokey" Joe Wood—the same Joe Wood who had had his ears pinned back the day before—now came on to pitch for the Red Sox. And for the next two innings, gave up but one walk and no hits. Matty, his elusive drop ball still picking up the corners and picking up outs as well, breezed through the eighth and ninth with just one man reaching base. Now it was on to the tenth. The most exciting inning in World Series play.

After retiring Snodgrass to start the Giants' half of the tenth, one of "Smokey" Joe's smokiest fastballs was intercepted on its way to the plate, by the same Red Murray who drove in the first run, and driven into the temporary stands in left for a ground-rule double. The next man up, Fred Merkle, also saw through Wood's smoke and lashed a liner, arrow-straight, into centerfield, right at Speaker. This is the moment Connie Mack had warned everyone about, the "single that goes into the outfield" that "should score a man from second" but won't against the nonpareil outfield. But Speaker, swooping down on the ball, juggled it, looking like a man with 28 balls in the air, two of which were his own and by the time he found the handle, Murray has crossed the plate and Merkle was ahugging second. Wood bore down however, and struck out Herzog on three pitches and induced catcher Chief Meyers to hit back to the mound to get out of the inning without any more damage.

Still, the damage had been done. And with the incomparable Matty on the mound, there was nary a Boston fan breathing with a soul that wasn't so dead that they could have whispered a single curseword about their native land. Down 2-1, they needed one run to tie and two to win. And against a pitcher who had given up just two runs in his last 18 innings, the task seemed hopeless.

Their collective disposition didn't improve when, seconds later, pinch-hitter Clyde Engle, batting for Wood, lifted a tall lazy, high fly to center, midway between rightfielder Murray and centerfielder Snodgrass. Snodgrass called "I got it," waved Murray off the ball and, regarding his spikes with more than a passing concern, moved almost imperceptibly to his left and camped under the ball. As the ball descended, the 2,000 or more Giant fans began waving their blue-and-white banners. But there was a small flaw in their ointment and that was the fly. For Snodgrass, who had enough time to study the stitches on its downward flight, treated the ball cavalierly and now was forced to watch as it dribbled out of his glove and onto the ground. By the time Snodgrass had retrieved his muff, Engle had all but walked into second.

Mathewson, watching the cranky letter "E" for error raised on the scoreboard, slammed his glove petulantly against his leg in a motion that was eloquent in its anger. Unhinged, the master pitcher, who had always interpreted his opposite number in an interesting manner, now misinterpreted completely the intent of the next batter, Hooper, thinking only of a bunt. But Hooper cracked the ball hard, on a line for the farthest corner of center-field. Snodgrass, who was playing a shallow center and backing up second, also anticipating a bunt, took off with the crack of the bat, seeking a chance to redeem the situation, if such a thing were possible. Running rather than flying, only because he had no wings, Snodgrass finally ran abreast of the ball in the deepest part of center, the coming of the ball and retribution arriving simultaneously. There was now one out. But still the Giants' pilot light was flickering, his control somewhat short of the magnificent standard he had set for years, and he walked Yerkes on four pitches, putting the winning man on base.

Into the batter's box now stepped the fearsome Tris Speaker, he of the .383 batting average and the most extra-base hits in the Majors for the past season. Mathewson came in with one of his Fadeaways and Speaker swung, catching the drop pitch on the end of his bat and fouling it high into the air. As the ball twisted down toward what was then known as the "coacher's box," first baseman Fred Merkle, who had the right of way, started for it. But then, hearing a voice call out "Meyers, Meyers" suddenly detoured. The voice belonged to Mathewson—although there is a body of opinion that holds it was Speaker, adding verbal footwork to his agility afield, who was calling for the Giants' catcher—instructing the Giants' catcher to come down the line to take the pop up.

Hearing his name from God-knows-where, Meyers, began racing down the line with a resolution but not with a speed that would allow him to head off the ball. Meyers arrived in the midst of a tightly-knit debating group all arguing who would take what and where, there to watch as the ball which Matty could have stuck in his back pocket and Merkle eyeballed into his glove fell to the ground with a resounding Plop! Matty, turning mauve with disgust and self-reproach, snatched at the ball, all the while arguing with his two brethren and emphasizing his remarks with angry gestures. As he passed Speaker, the Boston captain, feeling as giddy as Captain John Smith just after Pocahontas went his bail, shouted at Mathewson, "Matty, that play will cost you the game . . ."

Now Speaker stepped back into the box, rubbing out the lines as if obliterating an evil memory. And, true to his word, drove Mathewson's first offering into right to drive in Engle with the tying run and move Yerkes over to third, Speaker taking second on Devore's late throw.

Fate had slipped the Giants a bitter pill with the sugar coating on the inside instead of the outside. There was now the shocking, almost indigestible, knowledge that what had only seconds before looked like a Giant win was about to turn into a defeat. Mathewson, unable to swallow the realization, threw four balls somewhere in the vicinity of the plate to walk Duffy Lewis and set up the hoped-for double-play that would take him out of this nightmare. But there was to be no double-play; nor a waking. For the next batter up, Larry Gardner, hit a high and deep drive to right fielder Josh Devore to bring Yerkes home and bring defeat to the Giants.

New York sportswriters, echoing Hughie Fullerton's belief that "The world championship belongs in New York and Boston is perfectly aware of it," did everything they could to rationalize the loss of the Series. Protecting Mathewson as if he were a national treasure, they tied a can to Snodgrass' name for all ages, making him the scapegrace of the Series. But truth to tell, the Giants had been beaten by the laws of nature and Others with a capital "O". And there had been nothing McGraw, the Giants nor the press could have done about it.

5 Carlton Fisk's Home Run

Boston Red Sox vs. Cincinnati Reds, 6th Game, 1975 World Series, October 21, 1975

LIKE THAT BEVY OF BLIND MEN WHO TRIED TO DESCRIBE AN elephant by researching different parts of its anatomy, Game Six of the 1975 World Series is almost as capable of possessing as many different descriptions. Some of those New York *Times* columnist Dave Anderson characterized as "the more excitable critics," and who didn't remember baseball back in those pre-TV days when sports reporting still got all over your fingers not your eyes, called it "The greatest game in baseball history." Others, like Boston catcher Carlton Fisk, who had a heavy hand in fashioning its melodrama, called it, more modestly, "A fantastic game." And still others, like Cincinnati's Pete Rose, in a little bit of verbal byplay during the 11th inning, called it "Some kind of game."

However described, it was an utterly implausible game. And one of the most thrilling in the history of baseballdom.

The '75 Series pitted the Cincinnati Reds against the Boston Red Sox, two teams which hadn't won a World Series between them since back in those antedeluvial days before World War One (I). From start to finish it generated enough electricity to branch out and start more power companies than the TVA ever underwrote. And, not incidentally, served as a showcase for baseball's wares for millions-upon-millions of TV viewers, once again establishing baseball as the premier sport in America, its "National Pastime."

The bill of particulars in the case for excitement started in Game One of the Series. But it centered less around the game itself than the Red Sox starting pitcher, "El Senor Tiante," better known as Luis Tiant. Rumored to be anywheres between 34 and Medicare, Tiant had been one of those baseball rarities to go from 20 wins one season to 20 losses the next back in the late '60s. And then worse. Rescued from baseball's discard pile by the BoSox in 1971, Tiant had come into his own with back-to-back 20-game seasons in '73 and '74 and contributed another 18 to the Red Sox's pennant drive in '75.

But he also came into his own, almost literally, with a pitching motion that resembled that of a contortionist. Hardly one of a surgical nature, his style was one that saw him doing everything but holding out his arms to become a railroad crossing. Preceding his delivery with palsied hand movements, approximately ten in number gradually descending from clavicle to belt line, Tiant would wheel around in mid-delivery to look at the second baseman, hold him momentarily in his gaze, and then swing plateward, coming with the ball from everywhere but between his legs. The overall effect gave batters the impression they were trying to hit through an out-of-control Water Pik.

For their part, the Reds—baseball's highest-scoring team in 13 years, winners of the National League West by 20 games and victors in three straight in the Championship Series—couldn't interpret the human corkscrew's flights-of-fancy, unable to tell his pitch from his elbow. With an unrelieved black scowl framed by a malevolent Fu Manchu mustache that would disqualify him for high honors in a beauty contest, Tiant threw an equally villainous ball which rendered the Reds' weaponry less bats than divining rods as they flailed in the general direction of his deliveries. But the Reds' Don Gullett, while hardly as efficient, was just as economical in doling out runs. The game now went into the bottom of the seventh tied at zilch, thanks to great fielding plays by Cesar Geronimo and Carl Yastrzemski. Then, leading off the Red Sox's seventh, Tiant, batting in his first game in three years, singled. Two more singles sent Tiant whirling around third in the general direction of home—which he finally identified and touched after someone showed him where the unfamiliar pentagon was—the first of six Sox runs in the seventh. As cries of "Lou-ie, Lou-ie, Lou-ie" wafted down from the stands and smells of his between-innings Cuban stogie wafted out of the dugout, Tiant reduced the last six Reds' batters to putty to wrap up his five-hitter and give the Sox the first game in their quest for baseball's Holy Grail.

For the second game the Sox tapped their reigning "Spaceman" and left hander, Bill Lee. Lee, who had earned a growing reputation in and around Boston—and even beyond its three-mile limits, for that matter—as being another in that great list of left-handed flakes which included the likes of Rube Waddell, Rube Marquard, Lefty Gomez and Mickey Lolich amongst many, met the charge with a typical Lee-ism: "Well, what can you expect from a northpaw world?" Now the "Spaceman" fed the Reds his best changes of space, retiring the first nine Cincinnati batters as the Red Sox jumped off to a 1-0 lead. In the fourth, almost as if they had finally smelled the coffee and awakened to its aroma, the Reds scored their first run of the Series and tied the score at one. That's the way it stood until Boston's half of the sixth when two all-too-familiar events took place: First the man that Boston owner Tom Yawkey called "Boston's best all-around player," Carl Yastremski, acquitted his accolade and singled and scored the go-ahead run; and Cincinnati manager Sparky Anderson, called "Captain Hook" for good and sufficient reasons, lived up to his nickname by yanking Reds' starter Jack Billingham in favor of Pedro Bourbon. By the time Bourbon had been relieved, one out and one inning later, the frontal edge of a nor'easter had brushed the Boston shoreline, dumping its waters on Fenway Park and holding up the game.

Finally, after 27 long minutes, play was resumed with the score 2-1, Boston. Lee moved through the Reds' eighth giving up nothing more than Pete Rose's almost obligatory single, just the fourth hit off him all afternoon. Then, in the ninth, with the Fenway Park lights shining through the thickening gloom, Johnny Bench led off with an opposite-field double off Lee. Boston manager Barrell Johnson, stealing a page from his opposing number's managerial book, immediately yanked Lee and brought in reliever Dick Drago. But after Drago had retired Perez and Foster he gave up a run-tying, two-out single to Dave Concepcion, who promptly stole second and scored what turned out to be the winning run on Geronimo's double.

Suddenly the gloom had pervaded the stands as the Reds, with some last-inning heroics, had tied the Series. And established the underlying plotline for a Series with more comebacks than Frank Sinatra ever assayed.

After two games at that misshapened old duenna of a park called Fenway with its inviting Great Wall, the highest-scoring team and the best-hitting club in the Majors had nary a home run to show for their combined efforts. But with the Series moving back to Cincinnati's Riverfront Stadium for Game Three, the four-baggers began to come in rather generous potations.

Game Three saw no less than six homers, three a side, explode into the darkness like night rockets. Yet, it was not a long home run that would decide the contest but the shortest hit of the night.

As the two managers rotated their pitching crops, running in a new pitcher every time a batter ran the ball out of the ballpark, the two teams battled into overtime tied at five, courtesy of a ninth-inning, two-out homer off the bat of Boston's Dwight Evans. Leading off the Reds' tenth, center fielder Cesar Geronimo, already responsible for one of the six homers, singled to right, there to become the responsibility of Boston's fourth pitcher, Jim Willoughby. Cincinnati manager Sparky Anderson now ran in Ed Armbrister as the designated bunter for his fifth pitcher, Rawly Eastwick. What happened next was to become the centerpiece of an argument for as long as memory and video tape serve.

Now Armbrister, in the best tradition of a man carrying out his assigned task, laid down a bunt, directly in front of the plate. Then, almost as if admiring his handiwork, he stopped short in a here-I-am-and-here-I-stay fashion as Boston catcher Carlton Fisk charged forth at the ball, barely five feet in fair territory between the mound and the plate. Proving they also serve who also stand and wait, Armbrister less advanced toward first than retreated one step back, all the while trying to tuck his head under his armpit in a move to get out of Fisk's way. Fisk, more than somewhat distracted by Armbrister's amateur acrobatics, fought his way past and then threw the ball on into center field as Geronimo continued on to third and the late-starting Armbrister raced into second. Appealing to home plate umpire Marty Barnett that Armbrister, amongst other crimes to the senses, was guilty of "Interference," Fisk and the Red Sox lost the argument. And moments later, lost the game as well on a single by Joe Morgan off Boston's fifth pitcher, Roger Moret. That 6-5 win put the Reds up two-games-to-one in the Series.

Carlton Fisk tries to climb up, over and around Ed Armbrister in Game Three.

The Sox came back with Tiant in Game Four to try to even the score. But this time around El Senor Tiant was vincible, his motion, while still giving forth ineluctible lies, also gave forth nine hits and four runs. The Red Sox, however, put together six hits for five runs in their half of the fourth. Then Fred Lynn, the MVP rookie with all his dues paid, saved the game in the bottom of the ninth by making an over-the-shoulder catch of a Ken Griffey line drive with two men on to preserve Boston's 5-4 victory.

The fifth game belonged to the Reds' Tony Perez. Coming to bat in the bottom of the fourth, Perez had gone, in the words of announcer Joe Gariagola, "15-for-0." But all that changed as Perez caught one of Reggie Cleveland's fastballs and frescoed it into the lower deck of the left-field stands to tie the score at one. Then, in the sixth, Perez duplicated his performance—same pitcher, same spot—for a three-run homer to give the Reds a 6-2 win and a 3-2 Series lead.

All of which serves as the table setting for the main course, Game Six, arguably the most exciting game in World Series history. Or, at the very least, the most exciting since the advent of television, that 23″ (diagonal) magic lantern which transported more people to fantasyland that night than Aladdin's wish-giver ever had.

Outdoing even guests and fish, which after three days outwear their welcomes, Game Six was postponed for three days by the continued and unwelcomed presence of the same nor'easter which had held up Game Two. But the three-day postponement of Game Six provided the Sox with one advantage: They were able to bring back Luis Tiant, winner of Games One and Four; in fact, the only winner Boston had. And for the first four innings, looking like a man who had just taken a four-way cold tablet and figured he had three more ways to go to catch up with it, Tiant rode his herky-jerky hobbyhorse, shutting down the Reds on one hit and no runs. His opponent, Gary Nolan, who had had to retire from Game Three with a stiff neck, now had another pain in his cervic, this one man-made, given to him when Fred Lynn hit a three-run homer in the first inning for a 3-0 Boston lead.

The score was still 3-0, going into the fifth. But in their half of the fifth, the Reds, after having spent two-plus games groping for Tiant's gypsy pitches, finally began to decipher his ambiguous motions. The inning started innocently enough, with Geronimo striking out. But then Armbrister, that professional fly in Boston's ointment, worked Tiant for a walk and went to third on Rose's single.

Up to the plate strode Ken Griffey, the same Ken Griffey who had smote one of Tiant's offerings to straight-away center in Game Four only to be robbed of a hit by Fred Lynn's game-saving catch. This time Griffey duplicated his feat, driving the ball on a line to the farthest reaches of Fenway's dead center. Lynn, racing as if a catch could be made by will alone, took off in pursuit of the ball, hoping for a repeat of his Game Four heroics. However, this time it was not to be, as for the first time in the Series "The Wall" played a part in the goings-on. The ball and Lynn reached the concrete fence at the spot marked "379 feet" at the same instant, both striking it and ricocheting off with equal force. As Lynn, clearly the loser in the race, slumped to the ground like a marionnette whose strings had been cut, his right foot crumpled under his prostrate body, the ball bounced toward right field allowing the two baserunners to score and Griffey to wind up ahugging third.

As Boston fans, who normally possess an infinite capacity for taking hurt, contemplated the possibility of the loss of the second part of their great outfield—Jim Rice having broken his wrist in the final days of the pennant race and missing the Series completely—

a cathedral hush descended over the stands. Finally, after what seemed to be an eternity, a shaken Lynn was helped to his feet and, after answering some of the same questions put to a fallen fighter, was allowed to resume his, and all of Boston's fight. But his presence, while a force, couldn't stop "The Big Red Machine" from scoring the tying run scant seconds later when Johnny Bench drove a ball off the left-field wall, a ball played into a single by Yaz, who owned the copyright for fielding "The Monster."

Now cranked up, the Big Red Machine scored two more runs in the seventh on a double by George Foster and another in the eighth on a lead-off home run by Cesar Geronimo to go up, 6-3. That did it for Tiant, who now marched off, looking less like an actor given the hook than a star being given an encore by his adoring fans, to be replaced by Roger Moret.

However, this was a game with more than enough flows and eddies to disturb the wits. And now fate, trying mightily to balance the ledger, shifted her attentions to Boston's side, somewhat in arrearages. Fate's first entry in Boston's behalf came next to the name Fred Lynn, who led off Boston's half of the eighth by hitting a single that hit off the leg of Cincinnati's fifth pitcher, Pedro Bourbon. After Bourbon had walked third baseman Rico Petrocelli, he himself walked, yanked by "Captain Hook" and replaced with Rawly Eastwick. Eastwick promptly disposed of Dwight Evans and Rick Burleson for two outs. Now all that stood between him and the third out—as well as game, set and Series for all practical purposes—was pinch-hitter Bernie Carbo. But here Carbo was to have his name writ large by fate.

Carbo had hit fifteen homers during the season—plus one as a pinch-hitter in Game Three—nine of which had been hit over The Wall, no mean feat for someone swinging from the first-base side of home plate. Now, as he took his place in the batter's box to face the offerings of the right-hander Eastwick, the Red Sox three runs down and four outs away from extinction, Carbo had but one thought in mind: "Not to strike out, to put the ball in play somewhere." The count went to three-and-two and Eastwick came in with an inside pitch on the hands, jamming Carbo. Fighting it off with a duffer's swing Pete Rose called "The worst swing in World Series history," Carbo dribbled it just to the left of the plate, but far enough to stay alive. What he did with the next pitch was an entirely different story. With one of the most beautiful swings in Series history, Carbo met a fastball down the pipe and drove it as far as a ball can possibly go in Fenway, 400 feet to dead center.

As the ball began its long flight into the record books, a vague roar, almost subterranean in quality, began to make itself heard. Then it gathered momentum and erupted into a full 35,205-throated bellow in an intensely-partisan salute to the utterly absurd scenario being played out in front of them: The Red Sox were still alive!

But Carbo's three-run homer—tying as it did the game at six all and the Series record for pinch-hit HR's with two—was only a link in the natural chain of events. For the next three innings those 35,205 in the stands and the millions more in the Global Village were reduced to a state of disability as the heroics, coming in many sizes and shapes, continued to pile atop other heroics.

In the ninth, Cincinnati left fielder George Foster gunned down Boston's Denny Doyle at the plate with the potential winning run. In the eleventh, Boston right fielder Dwight Evans didn't so much break the laws of gravity as tested their elasticity with an improbable leaping catch of Joe Morgan's probable home run against the right-field barrier and then threw out the dumbstruck baserunner for a double play. And, in the twelfth, Boston catcher Carlton Fisk caught Johnny Bench's pop foul with a spinning, sprawling catch,

falling into the seats. Just when the normal bookkeeper's mind, reeling at the thought of any more heroics, was about to call it a night, Fisk came to bat in the bottom of the twelfth.

With the game long past the prescribed limit, the clock just two ticks short of 12:33 in the A. M. and everyone limp from the veritable smorgasbord of thrills heaped on their plates, the man known as "Pudge" dug in to face Cincinnati's eighth pitcher in "Captain Hook's" processional, Pat Darcy. Darcy's first offering was high, "Ball One!" Then he threw a sinker, down and in. Fisk swung, making contact with the ball and, getting his whole body behind it, drove it on a line, bound for The Wall, but borne on a capricious flurry of wind blowing directly toward the left-field foul pole.

Up in the scoreboard, NBC cameraman Lou Gerard was trying to avoid a giant rat that had been menacing his ankle all night. Unable to avoid the rat and capture a shot of the ball at one and the same time, Gerard now zeroed in on Fisk. What he got, and what the viewers at home got as well, was a reaction shot to end all

"Pudge" Fisk's home run swing without the added histrionics and hand-waving that accompanied his Sixth-Game blast

reaction shots. For there was Fisk, one step removed from home plate, watching the ball which was now being carried by that vagrant rover called the wind back toward the foul pole. As the ball wafted back some 15 feet or more, Fisk prayerfully exhorted the ball to stay fair with exhuberant hand movements unseen this side of a Roman traffic cop, taking an entire host of Walter Mittys along with him, courtesy of Gerard's shot. Finally, what Fisk would later call the "Question of fair or foul" was resolved in Fisk's favor as the ball cleared The Wall, micrometers inside the foul pole. The elated Fisk shot straight up in the air, arms extended, and then began his historic trot around the bases, making sure to touch each and every.

That single act signaled the start of the most riotous scene since the Storming of the Bastille as fans exploded onto the scene, clogging the basepaths and hugging each other in celebration of the unbelievable 7-6 Boston win. But what should have been the end of our story wasn't. For Fisk's heroics had merely meant there would be another day, another game, a "Best of One" World Series. And by the next day Fisk, Evans, Lynn Yaz & Co. had sadly run out of miracles, going down to a Series-ending 3-2 defeat in the ninth inning of the seventh game of the Fall "classic."

While the spoils belonged to the Reds, the glory belonged to both teams, neither of which had lost. For never had two teams acquitted that overused word "Classic" so well.

CINCINNATI	ab	r	h	po	a	e	BOSTON	ab	r	h	po	a	e
Rose, 3b	5	1	2	0	2	0	Cooper, 1b	5	0	0	8	0	0
Griffey, rf	5	2	2	0	0	0	Drago, p	0	0	0	0	0	0
Morgan, 2b	6	1	1	4	4	0	fMiller	1	0	0	0	0	0
Bench, c	6	0	1	8	0	0	Wise, p	0	0	0	0	0	0
Perez, 1b	6	0	2	11	2	0	Doyle, 2b	5	0	1	0	2	0
Foster lf	6	0	2	4	1	0	Yastrzemski, lf	6	1	3	7	1	0
Concepcion, ss	6	0	1	3	4	0	Fisk, c	4	2	2	9	1	0
Geronimo, cf	6	1	2	2	0	0	Lynn, cf	4	2	2	2	0	0
Nolan, p	0	0	0	1	0	0	Petrocelli, 3b	4	1	0	1	1	0
aChaney	1	0	0	0	0	0	Evans, rf	5	0	1	5	1	0
Norman, p	0	0	0	0	0	0	Burleson, ss	3	0	0	3	2	1
Billingham, p	0	0	0	0	0	0	Tiant, p	2	0	0	0	2	0
bArmbrister	0	1	0	0	0	0	Moret, p	0	0	0	0	1	0
Carroll, p	0	0	0	0	0	0	dCarbo, lf	2	1	1	1	0	0
cCrowley, p	1	0	1	0	0	0							
Borbon, p	1	0	0	0	0	0							
Eastwick, p	0	0	0	0	0	0							
McEnaney, p	0	0	0	0	0	0							
eDriessen	1	0	0	0	0	0							
Darcy, p	0	0	0	0	1	0							
Totals	50	6	14	33	14	0	Totals	41	7	10	36	11	1

```
Cincinnati ...........  0 0 0 0 3 0 2 1 0 0 0 0 — 6
Boston .............   3 0 0 0 0 0 0 3 0 0 0 1 — 7
```

aFlied out for Nolan in third. bWalked for Billingham in fifth. cSingled for Carroll in sixth. dHomered for Moret in eighth. eFlied out for McEnaney in tenth. fFlied out for Drago in eleventh. Runs batted in—Griffey 2, Bench, Foster 2, Geronimo, Lynn 3, Carbo 3, Fisk. Two-base hits—Doyle, Evans, Foster. Three-base hit—Griffey. Home runs—Lynn, Geronimo, Carbo, Fisk. Stolen base—Concepcion. Sacrifice hit—Tiant. Double plays—Foster and Bench; Evans, Yastrzemski and Burleson. Hit by pitcher—By Drago (Rose). Left on bases—Cincinnati 11, Boston 9. Bases on balls—Off Norman 2 (Fisk, Lynn), off Billingham 1 (Burleson), off Borbon 2, (Burleson, Petrocelli), off Eastwick 1 (Doyle), off McEnaney 1 (Fisk), off Tiant 2 (Griffey, Armbrister). Strikeouts—By Nolan 2 (Evans, Tiant), by Billingham 1 (Petrocelli), by Borbon 1 (Tiant), by Eastwick 2 (Evans, Cooper), by Darcy 1 (Carbo), by Tiant 5 (Bench 2, Perez 2, Geronimo), by Drago 1 (Geronimo), by Wise 1 (Geronimo). Pitching record—Off Nolan, 3 hits, 3 runs in 2 innings; off Norman, 1 hit, 0 runs in 2-3 innings; off Billingham, 1 hit, 0 run in 1 1-3 innings; off Carroll, 1 hit, 0 run in 1 inning; off Borbon, 1 hit, 2 runs in 2 innings (pitched to two batters in 8th); off Eastwick, 2 hits, 1 run in 1 inning (pitched to two batters in 9th); off McEnaney, 0 hits, 0 runs in 1 inning; off Darcy, 1 hit, 1 run in 2 innings (pitched to one batter in 12th); off Tiant, 11 hits, 6 runs in 7 innings (pitched to one batter in 8th); off Moret, 0 hits, 0 runs in 1 inning; off Drago 1 hit, 0 run in 3 innings; off Wise, 2 hits 0 run in 1 inning. ER—Boston 7, Cincinnati 6. Winner—Wise. Loser—Darcy. Umpires—Davidson (NL), Frantz (AL), Colosi (NL), Barnett (AL), Stello (NL), Maloney (AL). Time—4:01. Attendance—35,205.

6 Alexander's Strike-Out of Lazzeri

St. Louis Cardinals vs. New York Yankees, 7th Game, 1926 World Series, October 9, 1926

FATE, IT IS SAID, HAS A FICKLE HABIT OF BESTOWING ITS fame upon those it later takes by the scruff of the neck and hurls overboard. Or, at least, tries to. Take the case of Grover Cleveland Alexander, for instance.

By 1926, the man alternately called "The Great Alex" and "Old Pete" had been around for 15 years. His reputation had been partially built on his pitching record—328 wins, including eight 20-game and three 30-game seasons. However, his reputation was not based on his pitching prowess alone, for Alex was known for his prowess with the bottle as well, indulging in batches of unregulated and unstamped grape back in those days when the hand of Prohibition lay heavily on the land. Only trouble was Alex had somehow slipped through its all-enveloping fingers, taking to drink like a camel arriving at an oasis after a long day's journey in sand.

But even Alex could hardly have been as drunk as he was often reported to have been; otherwise, he would never have been able to assay the mound. Some of his most severe cases of the "shakes" came not from his battle with the bottle but from his bouts with epilepsy, a condition brought about by a beaning in his first year of organized ball. One time, after reading a newspaper story about another of his supposed drunken revels, Alexander looked up and smirked, "Good God! I was never as drunk as this fellow had to be who wrote this here story."

Still, it was felt by most that Alexander's greatness was behind him; that he was dissipated, drank too much, and because he had broken his ankle in spring training that year, that he was through as a big league pitcher at the age of 39—an age when most self-respecting gentlemen of the same age were home tending to their gardens and collecting their pension checks.

But it wasn't his dissipation, drunkenness or disability that finished him with the Chicago Cubs, supposedly the end of the line for Alex. It was what Cub manager Joe McCarthy viewed as his insubordination. On the occasion in question, the freshman manager was running down the strengths and weaknesses of the opposing batters on the Dodgers, telling Alexander how to pitch to each. When the name Rabbit Maranville, the ancient shortstop who only the previous year had been with the Cubs, came up, McCarthy said, "We'll have to switch signs whenever he gets on second . . . He's smart enough to remember our signals from last year." Alex looked up slowly, a provocative teasing smile forming around his mouth, his eyes wrinkled to a fine comedy effect and sarcastically said, "Well, now, if we thought there was much chance of this guy gettin' on second, we wouldn't have got rid of him, would we?"

By the time the Cubs had moved on to Philadelphia, Alexander's remark had earned him a place on the waiver list, tossed onto baseball's scrap heap like an antique without worth, there to be picked up by any team in inverse order to their current position in the standings.

The team that then stood—or more accurately sat—in fourth place on that magic day in June of 1926 was the St. Louis Cardinals. In the first 24 years of the Twentieth Century the

Cardinals had finished in the first division just five times, the same number of times they had finished last. After a typical sixth-place finish in 1924, the '25 Redbirds, under the leadership of manager Branch Rickey, seemed destined, like water, to find their own level again, and by Memorial Day were floundering with a 13-25 record. It was then that owner Sam Breadon decided to make a managerial change, kicking Rickey upstairs and naming his second baseman, Rogers Hornsby, as his field manager.

Hornsby had first come up to the Cardinals as an anemic 135-pound, 19-year-old shortstop back in 1915. The then-manager, Miller Huggins, himself hardly robust at 140 pounds, took a liking to this equally diminutive infielder and took him under his wing. Hornsby hardly looked like he was destined for baseball immortality when, in his very first Major League game, he struck out the first two times he came to bat and compounded his first day non-heroics by muffing his first fielding opportunity. Huggins took Hornsby aside and told him "You don't have the strength to get the bat around. Try choking up on it," and Hornsby did, raising his first year batting average up to .246 in 18 games. Still, he didn't impress Huggins, and by the end of the year, Huggins "farmed him out," sending him back to the Texas League from whence he had come. However, Hornsby, misunderstanding the phrase "farmed out," thought it had something to do with his conditioning and spent the off-season working on a farm, fleshing out his scrawny and undernourished body.

A now-heavier Hornsby made the club the following spring—as a third baseman. In one of his first games he came up against Grover Cleveland Alexander, who had won 31 games for the

YANKEES vs CARDINALS

1926

MILLER HUGGINS   ROGERS HORNSBY

WORLDS CHAMPIONSHIP SERIES

HARRY M. STEVENS, Inc. PUBLISHER   PRICE 25 CENTS

pennant-winning Phillies the previous year. With the Phillies far ahead, catcher Bill Killefer, who had played with Rogers' brother Everett in the Texas League said, "Kid, here comes a good fastball. Le's see what you can do with it." What Hornsby did with it was hit it against Baker Field's nearby left-field fence for a double. Figuring that if he could hit the Great Alexander, he should be able to hit anyone, a now-confident Hornsby raised his second-year average to .313, tops on the Cardinals and fourth-best in the National League. He was on his way to greatness.

Hornsby remembered that moment. And he remembered Alex, too. And even though he had heard that Alexander had suffered the wages of gin, he now wanted him for his 1926 team. He was supported in his decision by coach Bill Killefer, the same Bill Killefer who had caught Alex behind Hornsby that fateful day and had caught him for 11 hard years, long enough to know that Alex pitched better drunk than anyone else did sober. Together they went to Rickey, now the general manager, and asked him to claim Alex on waivers. After the four teams below them in the standings had passed, the Cardinals claimed the Great One, all 39 years of him, as per invoice, thus getting the pitching help they needed. And the linchpin that was to make the Cardinals the World's Champions.

Five days later Alexander pitched his first game for the Cards, facing his old team, the Chicago Cubs. Giving up only four hits, Alex beat the Cubs 3-2 in ten innings, and after the game, passing by his own mentor—and tormentor as well—Joe McCarthy, he tipped his slightly askew hat in his direction, a smile lighting up his well-worn map.

With Alexander contributing nine victories, Rhem 20, Sherdell 16 and Haines 13, the Cardinals went into the lead in early September and clinched St. Louis' first pennant on September 28 with two victories over the Giants, one of those, fittingly, by Alexander.

The 1926 World Series pitting the Cardinals against the Yankees was mammoth in every sense of the word. Its seven games captured the imagination of the public as no other sporting event ever had, and was not matched in greatest number of fans and greatest gate receipts by any Series up to that time. It also featured the greatest stars in all baseball and one of the greatest moments in all Series history.

The '26 Series will be remembered by most as the one in which Grover Cleveland Alexander struck out Tony Lazzeri with the bases loaded in the seventh and final game to preserve a St. Louis victory. Ironically most of those who recall it—either from being there or from memory—recall it incorrectly, placing that moment in the ninth inning of the final game. Almost no one remembers that it was also the Series in which Ruth hit three home runs in one game, or that Alexander won his two starts, or that the Series ended in a strange and bizarre play . . . just that Alexander struck out Lazzeri.

With Yankee ace left-hander Herb Pennock pitching three-hit ball, the Yankees won the opening game, played in New York's huge Yankee Stadium, 3-2. The second game went to the Cardinals, 6-2, as Alexander set down the last 21 Yankees after a third-inning single by Earle Combs. Game Three, back in St. Louis' Sportsman's Park, saw the Cards take the Series lead on "Pop" Haines' five-hitter. Yankee bats, quiescent during the first three games, exploded in Game Four, as New York, led by Ruth's three massive homers, blasted 14 hits off five pitchers to win 10-5 and even up the Series. Game Five was a rematch of the first game with the Yankees grouping three hits in the top of the ninth to tie it; winning it in the tenth for Pennock, 3-2, to take a 3-2 lead. Back in Yankee Stadium, Alexander evened up the Series with an eight-

Grover Cleveland Alexander awaits his call from the bullpen, Game 7 of the '26 Series.

hitter, never having to extend himself, as the Cardinals raked three Yankee pitchers for thirteen hits and a 10-2 win. All of which served as a table setting for Game Seven, one of the most famous in World Series history.

The Sunday game, played in the cold and dreary autumn weather of New York—which had given rise to the early-morning rumor that the game would be postponed—saw Jesse Haines, winner of Game Three, go against Waite Hoyt, winner of Game Four. Alex was consigned to the bullpen where he could spend the worst three hours of the afternoon sleeping off the hangover his celebrating the previous night had produced.

In the third, pitching carefully to Ruth, whom he had walked in the first, Haines tossed a tantalizing inside knuckleball. Timing his swing perfectly, Ruth provided the momentum for the ball to take flight and clear the bleacher fence, deep in right center, passing directly over the words "World's Champions" in the Gem razor ad. That should have been enough to insure Hoyt and the Yankees the game . . . and the Series.

But Fate, who had decided every seventh game of a Series since its beginning, once again determined the winner, this time pointing her capricious finger at two men named Koenig and Meusel. She began in the fourth inning when, after Jim Bottomley had singled with one down, Hoyt induced Cardinal third baseman Les Bell to drill a one-hopper straight at Koenig for what looked like a sure double play. But Koenig, in his haste to shovel the ball over to Lazzeri, standing on second, lost the handle on the ball and bobbled it, putting runners on first and second. For the next batter up, Chick Hafey, protecting the plate with a count of two strikes and no balls on him, managed to ineffectively poke at the ball and lift a weaker-than-weak fly into the left field in the direction of Bob Meusel. However, the two marked men, Meusel and Koenig, decided at that moment not to communicate, and the ball fell between, leaving the bases full of Cardinals. Bob O'Farrell, up next, hit a high fly towards left center where Meusel, having a stronger arm than centerfielder Combs, waved Combs off so that he could make the throw to the plate in an attempt to catch the slow-footed Bottomley. But even as he positioned himself under the ball, Fate, who had taken a liking to him once, decided to extend her visit and somehow caused the ball to pop out of his glove. Bottomley scored and the bases remained full of St. Louis for the next batter, Tommy Thevenow (Thevenow had the lowest batting average on the Cardinal team that year, and yet, was to be the batting star of the Series, even hitting a home run in the second game, his last homer in the Majors even though he was to play another 12 years), who hit Yankee pitching, catching one of Hoyt's fastballs with the end of his bat and looping a hit into right, scoring two more unearned runs.

The Yankees got one run back in the bottom of the sixth and came into the bottom of the seventh trailing 3-2. Combs opened the inning with a single and went to second on Koenig's sacrifice. Ruth was intentionally walked, his third free pass of the game, to put runners on first and second with only one out. Meusel, with an opportunity to redeem himself, hit one of Haines' knucklers directly at Bell, who turned it into a force play, throwing out Ruth at second. Gehrig was now up. His bat had won one game with a single and his double had helped to win yet another. After getting two quick strikes on Lou, Haines seemed to falter, and his next four pitchers were all wide, loading the bases.

Haines turned around to Hornsby at second and wiggled his hand at his manager, sort of a cross between "Come here" and "Something's wrong." What was wrong was that he had worn the skin off his index finger throwing his knuckler and was asking to be taken out of the game. Hornsby, who had left-hander Willie Sherdell warming up in the bullpen, wanted a right-hander to pitch to the next man up, Tony Lazzeri. Lazzeri, although only a rookie, had an awesome reputation for power, having hit 60 homers and driven in 222 runs at Salt Lake City the year before. Hornsby wanted a right-hander; and the best one he had was Alexander.

So Hornsby yelled out "Alexander," and after a momentary delay a familiar figure emerged from the left-field bullpen, hat at a rakish angle and slouched over, ambling toward the mound, but in no apparent hurry to get there. It was Grover Cleveland Alexander, coming in after pitching a complete game the day before and—as legend would have it—celebrating all evening.

As Alex approached the infield with all the signs of a hangover, Hornsby trotted out and gave him a cram course in the situation at hand. "Well, the bases are full, Lazzeri's up and there ain't no place to put him," the player-manager told his pitcher. "Well," said the unflappable Alex, "Guess I'll just have to take care of him then," and moved inexorably towards the mound, Hornsby at his side.

After just three warm-up pitches, Alexander was ready to go. He readjusted his cap, fooled around with his belt, and then turned to make sure all of his teammates were ready. The man who had once thrown only 76 pitches while winning a nine-inning game—and who pitched fast because he didn't want to "let those sons-of-bitches stand up there and think on my time"—was now ready.

His first pitch was low and away for a ball. He took the throw from O'Farrell and returned it, almost as if it were on a long rubber band, strike one. His next pitch was outside and Lazzeri caught it on the meat part of his bat. It looked like a home run all the way; then just before it went into the left-field stands, the ball curved, going foul by no more than ten inches. Fate had once again frowned on the Yankees.

Now, normally a man who has just ladeled your pitch into the wild, blue yonder would bear investigation. But not when Alex was pitching. It has been said that a great martini must be the correct mating of gin and vermouth at precisely the right moment, not a second too late, like the proper making of a pitch. Alex knew the secret of both, even if he did get the two occasionally confused. However, this time he didn't, and coming back with a low curveball which one writer described as something "the Singer Midgets couldn't have hit." Lazzeri fished for it and missed, leaving the three base runners completely stranded. The confrontation—and the inning—were over. And, although it was only the end of the seventh, the Series, for all intents and purposes, was over. In the eighth, Alexander retired the Yankees on a grounder, a foul fly, and a pop-up . . . one-two-three. All that stood between him and baseball history were the three batters he would face in the bottom of the ninth: Combs, Koenig and Ruth.

Combs and Koenig opened the ninth by both grounding out. He then faced Babe Ruth, who had single-handedly beaten the Cards in Game Four. Pitching ever-so-carefully, Alex ran the count to 3-2. Then the man who could throw a ball into a gallon tomato can from the pitcher's mound for fifteen minutes without missing threw a curve ball on the outside corner of the plate and started to walk off the mound, convinced he had gotten the job done. But plate umpire George Hildebrand called it "Ball Four," and Ruth had his fourth walk of the game.

Alexander wheeled around and shouted at Hildebrand, "What's wrong with that pitch?" Hildebrand called back, "Missed by this much, Alex," holding out his hands to show no more than two inches. "For that much," Alex answered, reassuming his position on the mound, "You might have given an old son-of-a-gun like me a break."

The "breaks" were still with the Cardinals. With Bob Meusel at bat, Alex delivered a curve to the exact spot where the last pitch to Ruth had been. This time Hildebrand signaled "Strike." It was to be the last pitch of the Series.

At that moment, some strange spirit moved Ruth to take off for second. If his move was calculated to be a surprise, it came as none to catcher O'Farrell, who rifled the ball down to Hornsby at second. Hornsby merely held out his glove to catch the throw and

Tony Lazzeri

Ruth lumbered into it. In a great swirl of dust and a riot of noise the Series was over.

Later when asked by one of the members of the press how he felt after striking out Lazzeri, Alex merely stared at the pencil-wielder and replied, "How do I feel? Go ask Lazzeri how he felt."

ALEXANDER CUTS YANKS' GORDIAN KNOT, 3 TO 2, IN LAST TWO STANZAS

Old-Time Hurler Puts Out Lazzeri and Allows Ruth to Take Base on Balls After Haines Had Passed Him; Koenig and Meusel Are Left Handed "Heroes" Through Fumbles; St. Louis Gets All Runs in Fourth Inning.

BY HENRY P. EDWARDS.

YANKEE STADIUM, Oct. 10.—Alexander the Great again came to the rescue today and the St. Louis Cardinals carried off the deciding battle of the world series.

It was in the seventh inning of the seventh game that he made his third appearance of the classic. The Cardinals led by a single run, but the bases were filled with American leaguers.

An American league crowd was yelling frenziedly as Tony Lazzeri, the Italian boy from Telegraph Hill, San Francisco, went to bat.

Game 7 October 10 at New York								
St. Louis	Pos	AB	R	H	RBI	PO	A	E
Holm	cf	5	0	0	0	2	0	0
Southworth	rf	4	0	0	0	0	0	0
Hornsby	2b	4	0	2	0	4	1	0
Bottomley	1b	3	1	1	0	14	0	0
L. Bell	3b	4	1	0	0	0	4	0
Hafey	lf	4	1	2	0	3	0	0
O'Farrell	c	3	0	0	1	3	2	0
Thevenow	ss	4	0	2	2	1	3	0
Haines	p	2	0	1	0	0	4	0
Alexander	p	1	0	0	0	0	0	0
Totals		34	3	8	3	27	14	0

Pitching	IP	H	R	ER	BB	SO
St. Louis						
Haines (W)	6⅔	8	2	2	5	2
Alexander (SV)	2⅓	0	0	0	1	1
New York						
Hoyt (L)	6	5	3	0	0	2
Pennock	3	3	0	0	0	0

St L.	000	300	000					
N.Y.	001	001	000					

New York	Pos	AB	R	H	RBI	PO	A	E
Combs	cf	5	0	2	0	2	0	0
Koenig	ss	4	0	0	0	2	3	1
Ruth	rf	1	1	1	1	2	0	0
Meusel	lf	4	0	1	0	3	0	1
Gehrig	1b	2	0	0	0	11	0	0
Lazzeri	2b	4	0	0	0	3	1	0
Dugan	3b	4	1	2	0	1	3	1
Severeid	c	3	0	2	1	3	1	0
a Adams		0	0	0	0	0	0	0
Collins	c	1	0	0	0	0	0	0
Hoyt	p	2	0	0	0	0	1	0
b Paschal		1	0	0	0	0	0	0
Pennock	p	1	0	0	0	0	1	0
Totals		32	2	8	2	27	10	3

a Ran for Severeid in 6th.
b Grounded out for Hoyt in 6th.

Double—Severeid. Home Run—Ruth. Sacrifice Hits—Bottomley. Haines, Koenig, O'Farrell.
Left on Bases—St. Louis 7, New York 10. Umpires—Hildebrand, Klem, Dinneen, O'Day.
Attendance—38,093. Time of Game—2:15.

The swing of "Poosh'em up Tony" Lazzeri, the party of the second part in the great 1926 confrontation

Alexander warms up before becoming the oldest pitcher ever to throw a complete Series game in Game 6.

7 Johnny Vander Meer's Second No-Hitter

Cincinnati Reds vs. Brooklyn Dodgers, June 15, 1938

IT'S WELL-NIGH IMPOSSIBLE TO CATCH LIGHTNING IN A BOT-tle once, let alone twice. But don't tell that to Johnny Vander Meer who exceeded the union rate for pitching no-hitters, bottling his lightning in two successive games. And, not incidentally, pitching the first no-hitter in a night game.

Night baseball had long been a novelty. As far back as 1880, two amateur teams had met at Nantasket Beach, Massachusetts, under arc lights strung along the perimeters of the playing field. Other nineteenth-century exhibitions were held at Fort Wayne, Indiana, in 1883, and Houston, Texas, in 1894.

Even though exhibition games continued at night—including a game between two local Chicago teams, Logan Square and Rogers Park, at Comiskey Park on August 28, 1910, when twenty 137,000-candlepower arc lights "made the diamond bright as day"—organized baseball could, and would, do without them.

Then, on Thursday, October 24, 1929, the stock market crashed with a resounding Thud! and everything changed. People with no money to spend and only despair to look forward to began shunning non-necessary entertainment, like baseball, Major League attendance plummeted. The minor leagues were in worse shape, if that was possible. Something had to be done to resuscitate the fortunes of "the National Pastime." And quickly.

Grasping for any straw in the fiscal storm, E. Lee Keyser, president of the Des Moines team of the Class A Western League, boldly announced at the 1930 National Association meeting his intention to be the first team in organized baseball to play at night. Investing more than $19,000 in the installation of a system of Little Giant generators, he planned his first night game for May 2, 1930. Keyser's idea soon took hold throughout the minors. Team after team tried what was then called "a scheme" as odd jewels began shining against the velvet of the night. *The Reach Official Baseball Guide* of 1931 duly noted the occasion, "The Western League had one of its best financial seasons in history. Electric lights saved the circuit at a time when conditions were quite shaky."

Des Moines was like an illuminated pebble thrown into a pond. Minor league ballparks soon began to take on the look of fireflies at twilight as ripples reached parks in Omaha, Oklahoma City, Topeka, Pueblo, Denver, Houston, San Antonio, Shreveport, Little Rock, Indianapolis and Buffalo. The Texas League, which had played only four night games during the first half of the 1930 season, saw 116 of the final 307 games played under the lights. And every team that experimented with night baseball profited because of it. They had chanced across a heretofore undiscovered marketing verity: 90 percent of all entertainment dollars were spent at night. It was now a brand new ball game because of night baseball.

Even while minor league baseball had lit a candlepower to show baseball the way, Major League owners, as unmoving as the faces on Mt. Rushmore, failed to see that way. It would take them five more years to light up their lives. And their pocketbooks as well.

The man who was responsible for finally leading the Majors out of their self-imposed darkness was Leland Stanford MacPhail. Known throughout the baseball world as Larry, MacPhail was a brash, gaudy promoter, as enterprising as he was energetic.

MacPhail had found a franchise which he could fix up if he were handy with money, the Cincinnati Reds. There, the owner emeritus, Sidney Weill, had made a small fortune out of a somewhat more substantial one and the bank, having had enough of a bad thing, called in its loan, repossessing the team. The bank, now threatening that "unless someone came to the front with some ready money, the franchise would be sold to some other city," was ready to listen to anyone with capital. What it found was someone with two, as in MacPhail, capital "M", capital "P," who, together with his "angel," Cincinnati radio executive Powell Crosley, took the team off the grateful hands of the bank.

MacPhail inherited a team that had finished in last place for the past three years and showed little or no chance for improvement, its players long in the tooth and merely playing through the fogbanks of memory. And although he rechristened old Redland Field Crosley Field in honor of the owner and applied liberal coats of cosmetic paint to her aging exterior, the fans continued to show their appreciation by coming dressed as empty seats. Obviously something had to be done. And fast.

So MacPhail petitioned the National League for permission to play some of his home games at night during the upcoming 1935 season. Unexpectedly, he received support from Sam Breadon, president of the St. Louis Cardinals who had an entirely different problem than that which MacPhail faced. Breadon faced competition from a softball league which played triple headers at night before as many as 10,000 fans for an admission of only 10¢. Promoted by former great George Sisler, it had become a tremendous success in the St. Louis area, where day games were played in that summer abattoir known as St. Louis weather which heated up to 120 degrees on a good day.

In order to pacify the unceasing racket of this New Turk, the National League voted to "permit a maximum of seven night games to each of its member clubs desiring the privilege." However, the Old Guard held fast, New York Giant owner Horace Stoneham announcing that the Giants would not play night baseball, either at home or away. It was, or so he believed, an unsuccessful combination, one in which accidents could occur. And further, the initial outlay of "not less than $40,000" wouldn't warrant the extra fans. Two other teams, Pittsburgh and Brooklyn, also announced that they had no intention of trying night baseball either.

After several postponements due to rain—an omen some took to indicate meant that had God but intended there be night baseball, he would have caused ballplayers to be born with miners' lamps atop their heads—President Franklin D. Roosevelt threw a switch on the night of May 24, 1935, illuminating the 632 lights rimming Crosley Field. And as 20,422 "oohed" and "aahed," the era of night baseball was ushered in. Baseball's dark age had been enlightened—both on the field and in the front office.

Vander Meer, at the top of his form.

Jump three years ahead to 1938. MacPhail has been unceremoniously dumped on his classic features by the Cincinnati club and has landed again on his feet, this time as head of the once-proud Brooklyn franchise, reclaiming the Dodgers from the Brooklyn Trust Company like a second-hand car. Bringing with him his patented talent for zaniness, MacPhail has sponsored a nonstop feast of automobile raffles, track meets, beauty contests and fashion shows, not only turning the club around but converting a bankrupt property into a gold mine. Now, returning like an old tiger to the place of his last-remembered beauty, night baseball, he petitions the bank to ante up $72,000 for lights and the National League for permission to become the second Major League franchise to offer night baseball. Permission granted. The first night game in Brooklyn's history, and MacPhail's first effort in his second city, is scheduled to take place June 15, 1938, against his former team, the Cincinnati Reds.

A scant four days before Brooklyn was to join Cincinnati in the world of the enlightened, a 22-year-old rookie, with hair the color of a smoked meerschaum and a blazing fast ball, named Johnny Vander Meer had pitched the first no-hitter for the Cincinnati Reds in 19 years, beating the-then Boston Bees. Even before third baseman Lew Riggs had thrown out Boston catcher Ray Mueller for the 27th and final out, the last piece had fallen into place for MacPhail's jollyhop the following Wednesday night: Johnny Vander Meer would be going for his second consecutive no-hitter on the occasion of the first night game in Brooklyn's history.

Vander Meer's no-hitter had been but the 66th in modern Major League history, with only six pitchers before him—Christy Mathewson, Cy Young, Frank Smith, Addie Joss, Tom Hughes

Vander Meer Twirls Second No-Hit Game

Cincy Hurler Triumphs, 6-0

No-Hit Game Against Boston Bees Last Saturday Is Duplicated Against Dodgers in Night Contest

Johnny Vander Meer flanked by his manager, Bill McKechnie, and catcher Ernie Lombardi who, in Vander Meer's words, "called every pitch" in his two no-hitters.

and Dutch Leonard—ever having pitched two. And none of those in succession. But the subtext was always there. The closest any pitcher had ever come to pitching back-to-back no-hitters had come in 1923 when Howard Ehmke, pitching for the woeful Boston Red Sox, was the recipient of a questionable decision by the official scorer. In his previous outing, Ehmke had pitched a no-hitter against the Philadelphia A's. Then he stood on the mound against Babe Ruth & Co. of the pennant-bound New York Yankees. The very first batter Ehmke faced, little Whitey Witt, reputedly the fastest man in all of baseball, hammered at the first Ehmke fast ball offered up and chopped the ball down the third base line where Sox third baseman Howard Shanks hugged it to his chest like a long-lost son, muffling it more than muffing it. Witt, who had gotten a good jump out of the batter's box, legged it out without even drawing a throw. Ehmke retired the next 27 men, no hits, no walks, no man to reach first. But despite the pressure on him to change his decision, official scorer Fred Lieb wouldn't change what he called his "doubtful call" and it remained a hit, albeit a "scratchy one."

Johnny Vander Meer would change all of that. And make baseball history as well on the night of June 15, 1938. Not incidentally, the night night baseball came to Brooklyn. And, officially to baseball.

As 40,000 Brooklyn fans pushed their way through the turnstiles at Ebbets Field that June night, they little knew—nor in many cases, to be truthful, cared—that they were about to see baseball history in the making. The game was incidental. The novelty of night baseball and the pregame fanfare, with all the shuffles that precede a major event, were the attraction. There were bands, dignitaries, and on the field Olympic Medalist Jesse Owens running against the clock, and everywhere General Electric lights turned night into day. It was a picnic, even if it was a nocturnal one.

After what seemed like an eternity—but in reality only twenty-five minutes after the scheduled starting time for the game, Mac-Phail holding up the game because people still were backed up at the ticket windows—the circus goings-on were suspended for the ballgame much to the displeasure of those who were still basking in the accomplishments of MacPhail and Edison, in that order.

While the lights illumined the green-and-white-and-earth brown designs of Ebbets Field below, Johnny Vander Meer, out of the night that covered him, began to take on the sparkle of a solitary star as inning-after-inning he shut out the Dodgers' lights. By the end of the sixth, it seemed that he was holding up a mirror to his last performance, with no Brooklyn batter reaching him for anything resembling a hit.

As the game moved into the seventh, with the result no longer in doubt, courtesy of a Frank McCormick three-run homer, the crowd sat tense and giddy with anticipation. Even as they did, the human moth who was fluttering around the flame of greatness was experiencing difficulties with his fast ball, the pitch that had brought him this far. First he walked Brooklyn third baseman Cookie Lavagetto and then first baseman Dolf Camilli. With the Flatbush Faithful now solidly behind the efforts of one of the enemy and cheering his every pitch, the first impulse of Lavagetto and Camilli must have been to walk over to Vander Meer and apologize on behalf of management. But even as Vandy's fastball was losing its speed, he found another pitch, a sharp-breaking curve, a pitch he had used no more than five times over the first six innings. With the Dodgers still looking for his fire, Vandy was able to get them with his smoke. And get out of the seventh.

In the bottom of the eighth, with strength pouring out of his every hollow, Vander Meer put the Dodgers down in order, retiring Woody English, batting for pitcher Luke Hamlin, Kiki Cuyler and Johnny Hudson. Now it was on to the ninth. And history.

Closing in on immortality, Vander Meer took his place on the mound for the bottom of the ninth with a deceptive air of indifference. His countenance was proof against emotion. But inside it was a thousand little kids jumping up and down at their birthday parties. The stands were no different as the 40,000, dreaming out loud, were on their feet, feeling the urgency of the situation. The first Brooklyn batsman up, left fielder Buddy Hassett, hit an easy bounder along the first base line which Vander Meer fielded, personally tagging out Hassett. One out. Now every voice cheered in support of "their" Vandy.

The celebration was a mite bit premature as Vander Meer, pressing mightily, tried less to convince Brooklyn hitters with his fast ball than to confuse them with his curve. He did neither. In rapid succession he walked Babe Phelps, Lavagetto, and Camilli again to load the bases. The stands fell silent as visions of what might have been and what was merged.

After a brief visit to the mound by Reds' manager Bill McKechnie who told his young charge, "You're trying too hard, John, . . . , just get it over the plate," Vander Meer went back to the chore at hand—the speedy Ernie Koy. Having built a bridge for his retreating enemies, Vandy now took pains to destroy it. Concentrating on throwing strikes, Vander Meer decided to stick to his guns, loaded or no, and threw Koy two fast balls. Koy took both for a count of one-and-one. Vandy came back with another fast ball and Koy sent it bounding toward third baseman Lew Riggs. Riggs fielded the ball cleanly and then, after due deliberation, threw the ball very c-a-r-e-f-u-l-l-y to catcher Ernie Lombardi for the force out at home rather than try for a double play around the horn. Lombardi had no chance of doubling the speedy Koy up at first, especially since Koy was running inside the first base line, blocking Lombardi's view of first and first baseman McCormick.

All the chips were now piled high on Red . . . and on the Reds pitcher. Into the box stepped Dodger shortstop Leo Durocher. Despite his nickname, "The All-American Out," Durocher had a well-earned reputation for delivering in the pinch. Still, Vandy faced him with an equal serving of equanimity and sang-froid, his composure such that his eyes appeared to be affixed to a little red spot on the end of Durocher's nose. Or lip, as the case may be. With his no-hitter now a tangible thing, his eyes fired and then the ball. There was a loud crack and the crowd groaned as Durocher swung mightily, lining a loud foul down the right-field line and back into the stands. Strike one. Vandy came back with yet another fast ball. Strike two. And yet another. This time plate umpire Bill Stewart, his vision blocked by the square block of granite in front of him named Lombardi, missed the call as the ball caught the outside corner of the plate. Ball one, strike two. Vander Meer reared back and let fly and Durocher's bat hit ball with a thwack. The ball took off on an arc to center field, where center fielder Harry Craft, who had saved Vander Meer's first no-hitter with a circus catch, now only had to camp out under the soft fly. As the ball came down, Craft's yawning glove engulfed it for the third out.

Johnny Vander Meer now had his twin hills from which he could look down on the rest of the baseball world. Equally important, by providing his own incandescence to match the brilliance that shown down on Ebbets Field that June night in 1938, he had taken both himself and baseball into a world of light.

8 Cookie Lavagetto's Hit

Brooklyn Dodgers vs. New York Yankees, 4th Game, 1947 World Series, October 3, 1947

IF BASEBALL IS A METAPHOR FOR A METAPHOR, AS HAS BEEN suggested, then the year 1947 was the year when baseball's stage was crowded to overflowing with more aspirations—past, present and future—than at anytime in its history.

On stage, taking their final curtain calls, were several performers whose careers had been extended by World War II, now less baseball figures than father figures, all waiting to hear the applause of earlier days—earlier days which would never be heard again. That thinning group with thinning enthusiasm and equally thinning hair who bowed out in 1947 included the likes of Spud Chandler, Mort Cooper, Nick Etten, Stan Hack, Billy Herman, Billy Jurges, Ernie Lombardi, Al Lopez, and Red Ruffing. Add to their ranks the names of two former stars whose careers had been cut short by World War II, Hank Greenberg and Cecil Travis, and a cast of characters with some of the most unrecognizable names this side of a Lithuanian phone book and you have the greatest mass exodus since the staging of Dunkirk.

Waiting in the wings, stage left—or stage right, depending upon their instructions—for their cue to come front and center were such future stars as Yogi Berra, Lou Brissie, Bobby Brown, Nellie Fox, Billy Goodman, Gil Hodges, Art Houtteman, Larry Jansen, Ted Kluszewski, Mel Parnell, Jackie Robinson, Al Rosen, Spec Shea, Curt Simmons, Duke Snider, Hank Thompson, Vic Wertz, and Eddie Yost amongst the many listed in baseball's long chorus line of newcomers.

Yet, despite the presence on stage of so many leading and supporting stars and stars-to-be, 1947 would be remembered as the year when, in one of the most recurrent themes in all of dramaturgy, three understudies stepped into the World Series spotlight and raised a slipshod performance into a sterling melodrama; when three men, cameo players all, crowded the stars off the stage and, in their last hurrahs, gained timeless fame: Bill Bevens, Al Gionfriddo, and Cookie Lavagetto.

It was only fitting that, in baseball's greatest transitional year ever, the two teams that would meet in the '47 Fall Classic were the New York Yankees and the Brooklyn Dodgers, the two teams then in the greatest state of flux.

For years the Yankees had been the very model of baseball consistency, the team of Ruth, Gehrig, and Combs and later Bill Dickey, Red Ruffing, and Joe McCarthy, all mainstays of greatness whose careers had been synonymous with the Yankees on a year-in-year-out basis. But by 1947 all were gone, Dickey and Ruffing leaving after '46 and McCarthy quitting in mid-season when it seemed the Yankees were changing managers with every home stand.

Going into the 1947 season the Yankee pinstripes had become less a baseball uniform than a rented suit as players, not unlike the omen in T. S. Eliot's poem, would come and go, talking of Joe DiMaggio—one of only three players, along with Phil Rizzuto and Tommy Henrich, to be a fixture at his position in both '46 and '47. With Yankee Stadium's revolving doors all but air-conditioning the whole of the Bronx, no fewer than 28 names that had once graced

the '46 roster were gone by Opening Day, '47, to be replaced by other names that included Yogi Berra, Ralph Houk, Vic Raschi, George McQuinn, Allie Reynolds and new manager Bucky Harris.

But the Yankees hardly held the copyright for harnessing the winds of change, the Brooklyn Dodgers seeing them and raising them threefold. Just days short of the start of both the trout and baseball seasons, the Dodgers' changing of the guard had started with their manager, Leo Durocher, being suspended by Commissioner Happy Chandler for "Conduct detrimental to baseball"— read, between the lines, "Consorting with known gamblers." And one day thereafter, Brooklyn general manager Branch Rickey had added yet one more element to that stirring pot known as the Dodgers by bringing up Jackie Robinson from Montreal, the first black pebble to break the lily-white waters of the National Pastime.

When several players made known their wishes to be traded rather than play with Robinson, Rickey tried mightily to accommodate them. Within a month of the opening of the '47 season, Rickey had sent pitcher Kirby Higbe, the Dodgers' biggest winner the previous year, along with catcher Dixie Howell and two other players, to their farm club, the Pittsburgh Pirates, for $100,000 and outfielder Al Gionfriddo, whom writer Dick Young suggested was thrown into the deal merely "to carry the money in a satchel from Pittsburgh." By the end of the year several other players had been ticketed to be delivered F.O.B. Pittsburgh and other places North, East, and West, as the restless winds of change scattered the Dodgers to the four winds.

And yet, even as these two teams were achanging, they also were a-gelling, both winning their respective pennants, the Yankees by twelve games, the Dodgers by five. For only the second time in World Series history, two first-year managers would be leading their troops into the Fall Classic: Bucky Harris of the Yankees and Burt Shotton of the Dodgers. Apparently, after 26 years of dues-paying membership in the managers' guild-with only eight first-division finishes and a combined .467 won-lost percentage to show for their collective efforts—the fresh air of change had done them both some good.

Those wolves in pinstripe clothing, oldfangled and newfangled alike, got off to a typical old-fashioned Yankee start, winning Games One and Two behind newcomers Spec Shea and Allie Reynolds, 5-3 and 10-3. As the Subway Series took its five-cent ride over to Ebbets Field for Game Three, not even the most rabid member of the Flatbush Faithful would have staked a token on Brooklyn's chances, the fates obviously having dictated that this was not to be that "Next Year" they had waited so long for.

Game Three saw Yankee manager Bucky Harris tempt these fates and attempt to reestablish the improbability of the calendar by starting Louis Norman "Bobo" Newsom, the second-oldest starting pitcher in World Series history at the age of 40. Newsom had a tenure about as long as a Hollywood bridegroom, retiring all of three men as the Dodgers fed on his offerings like sweetbreads-on-toast at a vegetarian's outing. With six runs in the second, the Brooks went on to a 9-7 third-game win. That set up the classic-to-be that would go down as one of the greatest games in Series, if not all of baseball, history.

As a rule, managers have never been very good listeners. Now, with pitchers sitting around like numbers at a meat market ready to take their turns, Harris and Shotton, deaf to the message delivered just the day before by Newsom, separated the chaff from the wheat and started the chaff in Game Four: Shotton going with Harry Taylor, a sore-armed rookie who had won 10 games earlier in the year before coming down with a stiff salary wing; and Harris countering with Floyd "Bill" Bevens, who had underwhelmed American League batters with a 7-13 record during the season.

Proving he was the stiff of which dreams are made, Taylor's very first pitch of the game was hit, without so much as a by-your-leave, by Yankee lead-off batsman "Snuffy" Stirnweiss into left for a single. Taylor was to render just 10 more pitches, fetching a total of one run, two hits, one walk and no outs before he was handed his pink slip four men into the first inning. But the Dodgers, thanks to a 6-4-3 double play that went from ReesetoStankytoRobinson, justthatfast, and some excellent relief work from Hal Gregg, managed to stagger out of the top half of the first down by only one.

On the other glove, Yankee starter Bill Bevens started off little better, walking the first Dodger to face him, lead-off batsman Eddie Stanky, and then Dixie Walker. However, both Brooklyn baserunners were left there as sojourners as Bevens retired Reese, Robinson and Hermanski.

Recovering from the edge of one disaster, Bevens soon proved himself adept at returning to the scene of others, issuing a walk here, a walk there, and a walk everywhere as he made giving up walks a vocation in itself. By the fifth inning, with the score 2-0, Yankees—courtesy of a fourth-inning triple by Billy Johnson and a follow-up double by Johnny Lindell—Bevens' walk total numbered six. And two of them were now perched on base, tributes to Bevens' attempt to make too much of a good thing. After being sacrificed into scoring position by Stanky, Spider Jorgensen made the first crack in the man-made dike by scoring on Pee Wee Reese's fielder's choice which sorely tested the fielding skills of Rizzuto. Now the score was 2-1, Yankees. But the Dodgers still were not on speaking terms with the word "Hit."

Bevens, with the knowledge that a pitcher cannot be too careful in his choice of pitches, continued to serve up heaping platefuls of fastballs, all unhittable and most unfindable. However, if the pitching wasn't airtight, the fielding was as inning-after-inning the Yankees conspired to preserve Bevens' no-hitter by catching every ball cast at them in the name of challenge: Lindell making a miraculous catch of Robinson's deep fly in the third; DiMaggio twisting his ankle while chasing down Hermanski's long drive in the fourth; and Henrich backing up to the fence to haul down Hermanski's towering ball in the eighth.

Going into the top of the ninth the official scorekeeper's somewhat unkempt scorecard showed the Yankees leading in every category save that of walks. That was the inning when the Yankees, still up 2-1, threatened to take things into their own hands and mercifully put an end to whatever suspense still remained.

Batting against the offerings of Hank Behrman, the third Dodger pitcher, Johnny Lindell opened up the inning with a single. After Behrman retired Lindell on Rizzuto's fielder's choice, Bevens laid down a sacrifice bunt in front of the plate which Bruce Edwards pounced on, only to throw belatedly to second in an attempt to get Rizzuto. When the next batter up, "Snuffy" Stirnweiss, singled to center, the Yankees had three on and only one out.

All of which served to bring to the plate Tommy Henrich, called "Old Reliable" for good and sufficient reasons. However, it wasn't his presence nor his nickname which gave Brooklyn fans cause for pause, but his storied part in "The Strike-Out Heard 'Round the World" six Series before when Dodger catcher Mickey Owen had lost Hugh Casey's third-strike pitch; and loosed the fury known as Yankee "Five O'Clock Lightning."

Brooklyn manager Burt Shotton, with the look of a Sunday school teacher who fully expected to be hit in the head by an errant spitball the second his back was turned, now turned his back on the past as well, and called in reliever Hugh Casey—the same Hugh Casey who had thrown either a spitball or a slider lo those six years earlier to Henrich, depending upon whom one listens to. Casey wound up and came plateward with exactly one pitch: The exact same pitch to the exact same batter in the exact same spot. This time, however, his effort begot him a bouncer back to the mound which he converted into an inning-ending double play.

As the teams changed sides for the Dodgers' last at-bat, the Brooklyn Sym-Phony, a five-piece band wearing tattered clothing and playing battered instruments, began tootling away at something that sounded like the current Broadway favorite, "You'll Never Walk Alone," in obvious tribute to Bevens and the walka-thon he was staging. On the mound, his brow knitted, his eyes glazed, stood Bevens, not hearing the band's tribute. Looking preoccupied, almost like an habitual loser at blackjack who had had a small run of luck but no place to cash in his chips so that he could quit as a small winner, he now would have to gamble his all on the last three outs to become the first man in Series history to throw a no-hitter.

The first man to face Bevens in the bottom of the ninth was Dodger catcher Bruce Edwards, who frescoed one of Bevens' fastballs somewhere in the direction of the left-centerfield fence. Left fielder Johnny Lindell raced back to the fence, there to hollow out the concrete with his backside and catch the ball for the first out as Dodger coach Jake Pitler, less in appreciation than frustration, threw up his hands. Only two more outs remained.

With the four walls of the stadium slowly closing in upon him like the sides of a coffin, Bevens gave new life to the Dodgers by walking the next man up, Carl Furillo, his tenth free pass of the afternoon, tying the Series record. Facing Spider Jorgensen, the proud possessor of two of those walks and the only Dodger run in captivity, Bevens came in with his staple, a fastball, and this time Jorgensen, trying too hard, fouled the ball off meekly down the first-base line where George McQuinn, white as the proverbial piece of linen, suffocated the ball in his mitt. Now Bevens was only one out away from immortality.

But even before Bevens would be allowed to continue that struggle for immortality, he had to stand down and wait whilst Brooklyn manager Burt Shotton made some of those chess moves with men that managers since time immemorial have made just one out away from extinction. First, he sent in a foot soldier, Al Gionfriddo, to run for Furillo, now camped out at first; then, he deputized his last left-handed pinch-hitter, Pete Reiser, to bat for pitcher Hugh Casey.

Pete Reiser was one of baseball's greatest tragedies, a promise unkept in spite of a greatness hinted at and an awesome talent. The League's leading batter at the age of 22, he was now all but finished at the age of 28, the victim of too many tape-measure crashes into too many immovable fences. Having re-injured his ankle sliding into second the day before, Reiser now hobbled to the plate looking like the only way he could run was if he had a month's notice. But even if he only had one leg to stand on and

Floyd "Bill" Bevens, the man who came one out away from immortality before his "cookie" crumbled.

popular prejudice, being what it is, running in favor of two, the unprejudiced Bevens showed him the same respect he had shown every other two-legged creature he had faced all afternoon, quickly falling behind two-and-one on three fastballs.

At that magic moment in time Bevens was concentrating on Reiser, paying almost as much attention to Gionfriddo as the average party-goer would pay to the shoulder strap on a stately blonde. All of a sudden, as Bevens came plateward with his fourth pitch to Reiser, Gionfriddo lit out for second, taking everyone, teammates included, by surprise. Yankee catcher Yogi Berra, who up to that point had viewed Gionfriddo's presence only as a rumor, took the off-speed pitch cleanly. But in those days before, in Yogi's own words, "Bill Dickey learned me all his experiences," he didn't seem to know what to do with it. He eventually unloaded it to Phil Rizzuto, covering second, but Gionfriddo slid under the throw and descending tag with a scorching belly-whopper for the Brooks' seventh stolen base of the Series.

The pitch to Reiser was, not incidentally, a ball, raising the count to three-and-one. And drastically changing the entire equation of the game. For now Yankee manager Bucky Harris decided to put his oar in and stir the already bubbling-over pot.

Possessing one of those faces that looked like it had already been waited on, Harris had gained some measure of fame for his managerial contributions while managing the lowly Washington Senators. One of those moments had come when he told his weak-hitting team, then facing the offerings of fireballing Bob Feller, "Go up and hit what you see; and if you don't see it, come on back." Now, unimpressed with the seriousness of Reiser's injury—in fact, as reporter Dan Daniel noted, "He had given it no thought when Reiser walked to the plate"—Harris ordered Bevens to pass the empty batter to the empty base on his left. In one move Harris had not only amended Bevens' total of walks to a record-setting ten, but had broken the first rule of the oldest "Book" in the world, the one which starts with, "Thou shalt not put the winning

run on base . . ." But then again, Harris had always viewed all such great truths as blasphemous, even those baseball purists held as inviolable as belching in church.

As the gimp-ankled Reiser less walked than limped down to first, the loud speaker erupted with "Miksis running for Reiser . . ." And then, even before the echoes had died down, added, "And Lavagetto batting for Stanky . . . Shotton, gambling his all now, called back perhaps the best getter-on-base in the National League and, having exhausted his supply of left-handed pinch-hitters, sent up a right-handed model, but one with enough power to bring across the two baserunners. And win the game.

Still just one out away from a guaranteed safe conduct into the Hall of Fame, Bevens reared back and released the ball from behind his right ear, a fast ball up and in tight. Lavagetto swung hard at the offering and missed. Strike one. Now Bevens and Lavagetto regarded one another with a collective dual resignation of their fates as Bevens rocked and came in with his 137th pitch of the game, a fast ball up and over the plate. Lavagetto, with an obvious disinclination to be the 27th out, swung again, waving his bat more in protection than in offense, and sent it on a line out toward right field.

The ball took off, headed for the wooden right-field fence, a crazy patchwork quilt of advertising signboards, each a voucher for some product or service then benefiting mankind. Right fielder Tommy Henrich, the middleman in the unfolding drama, began his marathon route from his original position over in right-center hoping to intersect the ball. As he ran, Henrich remembers thinking that "the ball is tagged very well and that it's going to reach the wall." Nearing the fence, Henrich had to figure out how to play the ball: Would it be catchable off the wall or would it hit too high up on the wall and have to be played on the rebound?

In the two ticks it took Henrich to get to the wall, somehow, someway, somewhere, the best-fielding right fielder of the decade managed to lose sight of the descending ball. When he picked up its flight again, it became apparent that the ball could be caught only by a man who could eat apples off a tree without using his hands. Telling himself to "Get the heck off that wall as fast as you can," Henrich tried mightily to put on the breaks and reverse gears after making one perfunctory stab in its direction. But owing to the eccentricity of the sloping Ebbets Field wall, the ball caromed off at an angle, hitting the heel of Henrich's glove and going back through his legs, leaving Henrich looking as if he were performing a fielding fandango.

Back in the infield, some 207 or so feet south of where Henrich and the ball were playing cat-and-mouse, the two pinch-runners, Gionfriddo and Miksis, both of whom had taken off with the hit, were now circling the basepaths. Easily scoring the tying run, Gionfriddo turned around and gestured frantically to Miksis to join him as Henrich finally fetched the ball and threw it forth weakly in the direction of McQuinn. With the ball coming homeward bound Henrich-to-McQuinn-to-Berra, Miksis was coming even more so, sliding across the plate in a sitting pose with the third and winning run.

It was victory wrested from defeat! Vaudeville turned into drama! And as Miksis sat stunned atop home plate and Bevens left the mound with as much haste as dignity allowed, his illusion of one second turned into his disillusion the next, the field turned into a bedlam, a Funny Farms East. Everywhere people could be seen overrunning the field, in the traditional ex-post facto goings-on, flailing away at other fans and players with more back-slapping than could be found at a Shriner's convention. And there, out in right field, stood hundreds more of the Faithful, all staring up at a parellelogram next to a sign advertising the movie "The Kid from Brooklyn," almost as if looking at a memorial to the slaughtered convention of never putting the winning run on base.

All Joe DiMaggio remembered from the chaotic scene was that "Umpire Larry Goetz automatically took out his whisk broom and dusted the plate, although it wouldn't be used again until the next afternoon."

Those three bit players, Bevens, Gionfriddo and Lavagetto, now all but finished players in every respect, had strutted upon baseball's stage and would leave it soon, never to be heard from again. But not before each had had one encore.

For the very next afternoon, with the Series now tied at two games apiece by Lavagetto's hit, the very same Lavagetto came to bat as a pinch-hitter against New York's Spec Shea with two out in the bottom of the ninth and the tying run on second. As Yankee pitcher Spec Shea stared down at the man who had been the litter bearer to Bevens' dreams, Joe DiMaggio, standing next to Tommy Henrich in the outfield, said, "For Christ's sake, say a prayer." But this time there was no magic in Lavagetto's bat as he struck out for the last out,—the one that had gotten away the day before—and the Yankees won the fifth game, 2-1, to go up three games-to-two in the Series.

The Series shifted back to Yankee Stadium for Game Six, that cavernous ballpark where left-center field honestly came by the name "Death Valley." It was to be there that Al Gionfriddo was to come back for one last bow. And what a bow!

With the score 8-5, Dodgers, in the bottom of the sixth, Gionfriddo was sent in to replace Miksis for defensive purposes. Now, with two men on and two out, Joe DiMaggio came up to face Brooklyn pitcher Joe Hatten. Dodger manager Burt Shotton, playing DiMaggio to pull the ball, gestured to the man he called "The Little Italian," waving Gionfriddo over to the line. Standing there, as he remembered, "positioned between the 315-foot marker and the 415-foot marker . . . awfully shallow," Gionfriddo watched as DiMaggio swung on a Hatten fastball and caught the ball on the meat of his bat, sending a shaft, straight as an arrow, toward the bullpen. Putting his head down, Gionfriddo began what well may have been the longest-running show in the history of baseball, racing, back to ball, to the spot where he could intersect its flight. Finally, with something that resembled a cross between a leap and a lunge, Gionfriddo went up with his right-arm fully extended, and grabbed at the ball, then just beginning to cross the bullpen fence, losing his cap but not the ball in the process. Up in the broadcast booth, Red Barber was in the process of describing DiMaggio's "home run," telling the nationwide audience, "Swung on and belted. It's a long one, deep to left-center. Back goes Gionfriddo . . . Back . . . back . . . back . . . back . . . He makes a one-handed catch against the bullpen! . . . Ohhhhhhh, Doctor. . . ." And down on the field, DiMaggio, then almost to second, for one split second allowed people a glimpse behind the normal curtain of his feelings by kicking at the dirt in frustration.

The Dodgers held on to win 9-6 and force a seventh game, a seventh game that saw Bill Bevens come back for his second Series appearance and hold the Dodgers to two hits in two-plus innings as the Yankees came from behind to win the deciding game 5-2 in the most excitement-packed Series in years, thanks to the efforts of three players then at their journey's end—Bevens, Gionfriddo, and Lavagetto, three players who would never play another game in the Majors.

Harry "Cookie" Lavagetto, a baseball legend in his last grab at the brass ring.

Dodgers' Only Hit Wins, 3-2, And Evens Series

Game 4 October 3 at Brooklyn								N.Y.	1 0 0	1 0 0	0 0 0
								Bkn.	0 0 0	0 1 0	0 0 2

New York	Pos	AB	R	H	RBI	PO	A	E
Stirnweiss	2b	4	1	2	0	2	1	0
Henrich	rf	5	0	1	0	2	0	0
Berra	c	4	0	0	0	6	1	1
DiMaggio	cf	2	0	0	1	2	0	0
McQuinn	1b	4	0	1	0	7	0	0
Johnson	3b	4	1	1	0	3	2	0
Lindell	lf	3	0	2	1	3	0	0
Rizzuto	ss	4	0	1	0	1	2	0
Bevens	p	3	0	0	0	0	1	0
Totals		33	2	8	2	*26	7	1

* Two out when winning run was scored.
a Walked for Gregg in 7th.
b Ran for Furillo in 9th.
c Walked for Casey in 9th.
d Ran for Reiser in 9th.
e Doubled for Stanky in 9th.

Doubles—Lavagetto, Lindell. Triple—Johnson. Stolen Bases—Gionfriddo, Reese, Rizzuto. Sacrifice Hits—Bevens, Stanky. Double Plays—Reese to Stanky to Robinson, Gregg to Reese to Robinson, Casey to Edwards to Robinson. Wild Pitch—Bevens. Left on Bases—New York 9, Brooklyn 8. Umpires—Goetz, McGowan, Pinelli, Rommel, Boyer, Magerkurth. Attendance—33,443. Time of Game—2:20.

Brooklyn	Pos	AB	R	H	RBI	PO	A	E
Stanky	2b	1	0	0	0	2	3	0
e Lavagetto		1	0	1	2	0	0	0
Reese	ss	4	0	0	1	3	5	1
J. Robinson	1b	4	0	0	0	11	1	0
Walker	rf	2	0	0	0	0	1	0
Hermanski	lf	4	0	0	0	2	0	0
Edwards	c	4	0	0	0	7	1	1
Furillo	cf	2	0	0	0	2	0	0
b Gionfriddo		0	1	0	0	0	0	0
Jorgensen	3b	2	1	0	0	1	1	1
Taylor	p	0	0	0	0	0	0	0
Gregg	p	1	0	0	0	0	1	0
a Vaughan		1	0	0	0	0	0	0
Behrman	p	0	0	0	0	0	1	0
Casey	p	0	0	0	0	0	0	0
c Reiser		0	0	0	0	0	0	0
d Miksis		0	1	0	0	0	0	0
Totals		26	3	1	3	27	15	3

Pitching	IP	H	R	ER	BB	SO
New York						
Bevens (L)	9	1	3	3	10	5
Brooklyn						
Taylor	**0	2	1	0	1	0
Gregg	7	4	1	1	3	5
Behrman	1⅓	2	0	0	0	0
Casey (W)	⅔	0	0	0	0	0

**Pitched to four batters in 1st.

9 Merkle's Boner

Chicago Cubs vs. New York Giants, September 23, 1908

TODAY, THREE-QUARTERS OF A CENTURY AFTER JOHNNY Evers' cunning exhibition of one-upsmanship on September 23, 1908, the remarkable thing is not just that this game is remembered, but that it is still discussed and argued in all its detail. It is not known as "Evers' Brilliant Play," but instead goes under the handle "Merkle's Bonehead Play."

The centerpiece in the drama, however, wasn't Fred Merkle, but Johnny Evers, a player the size of a hotwalker who already knew how to ride before the Chicago Cubs put him in the saddle back in 1902. The diminutive 5'9", 100-pound Evers looked more like a baseball bat with a thyroid condition than a ballplayer, albeit one differing radically in design, almost invisible from the side. But even then there was something about this walking case of malnutrition that hinted at greatness; a greatness that would soon take its place alongside Joe Tinker and Frank Chance in the most storied double-play combination in baseball.

Beginning with the melding of these three great players in 1903, the Cubs were to win 65.9 percent of their games through the eight years the double-play combination played together, a higher total than any team over a similar period of time in the history of modern baseball. Their interlocking fame became such that Franklin P. Adams of the New York *Globe* was moved to incorporate their names in his deathless verse "Baseball's Sad Lexicon":

> "These are the saddest of possible words,
> Tinker-to-Evers-to-Chance.
> Trio of Bear Cubs fleeter than birds,
> Tinker-to-Evers-to-Chance.
> Ruthlessly pricking our gonfalon bubble,
> Making a Giant hit into a double,
> Words that are weighty with nothing but trouble.
> Tinker-to-Evers-to-Chance."

Although the very words "Tinker-to-Evers-to-Chance" conjure up images of a double-play combination *par excellence,* the double play was hardly the bedrock of their fame. For, if the truth be known, while the Cubs, anchored by TE&C, led the National League in least errors and best fielding average for the four years from 1905 through 1908, they never once led the League in double plays. And, almost as if to prove that the double play and TE&C were not an item, in the 21 World Series games, the threesome played in the 1906, '07, '08 and '10 Series, only once did the scorekeeper ever get to inscribe a double play as going from "Tinker-to-Evers-to-Chance."

No, the reputation of the most famous threesome since Wynken, Blyken and Nod rested instead on other qualities, most notably on that intangible known as "leadership."

Led by first baseman-manager Frank Chance, "The Peerless Leader" in name and action, the Cubs were one of the greatest aggregations in baseball history, numbering among their number such stalwarts as: Joe Tinker, the party of the first part of the lyrical trio; master catcher "Noisy" Johnny Kling; third baseman Harry Steinfelt, the unsung member of the infield; outfielder "Wildfire"

Schulte; pitchers Mordecai "Three-Finger" Brown, Ed Reulbach, Orvie Overall and Jack Pfiester; and, of course, Johnny Evers, the hero of the piece.

A little chap who could get lost in a crowd of two, Evers was always guaranteed to insert his oar in the most bothersome manner. Called "The Crab" for good and sufficient reason, Evers had a ritual he went into whenever the call went against his Cubs. Sidling over to an umpire with an air of carelessness, the man who was no more than a splinter of bone and a hank of hair would jump up and down in front of the umpire, all the time wagging his jaw like a Gilbert and Sullivan chorus. While it looked to all like Evers was giving the umpire, in the argot of the day, a "hiding," what he was actually doing, between jumping around and screaming like a youngster with green-apple colic, was shouting greetings like "How's your wife?" thus saving himself the indignity of being summarily tossed out of the game—while, at the same time, prodding at the corners, like a sculptor seeking the grain of a rock, making his point.

Still, Evers had his run-ins with umpires. One of the most famous was the one he had with "The Old Arbitrator," Bill Klem. For the longest time Evers claimed that Klem owed him $5 on a bet the two had made and Klem had somehow neglected to pay. Evers, who had an elephantine memory to complement his mouse-like size, never let Klem forget, holding up five fingers whenever Klem glanced in his direction, or, when Klem was umpiring behind the plate, drawing a "5" in the dirt with the butt end of his bat or counting slowly to five whenever within earshot. One day Evers lost his temper in the presence of Klem, jumping up and down like Rumplestiltskin to prove his point. Klem heard him out and then handed Evers a five-dollar bill, saying, "Here's your five, Mr. Evers. And now you are fined $25." Without batting an eye, Evers pocketed the cherished bill and answered, "And it was worth it to bawl you out."

But even though Evers was viewed by many of his competitors as the type of man who, were he proprietor of a men's washroom, would reach for the last towel at the same time as his patrons, there was more to the man than his apparent antisocial behavior. Much More. For Evers was more dangerous in ways of warfare than the most terrible Turks. Believing that the curriculum of the ballpark is a wide one, Evers took to studying the rule book, less with an eye toward breaking the rules than merely testing their elasticity.

Evers also had an eye for other things as well. The Giants, from the years 1903 through 1908, had a pitcher named Luther Taylor and nicknamed "Dummy" for the obvious reason that he was deaf and dumb. Whenever Taylor pitched, the Giants would communicate with him through sign language. And whenever the Giants played the Cubs, Evers, a noted hand-pirate, would watch the strange goings-on intently, unable to decipher them as he had so many others. After several introductions to sign language, Evers took up its study, becoming so proficient he not only could converse fluently with his fingers but also could "listen" to the signs being flashed Taylor. Finally, when the Giants discovered Evers

had broken their code, they resorted to another set of signals, using sign language with Taylor only on social occasions.

Back in the first decade of the Twentieth Century, the National League was made up of the "haves" and the "have-nots." The "haves" were but three teams, the Cubs, the Giants and the Pirates, winners of every pennant from 1901, the start of "Modern" baseball, through 1913. The other five teams were fourth-class citizens. At best.

Of the three "haves," the two which had the greatest rivalry of aim were the Giants and the Cubs, two teams then known in the while-you-get-your-hair-cut weeklies as "blood enemies." When Giant manager John McGraw found out that Evers had stolen his team's signals to Taylor, he got into a long-range conversation with Evers in sign language about the propriety of taking advantage of a handicapped player. Evers, playing it for all it was worth, got so animated he "threw a finger out of joint replying to McGraw in a brilliant flash of repartee," according to Christy Mathewson in his *vers libre, Pitching in a Pinch.*

Determined not to let Evers, or the Cubs for that matter, give him the finger again, McGraw began revamping his club for the 1908 season, all the better to make a run at the team that had won two straight pennants. First he traded five of his over-the-hill gang to the Boston Braves for their manager, first baseman Fred Tenney, the originator of the 3-6-3 double play, and shortstop Al Bridwell. Then taking both heart and hint from Larry Doyle, who, upon being added to the roster the previous year, had said, "It's great to

be young and a Giant," McGraw went out to find more young talent and came up with Fred Snodgrass, Chief Meyers, Buck Herzog, Rube Marquard and Fred Merkle. Suddenly the team that had seemed so long-in-the-tooth in 1907 was an average three years younger. And ready to challenge the Cubs for the 1908 National League pennant.

McGraw's alchemy paid immediate dividends, the Giants breaking quickly from the gate and, in the best McGraw tradition, shooting to the front early in the season ahead of the Pirates and the Cubs, in that order. However, the Cubs, who had suffered a series of debilitating injuries early in the campaign, soon began to get whole. And back into the race as well.

Now it was the Giants' turn to fall victim to a series of injuries, starting with Fred Merkle's case of severe blood poisoning early in July and continuing on through the summer with Roger Bresnahan's sciatic rheumatism and not quite ending with lesser maladies, such as Turkey Mike Donlin's charley horse and Fred Tenney's tender rib cage. As the pennant race more limped than raced into September, the Giants still clung to a one-and-a-half game lead over the Pirates and a three-game lead over the Cubs. But their biggest hurt was yet to come.

On September 4, the Cubs played the Pirates at Pittsburg in a ten-inning game that would serve as a prelude to the more famous "Merkle" game three weeks thereafter. With the score tied at 0-0 in the tenth, the Pirates scored what appeared to be the winning run. But rookie first baseman Warren Gill, on first when the "winning" run scored, in a move that was part of baseball by all the sacred rights of established custom, if not the actual statute of limitations, detoured for the clubhouse when the run scored rather than proceeding on to second. Johnny Evers, observing the goings-on from his proximate position at second, was following Gill's course, thinking with him and one step ahead of him as well. Seeing Gill leave the geographic bounds of the basepath, Evers drew himself up to his full 5'9" and swelling with justifiable wrath, began yelling for the ball. Outfielder Solly Hofman retrieved the loose ball, throwing it to Evers who caught the ball and turned, simultaneously, toward umpire Hank O'Day, screaming that Gill be declared "Out."

O'Day, though, was the kind of character you couldn't suck in with a rash gesture. After first looking like a severe case of hoof and mouth disease had just been pointed out in his personal favorite in the herd, he weighed the question for a minute and then found it wanting, denying the appeal on the basis that he "had not seen it." And despite subsequent appeals by the Cubs to the National League president, Harry Pulliam, the Pittsburg win stood as part of the O'Day's business.

During the summer of 1908, the Cubs had put together a winning streak the size of a tablecloth. By Wednesday, September 23, they had closed the gap to mere percentage points of those walking wounded, the New York Giants. They were scheduled to play the Giants in New York in front of New York faithful. In front of umpire O'Day.

As Giant manager John McGraw entered the clubhouse before the game, he turned to his lame, halt and blind athletes and, in an effort to make light of the situation, called out, "How are the cripples? Any more to add to the list of identified dead today?" But it was no laughing matter to either McGraw or the Giants. Larry Doyle was recuperating in the hospital from a spiking; Donlin, limping around on a charley horse that wasn't getting any better; and Tenney bandaged from his waist down, in the throes of a lumbago attack. So, McGraw had to take Tenney out for the only time that season, penciling in rookie Fred Merkle at first base. And

Fate was soon to cut this man out of the herd and pin a can to his tail.

The darling of the multitudes, Christy Mathewson, would go for the Giants against Cub lefty Jack Pfiester, called "Jack the Giant Killer" for his mastery of the Giants over the years. But for the first few innings it was Matty's mastery that carried the day, the Wednesday matinee idol's famed "fadeaway" breaking off sharply and his fast ball blowing by Cub batter after Cub batter. Then, in the fifth, against the man he called "the worst man I have to face in the National League," Joe Tinker, Matty tried to get his "fade" by him. Tinker caught it on his extra-long bat and drove it out toward right-center field, in the direction of right fielder Mike Donlin. Donlin hobbled over to the ball, tried to arrest its progress with his foot, playing a sure double into an inside-the-park homer. Now the Cubs are up, 1-0.

The Giants come back with one of their own in the sixth on a single by second baseman Herzog which Cub third baseman Steinfeldt, with what the newspapers call "a particularly distressing throw," butchered into two bases. Then, after Bresnahan sacrificed Herzog over to third, Donlin shed his goat's horns by singling over second to score Herzog. The score stood 1-1 as 18,000 Giant fans "went out of their minds."

As the game went into the final innings, Mathewson seemed to pick up steam, not only setting down the Cubbies the rest of the way, but ending with a flourish, striking out Evers and Schulte in succession in the ninth.

Then it was Giants' turn. And Merkle's moment for immortality.

For the nonce, we defer to the write-up of the beginning of the ninth by writer W. W. Aulick of the *New York Times,* who wrote, in the quaint language of the day, "We fancy ourselves mightily in the ninth, after Devlin has made a clean single to centre. To be sure, Seymour has just gone out at first on a throw by Evers, but we have a chance. Devlin is on first, and the start is splendid. But here is McCormick with a drive over to Evers, who throws out Devlin at second, and we're not very far advanced—and two are out. Merkle, who failed us the day before in an emergency, is at bat and we pray of him that he mend his ways. If he will only single, we will ignore any errors he may make in the rest of his natural life. On this condition, Merkle singles. McCormick advances to third, and everybody in the enclosure slaps everybody else and nobody minds. Perfect ladies are screaming like a batch of Coney barkers on the Mardi Gras occasion, and the elderly banker behind us is beating our hat to a pulp with his gold-handled cane. And nobody minds."

At this moment in the action, Al Bridwell came to bat. Bridwell was to recall the moment later for oral historian Larry Ritter: "I

Fred Merkle, wearer of the Giants' first baseman's glove and baseball's eternal goat's horns.

stepped in the batter's box—I was a left-handed hitter—and as I was getting set, I saw Merkle edging pretty far off first base, almost as though he was going to try to steal. That didn't make any sense, so I stepped out of the box and looked at him and he went back and stood on the bag. I often think that maybe if I hadn't done that everything would have turned out all right." But return to first Merkle did and Bridwell stepped back into the box to face Pfiester. "Well, the first pitch came in to me," continued Bridwell, "a fast ball, waist high, right over the center of the plate, and I promptly drilled a line drive past Johnny Evers and out into right center field. Bob Emslie was umpiring on the bases and he fell on his can to avoid being hit by the ball. I really socked that one on the nose. A clean single."

As the ball streaked out toward right center field, all hell broke loose as the action spilled out onto the field . . . fans streaming out in the time-honored fashion of the day to (A) Congratulate the players, (B) Curse them out, (C) Touch them, (D) Carry them off in

---

SCORE OF THE CUBS-GIANTS GAME.

CHICAGO.

	AB	R	BH	TB	BB	SH	SB	P	A	E
Hayden, rf	4	0	0	0	0	0	0	1	0	1
Evers, 2b	4	0	1	1	0	0	0	4	7	0
Schulte, lf	4	0	0	0	0	0	0	1	0	0
Chance, 1b	3	0	1	1	0	1	0	11	1	0
Steinfeldt, 3b	3	0	0	0	0	1	0	1	1	1
Hofman, cf	3	0	1	1	0	0	0	0	1	0
Tinker, ss	3	1	1	4	0	0	0	3	7	2
Kling, c	3	0	1	1	0	0	0	5	1	0
Pfiester, p	3	0	0	0	0	0	0	1	0	0
Totals	30	1	5	8	0	3	0	27	18	4

NEW YORK.

	AB	R	BH	TB	BB	SH	SB	P	A	E
Herzog, 2b	3	1	1	1	1	0	0	1	1	0
Bresnahan, c	3	0	0	0	1	0	11	0	0	
Donlin, rf	4	0	1	1	0	0	0	2	0	0
Seymour, cf	4	0	1	1	0	0	0	1	0	0
Devlin, 3b	4	0	2	2	0	0	0	2	0	0
McCormick, lf	3	0	0	0	0	0	0	1	0	0
Merkle, 1b	3	0	1	1	0	0	0	5	1	0
Bridwell, ss	4	0	0	0	0	0	0	3	3	0
Mathewson, p	3	0	0	0	0	0	0	0	2	0
Totals	31	1	6	6	3	1	0	27	9	0

CHICAGO	0	0	0	0	1	0	0	0	0—1
NEW YORK	0	0	0	0	0	1	0	0	0—1

Home run—Tinker. Struck out—By Mathewson, 9. Bases on balls—Off Pfiester, 2. Double plays—Tinker-Chance (2); Evers-Chance; Mathewson-Bridwell-Merkle. Hit by pitcher—McCormick. Time—1:30. Umpires—O'Day and Emslie.

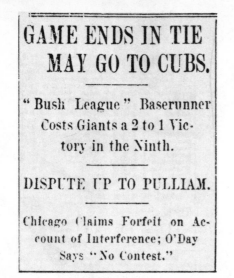

GAME ENDS IN TIE MAY GO TO CUBS.

"Bush League" Baserunner Costs Giants a 2 to 1 Victory in the Ninth.

DISPUTE UP TO PULLIAM.

Chicago Claims Forfeit on Account of Interference; O'Day Says "No Contest."

victory, or (E) All of the above. The players on the Giants' bench, having had enough of being crowded, trampled, and hustled by the hoi polloi, made it a practice to sprint from the bench to the clubhouse as soon as the game was over.

Merkle, a longtime benchwarmer, used to jumping off the bench at the end of the game and racing for the dugout, waited only long enough to see McCormick score, then took off with the rest of the Giants.

As soon as McCormick crossed the plate, everyone thought the game was over. *Everyone,* that is, except Johnny Evers. Suddenly in the madding throng on the field was Evers jumping up and down at second demanding the ball. Center fielder Hofman, who had somehow retrieved the ball from the onrushing crowd, excitedly threw the ball past Evers and past back-up shortstop Tinker, as well.

Umpire O'Day took notice of the goings-on. What he witnessed was the ball being passed back and forth like a parcel nobody wanted to pay postage on. Giant coach "Iron Man" Joe McGinnity, sensing the gravity of the situation, went after the ball. So did Kid Kroh, a third-string Chicago pitcher. McGinnity got to the ball first, but almost as quickly, Kroh and Tinker alighted atop him. McGinnity was able to wrestle free and throw the ball somewhere in the direction of the stands where six or more fans fell upon it. Kroh, in hot pursuit, knocked all of them galley-west, grabbed the ball, and sent it to Steinfeldt who, in turn, threw it to Tinker who ladled it to Evers. Evers then triumphantly stepped on second with a ball—although the Giants were later to claim it had come from the ballbag since McGinnity's throw had gone into the stands—and looked to O'Day for confirmation. O'Day, primed for the situation, declared McCormick's run did not count.

Meanwhile, there was still action aplenty on the field. Moose McCormick, after crossing the plate, noticed the activity going on at second and, figuring it was because Bridwell hadn't touched first, raced after Bridwell, then retreating to the clubhouse. Kicking Bridwell in his pride, McCormick hollered, "What's the matter? Don't you know where first base is?" The two then pushed their way back through the milling crowd to touch first base again. At home plate, Cub manager Chance and O'Day had formed a two-man debating society, arguing Chance's thesis that since the throngs couldn't be cleared from the field so that the game could continue, the game should be forfeited in favor of the Cubs. Everywhere else arguments were taking place as baseball's most disputed play was then being hotly discussed.

McGraw, whose normal reaction to umpires' decisions was a terse "The only good umpire is a dead umpire," was now enraged that the custom of the day had been changed to the custom of O'Day, and appealed O'Day's ruling to the National League president and then to the National Commission, the supreme court of baseball. He lost both times. The Giants, convinced the game had been rightfully theirs, refused to play any make-up game. But the Cubs, on the other glove, claimed the right to play for the championship, if necessary, at the end of the season. It was only after Giants owner John T. Brush urged the players to play the Cubs for the championship they thought they had already won that a play-off game took place.

That play-off game on October 8 need not have taken place nor would the name Merkle be enshrined in the Hall of Shame had not a series of events happened that brought the Cubs and the Giants to the wire in a flat-footed tie with 98 wins and 55 losses apiece.

Between the Merkle game on September 23 and the end of the season on October 7, the Giants lost several games that meant the difference between a pennant for New York and a tie with Chicago. Three of those were to Phillies' rookie Harry Coveleski who beat them every other day for a week for three of his four 1908 wins. Another came when the highly-celebrated rookie Rube Marquard was pressed into action, the Giants pitching staff threadbare, at best, and lost to Cincinnati, instantly turning from the "$11,000 Beauty" into the "$11,000 Lemon."

The play-off game was anti-climatic, in more ways than one. Despite the excitement leading up to the game, excitement that was responsible for the deaths of two spectators and the splintering of large portions of the Polo Grounds' fence by others clamoring to gain admission, the game itself would cause the 40,000 Giant fans a large amount of weeping and gnashing of teeth. The immortal Matty was less than mortal, his arm so dead it should have worn some of the crepe which bedecked the stadium.

The real turning point of the game came in the first inning, when Cubs' starting pitcher Jack Pfiester hit Tenney and walked Herzog. When the next man up, Bresnahan, struck out, Cub catcher Johnny Kling dropped the third strike. Conveniently at his feet. Herzog, perched on first, thought that an opportunity for advancement was at hand, especially since he heard screams of "Go on!, Go on!," and took off for second, then reversed his field, and was thrown out by Kling who proved that the only thing at hand was the ball. Oh yes, the man screaming, "Go on!, Go on!," was Cub second baseman Johnny Evers, who was playing behind Herzog.

The Giants were to score one run in their half of the first when Donlin doubled in Tenney. But Chance waived in "Three-Finger" Brown who managed to put at least one of his remaining digits in the dike to stop the Giants in the first with just one run—thanks to Evers' quick thinking. When the Cubs scored four runs in the third, wrapped around a triple by Matty's nemesis, Tinker, the game was all but over, Brown using his corkscrew delivery and excellent control to smother New York bats the rest of the way. The Cubs won the game, 4-2, and the pennant—and left the groundskeepers to pick up the pieces and the yellow journals to pick on Merkle.

While there were some who said that fate had played a dishonorable trick on Fred Merkle, there were more than a few who said that it had been Johnny Evers, a man whose grasp of strategy and tactics were second to none. Maybe that's why, years after he had finished playing, poet Ogden Nash penned: "E is for Evers/His Jaw in advance/Never afraid/To Tinker with Chance."

10 Don Larsen's Perfect Game

New York Yankees vs. Brooklyn Dodgers, 5th Game, 1956 World Series, October 8, 1956

GREATNESS, IT HAS BEEN SAID, TAKES ON MANY DISGUISES. But no more unlikely guest ever knocked at the door than Don Larsen, wearing what appeared to be a Halloween false nose to gain admission.

Before his moment in the sun, the most dazzling aspect of Don Larsen's career had been its total lacklusterness. He had pitched in the minors without distinction, in St. Louis without a team, and in Baltimore without a chance, capping his non-career with an incredible 3-21 record in 1954, one of the worst ever.

But one place Larsen had proven himself was in the Night Owl League, where he had gained timeless fame. A devotee of the life non-strenuous, Larsen had led the league in bourbon quarries visited, bed checks missed and nocturnal mishaps, including but not limited to, as lawyers are wont to say, wrapping his car around trees and other such florid libels against nature far after the bewitching hour. One of his managers, noting that it was always three o'clock in Larsen's soul, despaired, "The only thing Don Larsen fears is sleep." To many observers, it appeared that the only difference between this mummer by preoccupation and pitcher by occupation and the *Titanic* was that it had taken the *Titanic* longer to sink from sight.

However, there was one observer who was somewhat less jaundiced in his appraisal of Larsen than most: George Weiss, General Manager of the New York Yankees. What Weiss had seen was a big, strapping, 6'4" teddy bear of a man with a strong arm, a blazing fast ball, a snapping curve and a good change of pace. And if Weiss had any qualms about Larsen's well-earned reputation for never spilling a drop, they were more than compensated for by the fact that of Larsen's three wins in his disastrous 3-21 season in '54, two of them had come over the Yankees. Feeling, like Oscar Wilde, that "three addresses always inspired confidence, even in a tradesman," Weiss moved to give Larsen his third Major League address in three short years.

Wheeling and dealing, Weiss engineered a two-tiered deal that involved no less than 18 players shuttling between New York and Baltimore. The rolling stock coming to New York included youngsters Larsen, Bob Turley and Billy Hunter; going the other way to the Orioles were a flock of has-beens and never-will-be's which included the likes of Willie Miranda, Gene Woodling, Harry Byrd, Don Leppert, Kal Segrist, Ted Del Guercio and that famous oft-traded "player to be named later."

However, before Fate moved in mysterious ways its wonders to perform with Larsen, it almost didn't move at all, Larsen coming down with a sore arm in spring training '55. Manager Casey Stengel and Weiss, in concert assembled, decided that their non-fair-haired boy needed time in the sticks to work things out and sent him down to Denver, where newly-installed manager Ralph Houk could keep an eye on him. Houk did better than merely keep an eye on Larsen, keeping both eyes on him and an avuncular arm wrapped around his shoulders as well. Larsen responded to the treatment, pitching in 13 games and posting a 9-1 record with a 3.69 ERA. Brought back up to the Yankees, the prodigal Larsen continued his winning ways in the crucible of Major League competition, starting a lucky 13 times for a 9-2 won-lost record while lowering his ERA to 3.06.

With Larsen's nine late-season wins contributing mightily to their final kick to the wire, the Yankees broke the Indians' one-year stranglehold on the top rung of the American League and moved into the 1955 World Series against the Dodgers. However, this Series would belong to Johnny Podres, not Larsen. The point was brought home in Game Four when Larsen started and went four innings-plus, giving up five hits, including a two-run homer to Gil Hodges, in his only appearance. To make matters worse, in his last plate appearance Larsen fouled off a ball which hit Yankee owner Del Webb foresquare atop his head. This hardly looked to be the stuff World Series legends are made of.

Even before the first grapefruit had been thrown out in spring training the next year, Larsen had gone a long way towards reclaiming his momentarily lost reputation as a man who never let success go to his training. Apparently in search of genial bonhomie and other two-footed wild life at five in the morning, the man whose slogan was "Let the good times roll," rolled into a tree that was idly standing beside the road minding its own business. His rented car totaled and a ticket issued by a charitable member of the St. Petersburg constabulary for something called "Assumed speeding," Larsen blithely explained it away by saying he had fallen asleep at the wheel. Stengel, who had heard all the tales as far back as the Brothers Grimm, could only shake his head and mutter, "He's tired, but he ain't hurt." Then, as a way of making the punishment fit the crime, rather than fining his errant knight of nights, Stengel made him run wind sprints in the outfield for his use of wheels other than his own.

Stengel's faith in the man-boy his teammates fondly called "Gooneybird" was repaid as Larsen put together an 11-5 year in 20 starts with a .326 ERA, second-best on the staff behind ace Whitey Ford. Somewhere during the last month Casey Stengel, who managed the way a beagle chases a rabbit, instinctively, tampered with Larsen's delivery, making him pitch sans wind-up. That no-wind-up delivery would go a long ways towards helping Stengel avenge his previous year's Series loss to the Dodgers. And towards providing Larsen with a stellar brightness and stardom heretofore unhinted at.

In one of those little tricks history continually plays on us to see if we were really paying attention, Larsen's incomparable performance wasn't to come his first time out in the '56 Series. In fact, he was anything but perfect in his first appearance, reverting to vintage Larsen: Recovering from the brink of disaster and within scant minutes moving back again to the edge of another.

Given the ball by Stengel in Game Two in an effort to even the Series after Maglie had bested Ford in the opener, Larsen was staked to a six-run lead after one-and-a-half innings—on a first-inning single by Collins and his own single and Berra's grand slam in the second. But Larsen couldn't hold the fort, giving up four bases on balls and one hit before being given the hook in the bottom of the second. Some thought prematurely. The Dodgers were to come storming back and score a tying six runs in that second stanza, four charged to Larsen's open account and seven more against Larsen's six successors for the worst drubbing of a Yankee team in Series history.

Down no games to two, the Series shifted to the friendly confines of Yankee Stadium where the Yankees squared the Series with two wins behind Ford and Tom Sturdivant. Now the Series stood at two apiece. Larsen's moment had finally arrived.

Monday, October 8, 1956, broke bright and clear. A perfect day to see baseball and history-in-the-making. Also a perfect day to be seen, as expense-account hosts and their guests, as far from their Park Avenue abodes as the subways would allow them to go, commingled with the Calliphs from the Garment District and their out-of-town buyers, all shining with a special spit-and-polish as they leisurely strolled to their front-row seats, waving to people they didn't even know in the hopes of being recognized. For this was to be a New York experience: The first week-day World Series game at Yankee Stadium. And everybody who was anybody was there, arriving in time to be seen—as opposed to those at Ebbets Field, who arrived early to get their money's worth and be obscene. But even though thousands of deals would be made and hundreds of thousands of feet of prime New York realty would change hands, the day was not to belong to those business potentates, but instead to a young 27-year-old blond bear with the big ears and bigger grin, even then taking his place on the mound. And to the real fans.

The first man to step in against that 27-year-old was Junior Gilliam, the Dodgers' second baseman. Three days earlier Gilliam had faced the same Larsen and walked twice. Now, as Larsen made his first pitch of the game, a just-getting-acquainted pitch that was wide of the plate, it seemed as if the 64,519 in attendance were suffering through a severe case of *deja vu*. But then Gilliam fouled off the second offering by Larsen, took another ball and then a strike down on the corner. With the count 2-2, Larsen bent a fast curve over the low inside corner of the plate for a called strike three, catching Gilliam flat-footed. Umpire Babe Pinelli, punching his hand up in the air, thought to himself, "Oh-oh, Larsen's got it today."

That first out was like the first olive out of the jar: now they started tumbling out. Reese, after running the count to 3-2—the only Dodger all day who would see as many as three balls—also took a third called strike. And Snider, with a count of 2-1, lined the ball to right. That was 15 pitches and three outs.

Through the first three innings Larsen threw just 41 pitches off his no-windup delivery. But truth to tell, his delivery was in reality almost no delivery at all, his motion giving forth eluctible lies as he rocked back off his left leg, twirled his left forward, and then released the ball from his hands, held chest high, fasterthanyoucanreadthis. Dodger batters, thinking there was less in Larsen's delivery than met the eye, tried to time their swing, when they swang at all, and found themselves out-of-sync with the arrival of the ball. Coupled with his no-windup delivery, Larsen dealt in a form of insincerity known only to great pitchers, which he was on this, his day-of-days: When he promised one thing, he delivered another. The total effect had the Dodger bats rustling, almost sighing at the ball.

Larsen had now gone through the first three innings without hits, runs or fanfare, his economy of effort and efficiency of results matched by his opposite number, Sal Maglie, who less than two weeks earlier had pitched his own no-hitter against the Phillies. The only ball that had even vaguely resembled a hard hit off the

two had come back in the second inning when Jackie Robinson had smashed a liner off third baseman Andy Carey's glove which richocheted, faster than you can say "Jack Robinson," into the happily situated glove of shortstop Gil McDougald, who completed the 5-6-3 ground out by throwing out the fleet Robinson by less than a step.

However, their paths were to part in the fourth. After Larsen had set down the Dodgers on eight pitches in the top of the inning, Maglie, with two down, served up a breaking pitch to the eleventh man to face him, Mickey Mantle. Mantle arched the ball into the nearby lower right-field stands, just inside the foul pole at the 296-foot mark for a homer of the oriental variety.

Larsen came close to losing his place in history in the very next inning. Jackie Robinson opened the Dodgers' half of the fifth by flying out deep to right. Then Hodges, with a count of 2-and-2, caught one of Larsen's change-of-pace curves and drove it into the outer reaches of Yankee Stadium's center field area called "Death Valley." Mantle tore across the greensward with all the speed at his command and, at the last second, yawning glove at the ready, outran the ball and made the catch. The very next batter, Sandy Amoros, almost took a 1-1 pitch downtown, leaning into Larsen's off-speed delivery and rocketing a long towering drive in the direction of the right-field stands. At the last moment, the ball which promised to break up the no-hitter, and worse, hooked foul, fell into the stands for a long, and loud, second strike. Two pitches later Amoros grounded out meekly to second. Now Larsen was but 12 outs away from making history.

As the sixth flashed by in just 10 pitches, the arrogant Yankee fans, smug in their foreknowledge that they were entitled to win, it being their due as part of the territory, began to sit up and take notice. No longer was this just a game where they could go and accomplish their purpose of being able to tell everyone they had been there; this was suddenly becoming a game they could talk about afterwards.

Larsen too sensed he was closing in on immortality, having already cornered the market on its sound-alike cousin, twice removed, mortality. Thanks to a grace run in the bottom of the

N.Y. Hurler Retires 27 Hitters In Row

	1	2	3	4	5	6	7	8	9	10	R	H	E	AT BAT	8	POS.
BKLYN.	0	0	0	0	0	0	0				0	0	0	BALL	1	STRIKE 2 OUT 2
YANKS	0	0	0	1	0	1	0	0			2	5	0			

Don Larsen's Last Perfect Pitch

Ex-Oriole Beats Maglie, Gives New York 3-2 Series Lead

By LOU HATTER
[Sun Staff Correspondent]

New York, Oct. 8—Don Larsen created everlasting baseball history here today by pitching a perfect no-hit game, the first in 53 years of World Series competition, as New York defeated Brooklyn, 2 to 0 before 64,519 Yankee Stadium spectators.

told him they thought so too.

However, for some arcane reason never fully explained, those on the Yankee bench, while they may have thought he could, couldn't—and wouldn't—mention it. Larsen, sneaking down the dugout stairs for a quick smoke to quiet his nerves, asked Mantle, "Do you think I'll make it?" His center fielder merely looked at him with disgust and walked away without answering. Mantle went over to sit next to Billy Hunter, who asked Mantle to move to another seat. Mantle understood and did. Other players, wearing the expressions of ventriloquist's dummies, knowing something they dare not speak, merely smiled weakly in Larsen's direction and averted their eyes.

After Robinson led off the eighth by hitting back to the mound, Gil Hodges took his place in the batter's box, muttering to no one in particular, but overheard by both Berra and Pinelli, "I'll get this guy"—perhaps remembering that he had reached Larsen for a home run in the '55 Series and gotten the only hit off Larsen in his two innings pitched just three days before. With a 2-and-2 count, Hodges drove a low grass-cutting liner to the left of third baseman Andy Carey. Carey lunged for the twisting liner and speared it just off his shoe tops. Then, unsure of whether the third-base umpire had seen him, he made certain of the out by firing the ball over to first for insurance. The fans, a collective group of Madame De-Farges, now sitting at the foot of the guillotine Larsen was erecting, would drop one stitch from their knitting in the form of a loud roar with each out. They did so now, roaring for Carey and Larsen. Then after Sandy Amaros had ended the inning by flying weakly to Mantle in center they let out another. Three outs on 10 pitches. Only three more to go.

Now Larsen was on the threshhold of doing something that had never been done in 306 previous World Series games: pitching a no-hitter—although three men had come within one out. And more, a Perfect Game. As he took his place on the mound for the ninth inning, his knees caving, his brow wet with honest sweat like the village smithy and his breath that of a fish just removed from water, he called out, almost as if beseeching something from

sixth, he now had a 2-0 lead, if anyone was still counting. But it wasn't what was behind him that concerned him; it was what lay ahead.

A pitcher might convince himself he was a great pitcher by acting like one; and Larsen was acting like one now, throwing his curves at varying speeds and breaking off his change-of-pace curve sharply, almost as if he contradicted it in mid-flight. The Dodger batters were falling under the same delusion by taking Larsen at his own valuation, their bats suddenly taking on the consistency of charlotte russes. Imposing his will on everyone he faced now, he breezed through the seventh on just eight pitches. Only six more outs to go.

As Larsen walked off the field after the seventh, a deafening roar could be heard for his lion's heart. No longer did he constitute a majority of one who thought he could bring off the greatest performance in the history of the World Series. All 64,519 voices within, "Please help me get through this." But Larsen wasn't the only one giving pep talks to himself or to the Man Upstairs. For as the Yankee infielders finished their perfunctory infield warm-up, second baseman Billy Martin convened them, like four heads of state, and delivered three words: "Nothing gets through."

The first barrier to Larsen's place in history was Carl Furillo. As Larsen tried to get the ball by Furillo, Furillo hung tough, fouling the ball off, four times in all. In the almost cathedral hush that now engulfed Yankee Stadium, Furillo, finally tired of postponing destiny, flied out to right fielder. A giant roar went up and then almost before it started, it was over, as the Stadium once again fell into silence. As Larsen stood by with a case of rattling teeth and breath that sounded like that of a horse when the saddle is taken off, into the box stepped the penultimate batter in the scheme of things, Roy Campanella. Campy met Larsen's first pitch and drove it far down the left-field line. But as it tailed off into the seats, the apprehensive "o o o ohs" that had started with the flight of the ball turned into satisfied "aaaahs" as it went foul. On the next pitch Campy grounded out weakly to second.

With but one more out to go, Brooklyn manager Walter Alson sent up Dale Mitchell to pinch hit for his gallant pitcher, Sal Maglie. Larsen, reacting to the intense pressure, first turned ashen then mauve, his knees quaking, his breath coming faster. In the stillness surrounding him, his rasp could be heard by those on the field. Finally, after saying something to himself that sounded like a prayer, he let fly with a curve that broke high. Ball One. Working slowly, his every move now studied, Larsen came back with a fast ball. Over, 1-and-1. The crowd, now on its feet, let loose a cheer and then muffled it quickly lest they break the spell. Larsen toed

the rubber, picked up the resin bag for no reason whatsoever, then brought his hands to his belt in preparation for his next pitch. Mitchell swung and missed. It was 1-and-2. And another cheer rose and then fell, almost as if a choirmaster had waved it away. Larsen took a deep breath, looked in and came back with another fast ball. Mitchell, a slap hitter who had a reputation for protecting the plate, did so, fouling it off into the left-field stands, 1-and-2. Still, very still everywhere now. Larsen now prepared to throw a pitch he was never to remember throwing, his mind having blanked out. But throw it he did, his 97th pitch, a fast ball that umpire Babe Pinelli didn't "pick up until it was two-thirds in." The ball caught the outside corner of the plate, waist high. Mitchell made as if to slap out at it, lunging with his bat, but then froze. Almost as if in tableaux it could have been called either way, but Pinelli, playing out his lone hand, jabbed it in the air. "The third strike, and you're out."

The next thing 129,038 eyes remembered seeing was Yogi Berra catching the ball, Don Larsen catching Berra—who had engulfed him in the bear hug of an exhuberant child—and Mitchell, who struck out infrequently, if that, turning around to argue the call with Pinelli, who had already departed.

Later, one of those dandruff-scratchers known as a sportswriter, his pencil fluttering like a swallow, was to ask Larsen, "Was this the best game you ever pitched?" But his kind was not to be taken seriously. For most felt as did one of the deans of writers, Shirley Povich, who began his column the next morning, "The million-to-one shot came in. Hell froze over. A month of Sundays hit the calendar." It was all that. And more. Much more. It was the greatest single pitching performance in the history of baseball.

Yogi Berra and Don Larsen dance a "perfect" fandango of victory.

11 Hubbell's Five Consecutive Strike-Outs

1934 All-Star Game, July 10, 1934

THE BEST PLACE TO HIDE A NEEDLE IS NOT IN A HAYSTACK, but in amongst other needles. And there is no greater collection of needles than those polished, gleaming stars who gather each and every summer to shape the fabric of the midsummer dream game called the All-Star Game. This is the story of how one man, Carl Hubbell, threaded his way between all of those who have played in the All-Star Game to become the eye of that classic. And solidify the All-Star Game in the mind's-eye of the sports fan.

The All-Star Game jumped full-blown from the brow of Chicago *Tribune* sports editor Arch Ward back in 1933, both as a circulation-builder for the *Trib* and as an adjunct to the Century of Progress Exposition, then taking place in Chicago.

The game, then known as "The Game of the Century," had the blessings of baseball commissioner Kenesaw Mountain Landis, who saw the meeting of the cream of the two leagues in a dream game as a showcase for baseball. It would also be a method for raising moneys for the National Association of Professional Baseball Players, an organization which looked after the needy and ailing players. The game, according to those in the writing dodge, was "the first time since General Abner Doubleday conceived the game of baseball from rounders and cricket that two picked teams, representing the strength of two major leagues, ever met in midseason, when the players were at their peak of condition." Or some such pious dwaddle.

While the *Tribune* handled all balloting, Landis set himself up as proposer and seconder of the rules of the game, decreeing that each team have at least one representative on its league's roster, thus insuring that the rosters were twice as exclusive as Noah's list of eligibles and that those two grand old men of baseball, Connie Mack and John J. McGraw, be impressed into duty as honorary managers.

The capacity crowd of 49,000 in Chicago's Comiskey Park had looked forward to seeing every star in baseball's firmament in the advertised nine-ring circus. But they were to be disappointed as Mack started the Yankees' Lefty Gomez instead of the hoped-for Lefty Grove, and McGraw sent St. Louis' "Wild" Bill Hallahan to the mound for the National League instead of the Giants' Carl Hubbell, who only four days before had pitched eighteen scoreless innings against Hallahan's Cardinals. However, both Grove and Hubbell were to see action before the game was over, as were 28 other stars, as Mack continued his mastery over McGraw, repeating his victory of the last time the two had met in head-to-head competition, two decades before in the 1913 Series.

Mack's American League all-stars, then lower cased, won 4-2 on the strength of Babe Ruth's two-run homer in the third. And nothing McGraw could do, including throwing every round of ammunition in his bandillero and 17 of the 18 men on his roster into the fray—the only man held in reserve by McGraw was Hal Schumacher in case Hubbell ran into trouble in the last three innings—could alter that final result. Mack, who was out to win, had told his club at the pre-game meeting that it was against his instincts to "change a winning combination," and once in the lead

had played the rest of the game with virtually the same regular line-up with which he had started—leaving such stalwarts as Jimmie Foxx, Tony Lazzeri, and Bill Dickey on the bench for the entire game.

In just five ticks of the clock's long hand over the two-hour mark the first "dream" game was history. It was believed by many that it would be the last of its kind as well, an affair of no great moment that could be revived for every Century of Progress Exposition, but no sooner. But Commissioner Landis, encouraged by the excitement the first game had generated—and the receipts of $51,000, which were turned over to the players' charity fund—insisted that the idea not die aborning. Holding "that's a grand show, and it should be continued," Landis, despite some of the club owners who were underwhelmed with the idea of continuing the contest, pushed for its continuance. And, in those days, whatever Landis wanted, Landis got.

And so, at the bidding of Landis, "Son of the Ballgame of the Century" took place again in 1934, with nary a mention of the name by which it would become known: the All-Star Game. Cynical members of the press, who never recognized a trend until it was a tradition, viewed the game merely as an exhibition game for bragging rights and little else, and led off their pre-game columns with phrases like "So What?" But those in the writing dodge had had about as much chance of dulling the appetite of the baseball fan for the game as a down-on-her-luck palmist has of getting business by tucking her card into a passing coffin. And 50,000 fans showed up at the Polo Grounds for "Game of the Century" redux, or Number Two.

This time around they would see Hubbell start, and the year's wait was worth it. Hubbell, selected by National League manager Bill Terry to start in front of his hometown fans, was known for his screwball—a right-handed fadeaway that had the opposite effect of a normal lefty's curve, breaking down and in on left-handed batters and outward and away from right-handers—his great curve, and his sharp control. His style was such that it made demands on the batter as well.

Over the past six years, Hubbell had used his screwball and control to good effect, averaging 18-plus wins a year and issuing less than two walks per game. National Leaguers, who couldn't locate his offerings with a Geiger counter, had found that trying to hit Hubbell was like trying to mine coal with a nail file. Now it was to be the American Leaguers turn in the barrel.

With but minutes to go before they took the field, Hubbell and his starting catcher, Gabby Hartnett of the Cubs, were closeted in the clubhouse going over the American League batting order. After looking over the group of daguerrotypes and darker plates that made up the line-up: Gehringer, Manush, Ruth, Gehrig, Foxx, Simmons, Cronin, Dickey and starting pitcher Lefty Gomez—future Hall of Famers all—Hartnett paused and stopped. There wasn't a weak spot in the carload, with the exception of Gomez who was one of the weakest hitting pitchers in a field known for its weak hitters. But even Gomez had his moments, such as the one in

the previous summer's game when he singled in the American
League's first run in their 4-2 win.

Hartnett, his mind rebelling at the thought of having to pitch to
the aforenamed broadbacks—who had managed to pickle the ball
for a combined .327 average the previous year and were now
collectively flexing their muscles in the .350 range, not to mention
Gomez—finally, more in desperation than anything else, blurted
out, "Hell, let's use your screwball . . . they've never seen it
before!" Then, as if to make the meeting an official one, he added,
"We'll waste everything except the screwball. Get that over, but
keep your fast ball and hook inside . . . We can't let 'em hit it in the
air." That was it for the "meeting." Now it was out to the mound to
face the greatest collection of hitmen this side of Cicero, Illinois.

But if Hubbell was known to opposing batters for his screwball,
he was known to his fans as "Old Long Pants," his uniform looking
like he had a goodly deal of material left over which he had not
wanted to throw away. A lank and willowy six feet, Hubbell's long
woolen uniform reached below the knee and gathered at the
ankle, almost making a second garment for him. Now the man
with the villainous-looking uniform and the equally villainous
screwball stood ready to stand and deliver to the first batter up,
Detroit's "Mechanical Man," Charlie Gehringer.

Hartnett crouched down in his position and called for a "waste
pitch" so that Hub could get the feel of his first pitch. But it never
arrived, Hubbell having made it a little too good. Gehringer
opened the festivities with a single to center. One pitch, one hit.
From somewhere in the stands behind third a single voice could be
heard calling out, "Take him out!" It looked like it was going to be
that kind of day.

As Bill Terry took a few steps off first and hollered in, "That's all
right," Washington's Heinie Manush, who had led the American
League in hits the previous year, stepped into the batter's box.
Hubbell came in with two screwballs against the left-handed hitting
Manush. Manush swung twice and missed, two strikes and no
balls. But then, throwing "waste pitches," Hubbell missed the plate
four times and Manush, still unsure of what he had seen the first
two pitches, eschewed swinging at the final four offerings and
walked. Now Terry came to the mound, joined by third baseman
Pie Traynor, shortstop Travis and second baseman Frankie Frisch,
all to ask their "meal ticket," "Are you all right?" Hubbell, sounding like a little boy minimizing a bad report card, assured them he
was. Now he could hear his leather-lunged critic yelling down from
the stands, "Take him out before it's too late!" But the walk to
Manush would be the last installment on his dues. Now it was to be
the screwball, and nothing but the screwball.

With Gehringer and Manush now homesteading on first and
second, the man who stepped in to face Hubbell was the man who
had the original copyright on the home run, Babe Ruth. Knowing
that the "book" on Ruth was that his favorite pitch was one up a
little so that he could get his bat under it, Hubbell determined to
keep the ball around Ruth's knees, depriving "The Great Man" of
any chance for leverage, and hoping for a double-play ball. But if
Ruth labored under a delusion that he would get "his" pitch, he
wasn't to labor long. After wasting his first pitch, Hubbell, with
enough coolness to branch out and franchise it, came back with
three twisting screwballs around the knees. Ruth didn't even
bother to remove the bat from his shoulder. As plate umpire
Charles Pfirman punched the air for the third time signifying
"Out!," Ruth turned around to stare in disbelief and Hartnett stood
up laughing, paying no never mind to Gehringer and Manush,
then executing a heat double-steal and alighting unmolested on

"The screwball cometh," courtesy of Carl Hubbell

second and third.

The next man up was Lou Gehrig, the broad back of the Yankees, who that year would lead the league in homers and runs-batted-in. Now, as Gehrig stood in, his understated virility and dangerous bat threatening Hubbell, Hubbell, who could no more be melted than ice welded, threw Gehrig nothing but knee-high screwballs . . . four of them. Gehrig, now knowing what Hubbell threw even if its nature puzzled him, swung down on the fourth of the screwballs and missed. Two outs.

The vast throng now roared in tribute to Hubbell, the cheers replacing the earlier catcalls. And Gehrig, passing on his experience of trying to shovel smoke, offered the next batter, Jimmie Foxx, what little advice he could: "You might as well take a cut . . . it won't get any higher."

And so Foxx, a heavily-muscled man who was the broadest back of the American League's broadback attack, stepped in, determined to swing at Hubbell's offerings regardless of the consequence. Hartnett called, naturally enough, for what was working; and what was working was the screwball. As it came in, knee high, Foxx set his granite jaw and heavy muscles to the task and took a hefty swing. And missed. Hubbell stared in on the man who faced him, now looking like what Jack met at the top of the beanstalk as he swung the bat like a toothpick in anticipation of the next pitch.

Two more times Hubbell's left arm swung down in deliverance and two more times Foxx's bat swung to meet it. The first time Foxx nicked the ball for a loud foul. The second time, like an immense sail going limp in a chance of wind, he missed, almost failing from the force of the ball. The side had been retired on but 12 screwballs, so decimated that all that was missing was a note from their mothers explaining their emotional absence.

In the National League's half of the first, Frankie Frisch hit a homer—the National League's second in All-Star play, both by Frisch—and the National League, and Hubbell, took a 1-0 lead into the top of the second.

Now it was Aloysius Szymanski, better known as Al Simmons—or, more familiarly, "Bucketfoot," for his accentuated stance far back in the batter's box—who stepped to the plate to lead off the American League's second. Simmons, who would work himself into a self-induced rage before swinging, had endangered Junior Circuit third basemen for ten years, giving them cause to worry about their dentures if they got too close to his thundering bat. But there was no cause for concern this afternoon, as Hubbell, slowly suffocating Simmons with his screwball, struck him out. Then it was on to Washington's playing manager, Joe Cronin, who became merely another cipher on the scorecard, Hubbell's fifth straight strikeout victim.

American League Stars Defeat Nationals, 9 to 7

So What?					
NATIONALS—	AB	R	H	O	A	E
Frisch, 2b	3	3	2	0	1	0
W. Herman, 2b	2	0	1	0	1	0
Traynor, 3b	5	2	2	1	0	0
Medwick, lf	2	1	1	0	0	0
Klein, lf	3	0	1	1	0	0
Cuyler, rf	2	0	0	2	0	0
Ott, rf	2	0	0	0	1	0
Berger, cf	2	0	0	0	0	1
P. Waner, cf	2	0	0	1	0	0
Terry, 1b	3	0	1	4	0	0
Jackson, ss	2	0	0	0	1	0
Vaughan, ss	2	0	0	4	0	0
Hartnett, c	2	0	0	9	0	0
Lopez, c	2	0	0	5	1	0
Hubbell, p	0	0	0	0	0	0
Warneke, p	0	0	0	0	0	0
Mungo, p	0	0	0	0	0	0
Martin	0	1	0	0	0	0
J Dean, p	1	0	0	0	0	0
Frankhouse, p	1	0	0	0	0	0
Totals	36	7	8	27	5	1
AMERICANS—	AB	R	H	O	A	E
Gehringer, 2b	3	0	2	2	1	0
Manush, lf	2	0	0	0	0	0
Ruffing p	1	0	1	0	0	0
Harder p	2	0	0	1	0	0
Ruth, rf	2	1	0	0	0	0
Chapman, rf	2	0	1	0	1	0
Gehrig, 1b	4	1	0	11	1	1
Foxx, 3b	5	1	2	1	2	0
Simmons, cf lf	5	3	3	3	0	0
Cronin, ss	5	1	2	2	8	0
Dickey, c	2	1	1	4	0	0
Cochrane, c	1	0	0	1	1	0
Gomez, p	1	0	0	0	0	0
Averill, cf	4	1	2	1	0	0
West, c	0	0	0	1	0	0
Totals	39	9	14	27	14	1

W. Herman batted for Hubbell in third and played second for Frisch later. Martin batted for Mungo in fifth.

| Americans | 0 | 0 | 0 | 2 | 6 | 1 | 0 | 0 | 0 | 9 |
| Nationals | 1 | 0 | 3 | 0 | 3 | 0 | 0 | 0 | 0 | 7 |

Two of Hubbell's five victims: Al Simmons (l) and Babe Ruth

"The Meal Ticket," Carl Hubbell

There being some minor shortcomings allowed in the name of human nature, Hubbell, throwing an obligatory "waste" pitch to the eighth batter in the line-up, Bill Dickey, got one too close. And Dickey indulged Hubbell's momentary failing by hitting his mistake for a single, breaking his string at five straight.

That brought up the ninth man in the American League line-up, pitcher Lefty Gomez. As Gomez stepped into the batter's box like a condemned man, he muttered almost as an aside to Hartnett, "What the hell am I doing up here? You are now looking at a hitter whose average is .104." What he was doing up there was striking out, Hub's sixth strikeout victim in two innings, his sixth out of seven batters. (Later, Gomez was to grouse to Dickey, "If it weren't for you getting that hit, I would have gone down with the greatest hitters of all time!")

Hubbell was to complete his three-inning stint by getting Gehringer on a fly to right, forcing Manush to ground out, then, after walking the ever-dangerous Ruth, retiring Gehrig on a routine fly-out,. As the man they called "The Meal Ticket" walked slowly to the centerfield clubhouse, his afternoon's assignment over, the crowd to a man stood on its feet to give him a standing ovation, one that continued to go around the stadium, picking up crescendo every time it began to ebb. Three times the stands rocked in roaring appreciation of the greatest feat of spot pitching in history—27 strikes to 13 men with only five pitches hit in fair territory.

Well-nigh forgotten in the wake of Hubbell's unbelievable performance—and other such traditional ex-post facto adjectives—was the American League's 9-7 win. Finally finding their sea legs and batting eyes after the departure of Hubbell, the American League belted out 12 hits and 9 runs against Hubbell's four predecessors for a 9-7 victory.

Regardless of the outcome, however, the game belonged to Carl Hubbell and his screwball, one which had deprived five of the greatest batters in the history of baseball of their breath and caused their eyeballs to rotate in their sockets. It forever linked the names Ruth-Gehrig-Foxx-Simmons-and-Cronin together like pearls on a necklace, All-Stars, all in what was now officially the "All-Star Game," thanks to Carl Hubbell's performance.

12 Enos Slaughter's Dash to Home

St. Louis Cardinals vs. Boston Red Sox, 7th Game, 1946 World Series, October 15, 1946

WHEN AMERICA MARCHED OFF TO WAR IN 1941, BASEBALL was put on ice. Twelve million men and women, the greatest host of personnel ever marshaled, were under arms, including the likes of Ted Williams, Joe DiMaggio, Stan Musial, Hank Greenberg, Bob Feller, and other lesser novas. In 1942, baseball had no less than 71 Major Leaguers in the service of their country; in 1943, 219; in 1944, 342; and in 1945, 384.

Even though baseball's players had gone marching off to fight for democracy, baseball as an institution had stayed behind to fight the good fight on the home front. Given the "green light" by President Roosevelt in January of 1942, baseball, with a patriotic fervor, became part of the new national pastime, war. Indulging in fundamental jingoism and fund raising, baseball began sponsoring a war bond drive, a benefit for Army and Navy relief there, and everywhere a "Waste Fat Night," a "Smokes for Servicemen" or a "Scrap Metal Night." And there, seated right beside servicemen with enough medals and tinware on to qualify as one-man scrap drives, sat little kids who had brought in the requisite amount of scrap metal for their free admission—all enjoying the game of baseball, or what passed for same.

Those who wanted baseball in the proverbial "worst way," got it accordingly, as baseball stocked its rosters with draft-proof players of every description. With a famine sweeping over the land, scouts with proprietary alacrity began snatching up beardless puppy-youth who could throw a baseball the length of a playpen and throwing nets over bearded grizzlies who had been around since the first game of rounders. All applicants grudgingly accepted. It began to look as if baseball had emptied out the mission. Baseball even found a ghost or two of baseball past in the wake of all these vagrant guests: Babe Herman making a ceremonial appearance for the Dodgers and falling over first in his very first at-bat after an absence of eight years; and Pepper Martin coming back after a four-year hiatus to play for the 1944 World's Champion Cardinals. The talent was so inexpressibly dreary that the St. Louis Browns even won the pennant in the wartime season of '44, led by a 34-year-old pitcher, Sigmund Jakucki, who had an 0-3 record his last time around, eight years before. With the end of the war in 1945, it had become quite evident that the wartime accidents on the ballfield had almost equalled those on the battle-field.

Johnny came marching home along with Bobby, Teddy and hundreds of others. And as they were mustered out of the service, their replacements were mustered out of baseball, casualties of peace. Soon those who had once been forgotten, but not gone, were both, as baseball suddenly realized they were not quite the dish they had ordered.

New York Giants manager Mel Ott sounded the warning when he cautioned his by-now expendable troops: "You were all right when we had nothing better, lads, but mind your p's and q's now. . . . The pros are back."

The team that gained the most from the sudden influx of former servicemen who players was the Boston Red Sox. The Sox,

seventh the year before, were now picked to win the 1946 pennant, their ranks swollen with returning veterans Johnny Pesky, Bobby Doerr, Ted Williams, Dom DiMaggio, Tex Hughson, Mickey Harris, Joe Dobson, Hal Wagner, and others for a total of 17 returning servicemen. Together those 17 contributed 65 percent of the Red Sox 104 wins and 59 percent of their 1441 hits, leading them to the BoSox's first pennant since 1918 by a full 12 games over Detroit.

In the National League, the pennant race became a two-team cakewalk, as the two teams with the most returning veterans, the St. Louis Cardinals and the Brooklyn Dodgers, finished in a flat-footed dead heat for the pennant. Playing an unprecedented two-game playoff series to settle the matter, the Cardinals, with 15 returning veterans, beat the Dodgers, with only 13, by the same margin, two games to none.

The handicappers, figuring the Red Sox had more firepower—and more veterans—installed them as 9-20 favorites to win the Series. The Red Sox had tradition behind them too, having gone undefeated in their five World Series appearances. The Cardinals had a tradition, of sorts. In the eight Series they had played in, they had won only one opener, back in '34. And after Game One, won by a Rudy York homer in the 10th for a 3-2 BoSox win, the reverence due tradition increased.

Game Two saw the St. Louis manager come back with his left-handed screwball pitcher, Harry Brecheen, who held the Red Sox to four hits, breezing to a 3-0 victory and a 1-1 tie in the Series.

Through the first two games, Boston's municipal monument, Ted Williams, had just one hit in seven at-bats, that a single to right-center in the sixth inning of the first game. Troubled by a sore right elbow he had hurt before the Series, Williams was troubled by something else as well, the Cardinals use of the Williams Shift. In an attempt to distract Williams' attention from Sportsman's Park handy right-field pews, the Cardinals had employed their version of the Shift. The Shift, used for the first time that July by Cleveland manager Lou Boudreau who knew that "he could pop short flies to left for doubles all day long, but I was willing to take the chance as long as somebody else had to drive him in," had the Cardinal shortstop playing on the left side of the infield with the rest of the St. Louis infield, lock, stock, and third baseman, moving over to the right side. But rather than take advantage of the open left-field area, Williams chose instead to challenge the Shift, as he had done all season. With the same results.

Game Three in Fenway Park was over almost before it started, with Rudy York hitting a three-run homer in the first after Pesky had singled and Williams been given an intentional pass. Dave "Boo" Ferriss shut down the Cardinals for a 4-0 win and a 2-1 Red Sox lead in the Series. But the big news, at least as far as the Boston papers were concerned, was Ted Williams' bunt single down the third base line and into left in the third inning against the Shift. The next morning the papers trumpeted "Ted Bunts!" in 48-point type, relegating the news of the Red Sox's victory to smaller print below.

In contrast, Game Four was anything but a pitcher's game, the goings-on resembling a fungo-hitting contest more than a ballgame. As things got out of hand, with 29 hits pock-marking the Fenway surroundings, the game produced the greatest number of hit records in Series history. Not only did the Cardinals get 20 hits in the game, tying a 25-year-old record for most hits in one Series game by the 1921 New York Giants, but every man in the line-up for St. Louis hit safely with varying degrees of success. Three of them, Enos Slaughter, Whitey Kurowski and Joe Gariagola, all had four hits, tying the one-game hit record originally set back in 1903; a fourth player, Boston outfielder Wally Moses of the Sox also chipping in with four. When the dust had settled and the scoreboard operator revived, the final score read: Cardinals 12, Red Sox 3. And the Series score read two games apiece.

Things got back to normal, at least as far as the oddsmakers were concerned, as Boston right-hander Joe Dobson beat St. Louis in Game Five and the Red Sox moved to within one game of the Championship.

One small occurrence in Game Five which received only scant notice in the next day's write-ups, but was writ large on the Cardinals' chances took place in the fourth inning when one of Dobson's pitches nicked Enos Slaughter, catching him on the right elbow. Despite agonizing pain, he wouldn't, according to one writer's quote attributed to Slaughter, "Give nobody the satisfaction of knowin' I was hurt." By the time the "old warhorse" came to bat in the sixth, his elbow had taken on the look of an artificially-colored tomato and had approximated its size as well. Slaughter, who was a chronic .300 hustler, wanted to stay in, but being unable to swing the bat or throw, he went to St. Louis manager Eddie Dyer and, for the first time in his career, asked to be taken out.

On the train trip back to St. Louis, the club trainer spent the entire night treating Slaughter with hot and cold packs, but to no avail—even going so far as swathing his arm in an electric jacket and plugging it into the only electric outlet available on the train. Upon his return to St. Louis, the team physician, Doc Hyland, took Slaughter immediately to the hospital for an X-ray. The diagnosis wasn't good. "Eno," said Hyland, "I'm sorry to say you've got such a bad hemorrhage that if you get hit on it again the chances are I'll have to amputate." But Slaughter, a riverboat gambler at heart, would have none of that. He would play the cards dealt to him, no matter the consequences.

Back in St. Louis for Game Six, the Cardinals beat Mickey Harris and the Red Sox, 4-1, for Brecheen's second Series win. Slaughter, barely able to grip the bat, got one of the five hits in the Cards' big three-run third to seal the victory. Now it was on to the Seventh Game.

With Murray Dickson pitching for St. Louis and Dave "Boo" Ferriss pitching for the Sox, the two teams went into the fifth tied at one apiece. Then, in the bottom of the fifth, the Cards put together four hits for two runs and the lead, 3-1.

That's the way it stayed until the top of the eighth when Rip Russell, pinch-hitting for catcher Hal Wagner, singled. George Metkovich, pinch-hitting for Boston's second pitcher, Joe Dobson, followed with a double, moving Russell to third. Manager Dyer brought in his stopper, Harry Brecheen, to close the door on the rally—the same Harry Brecheen who had won the sixth game only 24 hours before. Brecheen, pitching to the top of the BoSox batting order, struck out Moses and forced Pesky to line out to right, Slaughter's throw holding Russell affixed to third. With the door almost closed, Dom DiMaggio opened it by driving a Brecheen screwball off the right-center field wall for a double, scoring both baserunners and tying up the score, 3-3. But DiMaggio, running out the double, twisted his ankle and had to be replaced by pinch-runner Leon Culberson. Culberson was to remain there as a soujourner as the next batter up, Williams, swinging for the nearby fence, popped up for the third out.

When the Red Sox took their field positions in the bottom of the eighth, Culberson went to center in place of the injured DiMaggio, Roy Partee replaced Wagner behind the plate and right-handed Bob Klinger replaced Dobson on the mound. All three were to play a part in history within scant minutes, as was the first batter up to face Klinger in the bottom of the eighth, Enos Slaughter.

Game 7 October 15 at St. Louis

Bos.	100	000	020	
St L.	010	020	01x	

Boston	Pos	AB	R	H	RBI	PO	A	E
Moses	rf	4	1	1	0	1	0	0
Pesky	ss	4	0	1	0	2	1	0
DiMaggio	cf	3	0	1	3	0	0	0
Culberson	cf	0	0	0	0	0	0	0
Williams	lf	4	0	0	0	3	1	0
York	1b	4	0	1	0	10	1	0
c Campbell		0	0	0	0	0	0	0
Doerr	2b	4	0	2	0	3	7	0
Higgins	3b	4	0	0	0	0	1	0
Wagner	c	2	0	0	0	4	0	0
a Russell		1	1	1	0	0	0	0
Partee	c	1	0	0	0	0	0	0
Ferriss	p	2	0	0	0	0	0	0
Dobson	p	0	0	0	0	0	1	0
b Metkovich		1	1	1	0	0	0	0
Klinger	p	0	0	0	0	1	0	0
Johnson	p	0	0	0	0	0	0	0
d McBride		1	0	0	0	0	0	0
Totals		35	3	8	3	24	12	0

a Singled for Wagner in 8th.
b Doubled for Dobson in 8th.
c Ran for York in 9th.
d Grounded out for Johnson in 9th.

St. Louis	Pos	AB	R	H	RBI	PO	A	E
Schoendienst	2b	4	0	2	1	2	3	0
Moore	cf	4	0	1	0	3	0	0
Musial	1b	3	0	1	0	6	0	0
Slaughter	rf	3	1	1	0	4	0	0
Kurowski	3b	4	1	1	0	3	1	1
Garagiola	c	3	0	0	0	4	0	0
Rice	c	1	0	0	0	0	0	0
Walker	lf	3	1	2	2	3	0	0
Marion	ss	2	0	0	0	2	1	0
Dickson	p	3	1	1	1	0	1	0
Brecheen	p	1	0	0	0	0	0	0
Totals		31	4	9	4	27	6	1

Pitching	IP	H	R	ER	BB	SO
Boston						
Ferriss	$4\frac{1}{3}$	7	3	4	1	2
Dobson	$2\frac{2}{3}$	0	0	0	2	2
Klinger (L)	$\frac{2}{3}$	2	1	1	1	0
Johnson	$\frac{1}{3}$	0	0	0	0	0
St. Louis						
Dickson	*7	5	3	3	1	3
Brecheen (W)	2	3	0	0	0	1

*Faced 2 batters in 8th.

Doubles—Dickson, DiMaggio, Kurowski, Metkovich, Musial, Walker. Sacrifice Hit—Marion. Left on Bases—Boston 3, St. Louis 4. Umpires—Barlick, Berry, Ballanfant, Hubbard. Attendance—36,143. Time of Game—2:17.

Slaughter inhospitably greeted Klinger with a single to right-center to open the inning. But when Whitey Kurowski, trying to sacrifice Slaughter to second, popped out, and Cardinal catcher Del Rice flied out to Williams, Slaughter seemed destined to be anchored there.

However, Slaughter had other thoughts. Figuring that Walker was hardly a long-ball hitter, having just 23 extra-base hits all season, Enos took it into his head to steal second, all the better to score if Walker got a hit. With his tail stretched straight, like a pointer's, his hind-quarters rocking with the motion of a cat preparatory to leaping, Slaughter timed Klinger's motion and took off. But as Klinger's pitch crossed the plate, Walker swung and poked a hit into center field. With a full head of steam, Slaughter approached second as the ball bounced into center field in the general direction of Culberson. Without breaking stride, Slaughter raced past second toward third, his ears standing straight up, like a greyhound's.

While Culberson, who was a half-step slower than the man he replaced, Dom DiMaggio, was busy chasing down the ball, which seemed to be possessed and moved away from him, Slaughter determined he could score. Once before, in Game One, the third base coach, Mike Gonzalez, had stopped him at third on a triple when the Red Sox were playing hot potato with the relay and the Cards had lost the game in extra innings. After that episode, Slaughter had complained to manager Dyer, who had given him the go-ahead, telling his frisky warrior, "If it happens again and you think you can make it, go ahead. I'll take the responsibility." This was the time he thought he could make it; there would be nothing that could stop him now, not Gonzalez, not a brick wall, not anything.

Moving like a cat that fully expects a half-brick to catch him in the back, Slaughter came thundering toward third and coach Mike Gonzalez's outstretched hands, a train gate trying to halt the runaway train named Slaughter. Culberson, after fumbling at the ball momentarily, finally corralled it on the greensward and threw it back to the relay man, Sox shortstop Johnny Pesky, who had taken two steps into the outfield to receive the throw. Without slowing up, his feet hollering "Gangway. Here I Come!" Slaughter shot through Gonzalez's train gate and barreled toward home, under his own instructions. Pesky, seeing Gonzalez's upraised hands and fully expecting Slaughter to arrest his mad tear at third, took the relay over his left shoulder, and then turned as slowly as a door back toward the infield. Pinky Higgins, the Sox third baseman, was shouting at Pesky. Bobby Doerr, the Sox second baseman, was also shouting. But so were 36,143 other voices, all of whom had first gasped at Slaughter's daring and then grasped the significance of his mad dash. Higgins' and Doerr's shouts were lost somewhere in the tumult that now engulfed Sportsman's Park.

The unhearing Pesky's first impulse was to turn toward second, toward Harry Walker, who had turned first and was now on his way to second. And while Walker gave Pesky pause, he failed for a nanosecond to see that Slaughter was moving like a greyhound who had just heard the word "bone" shouted from somewhere behind home plate. Finally, the urgency of the situation was impressed upon him, and Pesky, having turned half-way toward second, now had to turn again and threw the ball, off balance, toward home. But Slaughter, still three furlongs in front of the ball and gaining, thundered down the basepaths and down the corridors of time as well, sliding over an unprotected plate as Partee had to go two steps up the line to take Pesky's off-line throw.

Slaughter's mad dash had given the Cardinals their fourth run, carrying them to a 4–3 win in the game and Series and carried the man they called "Country" right into baseball's pantheon at Cooperstown as well.

Cards Take Top Honors Of Baseball

Score With Two Down In Eighth Inning to Whip Red Sox, 4-3

Harry Brecheen Pitching Hero

Joins Select Group Of Hurlers Who Have Won Three Games

Enos "Country" Slaughter, the man who ran straight into the Hall of Fame.

13 Medwick's Shower of Trash

St. Louis Cardinals vs. Detroit Tigers, 7th Game, 1934 World Series, October 9, 1934

THE 1934 ST. LOUIS CARDINALS WERE KNOWN TO ONE AND all as simply "The Gashouse Gang"—the result of a remark made by shortstop Leo Durocher, who, having been asked by New York *Sun* columnist Frank Graham if the Cardinals were good enough to play in the American League, had answered, "They wouldn't let us play in the American League; they'd say we were just a lot of gashouse players." But whether they were known as the St. Louis Cardinals or the Gashouse Gang, they were a curious sort of characters either way, sporting some of the most fanciful nicknames this side of the Seven Dwarfs: "Ducky" Medwick, Frank "The Fordham Flash" Frisch, Leo "The Lip" Durocher, "Pepper" Martin, "Wild" Bill Hallahan, "Ripper" Collins, "Sunny" Jim Bottomley, and, of course, the Deans, "Daffy" and "Dizzy."

But the most curious one of all was Jerome Hannah "Dizzy" Dean, an authentic American tintype who served as proof positive that baseball not only builds character but that it also builds characters. A man-boy of unusually high spirit (pronounced "spart" by Dean as in "Spart of St. Louis"), Dean could literally strut sitting down. Referring to himself in the third person in an early Norman Mailer-esque affection, Dean would call himself "Ol' Diz" or "The Great One," depending upon his mood. When he was farmed out before the 1931 season, less for seasoning than as an object lesson, he reportedly told his manager, "That's the fastest I ever saw a club lose 30 games." He was one of the most irresistible, irrepressible, irresponsible whackos ever to come down the baseball pike. But also one of the most talented.

Some of "Ol' Diz's" stories, all told with the breezy nonchalance of a hog caller, gained him enduring fame. Like the night he had come in late after celebrating his 25th win as a member of the Houston Buffs and encountered the Houston president also coming in at the same wee hour. Dizzy looked at the president knowingly and conspiratorially said, "Looks as if we's both a little late, Mr. President. If you won't say nuthin' to nobody 'bout seein' me, then I won't nuthin' bout seein' you neither." Or on why his formal education had never progressed past the third grade: "If I'd a went to the fourth grade, I'd a passed up my old man, and I didn't want to show Paw up." But even though his fast quips gained him fame far and wide, it was his fast ball that gained him the most renown. His fluid overhand motion made him virtually unbeatable, especially when he mixed his blazing fast ball with his excellent change of pace and his "curvie," which, in teammate Leo Durocher's words, "Breaks like a ball falling off a pool table."

Dean burst on the baseball scene in 1930, a 19-year-old whose wisdom had remained at a standstill while whiskers had just started to grow unabated. At the time one of the brightest aspects of his career was the dazzling uncertainty of it. Bought out of the Army by his father, Dean reported first to St. Joseph, where he won 17, then to Houston, where he won another eight, a total of 25 wins against only ten losses. Unfortunately for management, he also lived as big as he won, renting three rooms in three hotels simultaneously and spending money that he hadn't even been programmed to receive. Brought up by the Cardinals after they

had clinched the 1930 pennant, Dean got one turn and made the most of it, pitching a three-hit shutout in his major league debut. But even then manager Gabby Street knew what he was getting, suggesting to one of those offering congratulations on his find, "He's going to be a great pitcher, but I'm afraid we're not going to know from one minute to the next what he's going to do."

Cardinal management knew what to do with Dean the next year: Send him back to Houston, less for honing up skills as a pitcher, than for growing up as a person. But Dean, still marching to his own drummer, continued on his merry way, winning 26 games for Houston—including a double header against Fort Worth on a Sunday afternoon and another game on Tuesday to wrap up the Texas League championship—strike out a record 303 batters and compile an ERA of 1.53. By 1932 he was back with the Cardinals for good. Or bad.

Dean returned to the Cardinals slightly restrained, and delivered to his companions oral deductions of his own wisdom, proclaiming, "I might be dizzy here in a hotel lobby, but I'm not dizzy out there on the mound." Then he proceeded to back up his uncharacteristically muted bravado by winning 18 games, including three in five days against the New York Giants, and leading the league in strikeouts in his first year with the Cards. However, instead of his efforts helping the defending World's Champions to another title, the '32 Cards, beset by injuries and morale problems, plummeted to a tie for sixth.

The year 1933 was little better for the Cardinals as they moved up one notch in the standings and traded managers in midstream, Gabby Street for Frankie Frisch and a pennant to be named later. But Dean, besides almost driving Rickey sane—leaving him with powers barely those of respiration and locomotion between explosions of his favorite expletive deleted, "Judas Priest!"—won 20 games and again led the league in strikeouts. Dean also continued to pull up batters to study their roots. Once he purposely walked the potential last out of a game in order to get to Giant slugger Bill Terry and fulfill a promise he had made that morning at a children's hospital that he would strike out the Giant manager. "I hate to do this, Bill," he shouted to the benumbed Terry, "but I promised the kids I'd strike you out." He did, too.

Yet another vintage Dean episode had him wander into his opposing number's clubhouse to attend a meeting in which each of the Cardinal batters was being dissected. "Don't mind me," said Diz, taking a stool near the door, " 'cause Ol' Diz knows how to pitch to 'em, too . . . 'Sides, fair's fair, and when you're through, I'll tell you how I'm going to pitch to your fellas." On still another occasion, he promised the Braves nothing but fast balls, "Honest!," and beat them on a steady diet of same.

It got so that new manager Frankie Frisch could only groan when asked how he managed his "zoo's who" of baseball: "A sense of humor helps."

Before the '34 season Dizzy allowed as how "Me and Paul will win 45 games between us this year." It was a mighty tall order since Paul hadn't even made the team, just coming up from Columbus where he had won 22 games. But they did, with room to spare, Dizzy winning 30 and rookie Paul—for reasons known only to sportswriters called "Daffy"—won the other 19. It got so that one writer said of the '34 Cards, "When Frisch gets past the two Deans, Frankie experiences the sensation of stepping out of an eighteenth story window and turning left." For the Cardinals, they were the whole show.

But if the Deans were the show—especially Dizzy—more than occasionally they were also a "no-show." Once, after "Dizzy" and younger brother Paul (the sportswriter who named Paul "Daffy" did so more on balance than on facts, Paul being as quiet as "Dizzy" was gregarious) had lost a doubleheader to the Cubs on August 12, they both got lost. When Frisch counted heads that night, he saw nary a Dean head in sight. Hopping mad, he fined both brothers for their wildcat walkout, one of many. Hearing of the fines, the Deans refused to take the field when they rejoined the team two days later in Pittsburgh, and Frisch suspended them on the spot. "Dizzy" went on a rampage, tearing up two uniforms—one for the benefit of insistent photographers—and stalked out of the clubhouse, determined to lay his case before Commissioner Landis.

Landis, however, was not impressed by the Deans' case, and admonished them publicly as "willful little kids." Thoroughly chastened, they chased back home to pick up where they had left off. And pick up they did. With one of the Deans pitching almost every day, the Cardinals were back into a pennant fight they had practically abandoned hopes of winning.

Still, despite winning seven of their next eight games, the week of Labor Day found them seven full games behind the front-running Giants. However, their pumpkin was about to turn into a carriage plus six, with the two trace horses the Deans. The day it turned was September 21, in a double-header against the same

"Dizzy" Dean, proof positive, baseball builds character as well as characters.

Brooklyn Dodgers that were now bedeviling Terry's Giants, getting even with Terry for his ill-fated off-season taunt, "Are the Dodgers still in the League?"

With the two brothers scheduled to pitch, Frisch was going over the Brooklyn batting order, player-by-player. Dizzy, however, was having none of the strategy meeting, and after listening to every Frisch suggestion, finally said, "This is silly, Frank. I've won 26 games already this season and it don't look exactly right for an infielder like you to be tellin' a star like me how I should pitch." Then, with Frisch fuming that that he would "get his ears pinned back," he picked up his glove and shouted over his shoulder, "They ain't pinnin' Ol' Diz's ears back. I doubt if them Dodgers get a hit off either me or Paul today."

And "danged" if Diz was just "braggin'." He had a no-hitter into the eighth and finished up with a tidy three-hit shutout. But in the nightcap, Paul went him three better, limited the Dodgers to no hits to move the Cards to within three games of the top. In the clubhouse after the game, Dizzy went over to his younger brother, and in a hurt tone said, "Whyn't you tell Ol' Diz you were agonna pitch a no-hitter? If I'd a knowed that, I'd of pitched me one, too."

It was that kind of year, and with two games to go, the Giants stumbled—to the Dodgers, naturally!—and the Cards clinched the pennant on Dean's thirtieth win. His brother Paul won only 19, but they made good the spring training boast that "Me and Paul will win 45 games." It was now on to the World Series and the Detroit Tigers, who, under their scrappy player-manager Mickey Cochrane, had won their first pennant in 25 years by a comfortable seven games over the Yankees.

The Series will be remembered as one of Dean, Dean and more Dean—with more than a little garbage thrown in for good measure. It started with Dizzy pitching an eight-hitter in the first

game for an 8-3 win, a Tiger victory in the second, Paul winning the third, 4-1, and a Detroit victory in the fourth as they got 13 hits off five Cardinal pitchers, none of whom was named Dean.

However, Dizzy did make an appearance in Game Four, inserting himself as a pinch runner. Going down to second to break up a double-play, Dean was hit in the middle of the forehead by Tiger shortstop Billy Rogell's relay to first. He tottered, then he swayed and after a brief pause came down like a felled oak under the woodman's ax. Carried off the field semi-conscious, Dean was rushed to the hospital for X-rays, but was released after. In his own words, "The doctors X-rayed my head and found nothing."

With the Series tied at two games apiece, Dizzy came back to pitch—headache and all—but gave up seven hits, three of them for extra bases, and lost 3-1. The Tigers had the Series lead 3-2, with the last two games at home in the friendly confines of Navin Field.

Game Six saw Paul going for the Cards against Schoolboy Rowe, the winner of Game Two. But this was a different Rowe, and Paul Dean won his own game with a single in the seventh, forcing the Series into a seventh and deciding game.

In the clubhouse afterwards, Dizzy was wrestling his younger brother to the ground, hollering for all to hear, "You're the greatest pitcher the Dean family ever had."Then he pounded everyone else on the back and began all over again. In the middle of this bedlam a writer, taking his own life in his hands, approached Frisch and asked him who would start the seventh game: "Dean tomorrow—the other Dean?" Frisch, head down between his legs, exhausted from the struggle, looked up and muttered, "If I last till tomorrow, maybe. It'll be Dean or 'Wild' Bill Hallahan."

Chicago sportswriter John Carmichael turned around to view a new source of excitement on the other side of the locker room and espying Dizzy, wearing a pith helmet and swinging an inflatable rubber tiger over his head, said, to no one in particular, "Wild horses couldn't keep Dean off that mound tomorrow." But Frisch heard. And knew.

October 9, 1934, dawned as a misty, dreary day. But one man radiated sunshine, Dizzy Dean, who began warming up early, alternating pitches with shouts to his teammates, "Get me a couple of runs, that's all . . . I'll blank the blankety-blanks."

But for two innings nobody bothered to give Dizzy those two runs. And so, in the top of the third, after the "All-American Out," Leo Durocher, had followed form and flied out, Dean took things into his own hands, hitting a clean single down the left-field line. When Goose Goslin, figuring that most pitchers don't normally break their necks getting down to first, nonchalanted the ball, Dean took off for second, just beating Goslin's lobbed throw back into the infield. That piece of base running might well have turned the Series around. The next man up, Pepper Martin, bounced a ball down the first-base line on a straight line to the exact spot where Tiger first baseman Hank Greenberg would have been holding Dean on first—that is, if Dean had been bivouaced at first. Instead, with Greenberg over in his normal position, the fleet Martin beat it out for an infield hit, putting men on first and third with one out. Then Martin did what he had done so many times previously to Cochrane, stole second, and Tiger pitcher Eldon Auker had to walk Jack Rothrock to load the bases and set up a possible double play. The only trouble with that strategy was that the next man up, Frankie Frisch, hit a bases-clearing double to right field, and Diz had his "couple of runs."

The Cardinals were to go on to score four more runs in the inning—Dizzy even chipping in with a second hit—as Cochrane tried anything and everything to turn off the Cardinal machine. But it was like trying to stuff toothpaste back into the tube, as St. Louis

Joe Medwick being tagged out by Mickey Cochrane in 3rd inning of the Game 2, won by Detroit, 3-2, in 12 innings.

continued to score at will against six Detroit pitchers, adding two more in the sixth on a Pepper Martin single and a Joe Medwick triple.

Medwick's triple brought on the most uproarious—if not most memorable—moment in World Series history. For as he came sliding into third base, Tiger third baseman Marv Owen apparently spiked him, and Medwick lashed back with his foot, kicking at Owen. But, as the smoke cleared, all that could be seen was Medwick, laying on his back atop the base, kicking at the hometown favorite. Figuring that there must be something in the Geneva Convention which outlawed such doings, the Tiger fans, who had sullenly sat through a long, frustrating afternoon, now had something to get worked up over. When Medwick went out to left to take his place in the bottom of the sixth, he was greeted by the 18,000 fans in the wooden bleachers, all of whom seemed to be raining a thunderstorm of trash down on the field—including, but not limited to, cushions, bottles, lemons, tomatoes, and even their shoes. (Medwick was later to say, "I knew why they threw it at me. What I can't figure out is why they brought it to the ballpark in the first place.")

Four times Medwick was called off the field, only to reassume his position and ignite an even higher crescendo of frustration and hate. Finally, after twenty minutes of watching the greengrocers in the bleachers deposit their wares in Medwick's direction, Judge Landis had enough. Calling both managers and the two partici-

pants over to his box, he asked Medwick, "Did you kick him?" to which Medwick answered without batting an eye, "You're damned right, I did!" Then he turned to Owen and asked, "Do you know any reason why Medwick should have made such an attack?" Owen said he did not. Landis then excused Medwick for the rest of the afternoon, silenced Frisch's protests and ordered the game to continue.

But the conclusion was now a foregone one. Dizzy Dean would go on to win the most lopsided shutout in World Series history 11-0, giving up only six hits, and finish not only one of the most memorable World Series in history but one of the greatest years any player has ever had.

Joe "Ducky" Medwick, the object of Detroit's disaffection in the '34 World Series.

CARDS WIN SERIES, BEAT DETROIT, 11-0; TIGER FANS RIOT

DEAN EASILY THE VICTOR

Six Pitchers Used by the Losers Against Dizzy in Deciding Contest.

7 RUNS SCORED IN THIRD

Frisch's Double With Bases Filled Starts Drive—13 Men Bat in Inning.

WILD SCENES MARK GAME

Landis Banishes Medwick After Aroused Fans Shower Missiles on Player.

1934

Game 7 October 9 at Detroit

St. Louis	Pos	AB	R	H	RBI	PO	A	E
Martin	3b	5	3	2	1	0	1	0
Rothrock	rf	5	1	2	1	4	0	0
Frisch	2b	5	1	1	3	3	6	0
Medwick	lf	4	1	1	1	1	0	0
Fullis	lf	1	0	1	0	1	0	0
Collins	1b	5	1	4	2	7	1	1
DeLancey	c	5	1	1	1	5	0	0
Orsatti	cf	3	1	1	0	2	0	0
Durocher	ss	5	1	2	0	3	4	0
D. Dean	p	5	1	2	1	1	0	0
Totals		43	11	17	10	27	12	1

Pitching	IP	H	R	ER	BB	SO
St. Louis						
D. Dean (W)	9	6	0	0	0	5
Detroit						
Auker (L)	2⅓	6	4	4	1	1
Rowe	⅓	2	2	2	0	0
Hogsett	*0	2	1	1	2	0
Bridges	4⅓	6	4	2	0	2
Marberry	1	1	0	0	1	0
Crowder	1	0	0	0	0	1

*Pitched to four batters in 3rd.

St L. 007 002 200
Det.   000 000 000

Detroit	Pos	AB	R	H	RBI	PO	A	E
White	cf	4	0	0	0	3	0	1
Cochrane	c	4	0	0	0	2	2	0
Hayworth	c	0	0	0	0	1	0	0
Gehringer	2b	4	0	2	0	3	5	1
Goslin	lf	4	0	0	0	4	0	1
Rogell	ss	4	0	1	0	3	2	0
Greenberg	1b	4	0	1	0	7	0	0
Owen	3b	4	0	0	0	1	2	0
Fox	rf	3	0	2	0	3	0	0
Auker	p	0	0	0	0	0	0	0
Rowe	p	0	0	0	0	0	0	0
Hogsett	p	0	0	0	0	0	0	0
Brides	p	2	0	0	0	0	0	0
Marberry	p	0	0	0	0	0	0	0
a G. Walker		1	0	0	0	0	0	0
Crowder	p	0	0	0	0	0	0	0
Totals		34	0	6	0	27	11	3

a Flied out for Marberry in 8th.

Doubles—D. Dean, DeLancey, Fox 2, Frisch, Rothrock. Triples—Durocher, Medwick. Stolen Bases—Martin 2. Double Play—Owen to Gehringer to Greenberg. Left on Bases—St. Louis 9, Detroit 7. Umpires—Geisel, Reardon, Owens, Klem. Attendance—40,902. Time of Game—2:19.

14 Harvey Haddix's "Perfect Game"

Pittsburgh Pirates vs. Milwaukee Braves, May 26, 1959

ON THE EVENING OF MAY 26, 1959, THE IMPROBABLE AND the impossible were to merge in one of the greatest pitching exhibitions of all time: Harvey Haddix's 12-inning Perfect Game.

Haddix, who had come F.O.B., Pittsburgh, only the previous winter, was a smallish, wiry, jug-eared left-hander whose resemblance to another pitcher, Harry "The Cat" Brecheen, had won for him the nickname "The Kitten" from his then-Cardinal teammates. An ambiguous pitcher who threw something when he meant something else, Haddix had won 86 games during his previous seven-plus seasons in the Majors. But nothing he had done—or would ever do—would become him more than his performance the night of May 26, 1959.

On what was to become his night of nights, Haddix had been selected by Pittsburgh manager Danny Murtaugh to start against the biggest bats in the National League, the two-time pennant-winning Milwaukee Braves of Hank Aaron, Joe Adcock and Eddie Mathews. At Milwaukee County Stadium, no less.

Going into the game, Haddix hardly had a feeling of inevitability. In fact, if anything, the head cold he had been nursing for days left him with a queasy feeling. And with the hope that he could go five innings against the Braves. If that. But if not in the rosy glow of good health, Haddix was, at least, in the pink of perfection, as later events would show.

Haddix took the mound for the Braves' half of the first as 19,194 Milwaukee fans, filled with *gemutlich* and brautwurst, cheered on their Braves. Using his fast ball and curve to their best advantages, Haddix retired second baseman Johnny O'Brien on a grounder to short, third baseman Mathews on a liner to first, and Aaron on a fly ball to center. Three up, three down, but hardly anything to write home about, yet.

After Braves pitcher Lew Burdette had treated the Pirates likewise in the second, Haddix fanned Adcock, got left fielder Wes Covington on a ground to second and catcher Del Crandall on a grounder to third. Now it was six-up-six-down.

In the third, Haddix got lead-off man Andy Pafko on a fly to right. Then shortstop Johnny Logan caught one of Haddix's fast balls on the meat of his bat and drove it on a line out toward left. Pirate shortstop Dick Schofield, timing his leap, speared the ball. That out was to stand like a beacon light for nine more innings, as Haddix, now back in the groove, caught his opposing number, Burdette, for a called third strike. Nine-up-nine-down.

As the innings began to flash by with all the speed of destination signs on nearby I-94, Haddix, more a machine than a pitcher, continued to mow down the Braves, their outs coming three to a penny. Fourth inning: O'Brien called out on strikes; Matthews, fly to center; and Aaron, fly to center. Fifth inning: Adcock, ground out to third; Covington, fly to left; and Crandall, fly out to left. Sixth inning: Pafko, ground out to first; Logan, ground out to shortstop, Schofield, who threw him out with a long throw from the hole between short and third; and Burdette, strike out. That was 18-up-18-down.

But even as Burdette continued to return the favor, limiting the Pirates to a stingy single here and a miserly single there, the crowd in County Stadium began rallying behind the stranger in their midst, putting down their brautwurst just long enough to cheer and then going back to the business at hand, almost as if to say, "We might like Haddix best, but we love brautwurst."

The head cold had now given way to cold calculation as Haddix, mixing a fast ball that moved and a curve that cut the corners of the plate with all the precision of a surgeon's scalpel, continued to mow down the Braves in the seventh: O'Brien, ground out to third; Mathews, strike out; Aaron, ground out to third. It was 21-up-21-down.

Laying down layer-upon-layer of his masterpiece, the layers began flowing together as Haddix continued his mastery through the eighth, playing the Braves much like a fisherman plays a salmon: Adcock, strike out; Covington, fly out to left; Crandall, ground out to third. And 24-up-24-down.

Now, as he took his place on the mound for the ninth, the madding crowd gave him a roar and Haddix responded with a roar from his thoroughbred's heart. Pitching with a mixture of genius and genuflection, he struck out Pafko, got Logan on a fly to left and retired Burdette on a swinging third strike. The score, 27-up-27-down, no-man-reaching-first, as they used to say in the old days.

That should have been the end to the story, but wasn't. For although Lew Burdette had fallen far short of perfection—allowing but nine Pirate singles—he had held Pittsburgh at bay, holding them scoreless and forcing the game into overtime. And now Haddix, who had paid the ticket of admission to the hallowed halls of greatness, would have to pay his full dues by going farther than any man in the history of baseball to protect his Perfect Game.

With his Perfect Game in the so-called burlap, Haddix went to the mound in the tenth. Five times before, pitchers who had no-hitters through nine innings had lost them in the tenth—Earl Moore, Leon Ames, Jim Vaughn, Tom Hughes and Bobo Newsom—but all of them were far from perfect, especially Newsom. Now Haddix had to tread in heretofore unexplored waters.

For nine innings, rarely did Haddix have to use more than one eye to quell any disturbance. Now setting both eyes firmly on the object at hand, one of them burning calculation and the other a devine fire, he continued his mastery over the Braves in the tenth, although, truth to tell, the margin of safety was becoming narrower. First Del Rice, pinch-hitting for the aforementioned O'Brien, lofted a towering fly to deep center where Pirate center fielder Bill Virdon backed up near the fence to haul it in. Then Eddie Mathews, getting the idea, sent Virdon back again in almost the same spot for his high fly. Then Aaron grounded out to short. Now it was 30-up-30-down, farther than any no-hit pitcher had ever been asked to go, let alone one pitching a Perfect Game. But, then again, none of those who had previously pitched Perfect Games had ever had to go against Lew Burdette, the Braves pitcher with "The Moistest on the Ball," who continued to match Haddix, if not in hits allowed, then at least in runs allowed.

And so Haddix went into the 11th of the scoreless game, vowing now more than ever to keep the perfection of "Ten." He discharged his oath by getting Adcock on a grounder to short, Covington on a fly to center and Crandall on a line drive to center fielder Virdon, who had to reverse himself, making his feet go rickety-rack, and race in for the catch. Now it was 33-up-33-down. And still 0-0.

Going into the twelfth, Haddix was now certain that he had a no-hitter "because the scoreboard was in full view." What he wasn't certain about was "about it being a Perfect Game." Also, because the scoreboard only carried ten innings worth of ciphers, Haddix had also "lost track of the innings" as well. Yet the twelfth looked like the eleventh, which had looked like the tenth, which had looked like the ninth, which had looked like every inning before, as Haddix continued to serve up goose eggs for the scoreboard, retiring first Pafko on a bounce-back to the mound and then Logan on a fly to short left-center. Then, Burdette, the 36th man up, smashed a ground ball in the general direction of third baseman Don Hoak, who made a great stop of the ball and threw out Burdette. Now it was 36-men-up-36-men down. And still 0-0, . . . very still.

After the Pirates' lethargic bats had gone down in the top of the inning, Haddix came out to pitch what would for him be his unlucky 13th, and for baseball, one of the wildest finishes in the long history of wild finishes.

The unbreakable line had to end somewhere. That somewhere was now about to happen. The first man to step into the batter's box in the bottom of the 13th was Braves second baseman Felix Mantilla, coming to the plate for his first at-bat, having replaced O'Brien in the 11th. Poking at one of Haddix's curves, Mantilla slapped it at third baseman Hoak. Hoak, cuddling the ball like a first-born to insure its safety, almost as if he were studying the stitching, threw it in the general direction of Pirate first baseman Rocky Nelson. Low. And while Nelson was madly trying to sort the ball, which had hit him in the foot, out of the dirt and floor sweepings in front of him, Mantilla's foot alighted on first. Nelson, after picking up the ball, tagged Mantilla rather ungently, claiming that Mantilla, after crossing the bag, had turned left. However, umpire Frank Dascoli disallowed Nelson's protest and the first Milwaukee base runner in two hours and fifty-some minutes now stood perched at first.

Mantilla's presence on first not only meant that Haddix's

Harvey Haddix, the most "perfect" pitcher in the history of baseball

Perfect Game was history, but that the complexion of the game had changed. Radically.

The next man up, Eddie Mathews, then sacrificed Mantilla along to second, a natural progression on the science of base running, but one which the Braves had had no use for in the past 12 innings, having had nothing that even faintly resembled a base runner. With the ever-dangerous Hank Aaron up, good strategy and common sense both dictated that he be given a free pass to first, setting up the hopeful inning-ending double play. But that hope would never eventuate. For the next batter, Joe Adcock, who in four previous times at bat had had only a waving acquaintance with the ball—two strike-outs and two grounders—swung with a mighty swing at Haddix's second offering, a high slider right in his wheelhouse, and, trying to blast the ball into smaller, untidy pieces, smote the ball into the farthest reaches of County Stadium. Aaron, watching center fielder Virdon go back, back, back in deep right-center field and then throw himself frantically skyward in one desperate leap at the spot reading "375'"thought the ball had dropped at the base of the fence. Mantilla, sure that the ball had barely cleared the fence—which, in fact, it had—set sail for the forbidden reaches of home. But Aaron, after touching second, ran, as if out of an approaching storm, across the diamond, in the direction of the Milwaukee dugout. Meanwhile, Adcock, running head down, chugged along toward third.

Enter Fred Haney, the operating genius of the Braves, stage left, as he tried to push Aaron back out toward third to retrace his steps before the "homer" was discounted at less than face value.

Haddix Hurls Perfect 12-Inning Game, Loses In 13th

BUCS' HURLER IS BEATEN BY BRAVES, 2-0

Double By Joe Adcock Is Only Hit After Error, Walk

PITTSBURGH (N.)					MILWAUKEE (N.)				
	ab.	r.	h.	rbi		ab.	r.	h.	rbi
Schofield, ss.	6	0	3	0	O'Brien, 2b	3	0	0	0
Virdon, cf	6	0	1	0	bRice	1	0	0	0
Burgess, c	5	0	0	0	Mantilla, 2b	1	1	0	0
Nelson, 1b	5	0	2	0	Mathews, 3b.	4	0	0	0
Skinner, lf	5	0	1	0	Aaron, rf	4	1	0	0
Mazeroski, 2b	5	0	1	0	Adcock, 1b	5	0	1	2
Hoak, 3b	5	0	2	0	Covington, lf	4	0	0	0
Mejias, rf	3	0	1	0	Crandall, c	4	0	0	0
aStuart	1	0	0	0	Pafko, cf	4	0	0	0
Christopher, p	1	0	0	0	Logan, ss	4	0	0	0
Haddix, p	5	0	1	0	Burdette, p	4	0	0	0
Total	47	0	12	0	Total	38	2	1	2

aFlied out for Mejias in 10th; bFlied out for O'Brien in 10th.

Pittsburgh	.000	000	000	000	0—0
Milwaukee	.000	000	000	000	2—2

Two out when winning runs scored.
E—Hoak. A—Pittsburgh 13, Milwaukee 21. DP—Logan and Adcock; Mathews, O'Brien, Adcock; Adcock, Logan. LOB—Pittsburgh 8, Milwaukee 0.
2B Hit—Adcock. Sacrifice—Mathews.

	IP.	H.	R.	ER.	BB.	SO.
Haddix (L, 3-3)	12⅓	1	2	1	0	8
Burdette (W, 8-2)	13	12	0	0	0	2

Umpires—Smith, Dascoli, Secory, Dixon. Time—2:54. Attendance—19,194.

But it was all academic now. And the journals of record in their early-morning editions would read that Adcock had hit a double, driving in Mantilla for the game-winning run in a 1-0 victory.

However, while Adcock's "homer" wouldn't stand up as one, Haddix's "Perfect Game" would. In the face of those who quoted some old African proverb which held that leaving a log in water as long as you want will never make it an alligator, others, particularly those who were the keepers of baseball's eternal flame, ruled that indeed Haddix had pitched a Perfect Game—the most Perfect Game in baseball history. And, in the bargain, he had also made history of another sort: He would enjoy timeless fame for having suffered the toughest loss in baseball history, sacrificed upon the altar of futility.

The hitter and the hittee: Harvey Haddix shakes hands with Joe Adcock the day after Adcock's homer-double broke up Haddix's "perfect" game in the 13th inning.

15 The Game that Broke Joe DiMaggio's Consecutive Game Hit Streak

New York Yankees vs. Cleveland Indians, July 17, 1941

JOE DIMAGGIO WAS LIKE AN ARTICHOKE; THE MORE YOU peeled away, the more you discovered. Baseball's version of Rashomon, everyone saw something different to appreciate about this seamless performer. Afield, he was light as a cucumber sandwich. With concentration in his every move, he made conscious efforts with unconscious ease. Nothing fancy, nothing spectacular, mind you, merely a touch of class in his every move. At bat, he was, in the words of Bob Feller, "Simply the best there was," his textbook swing and flawless follow-through giving him an overall look of inevitability, almost as if a hit could be produced by will alone. In short, whatever he was, he was Hemingway's "Grace under pressure."

However, if all the opinions of DiMaggio's greatness were laid end-to-end, they still wouldn't reach a conclusion. With one exception: That his 56-game hit streak, which stands as one of baseball's greatest achievements, also stands as a monument to his greatness.

The moment and the monument began back in 1932 when Vince DiMaggio, then a first-year outfielder with the San Francisco Seals, suggested to his manager, Jimmy Caveney, that he take a look-see at his "kid brother who can play any position." His team running short of manpower at the end of the long Pacific Coast League season, Caveney agreed to take the look and put the "kid brother" in at shortstop for three games. The 17-year-old sandlotter got two hits—both for extra bases—and a contract for the 1933 season. That was the season Joseph Paul DiMaggio, by now converted into an outfielder, achieved what *The Reach Baseball Guide* called "nation-wide attention" by hitting .340, driving in a league-leading 169 runs and putting together a record hit streak of 61 straight games. It was also the season when young Joe "Beat his brother out of his job," according to Lefty Gomez, replacing his sore-winged older brother in the outfield and forcing the Seals to sell the lesser of the two DiMaggios to Hollywood before the season was out.

1934 saw the rangy kid continue to deal out great gobs of hits. By mid-season the Major League scouts had begun lining up outside the Seals' door, like stage-door Johnnies, prepared to offer anything and everything to woo him to their homesteads. It was during this particular period that DiMaggio, then hitting somewhere in the heady neighborhood of .360, was in Seattle to play the Rainiers, then managed by former Major League pitcher Dutch Reuther. Before one of the games, Reuther sent his trainer over to DiMaggio. "Dutch wants to know if you ever had any trouble with your left leg," the trainer inquired. "No. Why?," the astonished DiMaggio demanded. " 'Cause," the trainer answered, "Dutch says you drag it a little when you run." DiMaggio, not knowing what else to say, could only come back with, "Tell him he's nuts . . . I never hurt it, and I don't drag it."

Less than one week after Reuther's diagnosis-cum-augury, DiMaggio was getting out of a cab in front of his sister's house when "my left knee popped like a pistol. Four sharp cracks. I swear you could have heard it down the block." The Pop! was so audible that its sharp report was not only heard "down the block" but its echo in towns as far away as Chicago, Boston and Cleveland, all towns where once there had been interest in the great prospect. All of a sudden, the scouts who had encamped at the Seals' door folded up their tents and silently stole away, their interest in a player with a trick knee that "popped like a pistol" somewhat underwhelming. All but one, New York Yankee scout Bill Essick, who recommended to the head office, "Don't give up on DiMaggio."

Essick continued his DiMaggio watch. Less than two weeks later he called the Yankee offices again. "Buy DiMaggio," he told general manager Ed Barrow. "I think you can get him cheap. They're all laughing at me, but I know I'm right." No sooner had Barrow hung up on Essick than he called Seals president Charlie Graham. After inquiring as to the weather, Barrow asked whether Graham would consider selling DiMaggio; and if so, for how much. Graham, who before the Pop! heard 'round the baseball world, had had the price bid up as high as $75,000, now asked for $40,000. Barrow, with all the guile of a stud poker player and the finesse of an elixir salesman, offered $20,000 and finally got Graham to compromise at $25,000, five minor league players and the right to keep DiMaggio for the '35 season. For Barrow and the Yankees, it was the greatest buy in the history of baseball. And for Essick, the last laugh.

DiMaggio was well worth the wait, finishing out his injury-shortened 1934 season with a .341 average and then leading the Seals to the Pacific Coast League championship in 1935 with a .398 batting average, 34 home runs and 154 RBI's.

At the end of his last season with the Seals, DiMaggio signed on with a team of Major League all-stars playing in and around the Bay Area. Yankee scouts, anxious to try out their thoroughbred, imported the services of the great black pitcher, Satchel Paige, then taking the sun down in the south of California. Paige, with a pick-up team of townies behind him, pitched to the Big League stars as if he cared nothing for their reputations, striking out fifteen of them and allowing only 2 hits through the first nine innings. Then, in the tenth, DiMaggio, who had twice struck out and once fouled out, came to bat with the potential winning run on base and hit a single off Satchel's famous "Hesitation Pitch." The scouts were ecstatic, sending a telegram back east which read: DIMAGGIO ALL WE HOPED HE'D BE. HIT SATCH ONE FOR FOUR.

Reporting to a Yankee team that had won only one pennant in the last seven years, DiMaggio was viewed by most as the heir to Babe Ruth's crown as the Yankee superstar. But to some—like the grizzled right hander Red Ruffing, who stared at him and said, half laughingly, "So you're the great DiMaggio"—he was just another "Rook" trying to make it. Instead he was to make the Yankees.

But not immediately. For shortly after the exhibition season started, DiMaggio twisted his left foot. The Yankee trainer, Doc Painter, tried a new diathermy machine on his injured foot, telling the rookie to let him know if it got too hot. "I can stand the heat," DiMaggio told Painter as the trainer turned away to work on

**Joe DiMaggio, one of the most dependable
stories in all of sports.**

Ruffing's injured flipper. But when Painter took the bandages off, there was a big bubble on DiMaggio's instep, a blister that prevented him from playing Opening Day and several days thereafter.

Finally, the big day arrived, Sunday, May 3rd, against the St. Louis Browns. In DiMaggio's first at-bat, he hit a dribbler back to pitcher Jack Knott, who threw him out at first. In the second, DiMaggio came to bat against Browns reliever Earl Caldwell and hit a blooper to short centerfield that dropped in front of centerfielder Ray Pepper for a single, his first Major League hit. Up again in the fourth, DiMaggio struck out. But in the sixth, he tripled up against the centerfield boards, a drive that would have been a homer in any American League park but Yankee Stadium. He flied out in the seventh, but closed out his first day in the Majors with a single in the eighth, going 3-for-6 in his Big League debut. The next day the New York *Daily News* headline read: "Joe Gets Goin'!"

By the end of his first year, the man-child Ruffing had called "The Great DiMaggio" had batted .323 with 29 home runs, scored

132 times and driven in 125 runs. And the Yankees had won the World Series for the first time since 1932. In '37, he hit .346 and led the League in home runs, runs scored and slugging average. And the Yankees won the World Series again. In 1938, he batted .324 and the Yankees once again won the World Series.

New York is a town in which reputations are built larger than its tallest buildings. Having more than acquitted his build-up, DiMaggio was now one of those few whose deeds had made him grow taller than most such man-made monuments found on the Island of Manhattan. By 1939 his popularity had transcended the boundaries of New York. Now his classic features adorned the covers of several national publications, including *Life* Magazine; his name was captured in the headlines of the daily newspapers; and his exploits were embraced universally by Italians in a banquet of ethnic pride and adopted everywhere by those with an eye for diamond delicacies.

With his record beginning to read almost like a tour map of his achievements, 1939 saw the man the writers had taken to calling "The Yankee Clipper," "Joltin' Joe" and just plain ol' "Joe D." lead the American League in batting with a .381 average and win the Most Valuable Player Award. Not incidentally, for the fourth time since he joined them four years before, the Yankees again won the World Series.

The Yankees lost in 1940, finishing two games behind the Tigers and one behind the Indians. However, DiMaggio more than did his share, winning the batting title for the second straight time with a .352 average, finishing second in slugging average, third in runs batted in and in total bases and fourth in home runs.

But 1941 was to be DiMaggio's year, the year of his 56-game streak; a year when he would capture the headlines and hypnotize the nation as no athlete had since the heyday of Babe Ruth some 14 years before.

As with all such things, the streak began during an affair of no great moment. The only distinguishing feature for the starting point of DiMaggio's streak was that May 5th, 1941, was "Jimmy Dykes Day," a day held for the little third baseman who had put in 22 years hard for the A's and White Sox. With the pre-game festivities, such as they were, gold watch and all, out of the way, Eddie Smith, the stocky lefty for the ChiSox, gave up a single to DiMaggio in the first inning, leading to a Yankee run. It was to be the Yankees' only run all day as the White Sox won 13-1 and Smith held the Yankees to nine hits, one of them DiMaggio's. Still, it was the first olive out of the jar.

With the Smith hit as an appetizer, he now began a steady diet of hits, hitting with a repetitive monotony and startling variety against all manner of pitchers. Nine games into the streak he faced Boston's Earl Johnson in the seventh inning of a tight game at Yankee Stadium. With first base open and two men on, Boston's manager, Joe Cronin, forbade Johnson to walk DiMaggio, telling his left hander, "You can get him out." But Johnson couldn't and DiMaggio could, singling across the winning runs as his streak reached ten. DiMaggio's bat continued to ring with the music of hits as he hit any pitcher worth his resin bag, skewering the likes of Boston's Lefty Grove, Cleveland's Mel Harder and Bob Feller, Detroit's Hal Newhouser and Dizzy Trout and St. Louis' submariner, Eldon Auker. And still nobody took note of his hackneyed act.

Finally, twenty-four games into the streak, a few of the more ambitious pencil-pushers dug deep into the yellowing clippings of their memories and trotted out a few of baseball's genetic links to the past for DiMaggio to shoot at: Roger Peckinpaugh and Earle Combs, co-holders of the Yankee record for hitting safely in

Jim Bagby, Jr., the pitcher who closed the door on DiMaggio's last chance to extend his streak.

Lou Boudreau, whose sure hands turned DiMaggio's last bid for a hit into a double play.

Cleveland left hander Al Smith, who held DiMaggio hitless his first three times up, thanks to Ken Keltner.

consecutive games with 29; Rogers Hornsby, possessor of the modern National League record with 33; George Sisler, keeper of the American League flame with 41; and Wee Willie Keeler, architect of the all-time record, 44, set back sometime around the great flood, in 1897.

Now, with someone keeping score, DiMaggio assaulted each and every landmark. His 30th hit, breaking the Yankee record, came off Chicago's Johnny Rigney, a bad-hop single that bounced off the forehead of White Sox shortstop Luke Appling. One week later he passed Rogers Hornsby with a single off Detroit's Dizzy Trout. And still the beat and the beaten went on, with all American League pitchers now waiting in line like old taxicabs to take whatever route they were driven to on their way to becoming ciphers in DiMaggio's growing total.

As DiMaggio continued to be one of the most utterly dependable stories in all of sports, he began to take on the proportions of a myth-in-the-making, turning the nation into a nation of DiMaggio-watchers. Newspapers, with tasteful and painstaking devotion, headlined his daily hit production, crowds turned out to cheer his every hit, and pitchers, determining on their mortality not to add to

DiMaggio's immortality, tried to put an end to the little recreations his bat was enjoying.

In his 36th game, it looked like the streak would finally come to end. Hitless going into the eighth, DiMaggio came up against St. Louis rookie Bob Muncrief. Muncrief, pitching ever-so-carefully to DiMaggio, gave up a single. Afterward Muncrief was to say, "It wouldn't have been fair to walk him—to him or to me." And then added, "Hell, he's the greatest player I ever saw."

Two days later, DiMaggio's hit streak was once again in jeopardy. Three times he had gone to bat and three times had come away without anything even remotely resembling a hit against St. Louis' submariner, Eldon Auker, whose pitch was peculiarly striking to the optic nerve coming as it did from somewhere out of the grass on the third-base side of the mound. With the Yankees winning 3-1 in the bottom of the eighth and DiMaggio the fourth-scheduled hitter, it meant someone had to reach base for him to get a chance to keep his streak alive. The first man up, Johnny Sturm popped up. But when the second man up, Red Rolfe, walked, Tommy Henrich turned to the dugout from the on-deck circle and called out to manager Joe McCarthy, "Skip . . . If I hit into a double-play, Joe won't get up. Okay if I bunt?" There must have been some argument against it, but unable to marshal any pertinent facts, McCarthy agreed. And Henrich, as announced, bunted, sacrificing Rolfe over to second.

DiMaggio stepped into the batter's box, his air denoting a quiet but conscious reserve force if not authority. Spread-eagling his legs in that wide-apart stance that was his signature, he set his jaw in determination. Auker came in with his best underhand pitch and DiMadge smote it, a well-aimed shaft that went over the head of left fielder Harlond Clift for a double. Afterward DiMaggio, commenting on the hit which had preserved his negotiability at 38 games, said, "That ball was really tagged. Clift jumped high for the ball but afterward told me he wondered why he'd leaped because he couldn't have stopped it with a fish net."

Game number 40 was one in which DiMaggio could have used a fish net himself. The starting pitcher for the Athletics, Johnny Babich, had made known his intentions of dousing DiMaggio's dreams. "Even," remembered Joe, "if it meant walking me every time up." Facing DiMaggio the first time, the big righthander threw four pitches that couldn't have been reached with a fish net. Nor found with a geiger counter. The second time around Babich uncorked three more fastballs which only had a passing acquaintance with the plate. DiMaggio stepped out of the batter's box and glanced over at the bench. There Joe McCarthy was flashing the "Hit" sign, giving DiMaggio *a la carte* to hit the cripple if it was anywhere near the prescribed zone.

But the fourth pitch was anything but a cripple, a high and outside change of space that would have been a ball even to someone who could eat apples off a tree without using his hands. DiMaggio, who during most of his streak had been less a glutton than an explorer of the ball, now found his anger giving a roar to his thoroughbred's heart. Swinging without so much as a by-your-leave, DiMaggio got the fat part of his bat on the ball and rocketed it back toward the mound. Babich hadn't even finished his follow-through when the ball whistled through his legs. Perched on first with a hit in his 40th consecutive game, DiMag looked over at Babich and saw him shaking like an aspen from top of hat to bottom of cleat and then, in DiMaggio's words, "his face turned white as a sheet."

The next day, June 29th, found DiMaggio in Washington for a double-header against the lowly Senators. In the first game he faced knuckleballer Dutch Leonard whose delivery had all the outward appearances of a come hither-look that invited the batter in and when he arrived found nobody at home. However, DiMaggio's bat found its way in the sixth as he timed a Leonard knuckler for a double, tying Sisler's American League mark at 41.

But a funny thing happened to DiMaggio's bat on its way to a new American League record: It was purloined by a fan with little reverence for history-in-the-making, snatched from in front of the Yankee dugout between games of the double-header. DiMaggio, accustomed to a 36-ounce bat with a sandpapered handle which took off one-half to three-quarters of an ounce, found himself without his normal armament and went down three times against a journeyman righthander named Red Anderson. Then, in the seventh, he availed himself of Tommy Henrich's bat—which was actually a DiMaggio model—and singled to break Sisler's mark.

Two days later the bat, still full of hits, returned almost as mysteriously as it had disappeared, found by some good friends of Joe's who had discovered the identity of the misappropriator and made him an offer he couldn't possibly refuse. Just in time for DiMaggio to tie Keeler's record with hits in both ends of a double-header against the Red Sox.

The next day was like an abatoir in August, 94.8 degrees and climbing. Boston's scheduled starter, Lefty Grove, begged off passing through the furnace, citing something that sounded like "hot as Hades." His place was taken by Dick Newsome, a right-hander who would go on to win 19 games that year and who had already served up a single in Game #9 way back when the streak wasn't even a glint in the eyes of sportswriters. In his first at bat, Joe sent a drive as hot as the day into the outer reaches of right

DiMaggio's Streak Ended at 56 Games

SMITH AND BAGBY STOP YANKEE STAR

DiMaggio, Up for Last Time in Eighth, Hits Into a Double Play With Bases Full

M'CARTHYMEN WIN BY 4-3

Stretch Lead Over Indians to 7 Lengths Before Biggest Crowd for Night Game

Yankee Box Score

NEW YORK (A.)	ab.	r.	h.	po.	a.	e.		CLEVELAND (A.)	ab.	r.	h.	po.	a.	e.
Sturm, 1b.	4	0	1	10	2	0		Weatherly, cf.	5	0	1	4	0	1
Rolfe, 3b.	4	1	2	2	5	0		Keltner, 3b.	3	0	1	1	4	0
Henrich, rf.	3	0	1	4	0	0		Boudreau, ss.	3	0	0	2	3	0
DiMaggio, cf.	3	0	0	2	0	0		Heath, rf.	4	0	0	0	0	0
Gordon, 2b.	4	1	2	0	1	0		Walker, lf.	3	2	2	1	0	0
Rosar, c.	4	0	0	5	1	0		Grimes, 1b.	3	1	1	12	0	0
Keller, lf.	3	1	1	0	0	0		Mack, 2b.	3	0	0	4	7	0
Rizzuto, ss.	4	0	0	2	1	0		aRosenthal	1	0	1	0	0	0
Gomez, p.	4	1	1	2	1	0		bHemsley, c.	3	0	1	5	1	0
Murphy, p.	0	0	0	0	1	0		Smith, p.	3	0	0	0	0	0
								Bagby, p.	0	0	0	0	0	0
Total	33	4	8	27	10	0		cCampbell	1	0	0	0	0	0
								·Total	33	3	7	27	16	0

aBatted for Mack in ninth.
bBatted for Hemsley in ninth.
cBatted for Bagby in ninth.

New York .... 1 0 0   0 0 0   1 2 0—4
Cleveland .... 0 0 0   1 0 0   0 0 2—3

Runs batted in—Henrich, Walker, Gordon, Rolfe, Rosenthal 2.
Two-base hits—Henrich, Rolfe. Three-base hit—Keller, Rosenthal. Home runs—Walker, Gordon. Sacrifice—Boudreau. Double play—Boudreau, Mack and Grimes. Left on bases—New York 5, Cleveland 7. Bases on balls—off Smith 2, Bagby 1, Gomez 3. Struck out—By Gomez 5, Smith 4, Bagby 1. Hits—Off Smith 7 in 7 1-3 innings, Bagby 1 in 1 2-3, Gomez 6 in 8 (none out in ninth), Murphy 1 in 1. Passed ball—Hemsley. Winning pitcher—Gomez. Losing pitcher—Smith. Umpires—Summers, Rue and Stewart. Time of game—2.03. Attendance—67,468.

DiMaggio's Record Streak

Date	Opponent	ab.	r.	h.	2b.	3b.	hr.		Date	Opponent	ab.	r.	h.	2b.	3b.	hr.
May 15	White Sox	4	0	1	0	0	0		June 17	White Sox	4	1	1	0	0	0
May 16	White Sox	4	2	2	0	1	1		June 18	White Sox	3	0	1	0	0	0
May 17	White Sox	3	1	1	0	0	0		June 19	White Sox	3	2	3	0	0	1
May 18	Browns	3	3	3	1	0	0		June 20	Tigers	5	3	4	1	0	0
May 19	Browns	3	0	1	1	0	0		June 21	Tigers	4	0	1	0	0	0
May 20	Browns	5	1	1	0	0	0		June 22	Tigers	5	1	2	1	0	1
May 21	Tigers	5	0	2	0	0	0		June 24	Browns	4	1	1	0	0	0
May 22	Tigers	4	0	1	0	0	0		June 25	Browns	4	1	1	0	0	1
May 23	Red Sox	5	0	1	0	0	0		June 26	Browns	4	0	1	1	0	0
May 24	Red Sox	4	2	1	0	0	0		June 27	Athletics	3	1	2	0	0	1
May 25	Red Sox	4	0	1	0	0	0		June 28	Athletics	5	1	2	1	0	0
May 27	Senators	5	3	4	0	0	1		June 29	Senators	4	1	1	1	0	0
May 28	Senators	4	1	1	0	1	0		June 29	Senators	5	1	1	0	0	0
May 29	Senators	3	1	1	0	0	0		July 1	Red Sox	4	0	2	0	0	0
May 30	Red Sox	2	1	1	0	0	0		July 1	Red Sox	3	1	1	0	0	0
May 30	Red Sox	3	0	1	1	0	0		July 2	Red Sox	5	1	1	0	0	1
June 1	Indians	4	1	1	0	0	0		July 5	Athletics	4	2	1	0	0	1
June 1	Indians	4	0	1	0	0	0		July 6	Athletics	5	2	4	0	0	0
June 2	Indians	4	2	2	1	0	0		July 6	Athletics	4	0	2	0	1	0
June 3	Tigers	4	1	1	0	0	1		July 10	Browns	2	0	1	0	0	0
June 5	Tigers	5	1	1	0	1	0		July 11	Browns	5	1	4	0	0	1
June 7	Browns	5	2	3	0	0	0		July 12	Browns	5	1	2	1	0	0
June 8	Browns	4	3	2	0	0	2		July 13	White Sox	4	2	3	0	0	0
June 8	Browns	4	1	2	1	0	1		July 13	White Sox	4	0	1	0	0	0
June 10	White Sox	5	1	1	0	0	0		July 14	White Sox	3	0	1	0	0	0
June 12	White Sox	4	1	2	0	0	1		July 15	White Sox	4	1	2	1	0	0
June 14	Indians	2	0	1	1	0	0		July 16	Indians	4	3	3	1	0	0
June 15	Indians	3	1	1	0	0	0									
June 16	Indians	5	0	1	1	0	0		Total		223	56	91	16	4	15

Big Fred Toney of Cincinnati unleashes one of his fast balls on his way to a 10-inning no-hitter.

Jim "Hippo" Vaughn, the Chicago Cub ace and one-half of the greatest pitching achievement of all time

called by the king of Sweden "The Greatest Athlete in the World." Unfortunately, Thorpe had not exactly distinguished himself in the world of baseball. Starting his professional career back in 1911 with a team in North Carolina, Thorpe had had to forfeit his Olympic medals for playing under his own name, something amateur athletes like Eddie Collins had wisely avoided by adopting *noms de game*. Signed by the Giants in 1913, Thorpe had managed to hit only .194 in 66 games over the next three years.

Ever since the formation of the National League, the New York Giants and the Cincinnati Reds had had a two-team shuttle that continuously shuffled players—and even owners—back and forth. Cincinnati owner John T. Brush had once traded his franchise for the entire New York team. He had then traded his aging pitcher, Amos Rusie, to the Reds for a young pitcher named Christy Mathewson. Others who had been given one-way—and in some instances round-trip—tickets between New York and Cincinnati included Red Ames, Josh Devore, Bob Bescher, Art Fromme, Cy Seymour and "Turkey" Mike Donlin. And the current Reds' roster included several former or future Giants, including the manager Christy Mathewson, third baseman Heinie Groh, first baseman Hal Chase, outfielder Edd Roush, and Thorpe himself—who had come to the Reds only five days earlier and would be returned before the season was over. Ironically 1918 would also see Fred Toney going to the Giants.

Thorpe, his muscles rippling in his tight-fitting uniform, stepped into the batter's box and, swinging with all his might, topped one of Vaughn's offerings just to the side of the mound. Vaughn came off the mound and fielded the ball, but finding he had no play on either the speedy Kopf racing in from third or the even speedier Thorpe streaking to first, retained permanent possession of the ball.

That, as it turned out, was the game. For although Toney had the reputation of having a head of concrete, no one had ever disparaged his heart. And now, setting his marble, you-bet-I-can chin, he retired the last three Cubbies to face him in the bottom of the tenth, preserving his no-hitter.

In just ten ticks of the minute hand short of two hours, baseball history had been made, the feats of Toney and Vaughn not only making their way into the record books for all time, but almost forming an institution. And one of baseball's greatest games as well.

Toney and Vaughn Set World's Record; Former Permits No Hits in 10 Innings; Latter None in First Nine; Reds Win, 1-0

CHICAGO, May 2.—A world's record was established here today in a 10-inning game between Cincinnati and Chicago, when, after the game had gone nine innings neither club had registered a hit or run. Cincinnati won 1 to 0.

For the nine innings, Vaughn, assisted by remarkable defense, by the Chicago infield, did not permit a Cincinnati player to reach second base, and in this only slightly surpassed his pitching opponent, Toney, who allowed but one Chicago runner to reach second.

Vaughn struck out 10 Cincinnati batsmen, while only three were fanned by Toney.

The game was won when, in the the tenth inning, after one was out, Kopf singled, advanced to third when Williams dropped Chase's fly and scored when Thorpe hit a slow bounder to Vaughn.

The Cincinnati outfielders several times saved the game for Toney, Cueto on one occasion backing into the left field fence for Merkle's fly. The score:

CINCINNATI	AB.	R.	B.	P.	A.	E.
Groh, 3b	1	0	0	2	3	0
Getz, 3b	4	0	1	1	4	0
Kopf, ss	4	1	1	0	0	0
Neale, lf	4	0	1	1	0	0
Chase, 1b	4	0	0	12	0	0
Thorpe, rf	4	1	1	1	0	0
Shean, 2b	3	0	0	3	2	0
Cueto, lf	3	0	0	2	0	0
Huhn, c	3	0	0	8	1	0
Toney, p	3	0	0	0	0	0
Totals	30	1	2	30	10	0

CHICAGO	AB.	R.	B.	P.	A.	E.
Zeider, ss	4	0	0	1	1	0
Wolter, rf	4	0	0	0	0	0
Doyle, 2b	4	0	0	5	4	0
Merkle, 1b	4	0	0	7	0	0
Williams, cf	4	0	0	2	0	1
Mann, lf	3	0	0	1	0	0
Wilson, c	3	0	0	14	0	0
Deal, 3b	3	0	0	0	1	0
Vaughn, p	3	0	0	0	3	0
Totals	30	0	0	30	9	2

*Batted for Groh in seventh.

Cincinnati	000	000	000	1—1
Chicago	000	000	000	0—0

Stolen base—Chase.
Double plays—Doyle to Merkle to Zeider; Vaughn to Doyle to Merkle.
Left on bases—Chicago 2, Cincinnati 1.
First base on errors—Cincinnati 2.
Base on balls—Off Toney 2, off Vaughn 2.
Struck out—Vaughn 10, Toney 3.
Umpires—Orth and Rigler.
Time—1:50.

FRED TONEY

Fred Toney Fourth Twirler to Travel Ten Hitless Heats

Big Fred Toney of the Reds, who twirled 10 hitless innings at Chicago yesterday, is the fourth major league boxman to accomplish this rare feat. The others were Kimber of Brooklyn, McIntyre also of Brooklyn and Wiltse of New York.

Kimber's performance took place on October 4, 1884, when the Brooklyn club belonged to the American Association. He was pitching against Toledo and the game was called in the early portion of the eleventh inning on account of darkness. Neither side had crossed the plate. Not a hit had been made off Kimber in the 10 chapters.

Harry McIntyre of the Dodgers held the Pirates hitless for 10 innings, on August 1, 1906, but the game continued until the thirteenth frame when Pittsburgh won by a score of 1 to 0. Lefty Leifield being credited with the victory.

George Wiltse of the Giants held the Phillies hitless and runless, on July 4, 1908, New York winning 1 to 0.

Yesterdays' affair was the third of the season in the big show in which the no-hit stunt has been pulled. Eddie Cicotte of the Chicago Americans held the Browns without a bingle recently. George Mogridge of the New York Americans did the same feat at the expense of the world's champion Redsox.

He Nearly Made It

JAMES VAUGHN

18 Mickey Owen's Passed Ball

New York Yankees vs. Brooklyn Dodgers, 4th Game, 1941 World Series, October 5, 1941

THE PLIGHT OF THE BROOKLYN DODGERS IN 1941 INSTIGATES the moral reflection that life is made up of smiles, sobs and sniffles, with sniffles undoubtedly predominating.

The Dodgers of 1941 had at one and the same time one of the most colorful casts of characters ever to dot the baseball landscape and a patchwork team put together with lots of spit, hope, glue and *gelt* from the vaults of the Brooklyn Trust Co., which held the mortgage on this somewhat less-than-bluechip property. The last time Brooklyn had won the National League pennant was way back in the prehistoric days of 1920. However, they couldn't sustain their high water mark and immediately sought their rightful level, falling to fifth the following year and bobbing to the surface of the first division only four times in the next 18 seasons. But all that was before wheeler-dealer Larry MacPhail came on the scene. Playing monopoly for real, MacPhail went out into the marketplace and, in a manner later to be popularized by the siren Lola in "Damn Yankees," whatever MacPhail wanted, MacPhail got. He picked up Dolph Camilli for $50,000 from the Phillies, who were just trying to keep body and soul together; Kirby Higbe from the same impoverished Phillies for another $100,000; Billy Herman from the Cubs for two players and $65,000; Joe Medwick from the Cardinals for $125,000 and four players; Mickey Owen from the Cardinals for $65,000 and two players; Dixie Walker from the Tigers for the waiver price; and minor leaguers Hugh Casey, Pee Wee Reese and Pete Reiser for the going price, which translated into whatever it took.

Together this catalogue of store-boughts had gone through the season hollering and whooping and kicking everyone else out of their way, edging out the Cardinals by one game during their boisterous stretch drive. Over in the American League, God was apparently back in His heaven and all was again right with the world as the New York Yankees reclaimed their rightful perch atop the League for the fifth time in six years. Their match-up in the 1941 Series was less classic than catastrophic, at least for the Brooklyn faithful as their swashbuckling heroes less swashed than buckled.

The Series started routinely enough with the Yankees, per past performance charts, winning the first game, 3-2 behind Red Ruffing. Brooklyn bounced back to win the second game by the same score, a result less surprising when one considers that former Dodger Frenchy Bordagaray—once described by Branch Rickey as "either the greatest rotten third baseman in baseball or the rottenest great third baseman, but never in between"—got into the game as a pinch-runner for the Yankees, thus contaminating their noble pinstriped blood.

Fate, it has been said, has a fickle habit of bestowing its fame upon those it later takes by the scruff of the neck and hurls overboard. Now, as the Series took the IRT subway over to Ebbets Field, she was already conspiring against the Dodgers.

But it wasn't the scruff of the neck that fate had singled out; it was Billy Herman's rib cage. For as Billy Herman was taking batting practice before the third game, practicing the lost art of

pushing the ball into right field, he took an awkward cut at the ball and pulled a muscle in his rib cage, causing him to gasp like a fish. Herman tried mightily to play in pain, but it was of no use and the Dodger second baseman had to retire from play at the end of the fourth inning, not to return until the next-to-last inning of the Series.

Fate wasn't through with the Dodgers yet. Whirling around like a hose out of control, she finally took note of Freddie Fitzsimmons' left kneecap and pointed her finger in its direction. Fat Freddie was in the midst of pitching a masterful four-hit shutout, his pitching motion—a corkscrew delivery which consisted of a bend here, a move, a gesture there, and then from out of nowhere, for all the opposing batters knew from between his legs, came his pitch—giving Yankee batters the impression they were hitting through an electric fan. But all that was to change as Yankee pitcher Marius Russo caught one of Fitzsimmons' offerings and sent it rocketing back off his exposed knee. Fitzsimmons had to be helped from the field, his ache getting purpler by the second, to be replaced by Hugh Casey. Unfortunately, four of the first five batters to face Casey hit safely and the Yankees won the third game, 2-1.

All of this merely served as a throat clearing for Game Four, an improbable game which was to feature the most famous strike-out in baseball history.

Game Four saw Kirby Higbe go to the mound for the Dodgers against Atley Donald of the Yankees. By the fourth inning both had retired to sample the Lifebuoy in the clubhouse, each having surrendered six hits with Higbe giving up three runs to Donald's two. The Yankees had threatened to break the game wide open in the top of the fifth, loading the bases on a walk, a hit batsman and an infield single, but Hugh Casey had come in, tough and mean, and slammed the door shut. Then, in the bottom of the fifth, Pete Reiser had hit a two-run homer off Yankee reliever Marv Breuer to give the Dodgers a 4-3 lead. And with Casey blowing his hard slider past the Yankee bats, it looked like the Series would again be tied up.

Hugh Casey was born to be a relief pitcher. Beaming devastation from one eye and destruction from the other, Casey gave the overall impression of a man who could be arrested for assault and battery on the basis of nothing more than looks. While off the field Casey was a heavy drinker who on more than one occasion had not only fallen off the wagon but become a spectator to its passing as well, on the mound he was all business. A hard-assed Cracker, Casey believed that every man who took up arms against him in the batter's box was a lineal descendant of Jack the Ripper, or worse, U.S. Grant, and treated them accordingly, honing in on their collective jugular. His style was of a crudely surgical nature, but one which got the job done nevertheless. Pumping in an exaggerated manner, like a rusty water pump, Casey would first go down to his knees and then come up, throwing with manifest gusto.

As Casey mowed down the Yankees in the sixth, seventh and eighth, giving up but two hits—and one of those of the infield garden variety—Dodger fans became less scorekeepers than actuaries, plotting out the life expectancy of the Yankees on their scorecards. But fate wasn't through with their beloved bums yet.

Now it was the ninth and Casey had only three more outs to go. The first man up was Yankee first baseman Johnny Sturm who bounced one over to Pete Coscarart, filling in for Herman. The Ebbets Field Faithful erupted with a shreik heard down in the Gowanus. In stepped third baseman Red Rolfe who accommodated the Brooklyn fans by bouncing back to Casey. The glass slipper was now being measured for Brooklyn's foot as the stands gave forth with an explosion of noise.

The next—and, as Brooklyn fans would have it, the last—batter to face Casey was Tommy Henrich. As Henrich stepped to the plate, the klaxon and garbage pail-lid brigade known as the Sym-Phony band broke into loud, raucous sound, urging on the Dodger fans, who at that moment sounded like all of Solomon's wives after catching him out on the town with another woman. As the count worked itself to three-balls-and-two-strikes, the din got even louder. If that were possible. As Casey studied, Henrich and Henrich, in turn, stood ribbed and tense in anticipation, the sound momentarily subsided, with several of the more unruly making ready to storm the citadel, their legs already over the railings of the lower box seats.

Casey let fly with the pitch and Henrich, trying his best to guard the plate, began his swing belt-high, right where the ball's trajectory appeared to be taking it. But then the ball seemed to hit an air pocket and veered off its appointed route, sharply. Henrich, recognizing that the ball was out of the strike zone, tried to check his swing. But couldn't. He'd already committed and was around on it like a man swinging a broomstick. Mickey Owen put up his glove to

Tommy Henrick practices his patent "check swin

Catcher Mickey Owen, object of the fans' disgust

catch the final strike of the game and umpire Larry Goetz went up with his right hand as the sounds of the stadium gathered momentum and burst like an erupting volcano.

In the next nanosecond a queer sensation of disquietude fell like the plague over the stands as the full-throated cheers were stilled, caught up in 33,813 throats. Down on the field a fantastic table was playing itself out: Pitcher Casey was striding off the mound, his work apparently over for the afternoon; Umpire Goetz had his hand frozen in mid-air, still calling the third strike; Catcher Mickey Owen, his mask off, was running in a they-went-thataway

THE BREAK IN THE NINTH INNING WHICH GAVE THE YANKEES THEIR CHANCE

Mickey Owen chasing the ball (designated by arrow) after the sharp-breaking curve which Pitcher Hugh Casey threw for a third strike on Tommy Henrich got away from the Dodger catcher. Henrich, the bat still in his hand, is starting for first. Umpire Larry Goetz's hand is up after calling the strike.

———————

manner in pursuit of the ball; and Tommy Henrich, his bat still extended in his strike-out swing was looking over his right shoulder at Owen and the quickly-disappearing little white spot that had just been thrown by him.

As cheers turned first to groans and then to a wailing anguish, the faithful watched in fascinated horror as Henrich, who only an instant before had been prepared to throw away his bat in disgust, set sail for first, as happy as a martyr saved from the stake, while Owen, still chasing down the ball, madly pursued it all the way to the backstop near the Dodger dugout. All the while this little drama was playing itself out, the police guard had made a rush out onto the field to hold the crowd even then preparing to make their mad dash onto the field, almost getting in Owen's way.

To those up in the stands it was worse than a blunder; it was a crime. Now Dodger fans slumped in their seats spitting out the

name "Owen" like a four-letter curseword, which it was to them now, conveniently forgetting that earlier in the year the same "Owen" had set a National League record for accepting chances without an error and had set the all-time Brooklyn fielding record for catchers. But records didn't matter now, only that damned missed third strike which caused them to turn away with a severe case of rising nausea and a feeling of inevitability.

Down on the field, Hugh Casey once again reassumed the mound, the man he thought he had dead to rights perched safely on first, so full of life his breath would becloud a mirror. Perplexed, nettled and at sea by this sudden turn of events, Casey picked up first the resin bag and then the ball, which all of sudden felt heavier in his palm. But, for reasons as hard to explain as the non-appearance of deer on their well-advertised opening day, nobody came out to talk to him at that pregnant moment, leaving him alone to contemplate the unrehearsed, unplanned and unmitigated disaster that had just befallen him.

However, Owen's missed third strike was but a link in the natural chain of events. Fate was now moving none other than Joe DiMaggio—who in this, his year of years, already had hit in 56 straight games—into the batter's box. Before Casey could work off his frustration at the way Fate had treated him, DiMaggio singled to left, putting men on first and second. And all after the third out of the ninth inning.

Now feeling like Father Adam before the great apple run, Casey played momentarily with the ball, determined to stick his finger in the leaky dike now coming apart in the worst places. But unbeknownst to him, the Yankees had responded to their famed five o'clock wake-up call. The scales having fallen from their eyes, they were suddenly alive. And when Casey tried to come back with the same pitch that had gotten away from Owen only scant moments before, again with two strikes on the next batter, "King Kong" Keller, belted it high off the right-field wall, scoring both Henrich and DiMaggio. The dam had been broken.

Not too sanguine about seeing an epic-in-the-making, especially one at their expense, the fans sat stricken to dumb apoplexy as first Bill Dickey walked and then Joe Gordon doubled over left fielder Jimmy Wasdell's head for another two runs. Suddenly, in the greatest turnaround since Serutan, the team which had "won" the regulation game 4-3 was behind 7-4 long past the normal game limit. And still the beat and beaten went on as Phil Rizzuto walked. But finally, almost twenty minutes after the game was "over," Casey got his opposite number, pitcher Johnny Murphy, to ground to short for the fourth and final out.

Needless to say, the Dodgers, as dead as the proverbial mackerel, went down tamely in the bottom of the ninth and also went on the next day to lose the game and the Series.

That night and far into the next night, wherever there was an elbow crooked throughout the Borough of Churches a thousand questions trembled on the tongues of those Dan Parker labeled "The Flatbush fanatics." They wanted an explanation, and an explanation of the explanation, of the missed third strike.

But the argument was not one which would be settled in one bar sitting, nor in many, and persisted for years. Today history holds two explanations for that missed third strike. The first holds that Casey threw a low sharp curve that broke down and away and that Owen, lunging to his right and groping for the gypsy pitch, got the edge of his glove on the ball and caused it to glance off and bounce away. One observer, Billy Meyer, the-then manager of the Newark Bears and former big league catcher, always felt that "Owen tried to catch the ball with his knees together and didn't shift for the pitch." The other far more popular explanation holds that Casey threw a wet ball, or "spitter." One of those who supports this thesis is *Pee Wee Reese*, who said, "It was a little wet slider and the ball kind of broke real sharply to the right and kinda got by Owen's glove."

Whatever, it was a missed third strike. And the most famous strike-out in baseball history.

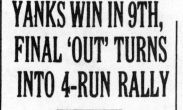

YANKS WIN IN 9TH, FINAL 'OUT' TURNS INTO 4-RUN RALLY

Game-Ending Third Strike Gets Away From Dodger Catcher, Leading to 7-4 Victory

---

KELLER IS BATTING HERO

Double, His Fourth Safety, Puts New York in Front—Victors Now Lead in Series, 3-1

By JOHN DREBINGER

It couldn't, perhaps, have happened anywhere else on earth. But it did happen yesterday in Brooklyn, where in the short space of twenty-one minutes a dazed gathering of 33,813 at Ebbets Field saw a world series game miraculously flash two finishes before its eyes.

The first came at 4:35 of a sweltering afternoon, when, with two out and nobody aboard the bases in the top half of the ninth inning, Hugh Casey saw Tommy Henrich miss a sharp-breaking curve for a third strike that for a fleeting moment had the Dodgers defeating the Yankees, 4 to 3, in the fourth game of the current classic.

But before the first full-throated roar had a chance to acclaim this brilliant achievement there occurred one of those harrowing events that doubtless will live through all the ages of baseball like the Fred Snodgrass muff and the failure of Fred Merkle to touch second.

Game 4 October 5 at Brooklyn								N.Y.	1 0 0	2 0 0	0 0 4				
								Bkn.	0 0 0	2 2 0	0 0 0				

New York	Pos	AB	R	H	RBI	PO	A	E
Sturm	1b	5	0	2	2	9	1	0
Rolfe	3b	5	1	2	0	0	2	0
Henrich	rf	4	1	0	0	3	0	0
DiMaggio	cf	4	1	2	0	2	0	0
Keller	lf	5	1	4	3	1	0	0
Dickey	c	2	2	0	0	7	0	0
Gordon	2b	5	1	2	2	2	3	0
Rizzuto	ss	4	0	0	0	2	3	0
Donald	p	2	0	0	0	0	1	0
Breuer	p	1	0	0	0	0	1	0
b Selkirk		1	0	0	0	0	0	0
Murphy	p	1	0	0	0	1	0	0
Totals		39	7	12	7	27	11	0

Pitching	IP	H	R	ER	BB	SO
New York						
Donald	*4	6	4	4	3	2
Breuer	3	3	0	0	1	2
Murphy (W)	2	0	0	0	0	1
Brooklyn						
Higbe	3⅓	6	3	3	2	1
French	⅓	0	0	0	0	0
Allen	⅓	1	0	0	1	0
Casey (L)	4⅓	5	4	0	2	1

*Pitched to 2 batters in 5th.

Brooklyn	Pos	AB	R	H	RBI	PO	A	E
Reese	ss	5	0	0	0	2	4	0
Walker	rf	5	1	2	0	5	0	0
Reiser	cf	5	1	2	2	1	0	0
Camilli	1b	4	0	2	0	10	1	0
Riggs	3b	3	0	0	0	0	2	0
Medwick	lf	2	0	0	1	1	0	0
Allen	p	0	0	0	0	0	0	0
Casey	p	2	0	1	0	0	3	0
Owen	c	2	1	0	0	2	1	1
Coscarart	2b	3	1	0	0	4	2	0
Higbe	p	1	0	1	0	0	1	0
French	p	0	0	0	0	0	0	0
a Wasdell	lf	3	0	1	2	2	0	0
Totals		35	4	9	4	27	14	1

a Doubled for French in 4th.
b Grounded out for Breuer in 8th.

Doubles—Camilli, Gordon, Keller 2, Walker, Wasdell. Home Run—Reiser.
Double Play—Gordon to Rizzuto to Sturm.
Hit by Pitcher—Henrich (by Allen).
Left on Bases—New York 11, Brooklyn 8.
Umpires—Goetz, McGowan, Pinelli, Grieve.
Attendance—33,813. Time of Game—2:54.

field only to have Stan Spence flag it down with a leaping catch. His second time up, he bettered that, frescoing the ball into center where his younger brother, Dom, made an acrobatic catch to rob him of a hit—and which prompted one writer to mutter, "Joe should sue his mother for that one." Then, in the fifth, exuding the only air that wafted over Yankee Stadium that day, his own air of inevitability, DiMaggio hit one where neither Spence nor brother Dom could go: Into the lower leftfield stands for a home run, his 13th during the streak. Returning to the bench, DiMadge was congratulated by his teammates and kidded by his Falstaffian sidekick, Lefty Gomez, who sidled up to DiMaggio and told him, "You not only broke Keeler's record, you used his formula . . . you hit 'em where they ain't.''

Having passed Keeler, writers began questioning whether there would be a let up. But not DiMaggio, the cylinders in his finely-tuned engine continuing to pump. And his bat pumping out hits against a smorgabord of pitchers that included Marchildon of the Athletics, Lyons of the White Sox, Niggling of the Browns and an assorted variety of cup bearers to his greatness as he added game-after-game to his glowing and growing totals. Mystery writer Raymond Chandler captured a fascinated nation's interest when he wrote: "Would he hit safely in every game forever? It seemed that way. And why not?" Why not indeed? But, unbeknownst to all, DiMaggio was now approaching journey's end with a single off Cleveland's Joe Krakauskas on July 16th, his 91st hit off a total of 43 pitchers in 56 games.

The next night the largest crowd ever to see a game of night baseball, some 67,000-and-change, gathered at Cleveland's Municipal Stadium to see DiMaggio add to his already legendary totals. However, the trip that had started two months and a day before finally came to a halt. But not without an intense fight to keep it alive.

As DiMaggio stepped into the batter's box in the first inning to face starting pitcher Al Smith, the Indians' third baseman, Ken Keltner, moved back near the edge of the outfield grass, almost as if he were daring DiMaggio to bunt on him. But DiMaggio, who hadn't bunted during his entire 56-game streak, did what he did

best, meeting the bat with sharp crack of ash on horsehide, sending Smith's second pitch rocketing down the third-base line. Keltner, with an agile move, lunged at the ball and backhanded it, the force of the hit taking him into foul territory. Finding his footing, Keltner got off a perfect throw to Cleveland first baseman Oscar Grimes to retire DiMaggio. Up again in the fourth, DiMaggio waited Smith out and walked. In the seventh, almost as if it were an instant replay of Keltner's crime against the senses in the first, DiMaggio again bruised the ball, sending yet another shot down to Keltner who corralled it as he had the first one and fired it across the diamond for another 5-3 ground-out, further drawing the tentacles of the octopus around DiMaggio's chances.

Three times unsuccessful, DiMaggio was to have one more chance. With the Yankee Clipper coming up in the eighth with the bases loaded, Cleveland manager Roger Peckinpaugh—the same Roger Peckinpaugh who only one month to the day earlier had owned half of the Yankees' record for most consecutive games hit safely in—pulled the lefthanded Smith in favor of righthanded relief pitcher Jim Bagby, Jr. With the count one ball and one strike on DiMaggio, the "Yankee Clipper" drilled a hot grounder deep toward short that took a bad bounce as it neared shortstop Lou Boudreau. But Boudreau, with that sharp sense of anticipation he was to become famous for, gauged the hop and shoveled the ball over to second baseman Ray Mack who continued it over to Grimes for an inning-ending—and streak-ending—double-play.

DiMaggio, who had built his monument with neither a boast nor a brag, now picked up his glove and trotted out to centerfield, his streak at an end, but his quiet dignity still very much intact, there being what one writer noted, "No kicking of dirt, no shaking of the head," merely "grace under pressure."

And whenever those with a tacit and tactical understanding of baseball hear someone invoke that old cliche "Records are made to be broken," they can feel free to mention three numbers that will stand as long as the game itself against any and all assaults: Gehrig's 2,130, Young's 511 and DiMaggio's 56. All are records of perseverance. And of greatness.

16 Babe Ruth's "Called Shot"

New York Yankees vs. Chicago Cubs, 3rd Game, 1932 World Series, October 1, 1932

DAMON RUNYON ONCE WROTE, "ABOUT 95 PERCENT OF ALL sports tradition is pure fiction. Lies, if you like. But harmless. Who the hell cares if long after a sport event the facts get a little twisted?"

Call them "pure fiction," "lies," or plain old myths, they are the coin of the realm for storytellers who shamelessly use them to embroider stories or make them out of whole cloth. In more recent years the ancient myths of Hercules, Oedipus and Ulysses have given way to those of more modern day heroes. Take the case of the old tosspot dime novelist Ned Buntline found under a Conestoga wagon, his face covered with flies, whom Buntline spruced up under the name "Buffalo Bill," and foisted on an unsuspecting public. Or of George Washington, whose fame rests more upon the fairy tales of his having hewn down a cherry tree and thrown a silver dollar across the Rappahannock—a feat not even Walter Johnson could duplicate—than on his actual accomplishments on the battlefield or in the office. Or a host of others whom mythographers, now known as publicity agents, have gussied up with revisionist trappings that fall under the categories of "pure fiction," "lies" and myths.

But of all the fields available to those who spin childlike tales, none has provided them with a more fertile field than that of sports. And particularly baseball.

Indeed, baseball's birth is one-half pure fiction, one-quarter lie and the rest myth. For, if the real truth be known, Abner Doubleday bears the same relationship to baseball as Santa Claus does to Christmas and the Easter Bunny to Easter. They are all delightful, childlike symbols; but hoaxes nevertheless.

One of the most romantic stories ever to come down the baseball pike had to do with the 1909 World Series when Ty Cobb supposedly—and here the word "supposedly" is stressed—stood on first and hollered down at Honus Wagner, "Hey, Kraut Head, I'm coming down on the next pitch." Wagner, in his autobiography, went on to tell the rest of the tall tale: "I told him to come ahead, and by golly, he did. But George Gibson, our catcher, laid the ball perfect, right in my glove and I stuck it on Ty as he came in. I guess I wasn't too easy about it, 'cause it took three stitches to sew up his lip."

However, the incident "remembered" by Wagner goes under these things covered in George Gershwin's song, "It Ain't Necessarily So." For in that 1909 Series between the Tigers and the Pirates, Cobb got on base nine times in 29 at bats, and tried to steal but three times, twice successfully—a theft of second in the first game and a theft of home in the second. The only time he was less than successful must be marked with an asterisk, his attempt to steal second in Game Four resulting in a run-down, culminating in first baseman Bill Abstein dropping the ball and allowing Cobb—whose theory was "if you keep them throwing the ball long enough, somebody is sure to throw it away."—to take second unmolested. But Wagner, who had a well-earned reputation for bellying up to the bar and telling his twice-told stories, continued to amuse his fellow salonnaires with his version of the Series, a version picked up by dishonest ventriloquists and made part of the warp and woof of baseball's growing legend, even if unsupported by the boxscores of that seven-game encounter.

Which brings us to one of the most endearing and enduring fables ever to dot the baseball landscape: Babe Ruth's "called" shot in the 1932 World Series.

While phrases like "fall feud" and "inter-league quarrel" have been used by some of the more imaginative pencil-pushers to describe the World Series, none had ever approached the 1932 confrontation between the New York Yankees and Chicago Cubs in acrimony and bitterness. The Yankees, back in the Series after a three-year absence, were now led by manager Joe McCarthy. McCarthy had managed the Cubs just two short years before and had been unceremoniously thrown out with but four games left in the season, Chicago trying mightily to repeat as National League champions and only a scant two games behind the Cardinals. According to his star left-hander Lefty Gomez, "McCarthy had us hopped up to pour it on the Cubs and lick 'em quick. He figured he hadn't got such a good shake in Chicago and said he'd like to get even. This was his chance!"

Besides McCarthy's desire for revenge, one other open item remained on the Yankees' agenda: The matter of Mark Koenig. The Cubs' road to the pennant had been a rocky one, highlighted by a dog-fight with the Pittsburgh Pirates and a change of managers in mid-stream, Charlie Grimm taking over for Rogers Hornsby in early August. But by far the most important element in their rollicking, brawling drive to the pennant was the addition of Mark Koenig to their roster in mid-season. On July 4th, the Pirates had taken a double-header from the Cubs and swept by them into first place. Two days later, second-year shortstop Billy Jurges was shot and wounded at Chicago's Carlos Hotel by showgirl Villet Popovich Valli. The matter was hushed up, euphemistically reported in the papers as an "untimely injury." But whatever it was, it put the Cubs in the position of desperately needing a shortstop for their stretch drive. After casting around for a replacement for Jurges the Cubs came up with one-time Yankee Mark Koenig, then on the San Francisco Missions, to which he had been relegated, like last year's suit, by the Detroit Tigers at the beginning of the year. Brought up on August 5, 1932, three days after Grimm had replaced Hornsby, all Koenig did was anchor the infield, hit a solid .353 in 33 games and spark the Cubs to the pennant. He also provided the spark for the ugly name-calling contest that went by the name "World Series," after it became known that the Cubs had voted the man who had powered their pennant drive but played for the Yankees for six years a mere half-share of their pennant and Series moneys, and voted Hornsby nary a sou.

The Series opened on September 28 at Yankee Stadium with name-calling the order of the day. While the Yankees directed phrases like "cheapskate" and other such calumnies at the Cubs, the bench-jockeys on the Cub bench retaliated with their own

Bobby Thomson, architect of the "Shot Heard 'Round the World" — Game #1.

Carlton Fisk waving home his game-winning home run in the '75 Series — Game #5.

Don Larsen, who pitched the only "Perfect Game" in World Series history in '56 — Game #10.

Joe DiMaggio, whose 56-game consecutive hit streak was broken in Game #15.

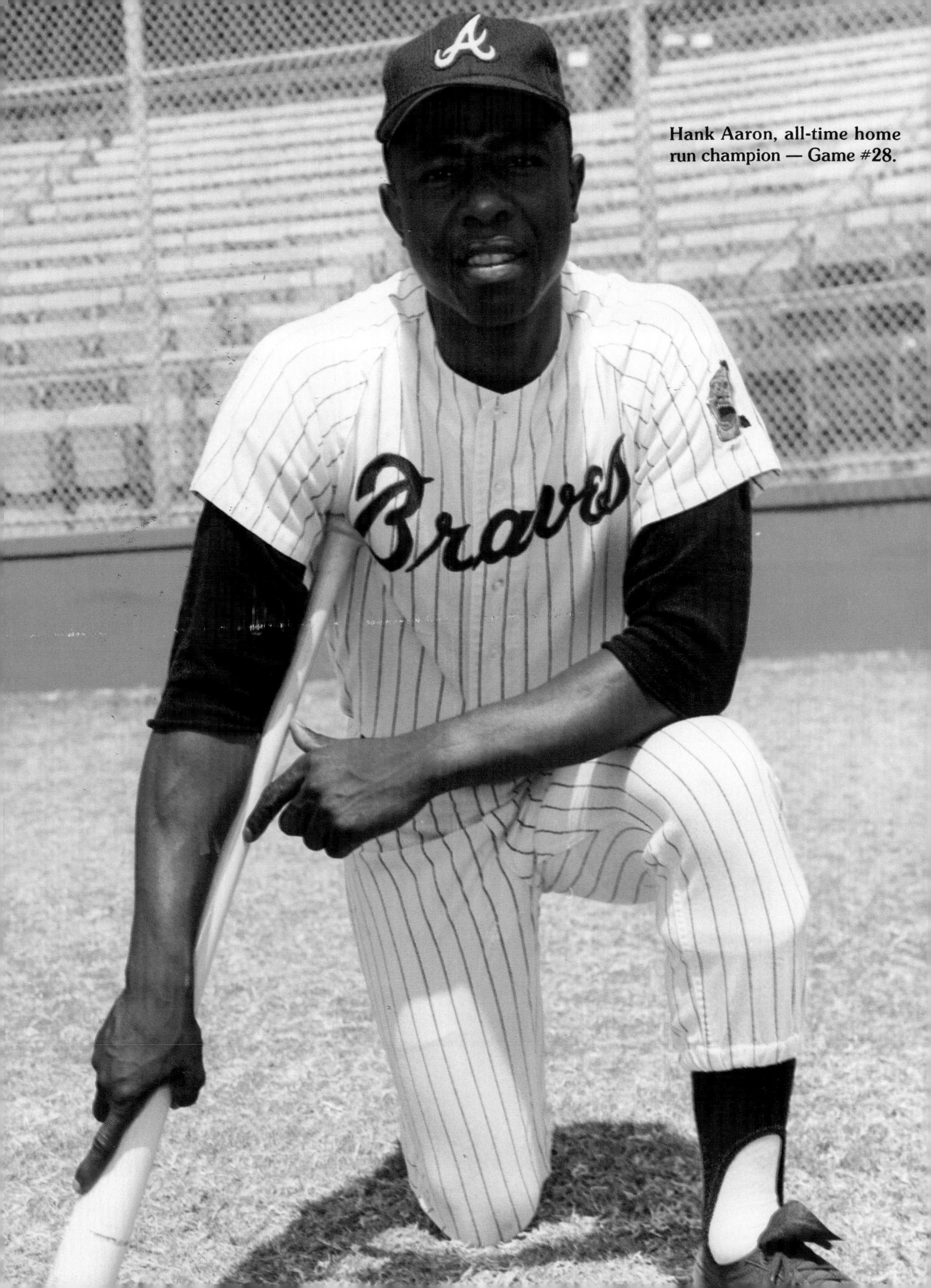

Hank Aaron, all-time home run champion — Game #28.

Three minor miracles, Cleon Jones, Tommie Agee and Ron Swoboda of the '69 Mets — Game #29.

Willie Mays, whose heroics sparked the Giants in a come-from-behind win in Game #30.

Reggie Jackson hits one of his three-homers-on-three-pitches in '77 — Game #40.

19 Ted Williams' Home Run

1941 All-Star Game, July 8, 1941

IN ONE OF HIS RARE UNGUARDED MOMENTS, TED WILLIAMS once drew back the curtain and allowed the world a brief glimpse of what made Teddy bat, saying, "All I want out of life is that when I walk down the street folks will turn and say: 'There goes the greatest hitter who ever lived.' "

And there were those who believed he was. Or at least the best since Ty Cobb and Joe Jackson. One of those was Jimmy Dykes, the old A's third baseman, who was often heard to comment, apropos of Williams, "Best damned hitter I ever saw!" And that covered a lot of ground, Dykes' career going in one era and coming out the other—starting in the late 19-teens when Cobb and Jackson were the two greatest hitters in the game and ending in 1939, Williams' first year in the Majors.

At spring training before the '38 season, eyeing all of his teammates-to-be with a defiant pride known only to youngsters and caring nothing for the reputations of his elders, Williams willingly imparted to all the benefit of his inexperience. When someone tried to put the puppy-youth in his place, telling him "Just wait 'til you see Jimmie Foxx hit," Williams rejoined, "Just wait until Foxx sees me hit!" Red Sox General Manager Eddie Collins, who had personally scouted and signed the gangly adolescent of some 19 springs and summers—there being no winters in his native San Diego—decided that even if Williams had been born with a silver bat in his hands, his swaggering self-confidence could use some refining. To render a severe pruning to his young sapling, Collins gave Williams a ticket back to the Red Sox's Triple A farm team in Minneapolis. But before he packed, Williams, with a strong presentiment, predicted that not only would he be back, but that he ultimately would draw a higher salary than the combined Red Sox outfield—a tandem that consisted of Ben Chapman, Doc Cramer, and Joe Vosmik, all .300 hitters. Williams would make good on both promises. And many more during his promising career.

Never one to duly allow fate to trample him beneath its iron heel, Williams demonstrated to one and sundry that he belonged back up in the Majors, redeeming the second part of his round-trip ticket by leading the American Association in no less than six offensive categories—batting, runs scored, home runs, total bases, RBI's and walks.

Williams continued his assault on American League pitchers in 1939 with a dismal monotony and startling variety, leading the league in RBI's with 145, the most ever for a rookie, batting .327, finishing second in doubles with the second highest total in history, coming in third in homers with 31, the second-highest rookie total in history, and finishing with 107 walks, the most ever for a rookie.

Of all the record-breaking statistics Williams amassed in his rookie year, the most amazing one was his walk total, testimony not only to his uncanny "eye," but also to the umpires' faith in the judgment of this raw rookie. Dykes, who had seen them all, could only marvel, "If he took a pitch, the umpires called it a ball. They figured he knew the strike zone better than they did." Williams studied pitchers like a scientist studying a lab specimen, giving thoughtful exploration of his opposite numbers and their offerings, all the while snapping his bat back and forth to circumscribe the strike zone. One pitcher who faced him in later years, Bobby Shantz, remembered Williams' forebearance in swinging at pitches that missed by less than the proverbial carpenter's anatomical hair. "Man, I threw him some wicked curve balls that didn't miss by more than a fraction, and he'd just stand there and look at them, and that bat would stay back, not budging an inch." Others marveled at his uncanny ability to sight the ball when it left the pitcher's hand, following it all the way in, almost as if he were studying the spelling of the name "Spalding," and then stepping back from anything that remotely resembled a brushback pitch, letting it merely go over his head like smelly well-oiled hair tonic, rather than having to throw himself at the ground in the normally accepted manner of escaping such errancy. And still others could recall that trying to get a fast ball past Williams was like trying to mine coal with a nail file.

But whatever it was about Williams—his eye, his batting prowess, or his seeming and seamless perfection in the batter's box—after only one year baseball writers and fans alike were using catchall phrases like "superstar" and "great" to describe this man who, at 6'3" and 146, had the appearance of a bat with a severe thyroid problem, a throwback to some giraffe ancestor. And 1940 would only add to his glow as he continued to add to his totals—raising his average to .344, third best in the League, finishing third in slugging average and total bases and leading the league in runs scored. But all that would serve merely as throat clearings for 1941, one of the greatest seasons any batsman would ever have.

For "all" Williams did during that last pre-War season was hit .406, 47 percentage points higher than the runner-up; lead the league in homers, runs scored, slugging average and bases on balls; and finish third in total bases and fourth in runs batted in. And while 1941 was known as the year of Joe DiMaggio's celebrated 56-game hit streak—a long-running show that ran from May 15th through July 16th—Williams actually outhit DiMaggio during the course of the streak, .412 to .408.

Even while DiMaggio was well on his way toward his 56 games and Williams on his way to his .406, the two would be teammates for one day as members of the 1941 American League All-Star team. That day, too, would belong to Williams in this his year of years.

The 1941 All-Star Game was but the ninth in the history of the Mid-Summer Classic, with the American League having held the upper hand in five of the previous eight Games. But National League manager Bill McKechnie, who had guided the National League to a 4-0 win the last time they had foregathered, was bidding to become the first manager in the short history of the Game to put together back-to-back victories. Using the same strategy as in the previous meeting, McKechnie almost carried it off. Almost, but not quite, thanks to Ted Williams.

With so many premier pitchers on hand, their talents were almost available at a discount. And McKechnie's strategy, simply stated, was to use them in just such a manner: Throwing his vaunted pitching staff into the fray in abbreviated stints, discounting the allowable three innings per pitcher at two apiece, thus keeping the American League batters off balance and their bats silent. It had worked in the 1940 Game, as McKechnie threw them at the American League with a bewildering rapidity, using Paul Derringer, Bucky Walters and Whitlow Wyatt for two innings apiece on the way to the first All-Star shutout in history.

Now McKechnie merely rotated the crops, using Wyatt first, then Derringer and then Walters for two innings apiece over the first six. However, this time, after six the American League had two runs to the National League's one, thanks in part to Bob Feller's three scoreless innings and Thorton Lee's three middle innings in which he gave up but four hits to the National League's big bats and one run—that coming on a double by Bucky Walters and two sacrifices—and Lou Boudreau and Ted Williams, both of whom had driven in a run.

In the top of the seventh the National League bid to break the Game wide open. With Washington right hander Sid Hudson now pitching, Enos Slaughter opened the Senior Circuit's half of the "Lucky Inning" with a single to left where Williams, practicing his best imitation of a sleight-of-hand artist, waved at the ball and waved Slaughter down to second as well. However, whether Slaughter's way station was first or second became academic when the next batter, Pittsburgh shortstop Arky Vaughan, arched one of Hudson's deliveries into the upper reaches of the right field stands for a two-run homer and a 3-2 National League lead.

Still the National Leaguers weren't through with Hudson, as Brooklyn second baseman Billy Herman followed with a double and was sacrificed over to third by Pirate catcher Al Lopez. Now, with a fine sense of history, McKechnie sent Joe Medwick up to bat for Walters. Those in Detroit's left field stands, their memories

hardly taxed by the passage of seven years and Medwick's last stand in the Motor City when he had stood in left field amidst garbage and other miscellanea thrown in his general direction by frustrated Tiger fans during the course of the last game of the '34 World Series, harried and hectored him with stimulant imprecations to his ancestry mingled with boos. But this time, despite the bad intentions he still harbored, all that Medwick could muster was one mighty swing and one mini tap back to Hudson. And after he had retired one more man, Hudson too retired from the game, bloodied and bowed.

After the American League had gone down docilely in the bottom of the seventh, the National League came to bat in their half of the eighth against Edgar Smith, the second White Sox left hander used by American League manager Del Baker. Smith gave up a double to big John Mize sandwiched in between strikeouts of Pete Reiser and Enos Slaughter. Then, in what looked like lightning striking a second time in the same place, Arky Vaughan, who was to hit only six home runs all year, smote another two-run homer to almost the exact spot as the one he had hit the previous inning—the first time in All-Star history any player had hit two in one game, a record which would stand until Williams hit two in 1946. Suddenly the score was 5-2, National League, and McKechnie's strategy looked as if it would pay off for the second straight year.

Unbeknownst to all, especially himself, McKechnie had altered his strategy. With a three-run lead and but two more innings to go, he would no longer stick with his original plan of throwing fresh pitchers in a befuddling variety at the American League, but instead was content to stick with the one he had brought in in the seventh, Cub right hander Claude Passeau.

The American League touched Passeau for one run in the eighth, courtesy of the Brothers DiMaggio, Joe getting his first and

The Splendid Splinter, Ted Williams, possessor of the sharpest eye in the history of baseball.

The swing that won the best All-Star Game in history

only hit of the afternoon—and, for those who were counting, even unofficially, the 49th consecutive game in which he had hit safely—and was driven in by younger brother Dom. But when Passeau struck out Jimmie Foxx to end the inning, McKechnie saw no reason why he should go to those who still sat in his bullpen, and which included the likes of Carl Hubbell, Lon Warneke and Cy Blanton.

Having weathered the storm in the eighth, Passeau got Philadelphia A's catcher Frankie Hayes on a pop-up to Herman to start the bottom of the ninth. It now looked like he could make it safely into port. But, in truth, he was an accident on its way to happening. Like the lion in pursuit of his prey who frivolously might set a paw upon a casual rabbit in its path, the American League now began to play with Passeau before swooping down on him in the person of Williams. First Cleveland third baseman Ken Keltner, sent up to bat for the aforementioned Smith, hit a bouncer which caromed off Braves shortstop Eddie Miller who had just replaced the hero Vaughan in the field for a scratch single. Then Joe Gordon of the Yankees followed with a single to right and Cecil Travis of the Senators drew a walk to fill the bases to overflowing. Now, as a feeling of inevitability gripped the 54,674 in Tiger Stadium, Joe DiMaggio took his place in the batter's box. But this moment was not to belong to DiMaggio, whose best effort was a scorching shot right at shortstop Miller. As the crowd groaned, sensing a game-

ending double play, Miller deftly fielded the hotter-than-hot grounder and shoveled it over to second baseman Billy Herman to get Travis for the second out; but Herman, in his haste to complete the double play and end the game, threw the ball wide of first base, pulling first baseman Frank McCormick off the bag. Safe at first on the fielder's choice was DiMaggio, Ken Keltner scoring with the American League's fourth run—the two to figure in history of yet another sort, DiMaggio's streak, in Cleveland nine days hence.

The moment now belonged to Williams. Moving into the batter's box with a marble you-bet-I-can look, Williams went through the batter's rites of swing, digging a little depression with the toe of his left foot, bouncing up and down and squeezing the handle of the bat until it seemed that sawdust would come out its end, all the while casting a look out at Passeau that would curl burnt toast. Passeau's first pitch came in, hard and fast. Williams, drawing a bead on it, swung mightily and the ball went high up in the stands, foul. The next two offerings were wide, and Williams, after appraising them closely for content through incurious eyes, eschewed swinging. The count now stood two-and-one. Passeau came back with one around the knees and Williams' bat unwound, almost independent of conscious effort, catching the ball at the last moment. The ball jumped off his bat on a line and carried straight out toward right field.

As Williams moved down the first-base line, following closely

Two On, Two Down When Bostonian Hits Ball Far Into Stands

Box Score of the Game

Thunderous Climax Before 56,674 Fans at Detroit Gives American League Sixth Victory

Vaughan Tilt's Previous Hero

Pirates' Shortstop Pounds Two Circuit Drives, Each With Man on Base, Earlier in Game

NATIONAL LEAGUE

	ab.	r.	h.	tb.	2b.	3b.	hr.	sh.	sb.	bb.	so.	po.	a.	e.
Hack, Chicago, 3b	2	0	1	1	0	0	0	1	0	1	1	3	0	0
Lavagetto, Brooklyn, 3b	1	0	0	0	0	0	0	0	0	0	0	0	0	0
Moore, St. Louis, lf	5	0	0	0	0	0	0	0	0	0	1	0	0	0
Reiser, Brooklyn, cf	4	0	0	0	0	0	0	0	0	2	6	0	2	
Mize, St. Louis, 1b	4	1	1	2	1	0	0	0	0	0	5	0	0	
McCormick, Cincinnati, 1b	0	0	0	0	0	0	0	0	0	0	0	0	0	0
Nicholson, Chicago, rf	1	0	0	0	0	0	0	0	0	0	1	1	0	0
Elliott, Pittsburgh, rf	1	0	0	0	0	0	0	0	0	0	0	0	0	0
Slaughter, St. Louis, rf	2	1	1	1	0	0	0	0	0	1	0	0	0	
Vaughan, Pittsburgh, ss	4	2	3	9	0	0	2	0	0	0	1	2	0	
Miller, Boston, ss	0	0	0	0	0	0	0	0	0	0	1	0	0	
Frey, Cincinnati, 2b	1	0	1	1	0	0	0	0	0	0	1	3	0	
Herman, Brooklyn, 2b	3	0	2	3	1	0	0	0	0	0	3	0	0	
Owen, Brooklyn, c	1	0	0	0	0	0	0	0	0	0	0	0	0	
Lopez, Pittsburgh, c	1	0	0	0	0	0	0	1	0	0	3	0	0	
Danning, New York, c	1	0	0	0	0	0	0	0	0	0	3	0	0	
Wyatt, Brooklyn, p	0	0	0	0	0	0	0	0	0	0	0	0	0	
aOtt, New York	1	0	0	0	0	0	0	0	0	0	1	0	0	
Derringer, Cincinnati, p	0	0	0	0	0	0	0	0	0	0	0	1	0	
Walters, Cincinnati, p	1	1	1	2	1	0	0	0	0	0	0	0	0	
cMedwick, Brooklyn	1	0	0	0	0	0	0	0	0	0	0	0	0	
Passeau, Chicago, p	1	0	0	0	0	0	0	0	0	0	0	0	0	
Total	35	5	10	19	3	0	2	2	0	1	7	*26	7	2

AMERICAN LEAGUE

	ab.	r.	h.	tb.	2b.	3b.	hr.	sh.	sb.	bb.	so.	po.	a.	e.
Doerr, Boston, 2b	3	0	0	0	0	0	0	0	0	0	0	1	0	0
Gordon, New York, 2b	2	1	1	1	0	0	0	0	0	0	0	2	0	0
Travis, Washington, 3b	4	1	1	2	1	0	0	0	1	0	1	2	0	
J. DiMaggio, New York, cf	4	3	1	2	1	0	0	0	0	1	0	0	0	
Williams, Boston, lf	4	1	2	6	1	0	1	0	0	1	1	3	0	1
Heath, Cleveland, rf	2	0	0	0	0	0	0	0	0	1	1	1	0	1
D. DiMaggio, Boston, rf	1	0	1	1	0	0	0	0	0	0	0	1	0	
Cronin, Boston, ss	2	0	0	0	0	0	0	0	0	0	1	3	0	0
Boudreau, Cleveland, ss	2	0	2	2	0	0	0	0	0	0	0	0	1	0
York, Detroit, 1b	3	0	1	1	0	0	0	0	0	0	0	6	2	0
Foxx, Boston, 1b	1	0	0	0	0	0	0	0	0	1	2	2	0	
Dickey, New York, c	3	0	1	1	0	0	0	0	0	0	4	2	0	
Hayes, Philadelphia, c	1	0	0	0	0	0	0	0	0	0	2	0	0	
Feller, Cleveland, p	0	0	0	0	0	0	0	0	0	0	0	1	0	
bCullenbine, St. Louis	1	0	0	0	0	0	0	0	0	0	0	0	0	
Lee, Chicago, p	1	0	0	0	0	0	0	0	0	0	1	0	0	
Hudson, Washington, p	0	0	0	0	0	0	0	0	0	0	0	0	0	
dKeller, New York	1	0	0	0	0	0	0	0	0	0	1	0	0	
Smith, Chicago, p	0	0	0	0	0	0	0	0	0	0	0	1	0	1
eKeltner, Cleveland	1	1	1	1	0	0	0	0	0	0	0	0	0	
Total	36	7	11	17	3	0	1	0	0	4	6	27	11	3

*Two out when winning runs were scored.
aBatted for Wyatt in third.
bBatted for Feller in third.
cBatted for Walters in seventh.
dBatted for Hudson in seventh.
eBatted for Smith in ninth.

SCORE BY INNINGS

National League .... 0 0 0   0 0 1   2 2 0—5
American League .... 0 0 0   1 0 1   0 1 4—7

Runs batted in—Williams 4, Moore, Boudreau, Vaughan 4. D. DiMaggio, J. DiMaggio.

Earned runs—National League 5, American League 7. Left on bases—National League 6, American League 7. Double plays—Frey, Vaughan and Mize; York and Cronin. Struck out—By Feller 4 (Hack, Reiser, Nicholson, Ott); by Derringer 1 (Heath); by Walters 2 (Cronin, Doerr); by Hudson 1 (Moore); by Smith 2 (Reiser, Slaughter); by Passeau 3 (Keller, Williams, Foxx). Bases on balls—Off Wyatt 1 (Williams); off Walters 2 (J. DiMaggio, Heath); off Hudson 1 (Hack); off Passeau 1 (Travis). Hits—Off Feller, 1 in 3 innings; off Lee, 4 in 3 innings; off Hudson, 3 in 1 inning; off Smith, 2 in 2 innings; off Wyatt, 0 in 2 innings; off Derringer, 2 in 2 innings; off Walters, 3 in 2 2-3 innings; off Passeau, 6 in 2 2-3 innings. Winning pitcher—Smith. Losing pitcher—Passeau. Umpires—Summers (A. L.), Jorda (N. L.), Grieve (A. L.) and Pinelli (N. L.). Time of game—2:23. Attendance—54,674.

the flight of the ball, the faint impersonal smile on his face gave way to a broad grin, giving him the look of someone who had just drawn to king's full. For what he had seen was the ball, still going on a straight line, hit the upper parapet of the right-field stands for a three-run homer, one long enough to qualify for two hyphens, as in well-hit-homer. Suddenly, there was Williams jumping up and down like a little kid at Christmas, clapping his hands and less running around the bases than hippity-hopping. Williams made it home to the thunderous roars of the crowd and the handshake of the man who met him at the plate to congratulate him for winning the game for the American League 7-5, Joe DiMaggio.

After the Game, the defeated McKechnie could only mutter, "Ted, you're just not human!" And in that year of 1941 he wasn't; but what he was, at least for that one year, was "the greatest hitter who ever lived."

20 Ten Runs in One Inning

Philadelphia Athletics vs. Chicago Cubs, 4th Game, 1929 World Series, October 12, 1929

WHEN NOAH WEBSTER FIRST PUBLISHED THAT GUIDE TO the spelling of words which could be located only if you knew how to spell them in the first place, the dictionary, he defined the words "Come back" as "a return to former prosperity or status." Had but Mr. Webster not keeled over 86 years before they came upon the scene, there is no doubt he would have illustrated the by-then hyphenated word come-back with a picture of the 1929 Philadelphia Athletics.

The 1929 Philadelphia Athletics represented not only "a return to prosperity and status" for the team itself, but also one for manager and guiding light Connie Mack—the only manager the team had ever had since Philadelphia joined the American League back in 1901. Only a few graybeards remember Connie's last championship team, a team Mack had gutted after their four-game series loss to the Boston Braves back in 1914. Since then, the A's had been an eighth-class power in the American League, holding permanent rights to the cellar for seven straight years and not shedding their eighth class status until 1922, when they moved, ever so imperceptibly, to seventh. Moving up the American League staircase one step at a time for the next three years, the A's finally broke into the first division in 1925, not incidentally the same year they brought up the greatest pledge class in history of baseball: Mickey Cochrane, Jimmie Foxx and Lefty Grove. By 1929 these three future Hall of Famers, together with a star-studded cast which included Al Simmons, Jimmy Dykes, Rube Walberg, George Earnshaw, Mule Haas, Bing Miller, Joe Boley and Max Bishop, had shown their pedigree, winning the pennant by 18 games over the defending World's Champions, the New York Yankees.

Their opponents in the '29 Series would be the National League pennant winners, the Chicago Cubs. On paper the 1929 Cubs were every bit as imposing as the Athletics. With Rogers Hornsby anchoring the infield and batting .380, a sub-par year by his standards, the team had hit .303 overall. Their outfield trio of Kiki Cuyler, Riggs Stephenson and Hack Wilson had combined to drive in 371 runs, led by Wilson's league-leading 159 ribbies. And their pitching staff featured the likes of Pat Malone, Charlie Root and Guy Bush, three of the four leading pitchers in the National League in winning percentage, wins, ERA, and innings pitched.

The man who best epitomized the Cubs and their spirit was a little fireplug of a man who had a build referred to in ready-made clothing catalogues as "portly": Lewis Robert Wilson, better known as "Hack," in tribute to the man reputed to be the strongest man in the world, George Hackenschmidt. Wilson, who somehow distributed 190 pounds and iron-band-like muscles over his 5'6" frame, was a bouser and carouser of the first water. And scotch as well. Called by Chicago sports columnist Warren Brown, "A high ball hitter on the field, and off," Wilson led the Cubbies on their merry way, bottled and otherwise. Someone once suggested that Wilson had never liked olives until someone had shown him how to mix them with gin and vermouth. Ever since, gin had been his tonic. And the tonic for the rest of the Cubs as they frolicked

through the National League, outdistancing Prohibition and the League by ten and one-half games.

A red-blooded, one hundred percent American sun still shone down from a clear Chicago sky that October day as the two teams warmed up for Game One of the Series. But there had stolen into the air a hint of autumnal weather, as a bracing wind worked its way through the stands. But it wasn't the bracing wind that was the topic of conversation; it was the pitcher warming up on the sidelines for the A's: Howard Ehmke. Ehmke, who was on the far side of 30 and nearing the end of the baseball road, had played little or no part in the A's total decimation of the rest of the league. What, wondered the onlookers, was he doing out there? Especially when the A's had such stalwarts as Lefty Grove, Rube Walberg and George Earnshaw—a trio that had won a total of 62 games for the A's between them. Even lesser lights like Eddie Rommel, Jack Quinn or Bill Shores, all of whom won more than 10 games, would have been understandable. But Howard Ehmke?

However, Connie Mack, stiff with the ramrod of conviction that comes from managing for 32 years, had decided that Ehmke would be his pitcher for Game One. How he decided was a story in itself, one which bears retelling. Back in late August, Mack had called for Ehmke. There Ehmke heard those saddest of all possible words, "Howard, this is bad news I have to give you. But I can't help it. I have to let you go." Ehmke stood staring at the "Grand Old Man of Baseball" through a veil of thinly-hinted tears. Finally, able to choke back the tears, he forced out the words he had been groping for, pleading for his last chance to smell the roses. "Gee, Mr. Mack, I've never been on a pennant winner before, and here this club is winning the pennant. I'd always dreamed that I could pitch in a World Series, and now you're giving me my release." Mack, a soft-bitten man whose will was strong even though his "won't" was weak, backed down ever so slightly, "Do you think you could pitch in a World Series?" And Ehmke replied, now hoping against hope, "There's one good game left in this arm." Mack, who was known for his fidelity, as well as his hunches, succumbed, "If you feel that way, all right. But I don't want you to take the next trip with the club. The boys don't want you around. They think you can't pitch anymore. I want you to stay home and when the Cubs are playing in Brooklyn and New York, go over there and scout them. And when they're here against the Phillies, I want you to watch them." Then, almost as an afterthought, Mack turned to Ehmke and asked, "Howard, tell me, which game you want to pitch against the Cubs and you'll pitch it." Ehmke, now sure of his ground even if he wasn't sure of anything else, answered quietly, "The first game, Mr. Mack. I want to pitch the first one."

And so the seldom-used control pitcher with no fast ball and even less reason for being on the mound took the field for the A's. The Cubs, fully prepared to face Lefty Grove and his blazing fast ball, were caught off guard and unawares by Ehmke's tantalizing off-speed pitches and near-perfect control. When the final batter, Chuck Tolson, pinch-hitting for Cub starting pitcher Guy Bush,

Philadelphia A's manager Connie Mack

struck out, it was Ehmke's 13th, a new World Series strike-out record. And a 3-1 win in the last game he would ever win in the Majors.

Ehmke was mere parsley on the plate of the A's, who now had the meat and potatoes of their pitching staff to throw at the Cubs. Game Two saw Mack send his leading pitcher, "Moose" Earnshaw, out to do battle with the Cubs. Earnshaw, staked to six quick runs, ran into trouble of his own in the fifth, giving up five hits and three runs. And so Mack, with an embarrassment of riches owing to his use of Ehmke in Game One, turned to the bullpen, bringing in his "Triple Crown" winner, Lefty Grove, to close the door on the incipient Cub rally. Grove did more than merely close the door, he locked it as well, striking out six—which, combined with Earnshaw's seven, gave the A's pitching staff 26 strike-outs in two days—and limiting the Cubs to three singles the rest of the way. Now it was back to Philadelphia with a 2-0 lead in games for one of the most memorable games in baseball history.

But history would have to wait. Momentarily. For Guy Bush beat George Earnshaw in a battle of curve balls in Game Three, 3-1, for the Cubs first win—and the first by the National League since Grover Cleveland Alexander struck out Tony Lazzeri, three long years ago.

Mack, who had played a hunch in Game One and gotten away with it, now played a second one. Only this time it damn near backfired on him. His hunch for Game Four was Jack Quinn, undoubtedly selected because he was the only man alive who remembered the man whose discovery of America was being celebrated that day, Christopher Columbus. Quinn, at 45 the oldest player in the Majors and the oldest ever to play in a World Series game, was a spitball pitcher who had been plying his wet trade since 1909, and had been given a dispensation for his unsanitary offering! Quinn used his spitter to good advantage for the A's during the season, winning 11 games, both as a starting and relief pitcher. However, the Cubs seemed to be hitting the dry side of the ball this October day, getting to Quinn and his spitter for seven hits and six runs in five-plus innings. They continued their unmerciful assault on his successors, Rube Walberg and Eddie Rommel, leading 8-0 going into the bottom half of the seventh. For all intents and purposes, that should have ended the competitive phase of the game.

The Cubs took the field for the A's half of the 7th, laboring under a torpor worthy of a python after its midday meal. With Charlie Root breezing along on a three-hitter, there hardly seemed

cause for concern when the first batter up in the A's seventh, Al Simmons, drove one of Root's fast balls high atop Shibe Park's left-field roof. Even Simmons was underwhelmed by his accomplishment, audibly muttering to himself as he returned to the dugout, "You dumb Polack, of all times to waste a home run!" But Simmons' homer had done more than merely break the serene and undisturbed existence of Root, it had also sounded the first gun of a rallying army.

The Cubs were still in their oh-hell-let's-go-fishing posture when the next man up, Jimmie Foxx, caught an outside pitch and drove it to right for a single. Bing Miller, the next batter up in the inning, lofted a fly somewhere in the general direction of Wilson in center. Apparently God was in his heaven and all was right with the world, and somewhere out there, communing with nature, was Hack Wilson who managed to lose the ball in the sun for a gift single, putting men on first and second. Wilson had done more than merely lose the ball in the sun; he had let the first olive out of the bottle. Now they all came tumbling out as Dykes singled, driving in Foxx for the second run and Boley singled driving in Miller. The score stood 8-3, for the nonce. But those three runs were merely throat clearings for what was to come.

The next man up, George Burns, pinch-hitting for pitcher Rommel, gave Root a momentary respite by popping out. Then Bishop singled over Root's head, Dykes scoring the fourth run of the inning. Suddenly, the Cubs' once insurmountable lead was halved.

By now the crowd had come to life, caught up in the spirit of the inning. The Cubs' bench came alive as manager Joe McCarthy, seeing his team come unstuck, began waving frantically to

Mickey Cochrane, a part of the Big Mack Attack

four or five pitchers warming up furiously in the bullpen. Over on the other side of the diamond, the A's bench also came alive. As the players pounded one another in the heat of the moment, third baseman Jimmy Dykes found himself pounding the person sitting on his left and turned to find, to his sorrow, that it was his venerable manager, Connie Mack. Surprisingly, Mack—who had never been heard to raise his voice in his almost biblical three score and ten years, his strongest emotion having been to once answer the sassy Dykes with an "And nuts to you, too, Mr. Dykes"— joined in, pounding first Dykes, then those around him, all the while cheering on his "boys."

McCarthy, apprehensively watching his pitcher and his team, come unstuck brought in veteran Art Nehf. Never did apprehension have more basis. With every pitch inviting some new diaster, one of Nehf's first offerings was hit by the first man Nehf faced, Mule Haas, somewhere toward Hack Wilson. This time Wilson didn't so much lose the ball in the sun as misplace it; and as he raced in pursuit of the elusive ball with all the agility of a man plowing his crops behind twin spavines, Bishop and Boley scored in front of Haas for three more runs. The score now stood or— searching in Mr. Webster's book for something more expressive— rested at 8-7, Cubs.

After the ninth man up in the inning, Mickey Cochrane, had walked, McCarthy, musing about the mutability of temporal affairs, again made his weary way to the mound to remove Nehf and bring in Sheriff Blake, hoping against hope that the nightmare would come to an end and the A's would just go away and leave the Cubs alone. Also leaving them with their 8-7 lead.

But it was not to be, Blake unable to stem the tide any more than his two predecessors. Simmons, starting the second installment of the batting order, continued the hit assault with another one, this time a single, moving Cochrane over to third with the tying run. Foxx chipped in with a chaser, his second single of the inning, and the score was tied. That did it for Blake. McCarthy, emptying his bullpen as surely as if he'd hollered "Fire"—which it was, by now an all-consuming conflagration—brought in Pat Malone, the starter and loser in Game Two.

Malone tried sticking his finger in the dike as one way of controlling the inevitable. But after he had plunked the first man he faced, Bing Miller, in the ribs to load the bases, the dike, or more accurately, Dykes, as in Jimmy, struck back. For the next man up after Miller was Dykes, who had singled and scored earlier on. Now Dykes smashed what the tabloids would call a hard "screaming" liner into the left-field corner at the base of the wall. Cub left fielder Riggs Stephenson chased the ball desperately, even managing to lay his hands on it. But the A's magic was still working and the ball bounded capriciously away from Stephenson's grasp for a two-base hit, Simmons and Foxx both scoring to make the tally now 10-8—unbelievably, the A's!

By now Philadelphia had exhausted itself. Joe Boley, who had earlier in the inning struck his head on the top of the dugout jumping up in excitement at the turn of events, came to bat still somewhat woozy. And struck out while the iron was hot. He was followed to the plate by Burns, who had entered the game as a pinch-hitter what seemed like an eternity ago and popped up for the first out of the inning, completed the cycle and the inning by striking out too. The damage had been done," the A's had staged the biggest inning in Series history.

Now Mack, who had started the afternoon by starting Jack Quinn, brought in Lefty Grove to pitch the eighth and ninth innings. Grove's elegant style and blazing fast ball bewildered the Cubs as he retired them in order, striking out four of the six he

faced, as the A's took a 3-1 lead in the Series.

The last game was a denouement, as the Cubs, still stunned by the sudden turn of events in the 4th game, were to be stunned again. This time they took a 2-0 lead into the bottom of the ninth, only to find that the A's had not run out of miracles. In the bottom of the ninth inning, Mule Haas hit a two-run homer and Bing Miller scored Al Simmons with the Series-ending run.

If the truth were to be known, the Series had actually ended for the Cubs in the seventh inning of the fourth game when the A's had staged the biggest scoring orgy in World Series history and the biggest "comeback" in baseball history in one of baseball's greatest games.

Jimmie Foxx, the man who looked like what Jack met at the top of the beanstalk

ATHLETICS' 10 RUNS IN 7TH DEFEAT CUBS IN 4TH SERIES GAME

Trailing, 8-0, Mackmen Unleash Attack That Beats McCarthy's Men, 10-8, Before 30,000.

15 MEN BAT IN ONE INNING

Four Pitchers, Root, Nehf, Blake and Malone, Used Before Athletics Are Retired.

DYKES'S DOUBLE DECIDES

Game 4 October 12 at Philadelphia

| | Chi. | 000 205 100 |
| | Phi. | 000 000 10 0 x |

Chicago	Pos	AB	R	H	RBI	PO	A	E
McMillan	3b	4	0	0	0	1	3	0
English	ss	4	0	0	0	2	1	0
Hornsby	2b	5	2	2	0	1	1	0
Wilson	cf	3	1	2	0	3	0	1
Cuyler	rf	4	2	3	2	0	0	1
Stephenson	lf	4	1	1	1	2	1	0
Grimm	1b	4	2	2	2	7	0	0
Taylor	c	3	0	0	1	8	1	0
Root	p	3	0	0	0	0	0	0
Nehf	p	0	0	0	0	0	0	0
Blake	p	0	0	0	0	0	0	0
Malone	p	0	0	0	0	0	0	0
b Hartnett		1	0	0	0	0	0	0
Carlson	p	0	0	0	0	0	0	0
Totals		35	8	10	6	24	8	2

a Popped out and struck out for Rommel in 7th.
b Struck out for Malone in 8th.

Doubles—Cochrane, Dykes. Triple—Hornsby. Home Runs—Grimm, Haas, Simmons. Sacrifice Hits—Boley, Haas, Taylor. Double Play—Dykes to Bishop to Foxx. Hit by Pitcher—Miller (by Malone). Left on Bases—Chicago 4, Philadelphia 6.
Umpires—Van Graflan, Klem, Dinneen, Moran. Attendance—29,921. Time of Game—2:12.

Philadelphia	Pos	AB	R	H	RBI	PO	A	E
Bishop	2b	4	1	1	0	2	3	0
Haas	cf	4	1	1	3	2	0	0
Cochrane	c	4	1	2	0	9	0	0
Simmons	lf	5	2	2	1	0	0	0
Foxx	1b	4	2	2	1	10	0	0
Miller	rf	3	1	2	0	3	0	1
Dykes	3b	4	1	3	3	0	2	0
Boley	ss	3	1	1	1	1	5	0
Quinn	p	2	0	0	0	0	0	0
Walberg	p	0	0	0	0	0	0	1
Rommel	p	0	0	0	0	0	0	0
a Burns		2	0	0	0	0	0	0
Grove	p	0	0	0	0	0	0	0
Totals		36	10	15	10	27	10	2

Pitching	IP	H	R	ER	BB	SO
Chicago						
Root	6⅓	9	6	6	0	3
Nehf	**0	1	2	2	1	0
Blake (L)	***0	2	2	2	0	0
Malone	⅓	1	0	0	0	2
Carlson	1	2	0	0	0	1
Philadelphia						
Quinn	*5	7	6	5	2	2
Walberg	1	1	1	0	0	2
Rommel (W)	1	2	1	1	1	0
Grove (SV)	2	0	0	0	0	4

*Pitched to 4 batters in 6th.
**Pitched to 2 batters in 7th.
***Pitched to 2 batters in 7th.

21 Podres' Win

Brooklyn Dodgers vs. New York Yankees, 7th Game, 1955 World Series, October 4, 1955

BY THE MIDDLE OF THE SIXTH DECADE OF THE TWENTIETH century, a tree had grown in Brooklyn (although there were those who held that the title of Betty Smith's book referred to a giant weed); Brooklyn's official flower, the forsythia, had bloomed yellow in more than a few garden spots, and Topps baseball cards had sprung forth in profusion from a Bush Terminal loft. But alas not one World Series flag had ever been raised in that famed borough.

In this baseball-mad borough the Dodgers were Everyman's religion and obsession. Their existence defined by the four walls of Ebbets Field, the lack of a World Series flag maddened them and tormented their manhood. It was almost as if life had been a promise unkept in spite of greatness hinted at. Seven times the team familiarly known to their faithful as "The Flock" or "Da Bums" had sallied forth to do battle in Series competition; and seven times had come back with tails clasped firmly between hindlegs. But every proud Brooklynite, worth his "hard-berled" egg, could be heard to utter, "Wait 'til next year."

Oppressed with the promises and the never-to-happens, each and every Brooklynite hoped he might once again get a chance to vent all the general rage and hate felt by the whole of Brooklyn from the days of Leo Durocher and before against the team that had beaten them five times—1941, 1947, 1949, 1952 and 1953—in the post-season classic: The New York Yankees.

Now it was 1955, another year and another chance. And the Dodgers, under Walter Alston, made the best of it, winning their first 10 games and 22 of their first 24. By the second week in May they were eight full games ahead of the second-place Giants. The rest of the pennant race was no race at all, but a cakewalk as the Dodgers won the pennant by 13 and ½ games, going away.

There was almost a tacit and tactical understanding that the Dodgers would once again face the Yankees in the World Series. Dodger fans, feeling a sense of mission like Robert the Bruce after coming up short seven times before, cheered in the name of "Oisk," "Skoonj," "Newk"—and hundreds of other players both past and present whose names escaped memory and pronunciation. They also cheered, as the regular season wound down, for the team they stood in permanent opposition to, hoping for a chance to erase the blot of humiliation that goes with being perpetual bridesmaids. Finally, after a pennant race worthy of the name, the Yankees edged out the Cleveland Indians for the American League title. And set up the hoped-for meeting in the fall classic.

But the first two games were a bitter pill for Dodger fans with the sugar coating inside instead of out. In the first game the Yankees hopped on Don Newcombe, the National League's leading pitcher, for six runs in five and two-thirds innings and held on for a 6-5 win despite Jackie Robinson's thrilling steal of home in the eighth inning. Game Two saw born-again Yankee pitcher Tommy Byrne drive in two runs and hold the Dodgers to five hits in a 4-2 win.

The two teams now moved locker room, stock and bat barrel

over to Ebbets Field for Game Three in what was beginning to look like a repeat of every year's nightmare. No team, according to baseball lore and its careful chroniclers, had ever come back after losing the first two games of a Series. This year looked to be no different, the Dodgers' performance almost closing on the road.

However, that old duenna named Ebbets Field, where dreams had been made and unmade in the past, was now about to witness the making of a new one. And a new star as well in the person of Johnny Podres, a young, flaxen-haired leftie who was to give himself and his teammates a birthday gift, a win.

With a change-up worthy of the name, Podres celebrated his 23rd birthday that 30th day of September by striking out six, walking two and giving up but seven hits in Brooklyn's 8-3 win. Other Dodgers shared in the festivities as well. One of those was Roy Campanella, who cut the cake for Brooklyn with a two-run homer in the first inning. Still another was Jackie Robinson, who not only loaded up the Dodgers' plate with a rendition of his famous will-he-or-won't-he hesitation routine off third in the second—forcing Yankee pitcher Bob Turley to walk Junior Gilliam on four pitches and forcing Robinson home in the bargain with the go-ahead run—but filled Brooklyn's plate to overflowing with an eighth-inning move that feinted Yankee outfielder Ellie Howard out of his socks, making Howard throw behind him as he took third on a two-base hit. But the icing on the cake was Podres' unexpected performance, made all the more a surprise party for the faithful by his mediocre 9-10 year; and one which might not have taken place at all had Don Newcombe not come up with a sore arm, disqualifying him from further mound appearances in the Series.

Suddenly manna fell from heaven as the Brooks won Games Four and Five with Duke Snider's bat a blasting cap, demolishing the Yankees with three homers and a double in two games. The curtain had come down on a three-game sweep at Ebbets Field, with scant time for refreshments and a stroll back to Yankee Stadium for Game Six with the Dodgers ahead, three games-to-two.

But winning in Yankee Stadium has always been akin to trying to take cheese from a set mousetrap. And winning the Series from the Yankees was even more difficult. The Dodgers had been ahead by the same margin in 1952, only to lose the last two games and the Series.

Tortured by such visions, Brooklyn fans could only watch in horror as the Yankees scored five runs off Karl Spooner in the first and waltzed to a 5-1 victory behind Whitey Ford, who was at his best, working the corners, low and outside, and holding the Brooks to four meaningless singles.

Now it was all down to Game Seven and to Johnny Podres, who, even while Dodger captain Pee Wee Reese was sitting, head down, in front of his locker after the devastating sixth game loss, came over to reassure the team leader. "Don't worry, Pee Wee, I'll shut them out tomorrow."

Indeed Alston had chosen Podres for the seventh game even before the sixth game had finished. The Dodgers had been here before, to the seventh and concluding game of the Series. And each time they had tracked it through the density and gotten it within their sights, only to hold their fire and lose the broad-antlered game. Now Alston gave the rifle to Podres with instructions not to hold his fire in pursuit of it.

Podres, warming up down the left-field line before the seventh game with third-string catcher Dixie Howell, was so cool he could

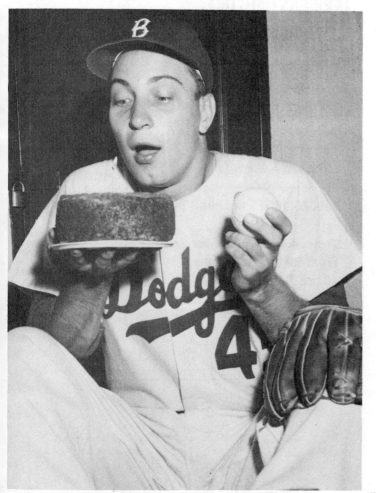

Johnny Podres, hero of the '55 Series, gets his 23rd birthday wish with a win in Game Three

no more be melted than ice welded. With that sensitivity an artist develops after a hundred or so recitals, he said to Howell, "Dixie, there's no way that line-up can beat me today."

Podres' swaggering braggadocio could be chalked up in part to his youth or even to the feeling that there were plenty of good pitches in his arm this afternoon. Or it might just have been the absence from the Yankees' line-up of their star performer Mickey Mantle, who had suffered a torn leg muscle.

The Dodgers, for their part, also had a healthy invalid list. For although Duke Snider, who had had to be removed from Game Six with a twisted knee, had returned to the line-up, Jackie Robinson had a strained Achilles' tendon in his right leg and was replaced with Don Hoak at third. Shuffling his line-up, Alston loaded the batting order with right-handed hitters, putting Don Zimmer in at second and moving switch-hitter Junior Gilliam to left in place of the left-handed hitting Sandy Amoros, all the better to counter the Yankees' starter, lefty Tommy Byrne.

Sandy Amoros flashes a winning smile.

For three innings the two left-handers gave one helluva performance, both holding their opponents scoreless. However, if the truth be told, like Orwell's pigs, while both were equal on the scoreboard, Byrne's performance was more equal as he held the Dodgers in check, giving up only two hard-hit balls, both outfield outs. Podres, however, had some of those moments that all Brooklyn rooters had come to dread. In the second he had given up a ground-rule double to Bill Skowron, who had been stranded on second when Podres retired Bob Cerv.

The third took all that Podres had. The Yankee half of the third started innocently enough, with Podres retiring Howard on a fly to Snider and then striking out his opposing number, Byrne, pulling the string on a change-up for a called third strike. Rizzuto then worked Podres for a two-out walk and moved to second on Billy Martin's single to right. Gil McDougald then hit a chopper down the third base line which Don Hoak would have had difficulty with had it ever gotten to him. But it never did, as Rizzuto, sliding into third, arms and legs all akimbo, was hit by the batted ball, retiring the Yankees—Dame Fortune credited with the assist.

Then, on a Campanella double and Gil Hodges single, the Dodgers finally broke through the Gardol Shield for a run in the fourth. Now Podres had something to work with. With the exception of one minor mux-ip in the fourth when Gilliam waived Snider off Berra's easy fly only to let it drop for a double, Podres kept the Yankees off-balance for the next two innings with a change of pace that was particularly striking. The Yankees showed Podres the consideration and forebearance his efforts demanded, waiving their weaponry in the general direction of his offerings. And little else.

The Dodgers added an insurance run of sorts in the top of the sixth on Reese's single, two infield sacrifices—one an error when Snider knocked the ball out of Skowron's glove—and Hodges' sacrifice fly. But even that was almost not enough. In the sixth, the Yankees and the fates were to test Podres' tensile strength and the weak hearts of Brooklynites everywhere.

During the Dodgers' quasi-rally in the top of the sixth, Alston, hungry for more runs, had inserted George "Shotgun" Shuba into the line-up as a pinch-hitter for the aforementioned Mr. Zimmer. Shuba grounded innocently to first, ending the inning. That innocuous substitution might have passed as unnoticed as it was unavailing had it not been for subsequent developments. For now,

having removed Zimmer from the game, Alston had to shift Gilliam back to his normal position, second, and here sent in his regular left fielder, Sandy Amoros. Before the afternoon was out, Amoros, and all Brooklyn, would remember his entry into the game.

With Amoros in left and Gilliam on second, the Yankees came to bat in their half of the sixth. Billy Martin, the first man up, worked Podres for a walk, only his second walk all day. The next man up, Gil McDougald, beat out a bunt down the third base line. Two men up, two men on and into the box stepped Yogi Berra, whose very presence seemed an accusation. This was the moment everyone had known was coming, the moment when Podres would be tested for his caving knee quotient.

Seeing the squat form of what looked like a genetic link to the Piltdown man move into the batter's box, the entire Brooklyn outfield moved over toward right, playing baseball's most danger-ous pull hitter to do his thing. Podres let fly with a pitch that was, in Podres' words, "High out over the plate, a fast ball that had something on it." Berra swung, not getting around on the pitch and sent it slicing out toward left field. On the pitching mound, Podres bent over and picked up the resin bag, saying to himself, "Well, there's one out." Then, turning around slowly he saw the ball continue to slice toward the line and saw Amoros racing after the ball. Podres thought to himself, "Jesus Christ, what's going on here?" What was going on here—or rather, out there—was that Amoros, pointed like a dog that sees a pheasant, had taken off after the ball at full tilt and, showing a profound contempt for body and wind, was racing to intersect the ball at the foul line in the left-field corner. Just as the ball began its descent, Amoros neared the dirt warning track at full speed, extending his right-handed glove for the ball and his left hand for balance against the onrushing railing. Again the Fates, which had taken a liking to Podres in the third, now turned upon him in envy and new admiration, enabling Amoros to make a catch the right-handed Gilliam could never have made.

As the cheers caught in the throats of those in Yankee Stadium, there to be replaced by screams of appreciation for Amoros' effort, the man who had now become litter bearer to the Yankees' hopes wheeled around, ball visible in his extended hand, in answer to Pee Wee Reese's frantic calls of "Give me the ball, give me the ball." Amoros threw it on the money, hitting Reese squarely in the chest with the ball. In less than one tick, Reese had turned around and fired the ball over to Hodges to catch McDougald, still backing and shifting at second, trying mightily to reverse his tracks, for the double play. One more out, Bauer on a grounder, and Podres and the Dodgers were out of the inning, thanks to Amoros, the Fates and Alston's substitution at the top of the inning.

The countdown was now on. Podres, going to his now-popping fastball, continued his mastery over the Yankees in the seventh and eighth innings, reducing their bats to matchwood. Now only three outs stood between Brooklyn and their cherished World Series flag. The first batter up, "Moose" Skowron, hit one back to Podres which caught in the webbing of his glove. Podres ran half-way with it to first, determining to throw Hodges "the glove with the ball in it" if he couldn't extricate it in time. Finally, he worked it out and retired Skowron. One out. The next man up was Bob Cerv, playing centerfield in place of the injured Mantle. Podres got him on a fly. Two out.

Now only Ellie Howard stood between Podres, the Dodgers and history. Trying to finish off Howard with a strikeout, Podres fired fast ball after fast ball at the Yankee catcher. Howard, protecting the plate, kept fouling off Podres' hard, rising fast balls. Campanella called for yet another. But Podres shook him off,

DODGERS CAPTURE 1ST WORLD SERIES; PODRES WINS, 2-0

He Beats Yanks Second Time as Team Takes Classic in 8th Try, 4 Games to 3

HODGES DRIVES IN 2 RUNS

Single in 4th and Sacrifice Fly in 6th Decide—Amoros Catch Thwarts Bombers

Sandy Amoros Gives Simple Explanation

NEW YORK, Oct. 4 (P) — The key catch of the 1955 World Series was made in the sixth inning when Sandy Amoros, fleet Brooklyn out-fielder, raced into the far left corner of Yankee Stadium to catch Yogi Berra's tricky high fly — and then doubled Gil McDougald at first, with Pee Wee Reese relaying the ball.

Two men were on and no-body out when the sensation-al catch and double play were made.

Amoros, a Cuban who talks little English, w a s asked afterwards if he thought he could catch the ball.

"I dunno," he said. "I just run like hell."

Game 7 October 4 at New York								
					Bkn.	000	101	000
					N.Y.	000	000	000

Brooklyn	Pos	AB	R	H	RBI	PO	A	E
Gilliam	lf-2b	4	0	1	0	2	0	0
Reese	ss	4	1	1	0	2	6	0
Snider	cf	3	0	0	0	2	0	0
Campanella	c	3	1	1	0	5	0	0
Furillo	rf	3	0	0	0	3	0	0
Hodges	1b	2	0	1	2	10	0	0
Hoak	3b	3	0	1	0	1	1	0
Zimmer	2b	2	0	0	0	2	2	0
a Shuba		1	0	0	0	0	0	0
Amoros	lf	0	0	0	0	2	1	0
Podres	p	4	0	0	0	0	1	0
Totals		29	2	5	2	27	11	0

Pitching	IP	H	R	ER	BB	SO
Brooklyn						
Podres (W)	9	8	0	0	2	4
New York						
Byrne (L)	5⅓	3	2	1	3	2
Grim	1⅔	1	0	0	1	1
Turley	2	1	0	0	1	1

New York	Pos	AB	R	H	RBI	PO	A	E
Rizzuto	ss	3	0	1	0	1	3	0
Martin	2b	3	0	1	0	1	6	0
McDougald	3b	4	0	3	0	1	1	0
Berra	c	4	0	1	0	4	1	0
Bauer	rf	4	0	0	0	1	0	0
Skowron	1b	4	0	1	0	11	1	1
Cerv	cf	4	0	0	0	5	0	0
Howard	lf	4	0	1	0	2	0	0
Byrne	p	2	0	0	0	0	2	0
Grim	p	0	0	0	0	1	0	0
b Mantle		1	0	0	0	0	0	0
Turley	p	0	0	0	0	0	0	0
Totals		33	0	8	0	27	14	1

a Grounded out for Zimmer in 6th.
b Popped out for Grim in 7th.

Doubles—Berra, Campanella, Skowron. Sacrifice Hits—Campanella, Snider. Sacrifice Fly—Hodges. Double Play—Amoros to Reese to Hodges. Wild Pitch—Grim. Left on Bases—Brooklyn 8, New York 8. Umpires—Honochick, Dascoli, Summers, Ballanfant, Flaherty, Donatelli. Attendance—62,465. Time of Game—2:44.

something only a fellow very sure of himself could get away with, and threw his bread-and-butter pitch, a change-up. Howard sent it, fittingly, to the man who had been a Dodger longest—and second-longest in the franchise's history—*Pee Wee Reese*, who engulfed the ball as a cat laps up cream and threw it somewhere in the direction of Gil Hodges. Hodges dug the ball out of the dirt; umpire Frank Dascoli went up with his right hand and "Next Year" arrived, all simultaneously.

Podres' 2-0, eight-hit win signaled the start of the most riotous scene this side of the storming of the Bastille as all of Brooklyn unleashed a pageant of nationalism for their borough. The un-graspable had happened, the Dodgers had given lie to the slander they couldn't win the World Series. And everywhere, from Atlantic Avenue to Prospect Park and back again, Brooklynites celebrated "with rockets red glare" the team that had prospected many times in search of a world's title and finally hit paydirt. This was that "Next Year" they had promised each other since they couldn't remember when.

Ironically, it would be the first and last World Series flag ever to fly in Brooklyn. Two years later Walter O'Malley packed that up with the team and moved them all to Los Angeles. But while it lasted, it was beautiful, and moved Pulitzer Prize-winning poetess Marianne Moore to write:

"Millennium, yes; pandemonium!"
Roy Campanella leaps high. Dodgerdom
crowned, had Johnny Podres on the mound.
Buzzie Bavasi and the Press gave ground;
the team slapped, mauled and asked the Yankees' match,
"How did you feel when Sandy Amoros made the catch?"

Amoros makes his famous catch.

**The winning style of Dodger Lefty
Johnny Podres**

22 Last Game of the '49 Season

New York Yankees vs. Boston Red Sox, October 2, 1949

IF THERE WAS ONE REGULAR-SEASON GAME WHERE EVERY-thing was reduced to its bare essentials, where both teams had to win on the final Sunday of the season because there was no Monday, no rent, no troubles, no use and no nothing, then it had to be the final game of the 1949 season between the New York Yankees and the Boston Red Sox. Return with us now, Dear Reader, to that thrilling one-game season of yesteryear when two teams met without even a blindfold, their final cigarettes dangling from their lips, to do battle for the pennant.

Even before the teams started their annual hegira to the south the professional pundits had installed the Red Sox as solid favorites to win the '49 American League pennant race. After all, or so the reasoning went, no team had won as many games in the previous three years than the BoSox. Coupled with that was the fact that the '48 Sox had led the Majors in runs scored and RBI's and despite not having a 20-game winner had finished in a flat-footed tie with the Cleveland Indians for the pennant. With an infield that had collectively driven in 399 runs and scored 415 runs and an outfield that had 322 runs and 289 RBI's, there was no reason to believe that anyone else was in their class.

Those same experts, trying mightily to regain their lost prestige after having picked Dewey to beat Truman in the fall election, tabbed the Yankees to finish third. At best. And when, only one week before opening day, Joe DiMaggio came up lame, calcium deposits collecting on his heel which had been operated on the previous winter causing him excruciating pain, their selection seemed justified.

The Yankees' new manager, Casey Stengel, registered nary a complaint with the pre-season pick, commenting in a voice which reminded the listener of a vehicle full of tin cans being dragged over gravel: "Third ain't so bad. I never finished third before . . ."

Indeed, Stengel's managerial record left something to be desired. In nine previous campaigns with the Brooklyn Dodgers and the Boston Braves-hyphen-Bees, the best he could show for his efforts were two fifth-place finishes. The sum of Stengel's career could be totaled up on both thumbs, one a quote and the other an award, both of the nature dubious. On managing the Dodgers, Stengel had said, "It was a tough business. Whenever I decided to release a guy, I always had his room searched for a gun. You couldn't take any chances with some of them birds." And while managing the Braves Stengel had been run down by an errant cab, prompting acerbic Boston writer David Egan to nominate the driver for the annual award given to "The Man Who Has Done Most for Boston." So much for his credentials.

Why then was this man with no managerial past and so little presence that John Drebinger described him in print as "A onetime hard-hitting outfielder, manager of both major and minor league clubs, sage, wit, raconteur . . . glib with a wisecrack," selected to run the most fabled team in all of baseball? It probably had something to do with his leading Oakland to the 1948 Pacific Coast League championship. Or, perhaps, it was his long friendship with the General Manager of the Yankees, George Weiss.

No matter the reason for his original selection, Casey would soon prove he belonged. His first conquest was of those members of the press who believed that few stories worth reading have ever been written that did not contain drink of some sort. Staying up and drinking themselves owl-eyed with the garrulous Casey, those of the fourth estate would find themselves getting cauliflower ears listening to strangely distributed words which only approximated the mother tongue and possessed the gutteral sound of an opera basso choking on a fishbone. Mixing his words—which were to become known as "Stengelese"—with his scotch, Casey would ramble on as if the morning paper had printed only one copy and he had it, getting up to only 1923 or so by the time rigor mortis set in on all.

But by far his most important victory was the one over the overwhelming odds which faced him. Not the odds posted by the winter "books" and those by the supposedly invincible Red Sox, but the odds against putting nine healthy men out on the field each and every day. For although Stengel, on the occasion of his appointment, had said, "I won't fail. I never had so many good ballplayers before," he would soon find he had less a roster of players, good or otherwise, than a serialized hospital chart filled with injured players.

Starting with DiMaggio's stabbing pain in his heel, Yogi Berra's facial lacerations, suffered when his car ran into an unforgiving palm tree during spring training, "King Kong" Keller's torn muscles in his side, Bob Porterfield's torn muscles in his arm and Snuffy Stirnweiss' severed nerve in his hand, Stengel's troops began to take on the look of the walking wounded. By the time the 1949 season finally limped through to its conclusion, the number of lame and halt on the Yankee roster approximated a World War II body count figure, with no less than 71 injuries present and accounted for. They didn't need a trainer, they needed a trip to Lourdes.

Unable to establish either a set roster nor a set pitching rotation, Stengel was reduced to moving his men around like pieces on a chessboard. Platooning his troops in a manner similar to that pioneered by his mentor, John McGraw, Stengel played Bobby Brown at third against right handers and Billy Johnson against lefties. Then he moved untried Jerry Coleman in at second to fill in for the injured Stirnweiss and Henrich in at first to fill the void left by the retirement of George McQuinn. With his players checking in and out of the line-up like weary salesmen into a motel, Stengel cajoled, manipulated and platooned his musical players. By the end of April, with no unconditional surrender to the undeniable facts facing him, Stengel had driven his team to ten wins in twelve games. And, taking another page from McGraw's book, Stengel had his Yankees off and winging in front of the pack.

The expected thunder from the north failed to materialize as the Red Sox got out of the gate slowly, winning but five of their first 11 games. By the end of April the Sox were four-and-a-half games back of the Yankees in the strange surroundings of sixth place, ahead of only the American League's two poor relations, the Browns and the Senators.

Both the Sox and the Yankees won 15 of their next 25 games as the Red Sox leap-frogged from sixth to second by Memorial Day, still 4½ back. However, the big news during the month of May was not the sudden reawakening of the BoSox on the field, but their off-the-field addition of outfielder Al Zarilla, brought over from the Red Sox's farm team, the St. Louis Browns, where he joined Brown expatriates Vern Stephens, Jack Kramer and Ellis Kinder in making the Red Sox a formidable team.

Then, one sunny morning in June, Joe DiMaggio, who had spent the previous two-plus months in seclusion anointing his aches and watching his bones mend, found that the pain he had experienced in something so simple as placing his heel on the ground had disappeared. Testing it first by taking batting practice and shagging fungos, he tried out the most famous heel since Achilles' by playing in an exhibition game against the Giants on June 27th. The next night, after 65 games on the disabled list, DiMaggio's name was penciled in on the Yankees' batting-order card for the first time that season.

Appropriately enough, the first three games DiMaggio played were against the Red Sox on their home turf, Fenway Park, which had always provided a safe haven for the Sox, in good times and bad. 1949 was to be no different, the Sox winning 61 of their 77 games in the Fens for a near-record .792 won-lost home percentage. Unfortunately for the Sox, three of those 16 losses came in DiMaggio's first three games back. And all directly attributable to DiMaggio. For all he did in the crucible of that three-game series was hit four homers, knock in nine runs and score five as he rewrote the legend of DiMaggio with his bat. And spark the Yankees to a three-game sweep.

The sweep extended the first-place Yankee lead to five-and-a-half games, eight-and-a-half over the Red Sox. And by July 4th, the traditional half-way point of the season, the pre-season favorites could be found only if the wrong end of the binoculars were used: Down in the small print that normally accompanies fifth place, 12 games off the pace.

But now Boston manager Joe McCarthy was whipping and driving, his team finally having found their bats—and other adjuncts of power. In a drive so late that its kind had theretofore been accounted for in train timetables only by an asterisk, July saw them win 18 of 30, August, 24 of 32. Suddenly, by September 1st, they were but two games back. And coming on under a full head of steam.

But the Yankees were hardly standing by with a case of rattling teeth. In fact, they weren't standing by at all. During that same Giant exhibition that saw DiMaggio make his reappearance to the playing ranks, Stengel had gone over to visit with the Giant first baseman, Johnny Mize. Casey, like a conman selling encyclopedias, had inquired first of Mize's health, asking the bulk who hovered over him, "How do you feel?" Mize had answered innocently, "Alright, but I'm not playing much." Stengel, now having his answer and his opening as well, replied, "If you were over here, you'd play." Mize looked down at the little man gnome standing next to him, his face that of a well-worn coin, and saying "Well make a deal," walked away.

And sure enough, even though the Red Sox were scouting Mize for the exact same purpose, on August 22nd, the Yankees sent the Giants $40,000 in coin for the services of Mize. Stengel now had his first baseman and could move Henrich back to the outfield.

But Mize was less to join the Yankees at first than join the ranks of their injured as six days later he pulled his right arm out of the socket. And, in the same game, Tommy Henrich, back in right field, collided with the wall and came out second best, suffering a traverse fracture of the second and third lumbar vertebrae.

While no casualty insurance company in the country would have then offered Casey a policy on his team, he continued to

Red Soxs' Big Guns: Ted Williams, Bobby Doerr, Dom DiMaggio and Vern Stephens

employ his extraterrestrial recuperative powers, together with more than a pinch of managerial chicanery, to keep them atop the American League. Barely.

On September 18th, with a two-and-a-half game lead in their pocket, the Yankees suffered what looked like the death blow to their pennant dreams: Joe DiMaggio came down with viral pneumonia.

The other shoe dropped eight days later, Monday, September 26th, when, in a hotly-contested game at Yankee Stadium, the Red Sox beat the Yankees 7-6 on a disputed squeeze play that scored Johnny Pesky with the winning run. The play not only gave the Red Sox the lead for the first time all season, it almost cost the Yankees the services of their utility outfielder, Cliff Mapes, who took exception to the call by plate umpire Will Grieve and cast aspersions not only on his parentage but on his integrity as well, asking him, "How much did you have on the game?" American League president Will Harridge, apparently taking pity on the plight of the Yankees, their bones stripped bare by pain and suffering enough, knew they could ill afford the loss of even a utility player and merely fined Mapes and ordered him to make a public apology.

With a toned-down Mapes and a bandaged-up Henrich back in the line-up, the Yankees fought back to tie the Red Sox on September 28th—thanks in no small part to Red Sox pitcher Mel Parnell's wild pitch in the ninth allowing the lowly Washington Senators to beat the Sox—and then fell behind again by a game two days later when they lost to Dick Fowler of the A's for the only time all year. Now there were but two days left in the season and the Red Sox were coming into Yankee Stadium needing only one win. The Yankees, who had long ago run out of safety bandages, had now run out of safety nets as well. For the first time in 45 years, two teams would decide the American League pennant in head-to-head combat, the last time, ironically, also being the Red Sox and the Yankees back in aught-four when the Sox won on Jack Chesbro's wild pitch.

Stengel, who had never been this close before, knew one thing for certain: His two starters would be Allie Reynolds and Vic Rashi. Beyond that nothing was sure. Yogi Berra was still wearying his teammates, protesting that his broken thumb prevented him from playing; Tommy Henrich was trussed up from head-to-foot, giving him the appearance of the runner-up in a King Tut look-alike contest; Joe DiMaggio was down 18 pounds from his bout with viral pneumonia, making him look like a refugee from a weight-reducing farm; and if the truth be known, the rest of the team wasn't feeling too well either.

The Yankees first chance to fill to their inside straight came on Saturday, October 1st, a day that had been designated "Joe DiMaggio Day" by a management grateful for all Joe D. had done for the Yankees, including retiring the mortgage on "The House that Ruth Built." DiMaggio, wearing a dissacted look that could be taken as evidence of his brittleness, acknowledged the cheers of the fans and the charitable donations of the local fat cats and well-wishers. Then he also acknowledged Joe McCarthy, the man who had led DiMaggio and the Yankees to the top of the American League heap with monotonous regularity, saying, "If we can't win the pennant, it's nice to know my old manager will win it."

And even before the fashionably late had found their seats it began to look as if McCarthy indeed might be better occupied having his only unadorned digit measured for his tenth pennant ring than bother with the game. For in the Red Sox first, as Reynolds struggled to find his pitching rhythm, the Red Sox combined two hits, one wild pitch and a sacrifice fly for a 1-0 lead.

In the third Reynolds found he had no rhythm at all and lost the plate in the process, giving up bases on balls to the first three men he faced and a bloop single, scoring the second Boston run.

Seeing his pennant hopes flash before his very eyes, Casey first assaulted the ears of those who sat near him, exceeding the spiel limit in number of four-letter words used in the course of a sentence, then set that face lined like the rind of a cantaloupe out toward the pitcher's mound. That was enough!, it seemed to be saying. Thrusting a pair of gnarled hands that looked as if they had been trampled on into his back pockets, he strode out to the mound, all the while staring at the ground. After what seemed like a marathon route to the mound, Stengel took the ball from Reynolds and motioned with his left hand for his ace reliever, Joe Page.

And so Page—he of the insolent manner, late nights and rising fast ball—ambled in from the bullpen to do battle with the Red Sox. In 59 previous outings Page had been the Yankees' stopper, winning 12 and saving another 27 games, although his average appearance lasted little longer than the wink of an eye, two innings per game. However, with everything riding on this one game, Stengel was ready, willing and able to throw Page into the fray early in an attempt to stem the tide. And Page was equally ready to go, as he told Casey, "A long way."

But Page's previous statistics were suddenly reduced to nothing more than mere window dressing as he walked the first two batters, the second on four straight balls, all high, to force in two more Boston runs. Raging at himself now, Page stomped off the mound momentarily. Finally, after getting control of both himself and his fast ball, he stepped back in. Pitching now with a conscious reserve force that had rarely evinced itself all season, he blew his rising fast ball by the next two batters to get out of the inning. And returned to the dugout down by four runs.

While the Red Sox, suffering from an almost terminal case of overconfidence, showed consideration and forebearance as they waved their weapons in the general direction of Page's rising fast ball from there on in, the Yankees got back in the game, scoring two in the bottom of the fourth and another two in the fifth. Suddenly the score stood at four apiece. Then, in the bottom of the eighth, the most unlikely Yankee of all, utility outfielder Johnny Lindell, caught one of reliever Joe Dobson's waist-high fast balls and drove it into the lower left-field stands for a home run and a come-from-behind 5-4 win for the Bronx Bombers.

As the Yankee clubhouse erupted in the mirth and clamor that can only accompany a next-day's coronation, and photographers shouted for Page and Lindell to get together for that proverbial "one more" shot, writer Garry Schumacher was heard above the din to say, "What I liked about this game is that the rogues won it." And outside the door to the clubhouse, where Mrs. DiMaggio sat demurely waiting for her famous son, Joe, to dress and join her, she refused an offer by the Yankees' traveling secretary to go upstairs where she "would be more comfortable," saying only, "Take me over to Dominic . . . he lose today."

But there would be a tomorrow; a final one-game season to decide it all.

Yankee and Dodger Stars light up the scoreboard.

YANKEES AND DODGERS WIN PENNANTS IN FINAL GAMES; 68,055 CHEER IN STADIUM

RED SOX DEFEATED

Raschi Pitches Yanks to American League Flag With 5-3 Triumph

BROOKLYN VICTOR BY 9-7

Conquers Phillies in 10th for National Loop Title—World Series Opens Wednesday

For that tomorrow Boston manager Joe McCarthy, believing that experience is the name everyone gives their mistakes and remembering all too well his ill-fated selection of Denny Galehouse a year ago to start the '48 Play-Off Game against the Indians, picked his ace right hander, Ellis Kinder. Kinder not only had 23 games in hand, but also had the hex sign on the Yankees, having beaten them four times during the season without a loss. For his part, Stengel came back with his 20-game winner, Vic Raschi, a pitcher of infinite non-charm and jest who, wearing a one-day's growth of stubble and a scowl, looked as hard-boild as a picnic egg. The one-game season would come down to a duel between two of the League's premier pitchers.

The game was to live up to its billing. And more. With both Kinder and Raschi throwing at the top of their games, the Yankees were to score on run in the first, a run that would hold up for seven-and-a-half innings. But nobody knew it then.

The run came after Phil Rizzuto, leading off for the Yankees in the first, drove a ball out into Yankee Stadium's sun field and Ted Williams, the Sox left fielder, momentarily lost it in the fierce noonday sun, playing a double into a triple. The second man up in the Yankees' first was "Old Reliable," Tommy Henrich. Henrich was not called "Old Reliable" for nothing, having won the very first game of the season for the Yankees with a homer and 20 of the first 40 Yankees' wins with the game-winning hit. But Kinder was different, Henrich knowing from past experience, "I can't hit Kinder nohow." Looking for a way, any way, to bring Rizzuto around, Henrich saw that the Sox were conceding the run, playing back on the right side of the infield. Figuring "that's how good I was against Kinder, about a ground ball's worth," Henrich choked up and hit what he called "a fourteen-hopper" to Doerr. And the Yankees had a 1-0 lead.

For the next six innings, as the fans sat nervous and tense on the collective edges of their seats and the pennant hung in the balance, the two pitchers threw goose-egg-after-goose-egg. Raschi, with a quick-breaking ball that today would be called a "slider," a fast-rising fast ball and a change-up curve of sorts his teammates called "Aunt Suzie," kept the Sox off balance and off the basepaths as well, giving up but two singles. The immense sail that had once driven the Sox had suddenly gone limp. For his part, Kinder reciprocated in kind.

But Kinder's kind was one run behind and in the eighth McCarthy sent up pinch-hitter Tom Wright to bat for him. Wright walked, but was immediately eradicated in a double play. And so, in the bottom of the eighth, McCarthy brought on Boston's other 20-game winner, Mel Parnell. The first man Parnell was to face was, as fate would have it, Tommy Henrich. And Henrich paid off yet another installment on his nickname by nicking Parnell for a home run and a 2-0 Yankee lead. After the next man up, Yogi

```
 BOSTON (A.)            NEW YORK (A.)
        ab.r.h.po.a.e.          ab.r.h po.a.e.
D. DiM'gio,cf 4 0 0 5 9 0  Rizzuto, ss. 4 1 2 1 7 0
Pesky, 3b...3 0 0 1 0 0  Henrich, 1b 3 1 1 10 0 0
Williams, lf.2 1 0 0 0 1  Berra, c....4 0 1 5 0 0
Stephens, ss.4 1 1 2 3 0  J. DiMa'gio,cf4 0 1 3 0 0
Doerr, 2b ..4 1 2 0 5 0  Woodling lf..0 0 0 0 0 0
Zarilla, rf ..4 0 1 1 0 0  Lindell, lf..2 0 1 1 0 0
Goodman, 1b.3 0 1 9 1 0  Bauer, lf-rf..0 1 0 0 0 0
Tebbetts, c..4 0 0 6 0 0  Johnson, 3b..4 1 2 0 0 0
Kinder, p...2 0 0 0 2 0  Coleman, 2b.4 0 1 3 1 0
aWright ....0 0 0 0 0 0  Mapes, rf-cf.3 1 0 3 0 0
Parnell, p..0 0 0 0 0 0  Raschi, p...3 0 0 1 0 0
Hughson, p..0 0 0 0 0 0
                          Total.....31 5 9 27 · 0
 Total....30 3 5 24 12 1
aWalked for Kinder in eighth.
Boston ........0 0 0  0 0 0  0 0 3—3
New York ......1 0 0  0 0 0  0 4 .—5
Runs batted in—Henrich 2, Coleman 3, Doerr 2.
Goodman.

Two-base hit—Coleman. Three-base hits—Riz-
zuto, J. DiMaggio, Doerr. Home run—Henrich.
Stolen bases—Goodman, Lindell. Double plays—
Coleman and Henrich; Rizzuto and Henrich; Doerr,
Stephens and Goodman. Left on bases—Boston 5,
New York 6. Bases on balls—Off Raschi 5,
Kinder 2, Hughson 1. Struck out—By Raschi 4,
Kinder 5. Hits—Off Kinder 6 in 7 innings,
Parnell 2 in 0 (pitched in 2 batters); Hughson
3 in 1. Wild pitch—Raschi. Passed ball—Berra.
Winner—Raschi (21-10). Loser—Kinder (23-6).
Umpires — Hubbard, Rommel, Berry, Summers,
Honochick and Hurley. Time of game—2:30. At-
tendance—68,055.
```

Berra, singled, McCarthy brought in Tex Hughson. DiMaggio, as weak as day-old ginger ale after his bout with viral pneumonia, hit into a double play. But the next three Yankees got on base against Hughson and then rookie second baseman Jerry Coleman, swinging late, brought all three home with a bloop fly to short right field that Al Zarilla just missed catching after a long and fruitless run.

With the score 5-0 against them and that tide in men's affairs now ebbing slowly out of them, along with everything else, the Red Sox came to at in their last at bat of the game. And of the season. Raschi, five runs to the good, now suffered a minor lapse, relaxing instead of bearing down and allowed the first two BoSox to get on base. One out later Bobby Doerr hit a long drive to center field. Where once DiMaggio would have flagged down such a drive with the style and grace that had made him famous, he now looked like he was swimming upstream, his moves lumbered with the baggage of a two-week convalescence and the loss of 18 pounds. The ball rolled by him for a triple as DiMaggio's legs knotted and he fell heavily, and suddenly the Sox were back in the game. DiMaggio, unable to argue with the undeniable, called time and, to the tumultuous roar of the understanding fans, removed himself from the line-up for the only time during his 13-year career.

Like the dying man who suddenly has some color come to his cheeks, the Red Sox were unwilling to concede. After Al Zarilla went down for the second out in the inning, first baseman Billy Goodman singled to drive in Doerr with the third run. Now, with the tying run at the plate in the person of catcher Birdie Tebbetts, both first baseman Henrich and catcher Berra neared the mound to offer some words of encouragement. But Raschi, hands on hips and tobacco chaw gripped tightly in his jaw, merely waved them off with a "Gimme the goddamn ball and get the hell out of here." And after giving Tibbetts a malevolent stare that would have melted butter, induced the Boston catcher to loft a high foul just behind first where Henrich waved off Coleman with an "I've got it! I've got it," and an extra "Get out of here!" And then took the foul for the third out. Game, set and pennant to the Yankees.

Fate had finally kissed the ugly toad and turned him into a pennant-winning manager on his third time around.

23 Roger Maris' 61st Home Run

New York Yankees vs. Boston Red Sox, October 1, 1961

IT HAS BEEN SAID THAT VICTORS ARE OFT UNDONE BY VIC-
tory. None more so than Roger Maris, a fiercely proud, private
man who flew into the public flame in 1961 and was badly burned
by the pretensions and trappings that went with daring to challenge
baseball's Gibraltar of Gibraltars, Babe Ruth's record of 60 home
runs in a season.

To fully understand the moment, and how to the victor go the
spoilsports, one must first understand Roger Maris—not an easy
task for anyone short of the owner of a psychiatrist's shingle—and
the place Ruth's record held in the hearts of the sports establishment.

First, Maris. Born in that heartland of isolationism, Fargo,
North Dakota, one week after Ruth had hit his last homer in
Yankee Stadium, Maris embodied all the virtues that made Mid-
westerners of Germanic stock famous: Rugged individualism, un-
swerving honesty and a stubbornness born of principle. Combined
with these three virtues were his guilessness and unsophistication,
two qualities that didn't play well East of the Hudson.

It was this straight-forward, no-bullshit approach that was to
cause baseball and its chroniclers to label Maris as a surly trouble-
maker throughout his career. And even before, if that were possible. For when his very team, the Cleveland Indians, tried to assign
their signee to their Class D Daytona Beach club, Maris steadfastly
refused to report, demanding that he be allowed to play in their
Class C Fargo-Morehead club, all the better to be near his friends
and his girl. When the Indians said "No," Maris wouldn't take
"No" for an answer and, digging in his heels like Balsaam's ass,
informed the Cleveland front office that no Fargo, no playee. The
Indians finally gave in and Maris repaid their trust in him by batting
.325 with nine homers and 80 RBI's.

Instead of advancing Maris up their minor league ladder, the
Indians braintrust wanted Maris to repeat his sojourn with the
Fargo-Morehead team his second season around. However, the
20-year-old Maris, who knew what was best for him and for his
employers, now demanded he be promoted. The Indians again
gave in to his demands, moving him up to its Class B team in
Keokuk, where Maris batted .315 with 32 home runs and began
proving his prowess in the outfield as well, leading the league in
putouts with 305.

His third year saw Maris again improve his standing in the
baseball community, moving up to Tulsa in the Class AA Texas
League. In his 25th game, Roger overthrew third and cost his team
a game. Tulsa manager Dutch Meyer, upset at his young right
fielder's throwing error, ordered a special post-game practice for
Maris, one in which he hit fungo-after-fungo in Maris' direction
which Maris was to fire to third. Finally, the enraged and embar-
rassed Maris had had enough and, tucking his glove, now worn
thin by its constant use, under his arm, marched off the field
despite the screams by Meyer to "Get back out there." But Maris,
fuming "I'll never take that abuse from anybody if I think it's
undeserved. . . . You've got to have enough pride to stand up for
yourself," walked directly to the clubhouse, not even passing

"Go." The very next day he was gone, demoted to Reading in the
Eastern League for some grafting on of skills. And manners.

Finishing out 1955 at Reading and 1956 at the Indians' top
farm club in Indianapolis, Maris was brought up by the Indians in
1957 as "Cleveland's Future Mickey Mantle." However, Maris
wasn't even "Cleveland's Future Roger Maris" in his rookie year—
one marked by the fracture of two ribs in an early-season injury
which caused him to miss 38 games—batting but .235 with just 14
home runs.

But even if Maris himself wasn't "working," something else
was, almost a wheel within a wheel. For even as Maris was
experiencing difficulties untracking himself, New York general
manager George Weiss, having seen Maris in Reading on one of
his many trips afield, had determined that Maris' sweet swing was
made for Yankee Stadium 's claustrophobic environs. And determined to have Maris in Yankee pinstripes.

However, Weiss knew that Cleveland general manager Frank
Lane would rather poke himself in the eye with a sharp pencil than
do business with the Yankees and Weiss. Now he had to resort to
some subterfuge to accomplish his purpose. And in this case
subterfuge was spelled K. C. A's.

Here an aside is in order to properly position both Weiss and
his dealings with the K. C. A's. The Kansas City A's were the lineal
descendants of the once-proud Philadelphia A's, bought by Chicago industrialist Arnold Johnson in 1955 and transferred
forthwith to Kansas City. Johnson had been introduced to the
pleasures of baseball by his business associate and fellow socialite
Dan Topping, who amongst other holdings owned the New York
Yankees. Topping, always anxious to help others who believed
business was merely the art of extracting money from others'
pockets without resorting to violence, recommended to Johnson
that he hire Parke Carroll, a man who had labored under Weiss for
the last 20 years in the backyards and vineyards of the Yankee
organization, as the A's new general manager; a suggestion Johnson wholeheartedly jumped at.

Weiss had the well-earned reputation around the League of
being the only living heart donor, his deals so stacked in his favor
that most general managers felt that dealing with Weiss was like
putting one's hand in a bag of snakes on the off-chance of pulling
out an eel. But while most GM's felt the necessity of having to
brush their teeth after talking to him on the phone, he now had one
in position who would listen to his former master's voice, Parke
Carroll. Soon their umblicius would be cemented into a bridge that
shuttled so many players between New York and Kansas City that
one-time Indian general manager Hank Greenberg was moved to
sarcastically comment, "It must be great to have your own farm
team in the same league."

Carroll, still knee-jerking himself off to Weiss' every wish,
immediately sent out feelers to Indians' GM Frank Lane on the
availability of Maris. What Carroll found was that Maris was
unhappy being platooned with Rocky Colavito and that Lane, like
Dickens' Barkis, was "willing." And so, on the final day of trading,

'58, Kansas City sent two players who had once been the property of the Yankees, Vic Power and Woodie Held, to the Indians for Maris. Maris would hit .247 with 19 homers the rest of 1958 and .273 with 16 more homers in '59 for the Athletics. But he was merely being held in storage until the wheel turned and the Yankees needed him.

That need came after the 1959 season, only the third time in 13 years the Yankees had failed to win the American League pennant. Losing had always galled Weiss, but finishing third was unthinkable. Hellbent on correcting what he saw as an injustice, Weiss now called in his debt to Carroll, a debt Carroll was only too happy to repay. Proving that man is the only animal that can be skinned twice. Weiss sent Carroll several players who, like prunes, had seen better days for Maris and two spearcarriers. Now he had his pull hitter.

But Maris also had something: His first misadventure with the New York press. For when the trade was announced, New York writers called Maris back at his home in Kansas City for his comments on the trade, fully expecting to hear how thrilled he was to come to New York. Instead, Maris, forthright to a fault, told them how much he liked it in Kansas City and then, with an assurance that bordered on effrontery, "I know that financially I can do much better in New York . . . therefore, I will go." That was to be the first salvo in the subtext that would color Maris' assault on Ruth's record two years hence.

1960 saw Maris his .283, 39 home runs, lead the League in RBI's and slugging average and win the coveted Most Valuable Player's Award. But it was also a year that saw his carefully-coded rules of privacy now in open conflict with what he perceived as the writers' prodding questions and he not only instinctively took a disliking to them, he showed it. The press responded in kind, Joe Trimble of the *Daily News* writing, "He doesn't take surly pills, he only acts that way."

Before the '61 season more than a few farsighted writers, as adept at reading baseball statistics as at reading the bottoms of their scotch-and-soda glasses, were already suggesting Maris had a good shot at breaking Babe Ruth's record. After all, they reasoned, wasn't his swing suitably tailored for Yankee Stadium's nearby right-field bleachers? And hadn't he just hit 39 homers in his first year there, one less than Mickey Mantle's League-leading total, thus becoming only the fifth man ever to hit that many in Yankee Stadium? And finally, or so their reasoning went, Maris' League-leading home run percentage, if extrapolated to accommodate the newly-expanded 162-game schedule, would mean at least 46 homers; and if 46, why not 60, or more? Bolstering their pre-season contention was Casey Stengel's off-season response to a reporter's inquiry about Maris' chances, the former Yankee manager answering, "Why shouldn't he break it? He's got more power than Stalin," the Stalin coming out, in pure Stengelese, "Stal-leen."

Ten games into the season, all the extrapolations, calibrations and predictions appeared to be just that as the mighty Maris still had not gotten homer one of '61. Then, in the eleventh game, on April 26th, the right fielder caught one of Paul Foytack's fastballs and drove it into Tiger Stadium's left-field stands for his first homer of the year. It was merely an hors d'ouvre of what was to become a steady diet of home runs.

Now the homers began to come in clusters, bunches, prides and schools as Maris added 11 more in May and, going into June, put together a string of six in six games. All of a sudden, with his fifteenth on June 4th off Chicago's Russ Kemmerer he stood only three games behind Ruth's pace of 1927 and almost even with

teammate Mickey Mantle, who had had seven early-season homers in the same time Maris had but one. And by June 9th, after Game Number 52, he had passed Mantle, 18 homers to 16, but still five games off Ruth's pace.

Maris, like June, now began bustin' out all over, driving a total of 15 out of assorted and sundry parks during the month. Nothing fancy, nothing spectacular, mind you, like Mantle's tapemeasure jobs, nor Ruth's never-to-be-found-again balls, but home runs nevertheless. And by July 1st he not only had a 28 to 27 lead over Mantle, but also a five-game bulge on Ruth. For the first time, sportswriters began to take note of Maris' pace, and believing there was more to Maris' swing that met the eye, began to eye Maris' efforts. When one of them approached Maris with the inevitable question, "Roger, do you think you can break Ruth's record?" Maris answered in his straight-forward manner, "How the fuck do I know?" Other writers, noting that Maris obviously wasn't running for prom king, began to view his behavior as surly; and worse, churlish.

As his home runs continued in rather generous potations, the 35th coming on July 15th in the Yankees' 86th game—a full 20

Maris Homers Day by Day

NR. NO.	GAME NO.	DATE	OPPOSING PITCHER AND CLUB.	WHERE MADE.
		APRIL		
1.	10	26	Foytack, Detroit (R)	Detroit
		MAY		
2.	16	3	Ramos, Minnesota (R)	Bloomington
3.	19	6	Grba, Los Angeles (R)	Los Angeles
4.	28	17	Burnside, Washington (L)	New York
5.	29	19	Perry, Cleveland (R)	Cleveland
6.	30	20	Bell, Cleveland (R)	Cleveland
7.	31	21	Estrada, Baltimore (R)	New York
8.	34	24	Conley, Boston (R)	New York
9.	37	28	McLish, Chicago (R)	New York
10.	39	30	Conley, Boston (R)	Boston
11.	39	30	Fornieles, Boston (R)	Boston
12.	40	31	Muffett, Boston (R)	Boston
		JUNE		
13.	42	2	McLish, Chicago (R)	Chicago
14.	43	3	Shaw, Chicago (R)	Chicago
15.	44	4	Kemmerer, Chicago (R)	Chicago
16.	47	6	Palmquist, Minnesota (R)	New York
17.	48	7	Ramos, Minnesota (R)	New York
18.	51	9	Herbert, Kansas City (R)	New York
19.	54	11	Grba, Los Angeles (R)	New York
20.	54	11	James, Los Angeles (R)	New York
21.	56	13	Perry, Cleveland (R)	Cleveland
22.	57	14	Bell, Cleveland (R)	Cleveland
23.	60	17	Mossi, Detroit (L)	Detroit
24.	61	18	Casale, Detroit (R)	Detroit
25.	62	19	Archer, Kansas City (R)	Kansas City
26.	63	20	Nuxhall, Kansas City (L)	Kansas City
27.	65	22	Bass, Kansas City (R)	Kansas City
		JULY		
28.	73	1	Sisler, Washington (R)	New York
29.	74	2	Burnside, Washington (L)	New York
30.	74	2	Klippstein, Washington (R)	New York
31.	76	4	Lary, Detroit (R)	New York
32.	77	5	Funk, Cleveland (R)	New York
33.	81	9	Monbouquette, Boston (R)	Boston
34.	83	13	Wynn, Chicago (R)	Chicago
35.	85	15	Herbert, Chicago (R)	Chicago
36.	91	21	Monbouquette, Boston (R)	Boston
37.	94	25	Baumann, Chicago (L)	New York
38.	94	25	Larsen, Chicago (R)	New York
39.	95	25	Kemmerer, Chicago (R)	New York
40.	95	25	Hacker, Chicago (R)	New York
		AUG.		
41.	105	4	Pascual, Minnesota (R)	New York
42.	113	11	Burnside, Washington (L)	Washington
43.	114	12	Donovan, Washington (R)	Washington
44.	115	13	Daniels, Washington (R)	Washington
45.	116	13	Kutyna, Washington (R)	Washington
46.	117	15	Pizarro, Chicago (L)	New York
47.	118	16	Pierce, Chicago (L)	New York
48.	118	16	Pierce, Chicago (L)	New York
49.	123	20	Perry, Cleveland (R)	Cleveland
50.	124	22	McBride, Los Angeles (R)	Los Angeles
51.	125	26	Walker, Kansas City (R)	Kansas City
		SEPT.		
52.	134	2	Lary, Detroit (R)	New York
53.	134	2	Aguirre, Detroit (L)	New York
54.	139	6	Cheney, Washington (R)	New York
55.	140	7	Stigman, Cleveland (L)	New York
56.	142	9	Grant, Cleveland (R)	New York
57.	150	16	Lary, Detroit (R)	Detroit
58.	151	17	Fox, Detroit (R)	Detroit
59.	154	20	Pappas, Baltimore (R)	Baltimore
60.	158	26	Fisher, Baltimore (R)	New York
		OCT.		
61.	162	1	Stallard, Boston (R)	New York

games ahead of Ruth's pace—the Maris watch began in earnest. But two days later something else happened that changed the face of the challenge: Ford Frick issued an official pronounciamento from his offices high atop Rockefeller Center that Maris would not be credited with a new home run record unless he broke Ruth's record in the first 154 games of this expanded 162-game season, thus effectively placing a protective shield around Ruth's 60 homers.

Enter Ruth, stage left, the second part of the story. Babe Ruth had been a special favorite of the sportswriters of his time, many of whom were still ambulatory, his boisterous well-met manner in the clubhouse and at the "speak" endearing to all who wrote about him. Throughout the years his legend had been propped up with reverential anecdotes, cut up and restitched according to the nostalgic preferences and requirements of chroniclers, all anxious to preserve, in their collective mind's-eye, that municipal monument that once was Babe Ruth. And his record.

Added to these reverential vestiges of the legend of Ruth was now Ford Frick's edict, prompted, it was suggested by a few writers, by the Babe's widow, Claire Ruth. Constantly in evidence, Mrs. Ruth had pressed the memories of her late husband between the pages of her mind, like the brittle, moldy roses of her youth, forever telling any and all connected with the establishment, "Records don't make the man, the man makes the records." And Frick, doing his best imitation of the three wise monkeys, had adopted Mrs. Ruth's stance, all the better to preserve the memory of the man he had served as ghostwriter in his beat days as a

sports writer for five-cent tracts.

Combined with the ghost of Ruth and with what writer Dick Young called an "asterisk"—or, as some detractors of Frick called it, an "ass-ter-kiss"—was Maris' challenge. Sure, others had challenged Ruth's record before, Jimmie Foxx and Hank Greenberg having climbed the mountain, only to fall short of the summit. But both Foxx and Greenberg had been superstars of the first magnitude. Mantle, they could accept; but Maris? With more than a taint of piety, the writers asked in print: How could a man with but a .258 lifetime average and 97 homers have the *chutzpah* to dare challenge the Great One's record?

Back when Ruth was Ruth and writers damned glad of it, he had hit home runs with such regularity and monotony that the sports pages had yawned at his feats, reporting them in matter-of-fact fashion. But with the coming of Foxx and Greenberg, newspapers had taken to charting the course of any aspirant's run at the record, running, almost as if it were a standard story, size nine, how many games "behind" or "ahead" of Ruth's pace the challenger was. However, because Maris' workmanship was far more arresting than his personality, they now added something else as well: searching interviews which transcended the four walls of the Stadium.

Suddenly, the privacy of Maris was compromised as writers flocked around him, doing everything but sticking pins into him to test his reactions. And as his home run total mounted, the beat reporters were joined by others, the bandwagon reporters, many of whom unearthed the same questions already asked of Maris but

Roger Maris' 61-

scarcely replanted them on a higher ground, more interested in hearing themselves ask the questions than hearing the answers.

As June turned into July and July into August, Maris' run at Ruth's record gathered momentum and burst on the nation's consciousness like an erupting volcano. Going into September, he had amassed 51 homers and was a full ten games ahead of Ruth's pace. Now the bandwagon reporters clambered all over him in the style of eater ants, taking pieces of his hide as well as interviews. Maris came to view the constant presence of writers as a survivor sport, even trench warfare. And reacted accordingly. When one writer asked, "If you were a pitcher, how would you pitch to yourself?" Maris bristled, thinking both question and questioner beneath his dignity, and retorted, "You nuts or something? Whaddya think I am?" To another, who asked him about the asterisk, he calmly responded, in his best imitation of Gertrude Stein, "A season is a season," and turned away. And to still another, who had asked "What would you rather do, break Babe Ruth's record or hit .300?" he answered the question with one of his own, "What would you rather do?" And when the reporter answered, "Hit .300," Maris, with a faint impersonal smile that seemed to cover something that passed for contempt, dismissed him with, "Well, it takes all kinds."

To the mounting pressures of the race against the asterisk and a press intent upon asking enough questions to require a forest of felled trees to reprint all of them each day came yet another byproduct of Maris' challenge to Ruth's record, controversy. Controversy has always been a part of baseball, being to the sport what garlic is to salad, an enlivening ingredient. Writers, frustrated by their inability to get through to Maris, turned to that old standby for their story line. They had researchers examine the official ball and compare it to similar products of the past, investigate the bats used, and assess the worth of the pitchers in both Ruth's and Maris' day. Now the questions pretended to be clinical, one writer asking Maris, "Roger, are you hitting more home runs because the ball is more lively?" Maris stared at his interrogator and, with an ugly scowl on his reddened face, snapped, "That's a lot of crap!" before staring at the suffocating crowd in front of his locker and mumbling, "The only time I'm by myself is when I'm in the John."

On the day of the 154th game—the last game in the gospel according to Frick to break Ruth's record—the stifling, choking magnifying glass of total coverage finally got to Maris. His face drawn, his eyes red, Maris came into the office of manager Ralph Houk and, shutting the door, fell into the couch opposite Houk's desk and burst into tears. "I can't handle this . . . I need help," he pleaded to Houk. Sobbing, he blurted out, "They keep asking the same questions . . . it never lets up." Houk, watching the decent man in front of him disintegrate, tried to offer some help, saying only, "It will . . . it will," less with conviction than with desire. Maris, convinced he was being sacrificed on the dual altars of tradition and journalism, shook his head. "Look at this," Maris said, baring his closely-cropped crewcut, "My goddam hair is coming out . . ." Houk now tried his avuncular best to offer some soothing advice, merely saying, "You gotta handle this all by yourself. Just get your hits and everything will take care of itself . . ."

It wasn't quite that simple. For even though Maris was to get his 59th home run that night as the Yankees clinched the pennant, the press, taking no note of Frick's fictitious asterisk, continued the hunt with Maris the prey.

With the second-highest total known to baseballkind, Maris now at least had one pressure off his shoulders, the asterisk. And with the pennant clinched, he could establish his own record at his own pace, a variation on Houk's advice. His next home run, his

Maris' Momentous Blast Wins Share of History

Yanks' Score

BOSTON (A.)	ab	r	h	rbi	NEW YORK (A.)	ab	r	h	rbi
Schilling, 2b	4	0	1	0	Richards'n, 2b	4	0	0	0
Geiger, cf	4	0	0	0	Kubek, ss	4	0	2	0
Yas'mski, lf	4	0	0	0	Maris, cf	4	1	1	1
Malzone, 3b	4	0	0	0	Berra, lf	2	0	0	0
Clinton, rf	4	0	0	0	Lopez, lf, rf	1	0	0	0
Runnels, 1b	3	0	0	0	Blanchard, rf, c	3	0	0	0
Gile, 1b	0	0	0	0	Howard, c	2	0	0	0
Nixon, c	3	0	2	0	Reed, lf	1	0	1	0
Green, ss	2	0	0	0	Skowron, 1b	2	0	0	0
Stallard, p	1	0	0	0	Hale, 1b	1	0	1	0
bJensen	1	0	0	0	Boyer, 3b	2	0	0	0
Nichols, p	0	0	0	0	Stafford, p	2	0	0	0
					Reniff, p	0	0	0	0
					aTresh	1	0	0	0
					Arroyo, p	0	0	0	0
Total	30	0	4	0	Total	29	1	5	1

aPopped up for Reniff in 7th; bPopped up for Stallard in 8th.

Boston	000 000 000—0
New York	000 100 00.—1

60th, came six nights later, on September 26th, against Baltimore's Jack Fisher. Now there was but one.

That one was to come on October 1st, in the Yankees' 162nd—and last—game. Batting in the first inning against Boston Red Sox rookie Tracy Stallard, Maris, fooled by a Stallard pitch on the outside of the plate, punched at the ball, flying out to Boston left fielder Carl Yastrzemski. As Maris stepped into the batter's box in the fourth, the crowd of 23,154, most of whom were clustered in the right-field stands, hoping against hope to catch Maris' 61st home run ball for which a $5,000 award had been offered, began to set up a chant.

Maris watched Stallard's first pitch go by high and outside for a ball. Stallard came right back with another pitch, this time low and inside, almost into the dirt, for ball two. Maris swished his bat a couple of times to delineate his strike area while Stallard studied the stitches on the ball closely. Now both men were ready. This time Stallard's pitch appeared to be right down the middle, waist high. Maris bat, almost with an instinct of its own, flashed in that rhymetic Maris swing and connected. Solidly. As the ball arced its way toward the right-field stand, some 300 feet away and about ten rows into the stands, an ear-splitting roar rent the air. But Maris was paying no attention to the roars, standing spellbound at the plate, almost using his magic bat as a vertebral cane, watching the flight of Number 61.

As the crowd roared and a 19-year-old mechanic from Staten Island named Sal Durante recovered the historic ball, Maris made his happy way around the basepaths. Returning to the dugout, he found the Yankee players forming a thou-shalt-not-pass phalanx across the entryway, forcing him back out onto the field for his encore in front of what were now clearly *his* appreciative fans. Three more times the Yankees repulsed his efforts to get into the dugout, each time pushing him back out to the field where he answered the fans' roars by doffing his cap and showing his golden blond crewcut.

Many summers have passed since 1961. Roger Maris is now gone. So, too, are Ford Frick and Mrs. Claire Ruth. And so is that notorious asterisk. For if you were to look at Roger Maris' record in *The Baseball Encyclopedia* you will find that Roger Maris is credited with 61 home runs with a sub-figure next to it, the number "1". And that is how it should be for the man who owns exclusive homesteading rights to the most home runs ever hit in a season, 61. No questions asked.

24 The Colossus of Rhodes

New York Giants vs. Cleveland Indians, 1st Game, 1954 World Series, September 29, 1954

NEXT TIME SOMEONE WHISPERS SOMETHING OUT OF THE side of their mouth that sounds like "Sure thing" and asks you to stake your rent money on same, feel free to quote liberally from the works of Damon Runyon, poet laureate of the misbegotten. Enunciated by Sky Masterson in *Guys and Dolls,* Runyon's thesis goes thusly: "When I was a young man about to go out into the world my father says to me a very valuable thing. . . . One of these days in your travels a guy is going to come to you and show you a nice brand-new deck of cards on which the seal is not yet broken. And this guy is going to offer to bet you that he can make the Jack of Spades jump out of the deck and squirt cider in your ear. But, son, do not bet this man, for as sure as you stand there you are going to wind up with an earful of cider."

Or, if you're hard pressed to remember Runyon, you can always invoke the name of the 1954 Cleveland Indians.

Draw up a chair and we'll tell you the story of the 1954 Cleveland Indians. And of cider in the ear. The '54 Indians were the winningest club in the history of the American League with a record 111 games won and a pitching staff that had just set the all-time ERA record. Going into the World Series that year against the New York Giants the Indians had been installed as the official 8-5 favorites undoubtedly by the same handicappers who had made Lady Godiva only a "show" bet in the great Coventry to-do. Unofficially, the odds were 2-1. And between friends you could find 13-5 money, most of it going abegging.

But even though their pitching staff had been both the mortar and the stuff of which teams are made—with Bob Lemon and Early Wynn leading the League in wins with 23 each, Mike Garcia leading in ERA and shutouts, minor divinities like Art Houtteman and Hal Newhouser contributing 15 and 7 wins respectively to the glowing totals and rookies Ray Narleski and Don Mossi throwing in 20 saves—the rest of the team bore the strictest investigation.

While a cut above the Immortal Casey's team—which possessed the dubious talents of Flynn, better known as a "lulu," and Blake, for purposes of rhyme called a "fake"—the Indians' cast of characters was not exactly Cooperstown-bound. With the notable exceptions of centerfielder Larry Doby, third baseman Al Rosen and catcher Jim Hegan, the remainder of the club was hardly a star-studded cast.

At the start of the season the Indians had fielded a team of the most well-unknown players in the whole of baseball. At short they featured George Strickland, he of the lifetime .230 batting average. At second, the steady but hardly sensational Roberto Avila. At first, Billy Glynn, who had all of five home runs in three seasons. In the outfield, a rotating repertory company of stock players to flank the exceptional Doby included the likes of Dave Philley, Wally Westlake, Al Smith and Dave Pope. And a group of Hall of Who? understudies who numbered amongst their number names like Sam Dente, Hal Naragon, Rudy Regalado, and Hank Majeski. In short, starting with short, the Indians were a mediocre team.

Proving that mediocrity is always at its best, Cleveland won 28

of its first 41 games and by June 1st was in first place by one game over the "Go-Go" White Sox with the five-time World's Champion Yankees three-and-a-half in arrearages. That was also the day that the Tribe made a trade which not only gave them a first baseman in Vic Wertz, but also would provide them with the power to power their way to the pennant.

Riding the strong arms of Lemon, Wynn, Garcia & Co., the Indians won 111 games, crossing the finish line a full eight games in front of the New York Yankees, who became only the fourth team in history to win 100 games without a pennant to show for their efforts.

However, those 111 wins were deceptive, some, like Orwell's animals, being more equal than others. For the American League of 1954 was, at best, an imbalanced League with the top three clubs winning the exact same number of games as the bottom five. And against the only other winning teams in the League, the Yanks and the ChiSox, the Indians had merely broken even in 44 games. Most of their record 111 wins had come at the expense of the little kids on the block, the have nots, whom they beat up with frightening regularity—Boston (20 wins), Washington (18 wins), Baltimore (19 wins) and Philadelphia (18 wins), for a total of 75 of their 111 wins.

Most of those 111 victories came as a result of Cleveland's magnificent mound staff, which not only established a new ERA mark of 2.78 but also led the League in complete games, least runs allowed and least bases on balls. The rest of the team's contributions, truth to tell, were adequate. At best. Parsing the offensive accomplishments, the Tribe was dead last in the League in doubles, triples and stolen bases, seventh in double plays turned, fourth in batting, third in least number of errors committed and second only in runs scored, runs-batted-in and slugging average. In fact, the only offensive category in which the Indians led the League was home runs, with 156, 30 fewer than the National League co-leader, the Giants.

The only members of the Tribe to show through offensively, suspended like a few pieces of fruit in a gelatin mold, were Larry Doby, who led the League in home runs and RBI's, Bobby Avila, who led the League in batting, and Al Rosen, who batted .300 despite an injured index finger. Other than that, the Indians finished the season at the plate as they had begun: Mediocre.

Still, the handicappers, not having done their homework nor held Cleveland up to the light for closer inspection, installed the Indians as a "sure thing" to beat the Giants. Never has baseball been plagued by so many false prophets; false prophets who now would get a dose of cider in the ear.

The party of the second part, the New York Giants, was as woefully undersold as the Indians overestimated. With their preseason trade for lefties Johnny Antonelli and Don Liddle giving form and flight to their pitching department—one which already housed the talents of righties Sal Maglie, Jim Hearn, Ruben Gomez and Hoyt Wilhelm—their infield anchored by Alvin Dark and their outfield roamed by such worthies as Monte Irvin and Don

Mueller, the Giants were already an excellent investment for those who liked to bet the 'dogs.

However, the cornerstone of the Giants was none of the above. It was a young centerfielder who mainlined excitement, his bat holding manna to distribute, his glove miracles to deliver: Willie Mays. Returning from two years of making sure the Nation could rest assured at night because his unit of the National Guard was awake, Mays had led the League in doubles, batting and slugging average and finished third in homers, hits and runs scored. But while his bat was thunderous, it was his lightning afield that was worth the price of admission. Playing with a little boy's delight, the man-child they called "The Say-Hey Kid" less ran than ranged the expansive caverns of the horseshoe-shaped Polo Grounds with a devil-Mays-care attitude, making a basket catch here, a magical cut-off there, and racing like the wind everywhere, making catches almost as if they could be produced by will—and Willie—alone.

Added to this more-than-credible collection of minor divinities and one superstar was one lesser nova, a left-handed pinch-hitter of extraordinary proportions, James Lamar Rhodes—known to all by the nickname oftimes attached to the surname Rhodes,

"Dusty." That year Rhodes had pinch-hit a total of 45 times, delivering in the pinch 15 times, many of those home runs. In fact, the Giants, as a team, had 10 pinch-hit homers, nine of which won ballgames. The first time Rhodes had come to the plate as a pinch-hitter for the right-handed hitting Monte Irvin, Brooklyn catcher Roy Campanella remarked, "Any club that's gotta pinch-hit for Irvin must be hurting." Rhodes showed just how much they were "hurting" by singling home the winning run.

Put them all together and you not only have the scene setting for a "cider-in-the-ear" tale, but the makings of another Damon Runyon line: "Between things human, it's mostly 6-5."

The first game of the 51st World Series was played on a day so soft you could almost wrap an infant in its folds. Fluffy, cumulus puffs of white hanging in the sky over the Polo Grounds contrasted with the brooding malevolence on the mound in the unrelieved dark looks of Giant starter Sal "The Barber" Maglie. But Maglie's dark countenance was soon approximated by the 52,000-plus partisans in the stands as the Indians scored two runs right off the bat in their half of the first, both on a Vic Wertz triple. Those who had the fine art of selling short down to a science might well have

Only the third time in Series history the two batting champions faced each other in the Series: Bobby Avila of Cleveland and Willie Mays of the Giants

been advised to leave their seats to get a few *shekels* down on the Indians.

But "The Barber's" razor-sharp control returned and soon things settled back to normal, as he held the Tribe to no hits, no balls-out-of-the-infield through the top of the third. Now it was the Giants' turn. Bunching three singles and a walk off Indian starter Bob Lemon, the "Jints" tied the score 2-2 in the bottom of the third, the big hit a two-run single by third baseman Hank Thompson.

And so the game progressed apace through seven with the Indians getting only four singles off Maglie and the Giants only three singles off Lemon. Now it was the Indians' eighth. And that magic moment that made this one of baseball's greatest games.

Maglie started the eighth off by walking Larry Doby. Then, after Al Rosen hit a single off shortstop Alvin Dark's hand and with the right-handed Vic Wertz—who had already had three hits in three at-bats off Maglie—coming up, manager Leo Durocher decided he'd seen enough and signaled for his left-handed reliever, Don Liddle. Liddle was to throw exactly one pitch, that one right in Vic Wertz's wheelhouse, to not coin a phrase.

Wertz caught the ball on the meat part of his bat and, getting his full trunk behind his swing, drove a heat-seeking missile which shot abruptly out of the unknown, destined for the deepest part of centerfield. Most outfielders wouldn't have been able to strike up even a waving acquaintance with the ball. But then again, most outfielders weren't Willie Mays, who normally covered enough ground to graze a dozen head of sheep. Now Mays took off, back to field, with the resounding crack of the bat, all the better to get a closer look at sheep and ball. The ball, not a parabolic blast which could twist slowly in the wind, there being none that day, cut through the air like a knife through the higher-priced spread, continuing on its unobstructed course—almost as if it had a date with a particular patch of grass far removed from the plate and was hurrying to get there. Commandeering his steed and heading that "somewhere," Mays continued one full furlong in front of the ball, running with resolution and almost running out of his uniform at the same time. He turned, in mid-stride, to look over his left shoulder for a nanosecond, as if he were trying to identify the object that was flying near him, and then turned his attentions back to his break-neck sprint. The ball now began its descent, ever so gently, heading for the green screen flanking the runway on the right-field side of center, 480 feet from where it had started. Just as it did, Mays flashed into sight, running as if he, and he alone, knew where it would finally come to earth. With his arms beautifully extended and his hands cupped, much like an end getting ready to catch a leading pass in the corner of the end zone, Mays caught up with ball and cradled it ever so gently, just a few feet shy of the screen.

The fans leaped off their seats, almost as if they suddenly had turned incandescent, bellowing in tribute to the great catch, one that would do justice to the memories of Sam Rice and Al Gionfriddo. But Mays was now about to see them and raise them one with a throw that would be the equal of his catch. While most balls are thrown with a downward tilt of the right shoulder north-north-west in direction, Mays now uncoiled like an ancient shot putter, his whole body swooping after the ball as he released rather than threw the missile, losing his hat and his balance in the process. And falling to the ground from his efforts.

The ball winged on its way, a mammoth throw equal to Wertz's mammoth hit, all the way to second baseman Davey Williams, who stood on the edge of the outfield grass at deep short. Larry Doby, the runner originally on second, had held up—his sixth

outfielder sense telling him against reason that Mays not only had a chance to catch the ball, but might well do so—forming a tight circle with Al Rosen, who had come down the line from first. Now Doby tagged up and moved to third while Rosen retreated to first.

Cleveland manager Al Lopez, having been denied the go-ahead runs on Mays' unbelievable catch—and throw—attempted to salvage something of the situation. Calling back the announced hitter, Dave Philley, Lopez inserted the right-handed hitting Hank Majeski in the line-up. Durocher, having lost what precious little hair he had left on Mays' catch, had had enough of Liddle and substituted right hander Marv Grissom. Lopez, in turn, called back Majeski and sent up left-handed Dale Mitchell to face Grissom.

"The Catch": Willie Mays outrunning Vic Wertz's gargantuan shot

Lopez's version of musical chairs worked, at least momentarily, as Mitchell worked Grissom for a walk to load the bases. But then Grissom got pinch-hitter Dave Pope on strikes and induced catcher Jim Hegan to fly out to Monte Irvin in left to strand the three little Indians as bereftly as Robinson Crusoe without a boat.

As Irvin raced in toward the dugout, still ahugging the ball, he turned to Mays and said, "Nice going, roomie. I didn't think you'd get to that one." Mays, with already enough great catches to last a lifetime, answered, in that casual tone of his, "I had that one all the way . . . had it all the way." Irvin could only stare and incredulously mumble, "Oh, you did, huh? Well, okay . . ."

Through the bottom of the eighth and into the ninth the two pitchers, Grissom for the Giants and Lemon for the Indians, kept their opponents' bats polite beyond indictment. Then came the tenth, and more drama.

Vic Wertz, leading off the Indians' top of the tenth, treated Grissom as he had Liddle and Maglie before him, smiting the ball on a wicked line into right-center. With the ball skipping on its merry out toward the wall—and inside-the-park home run territory—Mays intersected it, cutting it off after a particularly wicked low skip on a backhanded stab and holding Wertz to a long double. But the pinch-runner for Wertz was destined to perish on the basepaths as Grissom got Sam Dente, struck out pinch-hitter Billy Glynn and then escaped further damage when his opposite number, Lemon, lined out to Lockman at first.

Before the Giants took their turn in the bottom of the tenth, Mays stood in the on-deck circle studying the new Cleveland catcher, Mickey Grasso, who had just gone in to take over for Hegan. Noticing that Grasso bounced Lemon's last warm-up pitch to second on his throw, Mays asked Durocher if "it would be all right if I stole if I got on." Durocher, by now ready to do anything Mays wanted, simply said "Yeah" and went back to scratching his dandruff. Lemon got the first man up in the tenth, Don Mueller, who struck out but had to be tagged out by Grasso, who misplaced the ball on the third strike. That brought up Mays. Sure enough, Mays got on—on a walk—and promptly stole second.

Lopez now was reduced to having Lemon walk Hank Thompson intentionally to set up the possible inning-ending double-play; one made the more possible by the presence of Monte Irvin in the batter's box. But now Irvin was called back bu Durocher who, on a whim and a prayer, instructed "Dusty" Rhodes to "Get up there and hit one out."

Rhodes, whose intention upon entering the batter's box, had been "to take the first pitch," watched as Lemon hung a curveball. That did it. Rhodes, never one to keep an idea too long, changed his mind and less swung at the ball than merely browsed at it with his bat. The ball hung lazily in the air and then descended, no more than 257 feet, eight inches from home, Plop! into the first row of the shortest left-field bleachers in the Majors for a three-run homer, adjourning the proceedings *sine die*. As Rhodes rounded first, he chanced to look over at Lemon who now stood agonizing as if he had been struck in the heart by an Indian arrow. Grimacing, he angrily discharged his glove high in the air. All Rhodes could remember was "that Lemon's glove went farther than the ball." But the ball had gone far enough for three runs and a 5-2 Giant victory, the shortest home run and the longest out in World Series history conspiring to do in the Indians.

Now it was all downhill, the Indians collapsing like a balloon with the string removed as they stumbled through Games Two, Three and Four. The Series took on the look of an elementary, ailmentary and complimentary four-game blow-out as the Indians began to realize they indeed had had "Cider" squirted "in their

GIANTS WIN IN 10TH FROM INDIANS, 5-2, ON RHODES' HOMER

Pinch-Hitter Decides World Series Opener With 3-Run Wallop at Polo Grounds

LOPEZ NOTES MAYS'S CATCH

Says 'Longest Out, Shortest Home Run Beat Us'

New York, Sept. 29 (AP)—"The longest out and the shortest home run of the season beat us, that's all!"

Game 1 September 29 at New York

Cle.	200 000 000 0
N.Y.	002 000 000 3

Cleveland	Pos	AB	R	H	RBI	PO	A	E
Smith	lf	4	1	1	0	1	0	0
Avila	2b	5	1	1	0	2	3	0
Doby	cf	3	0	1	0	3	0	0
Rosen	3b	5	0	1	0	1	3	0
Wertz	1b	5	0	4	2	11	1	0
d Regalado		0	0	0	0	0	0	0
Grasso	c	0	0	0	0	1	0	0
Philley	rf	3	0	0	0	0	0	0
a Majeski		0	0	0	0	0	0	0
b Mitchell		0	0	0	0	0	0	0
Dente	ss	0	0	0	0	0	0	0
Strickland	ss	3	0	0	0	2	3	0
c Pope	rf	1	0	0	0	0	0	0
Hegan	c	4	0	0	0	6	1	0
e Glynn	1b	0	0	0	0	0	0	0
Lemon	p	4	0	0	0	1	1	0
Totals		38	2	8	2	*28	12	0

New York	Pos	AB	R	H	RBI	PO	A	E
Lockman	1b	5	1	1	0	9	0	0
Dark	ss	4	0	2	0	3	2	0
Mueller	rf	5	1	2	1	2	0	2
Mays	cf	3	1	0	0	2	0	0
Thompson	3b	3	1	1	1	3	3	0
Irvin	lf	3	0	0	0	5	0	1
f Rhodes		1	1	1	3	0	0	0
Williams	2b	4	0	0	0	1	1	0
Westrum	c	4	0	2	0	5	0	0
Maglie	p	3	0	0	0	0	2	0
Liddle	p	0	0	0	0	0	0	0
Grissom	p	1	0	0	0	0	0	0
Totals		36	5	9	5	30	8	3

Pitching	IP	H	R	ER	BB	SO
Cleveland
Lemon (L)	9⅓	9	5	5	5	6
New York
Maglie	**7	7	2	2	2	2
Liddle	⅓	0	0	0	0	0
Grissom (W)	2⅔	1	0	0	3	2

**Pitched to two batters in 8th.

* One out when winning run scored.
a Announced for Philley in 8th.
b Walked for Majeski in 8th.
c Struck out for Strickland in 8th.
d Ran for Wertz in 10th.
e Struck out for Hegan in 10th.
f Homered for Irvin in 10th.

Double—Wertz. Triple—Wertz. Home Run—Rhodes. Stolen Base—Mays. Sacrifice Hits—Dente, Irvin. Hit by Pitcher—Smith (by Maglie). Wild Pitch—Lemon. Left on Bases—Cleveland 13, New York 9. Umpires—Barlick(N), Berry(A), Conlan(N), Stevens(A), Warneke(N), Napp(A). Attendance—52,751. Time of Game—3:11.

ear."

Dick Young remembers when that realization finally dawned on the Indians. "There it was, the Giants ahead 3 games to 0, and Hank Greenberg, who was vice-president of the Indians then, no longer thinking about winning the World Series. All he wanted," wrote Young, who always seemed to be in the right place at the right time, "was to win Game 4 so that there would be Game 5, the Sunday game. There would be 80,000 people in the Wigwam for the Sunday game, and the Indians needed that." That was because, as Young pointed out, "The players' kitty gets most of the money from the first four games and it must go to five for the ball clubs to start making a profit." So saying, Young recalls Greenberg saying, "We're going to air-condition all our offices with the money from Game Five. That's why we have to win today . . . we just have to."

But Game Five and the air conditioning were more than wafting away from Greenberg's Indians, they were being blown away in a torrent of Giant runs as New York built up an early 7-0 lead over the shell-shocked Indians. Then the Tribe came back with three in the fifth and once again Greenberg could dream his dream of Game Five and air conditioning. But then Greenberg looked down at the Giants' bullpen and saw the Giants' ace left hander, Johnny Antonelli, warming up. Greenberg gasped, "He wouldn't! Leo wouldn't do that to us, would he?" Leo not only would, but did, bringing in Antonelli to shut the door on the Indians. And supply the last little bit of cider to what had once been the Indians' "sure thing."

25 Gabby Harnett's 1938 "Homer in the Gloamin'"

Chicago Cubs vs. Pittsburgh Pirates, September 28, 1938

THOSE FEW BASEBALL AFICIONADOS WHO REMEMBER "THE homer in the Gloamin'" can be entered on the head of a pin with more than enough room left over for a choir of angels. But suffice it to say that any old geezer around in 1938 who hasn't yet toppled over under the weight of his memories compares it to Bobby Thomson's "Shot Heard 'Round the World." And then some.

After all this time Gabby Hartnett's homer into what was then, in the argot of the time, called "The Gloamin'" grows strong and intoxicating in its memory, making it difficult to retain the essentials and reject the superficiality surrounding it. Even when reading the yellowing newsclips of the time. In order better to understand the moment one must start with the man: Charles Leo Hartnett, better known as "Gabby."

Hartnett reported to the Cubs on their Catalina Island spring training junket back in 1922 after only one year in the minors. This husky fireplug with the face of a fleshy Irish elf, a square torso and even squarer jaw that always seemed to be flapping in the slightest ocean wind was hardly the prototypical blushing, voiceless rookie, but one who spake in loud voices, giving all the veterans the benefit of his inexperience. It wasn't long before the baseball war correspondents who covered the Cubs were referring to this 21-year-old youngster whose very whisper caused bystanders to clap both hands to their ears as their only safeguard against going deaf as "That Gabby Guy." And of course, in the best tradition of newspapers, the phrase became condensed to "Gabby," gaining for Hartnett the classic appellation that superseded his own baptismal name.

But Hartnett's nickname obscured his skills, skills which extended far beyond his being the Cubs' unofficial noisemaker. For the 1922 Cubs had aboard one of the greatest pitchers of all time, Grover Cleveland Alexander. And Alex told manager Bill Killefer, himself a former batterymate of the great pitcher, that he liked the rookie and liked to pitch to him. Killefer also liked what he saw, telling those around him, "Boys, there's a catcher!" And when second-string catcher Tom Daly went down with an injury, the Cubs had their noisemaker-cum-catcher.

Hartnett soon proved Killefer correct, becoming one of the premier catchers in all of baseball. Possessing what many called "the best throwing arm in baseball," and one that was accurate as well, Hartnett threw a well-aimed shaft, lined like an arrow, to the base of his choice. Paul Richards, himself a catcher, remembered Hartnett's pre-game shows: "The fans used to come out early to watch infield practice just to watch Hartnett throw the ball around. He didn't go through infield practice as a matter of routine, he made a theatrical performance out of it because he knew the fans liked to see him pop that ball to second base and to third. And," marveled Richards, "you could hear it all over the park."

But Hartnett's showboating nearly wrote *finis* to his career in 1929 when, on the very first day of spring training, he tried to knock second baseman Rogers Hornsby off the bag with one of his bullet-like pegs. Suddenly the air was rent by the sounds of agony as the "pop" heard "all over the park" wasn't the "pop" of the ball but the awful-sounding "pop" of Hartnett's arm. The damage to his soupbone was such that it was feared for months thereafter he would never be able to throw again. However, the resilient Hartnett was able to return by the end of the season, catching one game and pinch-hitting in 27 more, including three games in that year's World Series.

1929 was to serve as a pivotal year for both Hartnett and the Cubs, the year in which both started streaks. Of sorts. For Hartnett, coming off his disabling injury of '29, 1930 was to see him start a string of eight straight seasons in which he caught 100 or more games, averaging 119 games behind the plate and .308 at the plate. And the Cubs, who had won their first pennant in 11 years in '29, were to begin a strange triennial custom—call it streak, if you will—of hopscotching to pennants every three years, winning the National League pennant in 1932 and 1935 behind their take-charge "holler" guy, "Gabby" Hartnett.

All of which brings us to 1938, the year Hartnett's endurance streak was to come to an end and the year the Cubs were "due" to win the pennant. And not incidentally, lest you think we've lost the thread of this story, the year of "The Homer in the Gloamin'."

The Cubs went into the 1938 season with high hopes. Their '37 edition had led the League in hitting—with Hartnett leading the team with .354—in slugging and in fielding and had even led the League itself before first baseman Ripper Collins went down with a broken ankle. But even with a healthy Collins returning in '38, the second-place Cubs still needed help, badly, in the pitching department if they were to make a run at the pennant. For their pitching staff had been one of inconsistency, underachievement, and disappointment, posting the third-worst ERA in the League and issuing the second-most bases on balls.

But even if the Cubs had an Achilles heel, they sure didn't have an Achilles wallet, by gum. Their president, Phil Wrigley, took care of that, throwing around Depression dollars whenever and wherever it could help his team—including, but hardly limited to, the disbursement of $135,000 for Chuck Klein in '34. Now he began to estimate the pitching talent throughout the League with the eye of a recruiting sergeant to see what was available to the Cubbies. And what to his wondering eye should appear but the form of that original baseball tintype, Jay Hanna "Dizzy" Dean of the Cardinals. Dean, who had had his toe splintered by a line drive off the bat of Earl Averill in the '37 All-Star Game had come back too soon after the injury, altered his pitching style and hurt his salary arm. Now St. Louis general manager Branch Rickey was shopping his damaged piece of merchandise around the League. Even though Dean's condition was well-known, Wrigley was willing, to the tune of $185,000 and three players, to give Dean a place on the Cubs roster, figuring him to be a spot pitcher. Plus one helluva gate attraction.

As the '38 campaign got off to its start, the Cubs got off to their usual stumbling start out of the gate. The surprise team was the Pittsburgh Pirates, who had ended the '37 season by winning their

104

last ten in a row and now picked up right where they had left off, moving smartly to the front of the pack and challenging for the lead. The Pirates were of suspect pennant pedigree, a team made up of the two Waner Brothers, Arky Vaughan, a rookie named Johnny Rizzo, a pitcher with the quaint name of Mace Brown and a cast of characters that could have escaped detection in a police line-up as ballplayers; in short, the whole was greater than the sum of its parts. Yet, on July 12th they charged into the lead and threatened to pull away.

By mid-July the Cubs still hadn't gotten untracked, their record only 45 and 36, and worse, they were falling behind the Pirates and the onrushing Giants with each and every game. In an attempt to make something—anything—happen, Wrigley changed his managers in mid-stream, a personnel move that had worked for the Cubs six years before when Charlie Grimm had replaced Rogers Hornsby 97 games into the season and rallied the Cubbies to the pennant. Now the same Grimm was replaced, 16 games earlier in the season, by none other than their most voluble player, "Gabby" Hartnett.

But Hartnett or no, the Pirates kept everlastingly at it, heading into September with a full seven-game lead over the Cubs. In fact, Pirate management was so confident of victory they commissioned the construction of a new left-field press box to accommodate the expected overflow of newspapermen at the forthcoming World Series.

Then, heading down the home stretch, the Cubs, awhooping and ahollering, began their patented cavalry stampede, one reminiscent of their charge in '35 when they won 21 in a row to capture the flag. Suddenly the Pirates had forged a small lead out of a somewhat more substantial one and by September 15th had watched it dwindle to just three-and-a-half games. That was to be the day the Cubs started their final kick to the wire in a rush that gave new meaning to the term "pennant drive."

The Cubs that day started their final swing through the East, one that would see them face Boston, New York, Brooklyn, and Philadelphia, respectively but not respectfully. And while three of the four abovementioned nines were then mired in the second division, any manager worth his line-up card could tell you that the apparent gifts of charity are oft encumbered with strings. The strings in this case were that the Cubs had to make up several earlier postponements, giving them back-to-back-to-back double-headers in almost every city.

The *tour de chance* started off on the wrong foot, a loss to Casey Stengel's Braves, then going under the alias "Bees," almost as if they were trying to escape the process server by changing their name. The next day the outlook for the Windy City nine was little better, the score standing 2-0, Bees, with but a few innings left to play when Hartnett came to bat with the bases loaded. As John Carmichael of the Chicago *Sun-Times* remembered it, "He hits a screamer into the stands that's foul by about ten feet. But Tiny Parker, the umpire, hollers, 'Fair Ball!' and all of us in the press box swoon and darn near fall out. Casey Stengel yowls bloody murder with the usual results. So we win that one."

Now it was on to the Polo Grounds where the Cubs swept a double-header from New York, effectively eliminating the third-place Giants from the race. And then over to Brooklyn, where, much to the Cubbies surprise, they lose the first game of the Sunday double-header, 4-3. In the second game, with darkness beginning to fall between raindrops, the Cubs take a two-run lead into the bottom of the fifth when outfielder Fred Sington hits a two-run homer to tie it up. But the Dodgers, as they say in Brooklyn, "ain't trew yet," and load the bases with one out in what has to be their last time at bat, darkness now shrouding the field. Brooklyn manager Burleigh Grimes sent up Gilly Campbell as a pinch-hitter. For the rest of the story we defer here to the eyewitness account of Mr. Carmichael: "What a belt he smacks! The ball goes a mile over Billy Herman's head toward right center but Billy jumps a mile into the air, spears the dang thing and it's a double play to save us our tie."

With a game scheduled the next day in Philadelphia, the Cubs couldn't stick around and play off the tie game. However, they did have an open date at the end of their Eastern swing, and now Brooklyn president Larry MacPhail and the Cubs themselves—knowing the only way they could ever hope to catch the Pirates was by winning and the Dodgers figured to be easy pickings—wanted to re-schedule the game. However, a make-up game at this critical stage of the season presented problems for Hartnett. The Cubs were to come off the road trip with three games at home against the Cards and then the Pirates and Hartnett knew "we had to win all three games in the series with Pittsburgh if we were to win the pennant." Coupled with that all-or-nothing philosophy was his nothing-or-all pitching staff, a staff that was now essentially two men, Bill Lee and Clay Bryant, the rest of the Cubs' staff having failed to stand and deliver—Larry French suffering an off-year, Charlie Root getting long in the tooth, and Dizzy Dean nursing a sore arm. Hartnett, believing the prospects for beating the Dodgers thick with possibilities but his pitching staff thin, declined the make-up game. All the better to face the Pirates with some semblance of a staff.

Now it was on to Philadelphia and the woebegone Phillies, a team of lambs in lambs' clothing. But the rains, which had forced the curtailment of the game in Brooklyn, were now on an unlimited run, causing a cancellation of the planned festivities in Philadelphia for three full days. So the Cubs sat around; so too did the Pirates, unable to play the Dodgers just two hours north. Finally the rains ceased and the Cubs got in a double-header on Thursday, Lee winning his 20th game with his fourth straight shutout in the opener and Bryant winning the second. But Pittsburgh also beat the Dodgers to retain their three-and-a-half game lead.

Gabby Hartnett practices his swing that will bring joy and victory to the Cubs.

The second twin bill against the Phillies on Friday, September 23rd, was, to quote John Carmichael, "a dilly. We're behind in both of them in the ninth inning. On each occasion Ripper Collins comes up to the plate with bases full. And on each occasion he wallops a tremendous shot to center field where Gib Brack circles under the ball, winding up with each fly bouncing off the back of his neck. So we win those two, thanks to Mr. Brack!" Even while Mr. Brack was being a pain-in-the-neck the second time around the Shibe Park scoreboard attendant was posting the score that showed that Cincinnati had beaten the Pirates. The Cubs were just two games back. And closing.

The Cubs returned home to the friendly confines of Wrigley Field to play a three-game set with the Cardinals. They beat the Cards 9-3 in the first game, but the Pirates won as well, leaving the margin at two games. Sunday it was the same thing, both Chicago and Pittsburgh winning. And on Monday, with the Pirates in the stands, the Cubs won the third game of the series behind Bill Lee, 6-3. Now, on the eve of the big head-to-head confrontation, the Pirates' margin of safety had been cut to but one-and-a-half games.

Hartnett, without a pitching staff to talk of—or to—now took a calculated risk. Going that "somewhere" whither his lucky mount might convey him, he selected Dizzy Dean to start the first game of the Pittsburgh series even though Dean had not pitched since September 13th nor started since August 13th. Hartnett felt that anything he got from Dean was like getting money from home without writing.

Dean, who no longer possessed the blazing fastball that had made him famous, now was reduced to pitching with his head and heart rather than his arm. And for eight innings that was more than enough as he threw what could best be described as a slow ball past bewildered Pirate batters. Going into the ninth two runs to the good, Dean was tiring, almost imperceptibly, but tiring nevertheless. One of those who noticed was catcher-manager Hartnett who, from his vantage point only 60′ 6″ away, could see that the once-"Great One" had nothing on the ball but his hand. Determining to take Dean out the minute he got into trouble, Hartnett called down to the bullpen to have his ace, Bill Lee, ready just in case.

That "in case" came with two outs in the top of the ninth when, after Dean had hit Pirate shortstop Arky Vaughan, third baseman "Jeep" Handley doubled to the wall in left center to put the tying runs on second and third. It was then that Hartnett resorted to Plan B, waving in Lee from the bullpen to pitch to catcher Al Todd. It appeared as if Hartnett had made the right decision when Lee fired a fastball past Todd for strike one and followed up with an off-speed pitch that caught Todd off-stride and forced him to foul it off. With a count of 0-and-2, Lee now endeavored to waste a pitch. But the waste pitch was "as wild a pitch as I've ever seen," recalled Hartnett and suddenly the Pirates were only one run behind with the tying run on third. But Lee, hitching up his belt and catching his breath at the same time, came back with another fast one, striking Todd out and ending the game with the Cubs the winners, 2-1. The Cubs were now only a half-game out of first.

Which brings us to what arguably can be called the most exciting game of the decade. In front of an announced crowd of 34,465—plus millions more who claimed ever after to have been in attendance—the Cubs jumped off to a one-run lead in the second on a hit and two Pirate errors. With Bryant, the number two man in Hartnett's one-two rotation, pitching masterfully, the lead held up into the Pirates' half of the sixth. But then Bryant, who had given up only one hit over the first five innings, gave up a home run to outfielder Johnny Rizzo, walked two and gave up two more hits as the Pirates scored thrice for a 3-1 lead. The Cubs came right back in their half of the sixth on doubles by Hartnett and Collins and a bunt single by shortstop Billy Jurges to tie it up at three apiece.

In the seventh the Pirates once again threatened, getting two singles off reliever Vance Page. Then, with men on first and third, one out, and Rizzo at bat, Page committed an obvious balk. Here we again call on that master old storyteller John Carmichael, who years later recalled the incident as if it had only just happened: "Umpire Dolly Stark starts to call it. But before he can even raise his hand, Page fires the ball to the plate. He never takes time to aim. He just throws. It whizzes past Rizzo's forehead and what doth that helpful citizen do but take a cut at the ball. Zing! In faster time than I can tell it, the ball flashes down to Herman and it's whipped to Jurges and then to Collins for a double play. The Cubs toss aside their gloves and everyone is in the dugout before anyone notices that Stark is frozen in that gesture of calling the balk. There's no one left on the field for him to call it on, so he puts his hand back in his pocket." The Pirates, of course, came racing out of their dugout *en masse* to argue the non-call, but succeeded only in using up time—time that would later become important as even in the seventh inning lights were beginning to spangle the city like popcorn bursting on the skillet and darkness was beginning to crowd perceptibly in upon the daylight.

However, the Cubs were unable to dodge the bullet in the eighth. Page picked up right where he had left off, allowing the first two Pirate batters in the inning to reach base. Hartnett, having had enough, now went to his bullpen, calling in Larry French. But French couldn't close the door, pitching to just one batter, Heinie Manush, who singled, driving in the go-ahead run. Hartnett again went to the bullpen, this time bringing in his stopper, Big Bill Lee, who was coming in for his second spot appearance in two days.

Gabby Hartnett: Baseball's most voluble player

Hartnett's Homer With 2 Out in 9th Beats Pirates

CUBS HALT PIRATES FOR 9TH IN ROW, 6-5

34,465 See Chicago Supplant Losers in League Lead With a Half-Game Advantage

---

ROOT WINS IN RELIEF ROLE

Lazzeri's Pinch Double Helps Tie Score in Eighth—Rizzo Connects for Corsairs

The box score:

PITTSBURGH (N.)

	ab.	r.	h.	po.	a.	e.
L. Waner, rf.	4	0	2	1	0	0
P. Waner, rf.	5	0	2	3	1	0
Rizzo, lf.	4	1	1	1	0	0
Vaughan, ss.	2	2	1	2	5	1
Suhr, 1b.	3	2	1	6	0	0
Young, 2b.	2	0	0	1	1	0
aManush	1	0	1	0	0	0
Thevenow, 2b.	0	0	0	1	3	0
Handley, 3b.	4	0	2	2	1	1
Todd, c.	4	0	0	2	1	1
Klinger, p.	4	0	0	0	3	0
Swift, p.	0	0	0	0	0	0
Brown, p.	0	0	0	0	0	0
Total	35	5	10	24	18	4

CHICAGO (N.)

	ab.	r.	h.	po.	a.	e.
Hack, 3b.	3	0	0	3	1	0
Herman, 2b.	5	0	3	3	3	0
Demaree, lf.	4	0	0	3	0	0
Cavarretta, rf.	5	0	1	0	0	0
Reynolds, cf.	5	0	1	5	0	0
Collins, 1b.	4	1	3	8	0	0
Jurges, ss.	4	2	1	1	1	0
Hartnett, c.	4	2	2	4	1	0
Bryant, p.	2	0	1	0	0	0
Russell, p.	0	0	0	0	0	0
bO'Dea	1	0	0	0	0	0
Page, p.	0	0	0	0	0	0
French, p.	0	0	0	0	0	0
Lee, p.	0	0	0	0	1	0
cLazzeri	1	0	1	0	0	0
dMarty	0	0	0	0	0	0
Root, p.	0	0	0	0	0	0
Total	38	6	12	27	9	0

*Two out when winning run scored.
aBatted for Young in eighth.
bBatted for Russell in sixth.
cBatted for Lee in eighth.
dRan for Lazzeri in eighth

Pittsburgh .... 0 0 0 0 0 3 0 2 0—5
Chicago .... 0 1 0 0 0 2 0 2 1—6

Runs batted in—Manush, Rizzo, Handley 3, Hack, Herman, Collins, Hartnett, Lazzeri. Two-base hits—L. Waner, Hartnett, Collins, Lazzeri. Home runs—Rizzo, Hartnett. Double plays—Thevenow and Suhr; Jurges, Herman and Collins; Hack, Herman and Collins; Lee, Jurges and Collins 10. Bases on balls—Off Klinger 2, Swift 2, Bryant 5, Page 1. Struck out—By Klinger 8, Bryant 1, Page 1. Hits—Off Klinger 8 in 7 innings (none out in eighth.; Swift 3 in 1-3; Brown 1 in 1 1-3; Bryant 4 in 5 2-3; Russell 0 in 1-3; Page 3 in 1 (none out in eighth); French 1 in 0 (pitched to one batter in eighth); Lee 1 in 1; Root 1 in 1. Wild pitch—Lee. Passed ball—Todd. Winning pitcher—Root. Losing pitcher—Brown. Umpires—Barr, Stark, Goetz and Campbell. Time of game—2:37.

Lee was greeted by "Jeep" Handley's single, driving in Pittsburgh's second run in the inning. Lee finally restored order by getting Al Todd to ground to Jurges who threw to Hartnett to nail Manush at the plate and then forcing Pirate relief pitcher Bob Klinger to hit into a double play. But the damage had been done. Pittsburgh now led 5-3.

However, the Cubs were far from through. As the shades began to enfold the field, the form of Ripper Collins, or something that passed for him, came to bat and ripped a single into right field. Jurges then walked and Tony Lazzeri, the former Yankee great, slashed a pinch double to right, scoring Collins with Chicago's fourth run and moving Jurges around to third. Stan Hack was then intentionally walked to load the bases and set up a possible double play. But Billy Herman, taking no notice of the strategy, drove a single to right, scoring Jurges with the tying run. However, Joe Marty, running for Lazzeri, was cut down at the plate on a perfect throw from Paul Waner to Todd. Pirate manager Pie Traynor now brought in the National League's ace fireman, Mace Brown, a mean-looking right hander whose hard stare was the equal of his fastball. Brown lived up to his reputation by inducing Cub outfielder Frank Demaree to hit into a double play and close out the Cubs and the inning.

By now the last fringes of daylight had been pushed aside by the coming darkness. The umpires, convinced that without legal interference the sunset would continue unchecked, allowed the game to go on for one more inning. Unbeknownst to all, that was all it would go.

With Charlie Root on the mound for the Cubs, the Pirates went down quietly in the top of the ninth, looking like men waving broomsticks at his offerings in the gathering gloom. Now it was the Cubbies' turn. And Gabby Hartnett's turn to take on a stellar brightness.

The Pirates took their places in the field not interested in the possibility of defeat. They were now playing for a tie; nothing more, nothing less. And with Brown throwing an almost invisible ball out there, it looked like a tie was what they would get for their efforts, especially when the first two Cubs in the bottom of the ninth went down with much ado. That brought up none other than the hero in our piece: Charles Leo "Gabby" Hartnett.

Hartnett, facing a sudden extinction not only of his lights but those of the Cubs as well, knew that a tie was damnably serious business. For if the game were called now, it would necessitate a double header tomorrow and the Cubs' overtaxed and threadbare pitching staff was in no condition to play another two-fer. Normally, the talented need not believe in miracles. But Hartnett was. And now did.

Barely visible in the tubular light of evening, Hartnett took his place in the batter's box and looked out somewhere in the direction of Brown. Brown, with a profound contempt for Hartnett's reputation, came in with his hard, fast one. Hartnett swung. And missed. Strike one. Returning the ball almost as if it were attached to a rubber band, Brown came back with the same pitch, same spot, so sure now that Hartnett couldn't find it with a geiger counter. This time Hartnett swung and got a piece of it. But that was all. Strike two.

One of the copybook maxims in the book of baseball is that a pitcher with an 0-and-2 count on the batter wastes a pitch, all the better to make the batter chase a bad ball. But Brown, obviously without enough light to read the book, eschewed all pitching etiquette and came back with a pitch that shot abruptly out of the unknown, almost a phantom pitch. However, the blackness was not so uniform that Hartnett couldn't pick up the white spheroid hurtling in his direction. Deciding to risk his luck rather than merely try it, Hartnett swung with everything he had, sending the ball hurtling back from whence it cometh, back into the blackness.

As the dark form outlined against the gray September skies made its way down toward first, the fans, most of whom hadn't the foggiest that the ball was then fast on its way toward the left-field bleachers, began to set up a small roar. Within seconds, the normal noises were accompanied by appropriate maltreatment of the vocal cords as sections of fans—in an early-day version of the wave—began screaming to others in the dark. And, as the Pirates moved slowly from the field, their chances fading away like a false dawn, the riotous assembly flowed over onto the field. By the time Hartnett got to second he "couldn't see third for all the players and fans there." No more valiant hero ever fought his way through the ranks of his followers as the crush of humanity on the field effected an almost complete strangulation of movement. Hartnett doesn't remember walking a step to the plate, but instead being "carried in," and ending his joyous marathon route by touching home plate. Looking up, Hartnett saw umpire George Barr taking a good look—he was going to make sure I touched that platter."

There was one more game to play with the Pirates. But, as Billy Herman said later, "We went out the next day and we could've beaten nine Babe Ruths." They did, beating the dispirited Pirates behind Bill Lee, 10-1. And, on Saturday, they won their 11th in a row and 21st in their last 24 games to clinch the pennant.

But the moment all remember was "The Homer in the Gloamin'." The moment that belonged to Gabby Hartnett, who, in darkness, took on a stardom loud and clear.

26 Bucky Dent's Play-Off Home Run

New York Yankees vs. Boston Red Sox, Play-Off Game, October 2, 1978

THE 1978 EDITION OF THE NEW YORK YANKEES WERE BASE-ball's continuing soap opera, less a version of "Dynasty" than "As My Stomach Turns."

The cast of characters in the Yankee potboiler included the most picturesque and improbable group of oddities this side of a Mack Sennett comedy. Only this group was tragicomedic; and played it for all it was worth.

The lead in the unfolding drama was played by George Steinbrenner, an owner with an obvious inclination to rock the boat, anytime, anywhere. Some held that since George owned the ball he could do anything he wanted. But the prevailing view was that by his constant meddling he committed crimes against the senses and others too numerous to mention. Some, like cartoonist Bill Gallo of the New York *Daily News,* took to calling him "General George Von Steingrabber," while still others pictured him as possessing a soul with all the properties of the underside of a flat rock. However he was perceived, this boat-rocker adhered to the philosophy that "A ship that sails on a calm sea gets nowhere. You've got to have a little turmoil."

Also playing a starring role in the continuing saga of the Yankees '78 was manager Billy Martin, a smoldering volcano in uniform who had never before allowed fate to trample him beneath its iron heel and kick him in the face with spiked shoes. Fighting back with everything at his disposal, Martin oftimes resembled a man born with a hangover, which was only fair, his having resorted to strong drink as a cornerman and found it to be both an adder and a subtractor of his talents.

Sharing the billing with these two estranged bedfellows was the third member of the starring triumverate, Reggie Jackson, playing the role of part cloud-buster, part bull-buster. Jackson, who possessed the look of one being eternally put upon, described himself immodestly as "The straw that stirs the drink" and couldn't resist stirring whenever he got the chance—thus becoming less a straw than the eye of the storm that gathered over the team.

The supporting cast included Thurman Munson, with so much will power he could eat only one potato chip, "Sparky" Lyle, who played pranks for the memory, Graig Nettles, who dealt in wrought ironies, Chris Chambliss, who went without saying, Mickey Rivers, a casual laborer, and a group of mistaken nonentities and assorted millstones.

Put them all together and you have a soap opera for those whose sensitivity comes out like hair on a comb, of a team which impacted one upon another, less in fusion than confusion. Perhaps the best review of the ongoing soaper was one rendered by new addition Goose Gossage: "After hearing all the stories last year, I thought they wore boxing gloves instead of fielders' gloves."

The season started off normally enough, by Yankee standards anyway. Based upon an offhand remark by Jackson—who had uttered those deathless words, "If I played in New York, they'd name a candy bar after me," when negotiating with the Yankees the year before—Standard Brands named a candy bar "Reggie!," although some of the Yankees insisted they had wasted their

money, there already existing a bar named after him, "Butterfingers." Now, on Opening Day, Standard Brands greeted the 50,000-plus in attendance at Yankee Stadium with free samples of their orange-wrapped candy. And when Reggie, obviously feeling the courage of his confections, blasted a home run in his first time at bat, the patrons, who looked upon the flat packets less as something to eat than something to throw, scaled them down on the greensward by the thousands, making it the first game ever delayed by candy bars.

But Reggie! bars doth not a season make, and within weeks the Yankees found themselves staring at the disappearing backs of the Boston Red Sox who were winning game-after-game without benefit of turmoil. The Yankees, meanwhile, had cornered the market on that precious commodity, their off-the-field struggles dominating headlines and serving as circulation-builders for the city's papers.

The turmoil had started during the off-season and continued, with more than a running start, into the '78 season. First, the cast of '77 had two major defections: Pitcher Mike Torrez, who had won two games in the '77 Series, decided he had been with the Yankees long enough to disturb him but not enough to settle his stomach, and left to go to Boston; and Gabe Paul, the general manager, who had had his fill of the spider's web of intrigue that surrounded the front office, had vacated his position, heading west to Cleveland as fast as his legs could carry him. And then there were the additions to the cast, including that of Gossage, which miffed Sparky Lyle beyond the niceties of the mother tongue, now having to play second-banana after being named "Fireman of the Year" in '77. Other members of the cast were less than pleased with their billing, one of whom, Ken Holtzman, called Steinbrenner "a fool" and pointed out additional defects in his spiritual make-up for paying him $165,000 a year to be a spectator. And everywhere everybody was screaming at everybody else in an off-Broadway take-off of what Sparky Lyle called "The Bronx Zoo."

And still the Red Sox kept winning, leading the Yankees by seven games going into their first three-game series June 19th.

The Yankees lost two of three to the BoSox to fall ever further behind in their first head-to-head meeting. But it was the last loss in the rubber game of the Series that brought the pot to a boil. That was the game that rookie Jim Beattie started for the Yankees, inserted into the starting rotation by Martin, desperate for any able-armed pitcher to help his injury-riddled staff. Beattie lasted but three innings, and by the sixth was on the first bus back to Tacoma on orders from owner George Steinbrenner, filtered through his new GM, Al Rosen.

Steinbrenner, who the previous year had given the four-letter word "Boss" new meaning—or, as one wag said, "Was boss spelled backward, double S-O-B"—with such significant contributions to team morale as issuing fiats to his team to get haircuts, now jumped back in with both feet. Claiming, "I won't put up with this much longer. I won't stand for what I see now," he threw in a few gratuitous barbs at the head of Alfredo Martin. Martin, taking

108

umbrage and cover at the shots rattling around his head, bitterly retorted, "I'm sick and tired of hearing about being fired. I give George 100 percent loyalty, and I expect it in return."

And still the Red Sox kept winning, leading the Yankees by 11½ games by the All-Star Game break, July 11th.

The situation, now almost beyond hope, beseeched something from Steinbrenner that was against his will: Thoughts of surrender. Preparing to run up the white flag, Steinbrenner barked, "We're playing horseshit. We're going to bite the bullet and go with the young guys." Then he made his expected but long-deferred speech to the team, telling them, "We're going to do it the way I want to do it and the way Billy has agreed is the proper way to do it. . . . I expect you to accept whatever role you're given without griping and do it the best you can."

One man who was not about to "accept whatever role" he was given was Reggie Jackson. And when the "straw" was relegated to the position of designated hitter, he became distraught. Coming to bat in a game on July 17th with a man on first and none out in the bottom of the tenth, Martin first flashed the bunt sign to Reggie and then wiped it off, ordering him to swing away. But Jackson, with a mind of his own, tried to bunt three times, the last two foul. Afterward, Jackson could only offer up lamely, "I was trying to advance the runner. I figured I'd get him over the best way I could. I thought I'd be helping the ball club." Then, as if to purge his soul of what was bothering him, he went on, "How can they say I'm a threat to swing the bat? I'm not an everyday player. I'm a part-time

player . . ." But soon, very soon, Jackson wasn't even than, Martin suspending him for five days for his insubordination.

But it was not enough, and the Red Sox kept winning, leading the Yankees by 14 games on July 17th.

In Jackson's enforced absence, the Yankees, led by pitcher Ron Guidry, won four consecutive games. And when an unrepentant Jackson rejoined the club in Chicago, Martin, incensed at the lack of contriteness on Jackson's part, kept him on the bench. Not incidentally, the Yankees won their fifth straight.

One always got the impression that Martin was so unrelenting that after he is called by the Great Umpire in the Sky he will have his ashes thrown in the face of those below. Now, his anger at Jackson so obsessive and his hatred so impelling, Martin was driven to throw ashes in Jackson's face. Unfortunately, the accumulation of frustration and rage which unleashed the dark side of Martin also caused him to make a throwing error, begriming

Bucky Dent, the improbable hero of the 1978 Play-Off

Steinbrenner as well in his now-famous reference to the two. "He's a born liar," Martin snapped, referring to the "straw" that had broken his camel's back. And then added, "The two of them deserve each other. One's a born liar, the other's convicted," referring to Steinbrenner's conviction for sub-rosa campaign contributions.

That tore it. Before Steinbrenner could make Martin another member of the growing fraterniy of ex-Yankee managers, Martin fell on his own sword, reading to the press from a note clenched in his quivering right hand that sounded more like a nervous breakdown on paper than a resignation: "I don't want to hurt this team's chances for the pennant with this undue publicity. The team has a shot at the pennant, and I hope they win it. I owe it to my health and my mental well-being to resign." Translated, it meant that Martin suffered from illness and fatigue; Steinbrenner was sick and tired of him.

And so, on July 17th, Bob Lemon was rushed in as the relief manager of the Yankees. "Lem" had the effect of calming the turbulent waters. Almost immediately the Yankees stopped afeudin', afussin', and afightin', and began ascramblin' after the BoSox, closing the gap to 6½ by the beginning of September and four by September 7th. That was the Thursday the Yankees arrived in Boston to take on the front-running Sox in a crucial four-game series. The four games would become known in the lore of New England as "The Boston Massacre," the Yankees winning all four by the one-sided scores of 15-3, 13-2, 7-0 and 7-4, and departed Boston tied for the lead.

With Lemon giving the Yankees a gentle hand ride home, the Yankees were to win 48 of the 68 games down to the wire under his easygoing leadership. The Red Sox, after being crushed four times in Boston, went on to Yankee Stadium where again they were treated as inferiors in station, losing two more times to the Bronx Bombers and falling three-and-a-half games back. But then, miraculously, the Red Sox found their legs and, whipping and driving, won 12 of their last 14—and eight in a row—to tie the Yankees on the last day of the season, forcing a one-game playoff, only the second one in the history of the American League.

The Boston weather that Monday afternoon was near perfect. And the announced crowd of 32,925, many of whom were people-horned into "The Fens," aisles overflowing to the danger point, expected their heroes, owners of the best home record in the Majors at 59-and-23, to be no less so. Cheering the every move of their idols, the fans roared every time one of them so much as touched the ball during the traditional pregame preliminaries, even reserving some of their noisy enthusiasm for the outfield wind sprints of starting pitcher Mike Torrez, whose erratic work during the past month had not necessarily endeared him to the loyal Red Sox rooters.

But on this day of days, Torrez was in the process of endearing himself to everyone who ever bled Red Sox red, besting the Yankees' "franchise," left-hander Ron Guidry, who had put together an incredible 24-3 record. Going into the top of the seventh, Torrez held a 2-0 lead thanks to a solo home run in the second by Carl Yastrzemski, Boston's patron saint, and a run-producing single in the sixth by Boston strongman Jim Rice.

Baseball historian Mike Nemec, in *The Ultimate Baseball Book,* remembers overhearing one of the Fenway faithful in the twenty-third row of Section 17 as Torrez lobbed a few plateward before the fatal seventh. "Pisses me off," said the patron, obviously less than pleased. "Fuckin' thing, you know? Zimmer's leaving him in. Lee's right—guy looks like a gerbil. Which would be all right if he didn't think like fuckin' Darrell Johnson. There was only one

time in his life that Johnson was too early pullin' a pitcher, and that was when he takes Willoughby out in the seventh game (of the '75 Series), inna goddamned ninth, and puts in that asshole Burton. And we lose. We'll blow this one, too. Wait and see if we don't blow this one, just like we did all the others."

Now it was the Yankee half of the seventh. Torrez, laboring somewhat, put Chris Chambliss and Roy White on. That brought up the somewhat less-than-formidable form of Bucky Dent, a .243 hitter with but four home runs and 37 runs batted in. Torrez reared back and fired and Dent, giving it all he had, drove the ball off his ankle and fell to the ground like a sunstricken horse. Boston fans almost felt sorry for the slight Yankee shortstop, now doubled up like a carpenter's rule in a sit-down-and-think-it-over position. Finally, after massaging his foot and assuaging the trainer that he was alright to continue, Dent reassumed his position in the batter's box. But he now had a new bat, one on-deck batter Mickey Rivers had given to the batboy to hand to Dent, saying, "Give this to Bucky. Tell him there are lots of hits in it. He'll get a home run." And unbelievably, he did get a home run, less smashing than looping a ball that cleared Fenway's Green Monster by no more than five feet, nestling in the screening just above the left-field wall.

Finally getting around to "pullin'" Torrez after Bucky had put a Dent in his team's chances, Boston manager Don Zimmer now replaced him with right-hander Bob Stanley. But Stanley, the proud possessor of a 15-2 record, couldn't stem the tide, failing to cross the first Rivers he came to, Mickey, who singled and was driven home by Munson for New York's fourth run and a 4-2 lead. They further padded their lead in the top of the eighth when Reggie caught one of Stanley's fastballs and drove it skyward in the direction of the centerfield bleachers and then, almost as if it were a punctuation mark to the entire season, detoured on his way back to the dugout in order to shake hands with the head of the unholy alliance known as the Yankees, George Steinbrenner.

The Sox came back with two of their own in the bottom of the eighth off flamethrower Goose Gossage, now on in relief of Guidry, and went into the bottom of the ninth down by one run, 4-5. Trying mightily to alter the course of the game, Rick Burleson worked Gossage for a one-out walk. Then Jerry Remy hit a low liner toward right field. Yankee right fielder Lou Piniella, losing sight of the line drive in the glare of the setting sun, stabbed at the ball and held the runners at first and second. Into the box stepped Jim Rice, who had become only the third man in baseball history to hit for over 400 total bases that year and had already driven in the second run. Gossage came in with his 100 mph smoker and Rice, swinging late, sent it out again to Piniella, who once again lost the ball and this time made a guess-what-I-found-in-my-glove move, catching the ball. Burleson, who would have scored on the fly had Piniella not corralled Remy's hit, now scurried over to third, only 90 feet away from tying the score. But Burleson was destined to become a permanent fixture at third as the next batter, the redoubtable Yaz, lifted a high pop foul that Graig Nettles fondled as it fell from the sky for the third out.

After 172 minutes, the tortuous season that had gone on for 163 games was over. And although both the Red Sox and the Yankees had won 99 out of their first 162 games, the Yankees had won the one game that had counted, the Play-Off game. Bob Lemon, who had been a participant in both American League play-off games—playing for Cleveland in '48 and managing New York in '78, both ironically played at Fenway Park—best summed up the win in this the Yankee's year of turmoil when he said, "This is even better than sex!" And fighting, too, for that matter.

27 Walter Johnson's Wet Farewell

Pittsburgh Pirates vs. Washington Senators, 7th Game, 1925 World Series, October 15, 1925

RAIN, DARK OF NIGHT AND OTHER CALAMITOUS ELEMENTS might a better mail delivery make, but those same conditions sure as hell don't abide to make a baseball game better. Take the final game of the 1925 World Series, called by New York *Times'* writer James Harrison, "The best and worst game of baseball ever played in this country."

The 1925 Series was a struggle between the old American League champs, the Washington Senators, and the Pittsburgh Pirates, winners of their first National League pennant since 1909. Before it was over it would become a struggle against the elements. But there is no need to embroider: Truth makes all things evident in the telling.

The party of the first part, the Washington Senators, were old in every sense of the adjective, repeating as American League champions for the second straight year and as long in the tooth as a team can be without stepping on their overbites. Owner Clark Griffith, looking at his championship team of returning graybeards, had, before the season started, determined to shore up what he considered to be his two weakest links: The pitching staff and centerfield. Called the "Old Fox" during his playing days, back when baseball was in short pants, Griffith decided youngsters weren't worth the gamble and instead raided the Old Players' Home for his pitching talent. During the winter he picked up Stanley Coveleski from Cleveland, Dutch Ruether from Brooklyn and Vean Gregg from Seattle, three rejects from the glue factory whose age averaged 36 years-and-change, an age when most self-respecting pitchers would be home in bed. His centerfield problems were not as easy to solve. After trying out such less-than-worthies as Roy Carlyle, Wid Matthews and George Rinehart in the center pasture, Griff traded Carlyle to the impoverished Red Sox for Joe "Moon" Harris, a 34-year-old journeyman who had been a consistent .300 hitter with some hint of power. Then, almost as if he meant to corner the market on those marked with crow's feet, Griffith picked up the likes of Mike McNally, Bobby Veach, and Everett Scott, total age 100 years young.

Together this group of gaffers, washing away the improbability of the calendar, outraced the young Philadelphia A's to the wire, winning by eight-and-a-half games—and a full 25½ over the favored Yankees, suffering through what has euphemistically been called "Babe Ruth's Bellyache," but which more than somewhat resembled a good old social disease. The Senators' pitching staff combined for 96 wins, led by 37-year-old Walter Johnson, the end of his career postponed by 20 wins. Added to that were the 20 more by 36-year-old Coveleski—who had been thrown away, like Othello's base Indian, by Cleveland and turned out to be a pearl richer than the rest of the tribe—Ruether's 18, "Old" Tom Zachary's 12 wins and Firpo Marberry's 15 saves. Offensively the "Nats" were led by Sam Rice's .350 batting average and 227 hits, "Goose" Goslin's 113 runs-batted-in and veteran Roger Peckinpaugh's .294 batting average and almost flawless play afield, winning for him the League's Most Valuable Player Award.

Their opponents, the Pittsburgh Pirates, were led by three Hall of Famers-to-be, Pie Traynor, Kiki Cuyler and Max Carey, who between them hit .340 with 595 hits, 367 runs, 203 extra-base hits, and 102 stolen bases. The Pirates had an evenly-balanced pitching staff, five pitchers winning 15 or more games, and possessed their own old-timer in the presence of pitcher "Babe" Adams, who had been a rookie when the club last appeared in the Series those 16 autumns ago.

But it was not to be the elements of pitching or batting which were to win this Series. Instead it was to be the elements themselves.

The first game of the Series was started, naturally enough, by that Washington monument Walter Johnson who faced "Specs" Meadows, the Pirates' 19-game winner. With an almost matter-of-fact delivery, Johnson, who late in his career had added a wide-sweeping curve ball to go with his unhittable fast ball, pitched a masterpiece, striking out ten Pirate batters and giving up but five hits, four of them meaningless singles, as the Senators beat Pittsburgh 4-1 for a 1-0 lead in the Series.

Game Two saw Washington's other 20-game winner, Coveleski, go against Pittsburgh's Vic Aldridge. For the first seven innings, Coveleski had the better of it on the scorecard, limiting Pirate bats to just four hits against the six Aldridge had given up, but fared no better than a 1-1 tie on the scoreboard. Then in the eighth, Washington shortstop Roger Peckinpaugh, who had kicked in one error in the first game, doubled his output, and a follow-up home run by the only man in baseball whose name ever sounded like a freight train picking up speed, Kiki Cuyler—but whose first name was merely a double contraction of the first syllable of his surname, used for calling his name on flyballs as in "Cuy-Cuy"— gave the Pirates a 3-2 win.

Kiki Cuyler, whose ground-rule double sparked the greatest comeback in Series history

Game Three, back in Washington after a day off for travel, was played before President Coolidge and 36,495 other paying guests, cramming every nook and crease of tiny Griffith Stadium, including the temporary stands. All, including Coolidge, got their money's worth, witnessing the most disputed catch in all of baseballdom, not to mention one of the greatest catches in World Series history.

To set the scene: Washington had just taken a 4-3 lead in the bottom of the seventh, courtesy of Washington's two Harrises, right fielder Joe driving in second baseman Bucky with the go-ahead run. Going into the top of the eighth, manager Bucky brought in his ace reliever, a curious piece of goods named Fred "Firpo" Marberry, described by his catcher, Muddy Ruel, as "a character," who on the mound would "kick up dirt, paw the ground with his spikes, fume, fret, then rear back, wave his big shoes in the batter's face, and blaze a fast-ball through." With two left-handed batters scheduled to come up for the Pirates in the eighth—first baseman George Grantham and catcher Earl Smith—manager B. Harris, concerned lest they catch one of Marberry's behind-his-violin foot fastballs and drive it to right, replaced the slow-moving J. Harris in right field with Earl McNeely and then inserted McNeely in center and moved the speedier Sam Rice over to right.

Sure enough, after Marberry's smokeballs had fired past the first two Pirate batters causing them to blink and then strike out in rapid succession, catcher Smith caught hold of one of Marberry's offerings amidship and sent it sailing on a line toward right center field. The ball, propelled by a cutting northwest wind, headed off in the direction of the temporary bleachers, just this side of Florida Avenue. Rice, like a puff of the same blustery wind, took off with the crack of the bat, back to the ball, trying mightily to catch up with the disappearing pellet. Turning slightly to his right, Rice caught sight of the ball and then returned to the work at foot, chasing it down. About 10 feet in front of the bleachers, Rice made a leap of faith, back-stabbing at the ball with his gloved left hand

Sam Rice, who made the greatest catch in Series history. Or did he?

over his right shoulder. Coming down five feet in front of the bleacher wall, Rice, with an obvious disinclination to slow down, hurtled the three-foot protective barrier like a river without banks and disappeared into the laps of the bleacher fans. What seemed like an eternity later, but was in actuality only about ten seconds, Rice, aided by now centerfielder McNeely, extricated himself from the mass of humanity and reentered the playing arena, holding up his trophy, or nontrophy as the case may be. Umpire Cy Rigler, who had run out to the spot where Rice had disappeared from view, now signaled Smith "Out." The Pirates put up a howl and a cry, claiming that the catch was "impossible" and that either McNeely or a fan must have retrieved the ball and handed it to Rice, but Rigler's decision stood.

What also stood was the controversy over the catch: one owner Clark Griffith called "A catch you are lucky to witness in a lifetime." For years Rice refused to answer directly whether or not he had actually caught the ball, always artfully side-stepping any such query with the non-answer, "The umpire called him out, didn't he?" But the Hall of Fame refused to take Rice's evasive non-answer for an answer and asked Rice, upon the occasion of his induction into Cooperstown in 1963, to finally settle the time-honored question of "Did he or didn't he?" Still Rice, wearing what sportswriter Shirley Povich called "the sardonic smile across the face of baseball," refused, holding both his secret and his smile. However, he did give the Hall of Fame a letter "to be opened after my death." The letter, finally opened after his death in 1974, gave Rice's version, a version in which he stated, "I had a death grip on it. . . . At no time did I lose possession of the ball."

To make a long story even longer, Rice's circus catch in the eighth and Marberry's clutch pitching in the ninth preserved the Senators' 4-3 win to give them a 2-1 lead in the Series. The next day Johnson came back with his second superlative performance as he rendered the Pirates' armaments harmless and threw a six-hit shutout for a Washington 4-0 win. Washington was now one game shy of winning their second straight World's Championship, leaving the Pirates' chances about as frosty as the weather, no team ever having come back from a 1-3 deficit.

But apparently no one bothered to tell the Pirates that they were close to Patrick Henry's second choice. And with whatever silent heresies of reason they could muster, the Pirates brought their once listless and phlegmatic bats to life to win Game Five 6-3 behind Vic Aldridge and Game Six 3-2 behind Ray Kremer. Now it came down to Game Seven; a game that would see Walter Johnson, Washington's two-time winner, go against Vic Aldridge, Pittsburgh's two-timer. And a game that would be packed with more thrills to the square inch than any game in World Series history.

But it was not the heroics of the two teams which would make this seventh and deciding game a memorable one, but something those cabalistic scratchings known as the boxscore never reflect: The elements. The game started in rain. Not in raindrops as far apart as currants in a cake sold at a neighborhood church bake sale, but a steady drizzle. By the third inning the drizzle went on an unlimited run, turning into gelid rain, downpouring diagonally from the west and turning the entire field into a navigable stream. By the seventh inning, the fog was so thick that outfielder "Goose" Goslin "could just about make out what was going on in the infield from out there in the outfield."

However, it wasn't the weather's shortcomings that did in Pirate starter Aldridge. Instead it was his own. After giving up a lead-off single to Sam Rice, the very first batter he faced, Aldridge retired Bucky Harris on a fly ball. That was to be the only man retired all afternoon before he himself was personally retired. For after getting Harris, Aldridge uncorked a wild pitch, walked Goslin, uncorked another wild pitch, walked Joe Harris and ditto Joe Judge for one run. Then, after Ossie Bluege singled to left to drive in Goslin with the second run, Aldridge was asked by manager Bill McKechnie to sample of the waters in the shower.

The fates did not take kindly to his replacement Johnny Morrison either, as the first man he faced, Roger Peckinpaugh, reached first on a catcher's interference call, bringing in run number three. Then Muddy Ruel was safe on second baseman Eddie Moore's fumble, the fourth Washington run of the inning crossing the plate. And if that weren't enough, when Ruel got down to first he became involved in what appeared to be a debating society mini-outing with Pirate first baseman Stuffy Mc-Innis, punctuated by shoves. Finally, after two hits, three bases on balls, two wild pitches, a catcher's interference call, a bobbled ground, a near-brawl and four runs, the inning mercifully came to a close after 24 long minutes. For 42,856 Pirate fans it couldn't have been soon enough.

With Walter Johnson on the mound and a 4-0 lead, it looked like Washington had the game in the bag, albeit a water-soaked one. And when Johnson got through the first two innings on just three rain-bespattered hits, it began to look like it was merely a matter of playing out the rest of the game for the sake of those masochists who demanded to see a game played out to its fullest and would have been better advised to start building their arks.

But that was to be the Senators' high-water mark. For in the third the heavens opened and a watery wash turned Forbes Field into an aquarium and the players into poor imitations of speckled trout. The most rain-swept area was that around the pitcher's mound, where once a proud mesa of dirt had stood. As he took the mound in the third, Johnson began to take on the look of a man treading water, which he was, losing his footing and unable to control his pitches, the gilt of his greatness washing off for all to see. That was to be the inning the Pirates began their swim upstream: A single, a double, another single and—almost as if there were footnotes and one could write Ibid.—still another single, all combining to produce three runs. Suddenly the score was 4-3, Washington.

Washington, however, also could take on the disguise of web-footed amphibians and, in the fourth, scored two more runs on a double by Joe Harris after two singles to increase their lead to 6-3. Pittsburgh still wouldn't walk the plank and fought back against Washington and the elements with one more run in the bottom of the fifth on two doubles by Carey and Cuyler to close to within two of the Senators. Then, in the seventh, Eddie Moore led off with an innocuous pop fly to short left that Peckinpaugh, part of what once had been a waterproof infield and which was now seeping along with the rest of the field, dropped for his seventh error of the season, an early two-base Christmas gift. Carey followed with his third double of the game and Pie Traynor brought him home with a triple, and suddenly the score was tied at six.

In an attempt to atone for his almost-terminal case of fumblitis, Peckinpaugh hit an eighth-inning home run over the low left-field fence off Pittsburgh's third pitcher, Ray Kremer, to make the score 7-6, Washington. But only for the nonce. For the gentle zephyrs buffeting the field had turned the field into a quagmire, with the pitching mound by far the worst—made all the more so by helpful Pirate groundskeepers who had taken to spreading sawdust all over the area so that Pittsburgh pitchers could get their footing

while denying Johnson any of the same. That mound of muck would prove to be Johnson's grave of mud before the eighth was over.

After retiring the first two men to face him in the eighth, more on the strength of his pedigree than his pitching, Johnson gave up his 13th hit, a double to Pirate catcher Earl Smith. Pitching now without grip, without traction and without hope, Johnson then rendered a pinch double to Carson Bigbee, hitting for Kremer, the ball shooting abruptly out of the unknown over the head of the unseeing Goslin and driving in the tying run. Johnson now gave up his only base on balls to Eddie Moore, putting men on first and second and bringing up Max Carey, who had been a one-man wrecking crew all afternoon, with three doubles and one single in his four at-bats. But Johnson, reaching down one more time into his not-so-distant past, prompted Carey to hit the ball in the direction of shortstop Roger Peckinpaugh. Peck, who already had been awarded the American League MVP trophy, now proved to be worthy of consideration for Most Valuable Player honors in the National as well, first plowing the infield for the ball and then throwing it away in an attempt to get a force at second.

"Old Barney," the great Walter Johnson, who could beat anything except the elements.

Johnson stood on the mound, such as it was, looking more like a body which had been found after several days at the bottom of the Monogahela than a pitcher. There were rain drops dripping off the beak of his cap into his eyes, almost as if they were salt tears of the first order. And well they might have been, Peck's eighth Series miscue all but dousing Johnson's dreams of a third World Series win; his flame now quenched by the rains and the fates.

Another whose dreams were being doused was manager Bucky Harris, now wrestling desperately with his dilemma: Whether to risk staying with the obviously staggering Johnson or bring in his ace reliever, Firpo Marberry. Knowing that the deficiencies of the day might not be supplied by the morrow, Harris, who would rather have plucked an offending eye than Johnson, determined to stake his all on the Big Train. And go down clinging to the wreckage.

However, the Big Train that had roared down the Major League tracks for 19 years was no longer an express, but a local which had stopped to take on water. Fondling the ball, which continued to get heavier and heavier as he held it in his hand, Johnson was now deciding whether to throw it, fling it or hold on to it for yet another second. With time measured only in raindrops, Johnson took his time, finally throwing the ball plateward. The batter, the aforementioned Kiki Cuyler, swung, his bat hitting the ball with the sound of a boat cracking up against a lighthouse, steering it down the right-field line into a tight covey of on-the-field spectators, all huddled like three thousand men in a tub. The umpires called it a ground-rule double. And waved in two runs, the go-ahead two runs to make the score 9-7, Pirates.

With the rain coming in fitful, virulent lines and darkness and the shroud of fog enveloping the field, it was all but impossible to find one's backside with both hands, let alone the ball. And the umpires, all stationed in the infield in those days before there were six assigned to World Series games, had to make their fair/foul calls from the infield. Goose Goslin remembered the ball years later for Larry Ritter: "The umpires couldn't see it. It was too dark and foggy. It wasn't fair at all. It was foul by two feet. I know it was foul because the ball hit in the mud and *stuck* there."

But the decision stuck. So too did the score at 9-7, Pittsburgh. And when Pirate reliever Red Oldham retired the Senators one-two-three in the top of the ninth—Goslin taking a third strike to end the game, the only time a World Series ever ended on a called third strike—the score, the game and the Series all became finalized.

The Pittsburgh Pirates had come back, twice, to win the Series, proving that even if the Series had been decided by the elements, the elements had not lacked for a champion.

1925

Game 7 October 15 at Pittsburgh

Was.	4 0 0	2 0 0	0 1 0			
Pit.	0 0 3	0 1 0	2 3 x			

Washington	Pos	AB	R	H	RBI	PO	A	E
Rice	cf	5	2	2	0	3	0	0
B. Harris	2b	5	0	0	0	6	3	0
Goslin	lf	4	2	1	0	2	0	0
J. Harris	rf	3	1	1	2	1	1	0
Judge	1b	3	1	1	0	6	0	0
Bluege	3b	4	0	1	0	0	0	0
Peckinpaugh	ss	*3	1	1	2	0	2	2
Ruel	c	4	0	0	1	6	0	0
Johnson	p	4	0	0	0	0	3	0
Totals		35	7	7	6	24	9	2

Pitching	IP	H	R	ER	BB	SO
Washington						
Johnson (L)	8	15	9	5	1	3
Pittsburgh						
Aldridge	⅓	2	4	4	3	0
Morrison	3⅔	4	2	2	0	2
Kremer (W)	4	1	1	1	0	1
Oldham (SV)	1	0	0	0	0	2

Pittsburgh	Pos	AB	R	H	RBI	PO	A	E
Moore	2b	4	3	1	1	2	0	1
Carey	cf	5	3	4	2	4	0	1
Cuyler	rf	4	0	2	3	4	0	1
Barnhart	lf	5	0	1	1	2	0	0
Oldham	p	0	0	0	0	0	0	0
Traynor	3b	4	0	1	1	1	3	0
Wright	ss	4	0	1	0	1	3	0
McInnis	1b	4	0	2	0	7	0	0
Smith	c	4	0	1	0	4	0	0
b Yde		0	1	0	0	0	0	0
Gooch	c	0	0	0	0	2	0	0
Aldridge	p	0	0	0	0	0	0	0
Morrison	p	1	1	1	0	0	0	0
a Grantham		1	0	0	0	0	0	0
Kremer	p	1	0	0	0	0	1	0
c Bigbee	lf	1	1	1	1	0	0	0
Totals		38	9	15	9	27	7	2

*Awarded first on catcher interference.
a Flied out for Morrison in 4th.
b Ran for Smith in 8th.
c Doubled for Kremer in 8th.

Doubles—Bigbee, Carey 3, Cuyler 2, J. Harris, Moore, Smith. Triple—Traynor. Home Run—Peckinpaugh. Stolen Base—Carey. Sacrifice Hit—Cuyler. Double Play—B. Harris to Judge. Wild Pitches—Aldridge 2. Left on Bases—Washington 5, Pittsburgh 7. Umpires—McCormick, Moriarty, Rigler, Owens. Attendance—42,856. Time of Game—2:31.

28 Hank Aaron's Record-Breaking Home Run

Atlanta Braves vs. Los Angeles Dodgers, April 8, 1974

AS WE DEAL IN THAT LIMBO OF MEMORIES THAT COMPRISE the whole of baseball, there are very few moments that stay with us. But there is one. It was an instance when time was separated and unified at the same time, when the record book and the flickering image on the 23-inch magic lantern in our living rooms became as one: Hank Aaron had just broken the most revered record in all of baseball, Babe Ruth's lifetime record of 714 home runs.

It was 9:07 P.M., April 8, 1974, when Aaron smote one of Al Downing's fast balls over the fence into the bullpen with his first swing of the nationally-televised game. And, as scoreboard lights flashed in six-foot numerals the now-magic number "715" over and over again and 53,775 fans stood in riotous assembly, millions more were told by ABC announcer Curt Gowdy, "He did it! He did it!" ending Aaron's long climb up the Baseball Everest that had stood for 39 years since Babe Ruth had hit his 714th and last career homer.

It was only fitting that the record had been broken 39 years after Ruth had established it, Aaron being 39 years younger than Ruth, less a day. Born in Mobile, Alabama on February 5, 1934, Aaron started life 686 behind Ruth. In fact, most people were that far behind Ruth, whose one-man monopoly on home runs had become such that when he pole-axed his 700th, off Tommy Bridges in Detroit on July 14, 1934, only one man, Rogers Hornsby, had 300, and that on the nose.

As the years passed, Ruth's record became a tour map, reading less as an atlas of his achievement than the outline of uncharted waters no man had ever traversed before. Or since. Hornsby had petered out at 301, Lou Gehrig had been struck down by disease with a total of 493, Mel Ott had finished with 511 and Jimmie Foxx had trailed off at the 534 mark. The '50s saw a brand new group take up arms against the towering record, and again fall short: DiMaggio with 361, Musial with 475 and Williams with 521. But still they kept coming, leap-frogging over others for positions on the home run all-time ladder somewhere behind Ruth.

While all these so-called "home run hitters" were falling short of the mark that Ruth set, it hardly seemed likely that the man destined to replace Ruth at the top of the homer mountain would be a wiry, trim line-drive hitter named Hank Aaron.

Aaron's first years in professional baseball, while giving promise of a great career, hardly gave promise of one whose career statistics would be generously dotted with home runs. Starting as an 18-year-old shortstop for Eau Claire in the Northern League in 1952, Aaron batted .336 with but 32 extra-base hits hidden amongst his 166 total hits—and only nine of those homers. The next year, at Jacksonville of the South Atlantic League, Aaron's bat came alive as the now-second baseman led the league in batting, hits, runs, doubles and RBI's with 22 home runs—good, but scarcely the stuff that would cause concern to the keepers of the Ruth flame.

The 1954 Milwaukee Braves—then only a year removed from Boston, the first team to move lock, stock and franchise in half a century—were a young team, abuilding and on the ascendancy. Their infield was made up of equal parts talent and youth, with Eddie Mathews, Johnny Logan, Danny O'Connell and Joe Adcock all holding down their positions. Very well, thank you. With no room at the infield inn, Aaron was moved to the outfield. But even though the young 20-year-old prospect had played the outfield during the previous winter in the Puerto Rican League, the prospects of his breaking into an outfield made up of Bill Bruton, Andy Pafko and the newly-acquired Bobby Thomson seemed bleak, at best. Then fate, in the form of a training camp injury to Thomson, intervened, and Aaron got his chance, starting the season in left field.

But Aaron's start was somewhat less than spectacular. Underwhelming might better describe it. "A typical rookie start," was the way he remembered his opening day performance against Cincinnati and Reds pitcher Joe Nuxhall, "0-for-4 or 0-for-5, I forget which." Like any rookie, he kept his bags packed, not knowing "whether I was going back to the minor leagues or not. It was terrifying . . ." But Aaron was, as he acknowledged, "fortunate to be playing for Charlie Grimm, who gave me a chance and stuck with me."

Then, in 1966, the Braves, who had been the first franchise to relocate, hopscotched again, becoming the first to relocate in a third city, this time carpet-bagging their way south to Atlanta. Almost undetected in the switch was the fact that Aaron was now playing in Atlanta Stadium with its more inviting left-field target, an area that would soon become known as "Home Run Alley." And, for the first time in his career, Aaron would begin hitting more homers at home than on the road—a pattern that had begun in his first year when 12 of his 13 homers were smote on the road and had continued for his 12 years in Milwaukee where only 184 of his 398 home runs had been hit, the other 214 coming on the road.

As Aaron continued to be a Swiss movement to be watched by all, his reputation grew amongst his peers, one of whom, Curt Simmons, said of him, "Throwing a fast ball by Aaron is like trying to sneak the sun past a rooster." Others found they may as well have tried to open up an oyster without a knife as get a pitch past him, as Aaron became an equal opportunity hitter, dealing up great gobs of homers with that quick flick of the wrists off all without regard to race, creed or uniform: 44 in 1966, 39 in 1967, and 29 in 1968.

Without any of those recognizable landmarks like "50 homers" that the minds of the fans and the press alike could wrap around, Aaron had quietly, almost too quietly, less continued his assault on Ruth's record than begun sneaking up on it. Like race-track bettors watching a front-running favorite, everyone had their eyes fixed on the highly touted heir-designate to Ruth, Willie Mays. Then, for the first time, some of those who had been following Mays began to notice something out of the corners of their eyes; that something was Aaron, who now had 510 homers to Mays' 587.

Mays himself thought "Aaron can do it. He is young and in good health, figures to have three to six more good seasons and plays half his games in the Atlanta park, which is favorable to home run hitting." Others weren't as convinced. Ernie Banks ventured, "To stay even with Ruth's pace, he would have to average more than 40 homers in each of the next five seasons, and that's asking a lot of any player, much less one who is in his upper 30's."

But still Aaron, without the fanfare of Mays—whose personality was now far more arresting than his workmanship—continued to add to his growing total, hitting another 44 in 1969, 38 in 1970 and 47 in 1971. Not only had he averaged the "more than 40 homers" Banks had thought necessary to "stay even with Ruth's pace," but also had closed the gap on Mays to only seven homers, 646 to 639. And with Mays now reduced to cameo parts, a myth betrayed by the rust that now encased his once-magnificent body, Aaron's passage of Mays seemed inevitable within the year. But Ruth? That still seemed far-fetched, especially to those romanticists who clung to their former values like captains to the mast of a ship going beneath the breakers.

Unconcerned with the brouhaha his attack on baseball's most legendary record was generating, Aaron, who could no more be melted than ice welded, went on about his task with a workmanlike mien, delivering another 34 homers in 1972. Now the cumulative total, clicking off like a taxi meter, read 673. And the Aaron watch began in earnest.

The 1973 baseball season saw the first members of the press vanguard flock into Atlanta, all but trampling him—but Aaron, his countenance proof against emotion, went about doing what came naturally: Hitting homers. Aided and abetted by a 1973 Atlanta line-up that saw second baseman Davey Johnson stroke 43 homers and third baseman Darrell Evans another 41, Aaron, with pitchers unable to pitch around him, had another of those "average" 40-homer seasons.

The 1973 season also saw something else as well as "the Aaron watch"—something not nearly as pretty. Babe Ruth had generated a depth of affection and a hold on the public consciousness that not only outlasted his career, but his lifetime as well. So for anyone, let alone a black man, to dare challenge his most cherished record was unthinkable to all too many. Some, rallying under the banner marked "baseball purists," tried to explain away Aaron's challenge to Ruth's record in terms not worth knowing, citing fewer at bats, modern ballfields, etc., etc., ad nauseum. Others, even more antisocial, viewed Aaron less with esteem than evil gleam and turned the occasion into a nasty name-calling contest, parading out all the time-dishonored abusive epithets of bigotry, shouting words like "Nigger" and "S.O.B." from the stands and sending Aaron anonymous letters from anonymous letter writers.

Less hardy souls wouldn't have made it. But Aaron, with a bearing that would earn him direct and safe conduct into the Hall of Fame, determined that "The more they push me, the more I want the record." And then he responded the only way he knew how: With his bat, stroking ball-after-ball out of the park with monotonous regularity. By the end of the 1973 season his 40 homers had left him but one home run shy of the magic "714" mark.

On April 23rd, in his seventh Major League game, Aaron got his first Major League home run, driving one of Vic Raschi's fast balls into the outer reaches of Sportsman's Park. But even though he followed that up with another two days later against St. Louis' Stu Miller, by September 5th he had only 13 home runs to go with his six triples, 27 doubles and 85 singles. That was the day he broke his ankle in a game against Cincinnati and ended his first season prematurely. But not before he had paid off handsomely on

Grimm's patience, keeping everlastingly at his hitting and driving the ball to all fields with that quick wrist swing which allowed him to wait until the very last split-second before swinging. And which, in time, would become as famous as the name of its possessor.

But even though his first year had been a creditable one—with 69 RBI's and a .280 batting average—there were those who thought his worth so small, his potential so minute and his fear so large he might not survive. One of those was Aaron, who spent the off-season fretting "whether or not the broken ankle would mend properly and, even if it did, whether I would hurt my hitting by favoring it." However, Aaron not only erased all doubts in 1955, but also established himself as a star—albeit not yet one of baseball's superstars, merely one of the lesser nova variety—by batting .314, driving in 106 runs and raising his home run total to 27. Still, after two years, he was 674 home runs behind Ruth and so far removed from the top of baseball's home run mountain that even Sir Edmund Hillary couldn't help him find it.

By 1956, Aaron began demonstrating to one and sundry that he was now a full-fledged star, even if a part-time home run hitter. Playing with intensity and concentration in his every move, Aaron led the League in batting, hits and doubles even while his home run production slipped a notch, down to 26. His batting now was drawing comparisons to Rogers Hornsby, not Ruth, manager Fred Haney calling him, "The greatest right-handed hitter since Hornsby." Others, observing that Aaron "operates the same way Hornsby did, just meeting the ball wherever it's pitched and counting on his wrist power to give it a ride," also made the inevitable likening.

But if those who had come to view Aaron's handiwork as that of a non-home run hitter were laboring under a delusion, they were not to labor long. For in 1957, the day after his home run against Cardinal pitcher Billy Muffett had given Milwaukee its first-ever pennant, Aaron went to bat in the first inning against Sad Sam Jones, tied with Ernie Banks for the National League lead, and hit a grand slam homer—ironically his first grand slammer ever—to win the National League home run title with 44, a repeating decimal in the home run total of this man who wore Number 44 on his back. Thus Aaron became only the fourth man in baseball history ever to lead his League in the categories of batting, hits, runs, RBI's, doubles and homers, the other three being the afore-mentioned Hornsby, Nap Lajoie and Ty Cobb. Not bad company for a player with but four years of on-the-job experience.

Forming the greatest 1-2 batting twosome in history with teammate Eddie Mathews—a tandem that would see the two Brave batters smite a total of 863 homers between them in 13 years, four more than Ruth and Gehrig as teammates—Aaron began bruising the ball at a hardy pace, hitting 288 homers over the next eight years, thus giving him a total of 398 after his first dozen years in the Majors—89 more than Ruth had in his first twelve years if anyone was counting, which they weren't.

However, the glow of Aaron's accomplishments had been hidden under that bushel basket called Milwaukee. Had he but practiced his feats of bat in a New York or a Los Angeles or even in nearby Chicago, they would have been well chronicled by the press. Instead, he was as overlooked as Whistler's father, those members of the fourth estate who looked upon themselves as the movers and shakers of opinion devoting their attentions to players who had an association, past or present, with the three media epicenters: Like Willie Mays, Mickey Mantle and Ernie Banks.

1974 brought a full-fledged media circus. Now the chasing of 715 and the ghost of Ruth took on new proportions. Hundreds of members of the press, falling all over themselves to come up with some new angle, unearthed Guy Bush, the pitcher who had thrown Ruth his 714th home run ball, interviewed Mrs. Babe Ruth, and even, in their wretched excess, came up with the only humorous line attributed to Aaron in his 20-year-career—his rejoinder to Yogi Berra in the '58 World Series when Berra pointed out that his bat was turned around and the trademark wasn't showing: "Yogi, I came up here to hit, not to read."

Atlanta management, treating the event with all the seriousness of the Second Coming, issued a media guide that seemed to ignore the existence of anyone else on the Braves' roster. Instead, they provided everything anyone could ever want on the subject of Henry Aaron without asking—including, but hardly limited to, trivia, landmark dates, bio material, and other absurdities.

Then, with all the seriousness of a fourth assistant to the assistant district attorney delivering an indictment, Braves' management issued the most misleading misdirection since Douglas "Wrong Way" Corrigan filed flight plans for California and wound up instead in Ireland, proclaiming, "We owe Braves fans the

Aaron adds another on his way to the top of the Home Run Mountain

Aaron Hammers No. 715

opportunity to see Hank break Ruth's record." Several of the more cynical could only echo Mets' second baseman Bud Harrelson's comment, "Hell, if they really wanted to do it for Braves fans, let them play in Milwaukee." And baseball Commissioner Bowie Kuhn, without bothering to read between the lines—which, when rubbed with lemon juice, read: "We stand to make a helluva lot more money that way"—ordered Atlanta to have Aaron in the starting line-up during their opening three-game series in Cincinnati.

And so Aaron, equal to the pressure and publicity surrounding his assault on Ruth's record, stepped to the plate on Opening Day against Cincinnati's Jack Billingham and with the first swing of his 34¾-ounce bat sent homer number 714 soaring on an arc over Riverfront Stadium's left-center field wall at the 400-foot mark.

Now Aaron and Ruth stood together on a sparsely populated crest, one marked with the sign "714." Four days later, Aaron would stake out a still higher peak.

In front of the largest crowd to see the Braves since they had migrated to Atlanta eight years before, Aaron led off the second inning for the Braves against the Dodgers' Al Downing. Downing, wearing Number 44, threw a ball and then a called strike to Number 44 of the Braves, followed by three more balls. As Aaron made his way to first, 53,775 voices exploded in boos, having been deprived of seeing history made. Seconds later, Aaron was to provide history of another sort, coming home to score his 2,063rd run on Dusty Baker's double, breaking the National League record for runs scored and moving him into third place behind American-Leaguers Cobb and Ruth on the all-time list.

However, the restive fans had not come to see Aaron simply break a National League record, they had come to see him break *the* record, Babe Ruth's all-time home run record. In the fourth, they were to get another chance when Aaron came to the plate for the second time, his eighth time all season. With Darrell Evans on first, Aaron moved into the batter's box as serene and unmoved as

an oyster on the half shell, almost oblivious to the noise engulfing him. Downing came in with "Ball One," inside, and then came back with a pitch that didn't quite stay outside Aaron's strike zone. Aaron took his first swing of the night. The crowd jumped to its feet, their voices exploding into the air as the ball arched its way toward "Home Run Alley" and the hundreds of fans lined up against the railing hoping against hope to catch the ball valued as high as $25,000. However, the trajectory of the ball took it just short of the left-field seats, falling against the auxiliary scoreboard in the Braves' bullpen, where Atlanta relief pitcher Tom House snared it on as good a fielding play as he would make in his eight-year career. As the unemotional Aaron made his way around the bases, he allowed himself one well-earned smile and said, to no one in particular, "Thank God it's over."

The quest was finally ended. Downing had become the Omega to Raschi's Alpha. And the all-time home run leader had become the first name in baseball as well as the first name in the Baseball Encyclopedia: Hank Aaron.

LOS ANGELES (N.)					ATLANTA (N.)				
	ab.	r.	h.	bi.		ab.	r.	h.	bi.
Lopes, 2b	2	1	0	0	Garr, rf	3	0	0	1
Lacy, 2b	1	0	0	0	Lum, 1b	5	0	0	1
Buckner, lf	3	0	1	0	Evans.....	...	..	..	.
Wynn, cf	4	0	1	2	Evans, 3b	4	1	0	0
Ferguson, c	4	0	0	0	Aaron, lf	3	2	1	2
Crawford, rf	4	1	1	0	Office, cf	0	0	0	0
Cey, 3b	4	0	1	1	Baker, cf	2	1	1	0
Garvey, 1b	4	1	1	0	Johnson, 2b	3	1	1	0
Russell, ss	4	0	1	0	Foster, 2b	0	0	0	0
Downing, p	1	1	1	1	Correll, c	4	1	0	0
Marshall, p	1	0	0	0	Robinson, ss	0	0	0	0
Joshua, ph	1	0	0	0	Tepedino, ph	0	0	0	1
Hough, p	0	0	0	0	Perez, ss	2	1	1	0
Mota, ph	1	0	0	0	Reed, p	2	0	0	0
					Oates, ph	1	0	0	1
Total	34	4	7	4	Capra, p	0	0	0	0
					Total	29	7	4	6

Los Angeles ....003 001 000—4
Atlanta ....010 402 00x—7

E—Buckner, Cey, Russell 2, Lopes, Ferguson. LOB—Los Angeles 5, Atlanta 7. 2B—Baker, Russell, Wynn. HR—Aaron (2). S—Garr. SF—Garr.

	IP.	H.	R.	ER.	BB.	SO.
Downing, (L, 0-1) ...	3	2	5	2	4	2
Marshall	3	2	2	1	1	1
Hough	2	0	0	0	2	1
Reed (W, 1-0)	6	7	4	4	1	4
Capra	3	0	0	0	1	6

Save—Capra (1). Wild pitch—Reed. PB—Ferguson. T—2:27. A—53,775.

Number 715

29 The Mets' Miracle Win

New York Mets vs. Baltimore Orioles, 5th Game, 1969 World Series, October 16, 1969

Somewhere it was once written that long after an injured guy has forgotten how he was hurt, he'll remember who gave him a crutch. So it was with New York's National League fans, orphaned when the Dodgers and Giants left town in 1957. Suddenly, they had lost their sense of identity; and worse, their heritage. But even in their grief they wouldn't be caught dead in Yankee Stadium, where watching those guys in pinstripes who monotonously won all the time was "like rooting for U. S. Steel."

Dodger and Giant fans had never been the type to flock to a winner. They had faithfully stuck with their teams year after year, come hell or high jinx. And so, when the Dodgers and Giants went west after a combined total of 136 years in the National League, you would have thought some of those baseball-starved fans would have given in to an old urge and surreptitiously crept into Yankee Stadium, even if it was just for a "fix" to keep their old habit going. But the Yankees, as one of the team officials remembered, "offended a lot of people in the old days." And even though they were on their way to their ninth pennant in ten years, the Yankees actually drew 68,700 *fewer* fans in 1958 than they had the previous year when the Dodgers and the Giants had been in town.

No, the National League fans needed one of their own, a team they could support. The New York Mets, made of whole cloth in 1962, provided them with that crutch. And the fans, acting as if they hadn't yet found out Adam had been dispossessed, flocked to them.

The Mets back in those days were a team only in the same way a raisin can be classified as a fruit, technically and without reason. They were an expansion team of has-beens, never-wases and those who weren't even household names in their own households. Possessing all the paraphernalia of losers, they used slabs of Swiss cheese for bats, their double play combination could best be described as Chacon-to-Neal-to-the-parking-lot, and, on the whole, they looked like a road company for the Little League finalists. In fact, their total inadequacy could best be illustrated by the plight of center fielder Richie Ashburn, the anchor† of the 1962 Mets' outfield—such as it was. Ashburn played between two men who would never qualify for speed merchants, Gus Bell and Frank Thomas, and behind shortstop Elio Chacon. On more than one occasion, Ashburn, calling for the ball in the traditional, "I've got it!" would find Chacon, who didn't understand English, banging into him. Not wanting to spend the entire season sitting home watching his bones mend, Ashburn finally worked out a set of signals with Chancon that would have him calling out, *"Lo tengo"* all the better for the Spanish-speaking shortstop to *comprendo* and pull up short of a collision. The first time Ashburn camped out under a tall fly, he shouted out the agreed-upon, *"Lo tengo"* to wave off Chacon, only to find himself in a collision with Thomas who didn't understand Spanish. It was to be that kind of team; and that kind of year, as the woeful Mets lost 120 games.

But the attraction of the Mets was not just being a team of men forgotten but not gone. It was their packaging. And how they captured the hearts of New York. The Yankees were doing everything they could to alienate the typical New York fan, including confiscating banners and bedsheets within the stately confines of their pleasure palace with all the efficiency of S. S. troops and putting Casey Stengel, a man made out of gingerbread who looked like he had stepped right out of the pages of a Hans Christian Andersen fairy tale gone wrong, out to pasture. On the other glove, the new kids on the baseball block, the Mets, were making all the right moves. For openers they hired Stengel to run the team. Then they acquired the rights to play in the Polo Grounds, that duenna of major league parks and one which tugged at the heartstrings of every dyed-in-the-flannel National League fan. Next, they drafted one of the most popular Dodger stars of all time, Gil Hodges, in their first draft—a draft that saw them choose catcher Hobie Landrith as their first choice, because, as Stengel suggested, "Without a catcher you'll have all them passed balls." And, finally, they obtained the Yankees' former training site, St. Petersburg, as their spring headquarters. The Mets had arrived, if not on the field, at least in the hearts of New Yorkers, where it counted.

While the word the most punctilious stylist would have chosen to describe the Mets on the field was "terrible," they continued to capture headlines, mainly because their field leader was Casey Stengel, that loveable, gnomish man who, like Old Man River, just kept rolling along. Stengel, who knew that many placed called "Watering Holes" are provided in New York where men could repair for the purpose of extricating themselves from sundry and divers difficulty, found each and every and dragged friendly newsmen with him, exasperating them throughout the night with a lot of quotations from the past and double-talk of the future. But whatever Casey did, it begot the Mets ink in the papers the next day, far more than that accorded the Yankees, who were just doing what came to them naturally, winning.

Stengel coined the word "Amazin' " to somehow cover that skim milk in Mets uniforms attempting to masquerade as cream. But, truth to tell, it was the Mets' fans who were truly "Amazin'." Some were caught up in the role reversal of rooting for the underdog, seeing in the Mets an identifiable champion for all its lost causes. A strike-out with the bases empty was accompanied by cheers; a one-base error was enough to generate a "Let's Go Mets" chant; and a walk was enough for hosannahs. Together those who were searching for their own identity or a vicarious one all came out to the Polo Grounds to cheer even the weakest of ground balls, carry their illegible banners around the stands and follow their heroes. These fans were what New York *Daily News* columnist Dick Young called "The New Breed." And they were the making of the franchise.

During that first year the Mets traded their first draft choice, Landrith, to the Baltimore Orioles for a man who would become enshrined in lore and legend as the prototypical Met: Marvelous Marvin Throneberry. Not only were Throneberry's initials an acronym for the team (Marvin Eugene Throneberry, M. E. T.), but his exploits, more than those of any other player, epitomized the loveable ineptitude of the team. (On one occasion Throneberry hit what appeared to be a home run out of the park, only to be called out for failing to touch third. When asked why he hadn't appealed to the umpires, Stengel could only answer: "Hell, he missed first and second, too.") Soon T-shirts started blossoming like spring crocuses spelling, four across, "M-A-R-V," and then, when Throneberry, whirling around like a Water-Pik out of control, would make one of his inexplicable plays, they would reverse themselves to read: "V-R-A-M."

By 1963, the Mets had improved vastly, from terrible to just plain bad, losing "only" 111 games. And 1964 saw them improve again, if losing two fewer games is an improvement. That was the year that Met pitcher Tracy Stallard, who won 10 while losing a league-leading 20, got in on the growing spirit of Mets-amania when, after his team had scored six runs in the top of the ninth to give him a 19-1 lead, said, "That's when I knew I had them." By 1965, Casey Stengel had stepped, or rather hobbled, down, his ancient hip fractured in a fall. His torch-cum-crutch was handed over to coach Wes Westrum, former Giant catcher, who brought the Mets home dead last yet again, only 15 games out of ninth.

But something was happening, ever so imperceptibly. For among those long in the tooth, every now and then a young prospect could be sighted, bobbing to the surface. By 1966, the Mets could boast of an Ed Kranepool, a Ron Hunt, a Ron Swoboda, a Jerry Grote and a Tug McGraw. By 1967, Cleon Jones and Tom Seaver joined the team. And by 1968, Jerry Koosman, Nolan Ryan and Bud Harrelson. 1968 was also the year when Gil Hodges came back to the Mets as manager. And although the Mets finished in ninth place with a 73-89 record, all was in place for the most "Amazin'" year in baseball history: The Year of the 1969 Mets.

1969 was a year that would go down in history in more ways than one: It was the year when technological history was made as Man walked on the moon for the first time; and it was also the year

**Gil Hodges,
Miracle Maker**

when baseball history was made as the Mets romped to their first pennant ever. And the first championship of any sort for an expansion team. It was a feat that did not exactly beggar description, but it certainly had that word on the lookout for the mendicancy squad.

Only once before had such an improbable scenario taken place: Back in 1914 when the Boston Braves roared from last place on July 4th to take the pennant and then sweep the supposedly invincible A's in the Series in four straight games. That was enough for the Associated Press, in their half-century poll, to call it "The Greatest Upset of the 20th Century." But the Braves had nothing on the Mets. Both teams had had a .451 won-lost average the year before their unbelievable season, the Braves finishing in fifth place, the Mets in ninth. But the Braves had had a .251 team batting average the year they pulled off their "Greatest Upset," the Mets' team average was only .242; the Braves had had two twenty-game winners, the Mets one; and the Braves franchise had at least had a winking familiarity with the first division, finishing in that rarified atmosphere once; to the Mets, a pennant race had only been a rumor. *Theirs* was the most impossible dream.

Starting in the summer when they stood, literally, nine-and-a-half games behind the Cubs, the Mets put on a torrid stretch drive, culminating in a sweep over the Cubs in a head-to-head series in early September—highlighted by Tom Seaver's one-hitter, a dying quail single by Jimmy Qualls in the ninth all that separated him from a perfect game—to put them over the top, on their way to the Eastern Division championship by an "Amazin'" eight-game margin. The Mets then continued their miracle antics by sweeping the Hank Aaron-led Atlanta Braves in three games in the first Championship Series ever played and made their merry way to the World Series. And the Baltimore Orioles. But even the most foolhardy, even those who believe in miracles, would never have scripted what happened next. For it was believed by most observers that the team which had won the National League pennant in a breeze—and captured the imagination of the nation in the process—would run out of miracles when it came to the World Series.

The 1969 Orioles came into the World Series as heavily favored as the A's had been in 1914, having won the Eastern Division of the American League by no less than 19 games and having swept the Minnesota Twins in their divisional Championship Series. Earl Weaver had put together a squad that tottered on the brink of dynasty, one which included Brooks Robinson, Mark Belanger, Boog Powell, Paul Blair, Mike Cuellar, Dave McNally and Jim Palmer, plus a cast of supporting players who could step in and pick up the slack at any time. But dynasty was to meet destiny; and in this case, dynasty was to come out decidedly on the short end.

However, it looked bad for destiny in the first game of the Series, as Don Buford, the first man up in the Orioles' half of the first drove Tom Seaver's second pitch over the right field fence, and the Birds, behind Mike Cuellar, coasted to a 4-1 victory. But Fate, which has an unnerving habit of jangling whatever strings are near at hand, now began to jangle those marked "Mets," and the Mets' magic resurfaced.

Game Two saw Jerry Koosman pitch a two-hitter and even up the Series. And then it was all Met magic from there on in, as the Series took on a dog-bites-man plot line. Back in the friendly environs of Shea Stadium for Game Three, the Mets turned the tables on the O's, Tommy Agee, the first man up in the bottom of their first, driving one of Jim Palmer's fast balls over the center field fence. Pitcher Gary Gentry then added two more with a double in the second. And then Gentry and Agee combined to hold the lead,

Gentry holding the Orioles to four hits and Agee making a sensational diving backhanded catch of Elrod Hendrick's sinking liner in the fourth at the base of the wall and coming back to snare a Paul Blair liner in the seventh as he slid on his belly somewhere out there in deep right-center field, leaving a total of five Baltimore baserunners on the base paths, there to stay like ice on a pond in the dead of winter.

Game Four was a redux of Game One, with Seaver and Cuellar going at it again. In the second, Don Clendenon homered to give the Mets a 1-0 lead, a lead which held up for eight and two-thirds innings. But in the ninth, Baltimore suddenly came to life, and after Blair had flied out to Swoboda, Frank Robinson singled to left, and Boog Powell singled to right, sending Robinson to third. Then the Robinson of the second part, Brooks, swinging late on a Seaver fastball, drove a sinking line drive somewhere in the direction of Ron Swoboda in right center. Swoboda, stealing a page out of Agee's book of magic, made a diving catch to retire Robinson, Brooks, with Robinson, Frank, coming in after the catch to tie the score. Almost as if he were parroting Jimmy Durante's "You ain't seen nuthin' yet, folks," line, Swoboda then repeated his act by robbing Ellie Hendricks of a hit with a running catch of his inning-ending line drive to send the game into the bottom of the ninth, tied 1-1. But even though the Mets managed two hits off Baltimore reliever Eddie Watt, they couldn't manage to score, and the game went into extra innings. And into the realm of the "Amazin'."

After the Mets retired the O's in the top of the tenth, the Mets started with Oriole left fielder Don Buford misplaying Jerry Grote's short bloop fly into a double. Now the game became less a baseball game than a game of chess as the two managers jockeyed players and percentages. First Mets manager Gil Hodges sent in Rod Gaspar to run for Grote. As he did, Oriole manager Earl Weaver sent in instructions for reliever Dick Hall—who had just come in to the game in relief of Watt, who, in turn, had come in in relief of Cuellar—to walk the normally weak-hitting Al Weis (who had hit but .215 during the year, but catching the Mets' magic had hit .455 in the Series) in order to set up a possible double play with

Jerry Koosman, on his way to a win in Game Four

Tom Seaver, alias "Tom Terrific"

Game 5 October 16 at New York

Baltimore	Pos	AB	R	H	RBI	PO	A	E
Buford	lf	4	0	0	0	1	0	0
Blair	cf	4	0	0	0	3	0	0
F. Robinson	rf	3	1	1	1	2	0	0
Powell	1b	4	0	1	0	6	0	1
b Salmon		0	0	0	0	0	0	0
B. Robinson	3b	4	0	0	0	1	4	0
Johnson	2b	4	0	1	0	1	0	0
Etchebarren	c	3	0	0	0	8	0	0
Belanger	ss	3	1	1	0	2	1	0
McNally	p	2	1	1	2	0	0	0
a Motton		1	0	0	0	0	0	0
Watt	p	0	0	0	0	0	0	1
Totals		32	3	5	3	24	5	2

New York	Pos	AB	R	H	RBI	PO	A	E
Agee	cf	3	0	1	0	4	0	0
Harrelson	ss	4	0	0	0	1	6	0
Jones	lf	3	2	1	0	3	0	0
Clendenon	1b	3	1	1	2	8	0	0
Swoboda	rf	4	1	2	1	5	0	0
Charles	3b	4	0	0	0	0	1	0
Grote	c	4	0	0	0	5	0	0
Weis	2b	4	1	1	1	1	2	0
Koosman	p	3	0	1	0	0	1	0
Totals		32	5	7	4	27	10	0

Bal. 003 000 000
N.Y. 000 002 12x

Pitching	IP	H	R	ER	BB	SO
Baltimore						
McNally	7	5	3	3	2	6
Watt (L)	1	2	2	1	0	1
New York						
Koosman (W)	9	5	3	3	1	5

a Grounded out for McNally in 8th.
b Ran for Powell in 9th.

Doubles—Jones, Koosman, Swoboda. Home Runs—Clendenon, McNally, F. Robinson, Weis. Stolen Base—Agee. Hit by Pitch—Jones (by McNally). Left on Bases—Baltimore 3, New York 6. Umpires—DiMuro, Weyer, Soar, Secory, Napp, Crawford. Attendance—57,397. Time of Game—2:14.

Seaver scheduled to bat. But Hodges, turning the chess game into one of leap frog, called on the left-handed hitting J. C. Martin, his reserve catcher appearing in his first Series game, to pinch-hit for the right-handed hitting Seaver against the right-handed throwing Hall. As Martin made his way to the plate, Weaver continued the game of musical players by calling on left-hander Pete Richert to face Martin. Finally, the official scorer, having gotten cramps writing down the changes, had entered all of them in the official boxscore, and the game was ready to continue. Richert came in with the pitch and Martin bunted it toward the mound. Richert jumped off the mound and fielded the ball. After looking first at third and then at second, Richert saw he had no play at either base. He then threw the ball toward first where it hit Martin's wrist as the catcher chugged down the line illegally in fair territory and caroomed into foul territory, the winning run scoring. The Mets Magic had continued.

The fifth game was a declincher, the result a foregone conclusion, as the Mets and Magic triumphed 5-3 to wrap up the greatest upset in the history of baseball. Finally, the Mets could throw away their crutches. They had walked on water.

Mets Win, 5-3, Take the Series

New York welcomes its conquering heroes.

30 "1951" Play-Off Revisited

San Francisco Giants vs. Los Angeles Dodgers, Play-Off Game, October 3, 1962

IN ONE OF HIS RUBAIYATS OF THE JACK DANIELS AND BRANCH water, Dan Jenkins took a Texas-eye view of the rest of the country as seen from down under and called our bicoastal regions "The left coast and the right coast." Using Mr. Jenkins' imaginative description, the left coast recreated one of the right coast's most memorable moments, the Bobby Thomson "Shot Heard 'Round the World," with their own version, the 1962 Giant-Dodger Play-Offs, a little three-act outrage for all those drugged by the scent of the reconstituted past.

Much had happened since the Giants and the Dodgers met in the Play-Offs the first time around those eleven years before. For the 1951 Play-Offs had taken place on the right coast, the East Coast, in two places called the Polo Grounds and Ebbets Field, two once-proud baseball parks that now stood as vestigial reminders of what was, offending the residual sense of memory of millions of New York and Brooklyn fans. For, in 1957, six seasons after one of the most glorious moments in all of sports, Brooklyn president Walter O'Malley, treating the fans of Brooklyn like widow-and-orphan oppressors with incipient Bright's Disease, upped and moved his entire operation to Los Angeles, taking the team, lock, stock and memories, to the left coast. Along with his traveling companion, Horace Stoneham and his franchise, the New York Giants. Suddenly, after three-quarters of a century of wedded bliss between a city and its teams, it was over, and, in a take-off on Bill Terry's famous baseball question, neither Brooklyn nor New York were "still in the League."

By 1962 baseball, not unlike the man who had to loosen his belt continuously to ingest more and more food, had taken to expanding its own horizons by seating more and more cities at its own exclusive dinner table. Starting in 1962, the National League numbered ten in its seating arrangement and went to a 162-game schedule to determine its winner. But it was to take three more games—the most games ever played by a team in all of base-balldom—to finally come up with a winner in one of the most exciting three-game sets this side of Brooklyn and New York.

The two teams involved, as always seemed to be the subtext when this sort of thing occurred, were the Giants, now of San Francisco, and the Dodgers, now of Los Angeles, locked in a rivalry that challenged, in one sentence, history, Noah Webster and Rand-McNally. And, like good wine, the rivalry traveled very well indeed from right coast to left coast.

But the '62 Play-Offs should never have taken place. Holding a four-game lead over the second-place Giants with but one week left in the season, the Dodgers looked like sure things. Especially with Maury Wills supplying the fire-power on the basepaths and Tommy Davis ditto in the batter's box. Just when it looked like the Dodgers could cruise home on their batteries, they all but shut them down completely, their good performances so few they could be suspended like fruit in Jell-O. Losing eight of their next eleven games, the Dodgers moved backward to just two games ahead of the Giants. And were closing fast. For their part, the Giants weren't so much winning it—with Willie Mays wandering off third thinking

there were three out when there were only two and other such heads-down plays—as much as the Dodgers were blowing it as completely as a pyromaniac sneezing on his last match.

Now the pennant came down to the final two games of the season: The Dodgers versus the Cardinals and the Giants versus the expansion Houston Colt .45s. In one of those absolutely, positively, I-swear-my-hand-to-God truths, Willie Mays told of being approached by Houston second baseman Joey Amalfitano, who only the previous year had been with the Giants. "Can you score a run?," Amalfitano asked Mays. Taken aback by the question, Mays answered, "Yes," and then quickly amended his answer to read, "Well, at least I think we can." "Then you've got the pennant," Amalfitano responded, "because those Dodgers are *never* going to score another run." Sure enough, while the Giants were winning, the Dodgers were being blanked by the Cards for their ninth loss in 12 games. Now only one game separated the two.

The next day Mays hit a mammoth home run off Houston pitcher Dick Farrell, his 47th of the year, as the Giants won 2-1 to preserve their negotiability. Retreating to their clubhouse to await, like a curbside taxi, whatever destination the fates had in store for them, they huddled in a tiny knot around the radio to hear the end of the Dodger-Cardinal game. There they heard Dodger announcer Vince Scully describe the Dodgers continuing to make too much of a bad thing, their bats practicing obsequies and other servilities as they extended their scoreless streak to 22 innings and lost 1-0.

For the first time in history a team had backed into the Play-Offs, winning while the front-runner was losing. And for the fourth time in four National League Play-Offs—1946, 1951, 1959 and now 1962—the Dodgers were involved, this time against their opponents from eleven years before, the Giants.

To author Roger Angell it was "A Tale of Three Cities." But to millions of others, protecting the yellowing clippings of their memories, it was a repeat of baseball's most memorable fiction, the 1951 Play-Offs, played by that bedrock of rivalries, the Dodgers and the Giants, now two left coast stepchildren.

For those who remembered 1951 and whose tour map included stopovers at memories, there were three nostalgic links to the past whose very presence brought back evocations of the last time these two teams had foregathered in the Play-Offs: Willie Mays, a rookie in '51 and now the caretaker of the shrine for all Giant and Dodger fans everywhere; Alvin Dark, the shortstop on the '51 Giants and now manager of the '62 left coast version; and, the most interesting of the memories in uniform, Leo Durocher, who had been the manager of the '51 Giants and now served as coach for the Dodgers. All three would now take a part in the ancestral rite being revisited on the left coast but which had more of a meaning for those on the right coast who were suckers for such a rite.

There were other common denominators, most notably the calendar which marked Monday, October 1st as the starting date for both Play-Offs. Now, with the first game scheduled, courtesy of a flip of the coin, for San Francisco's wind tunnel, also known as Candlestick Park, Giant manager Alvin Dark was engaged in a pinch of early-morning managerial chicanery on *this* Monday. Recognizing that feet had brought the Dodgers in—particularly those of their Wills O' the Wisp, Maury, who had broken Ty Cobb's 47-year-old stolen base record with 100 thefts, most of them in what Dark called "the brickyard," Dodger Stadium—he determined that feet would not take them out and had the infield watered down, all the better to neutralize Wills' speed.

But as they say on the right coast, he shoulda stood in bed for all it mattered. For the Dodgers not only didn't score, keeping their string of scoreless innings intact, but barely got on base against Giant left-hander Billy Pierce. Playing with glazed eyes that had a dead fish look, they walked through the formalities, getting only three hits and one walk, none of the above by Wills. The Giants, for their part, got to Dodger starter Sandy Koufax who was coming off the injury list to make his first start since mid-July when he had gone down with a circulatory problem in his left index finger. Pressed into duty by Dodger manager Walter Alston, who gambled he could come back and stop the Dodger skid, Koufax lasted one-plus innings, giving up three runs and two homers by Mays as the Giants coasted to an 8-0 win. And a 1-0 lead in the Play-Offs.

The Play-Offs now shifted to that musical version of New York, Los Angeles, and to the Dodgers' first-year stadium, known to the locals as Dodger Stadium and Chavez Ravine and to cynics as the Taj O'Malley. With that nauseous feeling of inevitability that comes from watching your heroes suddenly develop an acute aversion to stepping on home plate, the smallest crowd ever to see a Play-Off game came out, only 25,231, fleshed out by the normal complement of obligatory celebrities, there to see as well as be seen.

Juan Marichal, San Francisco's starting pitcher in the Third Play-Off Game, fires on plateward

For five innings the Dodgers, in the words of master writer Roger Angell, "displayed the muscle, the frightfulness, and the total immobility of a wooly mammoth frozen in a glacier." The Giants meanwhile, "finding the beast inert, fell upon it with savage cries and chopped off steaks and rump roasts at will," building up a 5-0 lead against Los Angeles starter Don Drysdale.

Trailing by five and scoreless in 36, the Dodgers finally deserted their utterly dependable scenario in the sixth, bringing their once-frozen armaments to life. The inning started innocuously enough with Junior Gilliam working a tired Jack Sanford for a walk. That was enough for Dark, who replaced Sanford with reliever Stu Miller. But Miller rendered a double to Duke Snider and an outfield fly to Tommy Davis to fetch home the first Dodger run since Angell's troglodyte age. One walk, one hit-by-pitch, one error, two singles, one double and two Giant pitchers later, the Dodgers had six more runs and a 7-5 lead. The Giants came back with two of their own in their half of the eighth to tie the score. But, in the bottom of the ninth, the Dodger batters worked three Giant pitchers for three walks to load the bases and then won the game on a short outfield fly which saw Wills dashing home ahead of Mays' strong throw for an 8-7 Dodger win.

There would be a third game, eleven years to the day after the "Shot Heard 'Round the World."

Although one look at the calendar should have told those looking for an omen that twice before on this date the Dodgers had lost the final canto of a Play-Off, 45,693 non-believers in the fates came out to Dodger Stadium on Wednesday, October 3rd to see what had been billed in the local papers as "The Sudden-Death Duel for the Pennant." What they saw instead was a suicide pact. Acting like some of life's losing stuntmen, the Dodgers shot themselves in the foot with three ghastly third-inning errors to gift-

Willie Mays, who sparked the Giants in a come-from-behind win in the third game of the Play-Offs

Sandy Koufax, the Dodgers' starting pitcher in Game One of the Play-Offs

wrap two runs for the Giants. Wounded but still alive, the Dodgers got back one of their own in the fourth off Giant starter Juan Marichal when the Giants couldn't pull the trigger on a double-play, giving them back half of their gift. Going into the sixth the score more sat than stood at 2-1, Giants.

The duel turned, for the first time, in the sixth. After Dodger starter Johnny Podres had given up three singles to load the bases with none out, the Dodgers escaped the bullet when reliever Ed Roebuck came in to retire the side on two enfeebled ground balls to Wills. Inspired by their efforts afield, the Dodgers came to bat in their half of the sixth ready to pick up their sputtering weaponry. After that old expatriate Duke Snider had singled, homegrown hero Tommy Davis, eschewing his bat and employing instead a howitzer, drove one of Marichal's offerings into the wild Dodger-blue yonder for a two-run homer—Snider, scoring ahead of Davis, jumping on the plate with both feet to make sure it didn't move—and a 3-2 Dodger lead.

In the eighth the Dodgers added yet another run on the baserunning pyrotechnics of one Maury Wills, now the base-stealing champion of both coasts. Wills, setting up shop on first with his fourth single off Marichal, promptly set out for second on the first pitch to Junior Gilliam, and, propelled by his own spark of devine fire, slid into second far ahead of catcher Ed Bailey's throw. Whereas only the day before Bailey had fired his throw down to second trying to catch Wills and instead thrown it on a line into center, directly at Mays who had thrown out Wills at third on his attempt to stretch his stolen base, the now-flustered Bailey, seeing Wills light out for third, overthrew the outstretched glove of third baseman Jim Davenport into left field, far away from any help Mays could bring to bear. Arising joint-by-joint, almost as a carpenter's rule opening up, Wills picked himself up, dusted himself off,

and started all over again—for home, with the Dodgers' fourth run.

So, just as it had eleven years before, it all came down to the ninth. But unlike Durocher, who eleven years before had employed his cauliflower tongue to indulge his troops in one of his "Win-this-one-for-the-Gipper" speeches, Dark, who had led off that ninth inning eleven years before with a single, merely said "Matty, get your bat," selecting Matty Alou to pinch-hit for reliever Don Larsen. As Alou dragged a pale ashen bat that looked as long as he was to the plate, Durocher, remembering the echoes of an earlier day, stared out of the Dodger dugout with that cold marble face that chilled the noonday. Without waiting for a proper introduction to Ed Roebuck or his pitches, Alou, M., brief and business-like, hit the first pitch for a single. However, this last gasp seemed exactly that seconds later when Harvey Kuenn's grounder erased Alou at second on a fielder's choice. But then the second of Dark's reinforcements, Willie McCovey, batting for second baseman Chuck Hiller, got a pinch walk to put the tying runs on. And when Roebuck's control continued to be a stranger and he walked Alou, Felipe, to load the bases, it brought to the plate the hero-designate, Willie Mays.

Mays, who eleven years ago had been in the on-deck circle when Bobby Thomson hit his dramatic home run "praying that it wouldn't have to be me to come up with the bases loaded in the ninth," was now a lusty combatant instead of a raw rookie, and "prayed it would be me . . . I *wanted* to hit!" And hit he did, bruising the ball more than a bit and it, in turn, bruising Roebuck's leg as it caromed off the Dodger pitcher for a run-producing single, making the score 4-3 and leaving the bases loaded.

Dodger manager Alston, trying mightily to stuff the toothpaste back into the tube, now called on the winner of the second game in

Box Score of 3d Playoff Game

SAN FRANCISCO (N.)	AB.	R.	H.	RBI.	PO.	A.	LOS ANGELES (N.)	AB.	R.	H.	RBI.	PO.	A.
Kuenn, lf......	5	1	2	1	2	0	Wills, ss........	5	1	4	0	3	0
Hiller, 2b.....	3	0	1	0	4	1	Gilliam, 2b-3b..	5	0	0	0	3	1
bMcCovey	0	0	0	0	0	0	Snider, lf......	3	2	2	0	2	0
cBowman, 2b..	0	1	0	0	0	0	Burright, 2b....	1	0	0	0	3	2
F. Alou, rf....	4	1	1	0	4	0	eWalls	1	0	0	0	0	0
Mays, cf......	3	1	1	1	3	0	T. Davis, 3b-lf.	3	1	2	2	1	1
Cepeda, 1b....	4	0	1	1	8	0	Moon, 1b.......	3	0	0	0	8	0
Bailey, c......	4	0	2	0	3	0	Fairly, 1b-rf...	0	0	0	0	2	0
Davenport, 3b.	4	0	1	1	2	4	Howard, rf.....	4	0	1	0	0	0
Pagan, ss.....	5	1	2	0	1	1	Harkness, 1b..	0	0	0	0	0	0
Marichal, p....	2	1	1	0	0	0	Roseboro, c....	3	0	0	0	3	1
Larsen, p......	0	0	0	0	0	1	W. Davis, cf...	3	0	0	0	2	0
aM. Alou.......	1	0	1	0	0	0	Podres, p......	2	0	0	0	0	2
dNieman	1	0	0	0	0	0	Roebuck, p....	0	0	0	0	0	0
Pierce, p.......	0	0	0	0	0	0	Williams, p....	0	0	0	0	0	0
							Perranoski, p..	0	0	0	0	0	0
Total	36	6	13	4	27	7	Total	35	4	8	3	27	14

aSingled for Larsen in 9th; bWalked for Hiller in 9th; cRan for McCovey in 9th; dStruck out for M. Alou in 9th; eLined out for Burright in 9th.

San Francisco Giants................. 0 0 2   0 0 0   0 0 4—6
Los Angeles Dodgers................. 0 0 0   1 0 2   1 0 0—4

Errors—Marichal, Podres, Roseboro, Gilliam, Pagan, Bailey, Burright. Double plays—Gilliam, Wills and Moon; Wills and Moon; Wills, Burright and Fairly. Left on bases—San Francisco 12, Los Angeles 8.

Two-base hits—Snider, Hiller. Home run—T. Davis. Stolen bases—Wills 3, T. Davis. Sacrifices—Hiller, Marichal, Fairly. Sacrifice fly—Cepeda.

	IP.	H.	R.	ER.	BB.	SO.	HBP.	WP.	Balks
*Marichal	7	3	4	3	1	2	0	1	0
Larsen (W, 5-4)	1	0	0	0	2	1	0	0	0
Pierce	1	0	0	0	0	0	0	0	0
†Podres	5	9	2	2	1	0	0	0	0
Roebuck (L, 10-2)	3⅓	4	4	3	3	0	0	0	0
Williams	⅓	0	0	0	2	0	0	0	0
Perranoski	⅓	0	0	0	0	1	0	0	0

relief, Stan Williams, to come out of the bullpen and put out the raging fire. But Orlando Cepeda met Williams' fire with some of his own, hitting a deep fly to right that scored the tying run and advanced Alou, F., to third. Williams personally insured that the margin of safety would become even narrower by uncorking what was less a wild pitch than a tame one with a miss, the miss being that of Johnny Roseboro who allowed the ball to skip a few feet away from him and Mays to skip down to second unmolested. With men now on second and third, Alston ordered Williams to intentionally pass catcher Ed Bailey to load the bases and set up a force play.

But all such gifts of charity some encumbered with debts to be paid later. And as Dodger fans set up a low hum, almost one which emulated the keening sound of those eternally put upon, Williams, never renowned for his control and now beset by visions of becoming a latter-day Ralph Branca, paid that debt by throwing an inside pitch to Giant third baseman Jim Davenport on a 3-1 count, walking across Alou, F., with the tie-breaking run. Yet another run came scampering across the plate on an error in the person of Willie Mays and suddenly the Giants had four runs, the same number they had scored in the ninth inning to those eleven years ago. And a 6-4 lead.

The difference—with the notable exception of a dramatic home run, a la Bobby Thomson—between this time around and the last time was that now the Giants had to go out and protect their newly-minted lead in the bottom of the ninth. Now Dark brought in the winner of the first game, Billy Pierce, to draw the tendrils of the octopus around the Dodgers' chances. Pierce delivered as advertised, setting the Dodgers down as docilely as he had in the first game.

The last ball went, naturally enough, to Willie Mays in straight-away center, a ball that held up almost as if it were suspended from one of the fluffy cumulus puffs of white with gray that had hung over the Stadium all afternoon. This time Mays would not resort to one of the basket catches that had made him famous, catching it like a grocery clerk catching an overripe tomato in his outstretched apron; this time the keeper of the Giant-Dodger Play-Off flame would cradle it securely in his glove and race back to the infield with his trophy.

The 1962 version of the 1951 Play-Offs was finally over with almost the exact same result, although without benefit of a home run of the dramatic impact of Bobby Thomson's. But then again, the left coast was always more laid back, leaving all such dramatics to the right coast.

Giants Win Playoff, 6-4, in 9th; Oppose Yanks in Series Today

The Giants stayed alive down the stretch on the heroics of Willie McCovey and Mays, among others.

31 Lou Boudreau's Great Day

Cleveland Indians vs. Boston Red Sox, Play-Off Game, October 4, 1948

ONE OF THE MOST RECURRENT THEMES IN DRAMATURGY IS that of the man cast out who ultimately comes back to reward those who have thrown him out. In a story line as timeless as a blade of grass, going all the way back to Joseph of the technicolor coat, many's the outcast who has come back. Handsomely. One who almost fit into that category was Lou Boudreau. Almost, but not quite. And therein lies a tale worth telling.

But before we get to Boudreau, we should start at the beginning. In this case, that means Bill Veeck, who, on June 22, 1946, purchased the Cleveland Indians for $2.2 million. The entry of the new owner on the American League block was greeted by columnist Red Smith as "One of the best things that could have happened to the American League," noting that he brought to baseball two qualities it hasn't had in a long while: "A business administration under a young and lively guy who never has had any business except baseball, and promotional methods that are fresh, original, intelligent, enthusiastic, uninhibited and imaginative."

Will Harridge, the president of the American League and head of the Old Guard's Welcoming Committee, greeted Veeck's entry into the ranks with a touching, "But, of course, you're going to cut out the gags," remembering all too-well his little adventures as head of the Milwaukee franchise in the American Association some three years earlier. The so-called Old Guard, a group of men whose idea of a good time was wearing brown shoes, viewed anything that wasn't 110 percent pure and unadulterated baseball as kippered baseball, unworthy of them.

But Veeck, who believed that "Baseball was the best entertainment buy, dollar-for-dollar," was prepared to use "the gags" to sell the product. He unveiled a dynamic duo in the coaching boxes in the persons of contortionist Max Patkin and comedian Jackie Price. He gave away hard-to-get nylons, pushed Bob Feller to break the all-time strike-out record, and showered the fans with promotions and the field with fireworks.

With wartime restrictions lifted, attendance in the Major Leagues—still measured by the 1920 record—soared to 18-and-a-half million in 1946, up 69 percent over 1945. But Cleveland's attendance climbed even more. When Veeck took over the team attendance stood at only 289,000. At season's end, attendance figures stood at 1,057,289, up an astonishing 89.4 percent over 1945 and surpassing the previous Cleveland record set in 1920 by some 150,000. One Sunday afternoon the second largest crowd in Major League history showed up at Municipal Stadium to watch the Indians play a double-header against the Yankees. Apparently what had been called "bush" in the bush leagues worked just as well in Cleveland.

The team itself was hardly able to match Veeck's pyrotechnics, finishing sixth while compiling the lowest batting average and the second lowest run production totals in the League.

With the team about to move into large Municipal Stadium from small League Park for all its home games, something would have to be done to shore up the weak Indian team before "the

gags" would even take. Veeck's entire marketing premise was based on one factor: "You start with a product." And in this case the Indians were an inferior product at best.

One of the first trades the tireless and tieless Veeck put together to give the team some muscle was the "almost" trade of player-manager Lou Boudreau to the Browns for shortstop Vern Stephens and a cast of thousands. But the Tribe's new chieftain sorely underestimated Louie's popularity.

Ever since Boudreau first came off the University of Illinois campus as a handsome and personable puppy youth to capture the starting shortstop position and the imagination of Cleveland fans, he had been the most popular Indian to populate their teepee since the days of Tris Speaker. A perennial all-star at short, Boudreau had led the League in fielding every year since he became a fixture at short back in '39, and had added League-leading figures in putouts four times, double plays three and assists two. And although sportswriter Stanley Frank had called him, "The slowest ballplayer since Ernie Lombardi was thrown out trying to stretch a double into a single," Boudreau had not had to stretch all that many, twice leading the League in two-baggers of the legitimate variety and, almost as if to prove he had lightning in his bat to go with his thunder afoot, had led the League in batting in 1944 with a .327 average. Added to his fielding prowess and his batting power, Boudreau had also gained fame as the youngest manager in the history of Major League baseball, taking over the reins of the Indians in 1942 at the tender age of 24. Granted, over the succeeding five years his managerial won-lost record of less than .500 was unlikely to kindle comparisons with John McGraw, he still was considered Cleveland's leading citizen. But the real cornerstone of his popularity was his youthful Gallic good looks, a handsomeness that captured the public imagination in a manner normally reserved for leading men of the Clark Gable, persuasion.

In short, any plan to move Lou Boudreau was looked upon by the citizenry of Cleveland as comparable to the moving of a civic monument. Which he was.

When the news of the proposed Boudreau-for-Stephens deal hit the headlines, Cleveland fans, especially the women who had fallen in like with Boudreau's matinee idol features, rallied to his defense demanding he be kept. Veeck, who had a tacit and tactical understanding of the worth of headlines, not only called the trade off, he donned sackcloth, beat his breast in a public *mea culpa* admission of his mistake and retained Boudreau, even giving him a raise to boot instead of the boot.

Instead of trading away his local hero, Veeck traded pitcher Allie Reynolds to the Yankees for Joe Gordon, picked up Gene Bearden in another trade with the Yankees, acquired old Milwaukee outfielder Hal Peck from the A's, bought Bob Kennedy from the White Sox and added Johnny Berardino and Bob Muncrief from the Brownies. The job of building a creditable team with Boudreau still at the helm had begun.

In 1947 the Indians improved their team batting average by 14 percentage points, increased their home run output by 33 and their runs scored by 150. And moved up to fourth. Attendance, sparked by the team's better play, the use of Municipal Stadium for all the Indians' home games and more Veeck promotions, climbed almost another half a million—the largest increase in the Majors—to 1,521,978. The Veeck method of merchandising the National Pastime was succeeding in spite of the doubting Thomases, Griffiths, Comiskeys and Harridges.

1948 was to be the Indians' year. On the field and in the front office as well.

As the Indians made their first run for the pennant in 28 years, Municipal Stadium began to take on the look of The House that Veeck Promoted Hell Out Of, with more than 2.6 million baseball-and promotion-mad fans flocking to the ballpark to see the Indians. And the promotions. One of those promotions had something else going for it, a little incentive on the side as Veeck threw a party for Kenny Keltner, the Cleveland third baseman. Keltner, who had just broken the record for the most games ever played at third for Cleveland in this his tenth full season as an Indian could use, or so Veeck reasoned, a little bit of psychological encouragement. And so a Kenny Keltner "Night" was given to render aid and comfort to one of the important cogs in the Indians' wheel. Apparently the treatment "took" as Keltner went on to enjoy his greatest year, a year which saw him hit more homers, score more runs and drive in more than ever before.

But even though Keltner had responded the way Veeck knew he would, one who responded differently was a plant foreman at the local Chevrolet plant named Joe Earley. Earley wrote a letter to the editor of the Cleveland *Press* asking, "Why not honor the guy who pays the freight?" instead of the high-priced stars. And so, Good Old Joe Earley Night was held. It had all the trappings of what was to become known as Fan Appreciation Night as orchids, flown in from Hawaii at a cost of $30,000, were given to the first 20,000 women entering the park and Good Ole Joe was given enough gifts to pay the freight from Cleveland to at least New York and back several times over, including an automobile, a refrigerator, a stove and a "house." Well, a house of sorts, for Rudie Schaeffer owned a piece of property out in Brecksville, Ohio, halfway between Toledo and Akron and one of the houses on the property was an outhouse that wasn't really needed. "So," remembered Rudie, "we gave it to him."

But that wasn't all Veeck gave the fans. He gave them fireworks, clowns, giveaways, and, not incidentally, a great team. Wheeling and dealing to bolster a pitching staff that already included the likes of Bob Feller, Bob Lemon and the rookie phenomenon Gene Bearden, sportshirt Bill bought Russ Christopher from the A's on April 3rd, left-hander Sam Zoldak from the Brownies just before the June 15th trading deadline, and then, still seeking help, dealt with the Kansas City Monarchs of the Negro League on July 7th for the ageless Satchel Paige, described in the press release as "40 or older"—but who once dismissed a question about his age with "If you don't know how old you are, how old would you be?"

It was this pitching staff that established one American League record and tied another by pitching four straight shutouts and 47 consecutive scoreless innings that August with Lemon, Bearden, Zoldak and Paige pitching back-to-back-to-back-to-back shutouts and Feller and Lemon tacking on scoreless innings on both ends of the skein.

Coupled with an outstanding pitching staff that led the American League in ERA, shutouts, saves and least runs allowed, the Indians also possessed an airtight defense that led the League in fielding and an explosiveness at the plate. With youngsters Larry

Doby, Eddie Robinson and Dale Mitchell joining in the hit parade along with veterans Boudreau, Keltner and Gordon, the Indians led the League in hits, home runs and batting.

Going into the last day of the season, the Indians had parlayed all of the abovementioned into a one-game lead over the Boston Red Sox, clinching a tie for the pennant on Gene Bearden's 19th win, an 8-0 victory over the Detroit Tigers. But here fate, and its handmaiden, Hal Newhouser, had conspired against the Indians as Newhouser outdueled his nemesis Bob Feller in front of 75,000 pennant-hungry fans who had turned out to watch Cleveland win its first pennant since Warren Harding was in office, nearly three decades before. Meanwhile, the Red Sox were beating the Yankees to finish the season with an identical 96-58 mark, forcing the first Play-Off game in American League history.

The Play-Off Game was scheduled for Boston, the result of a coin toss earlier that month in the offices of American League President Harridge when it appeared that there would be a three-way tie between Boston, Cleveland and the Yankees. Now, like Agatha Christie's dwindling number of Indians, there were just two and Boudreau, hoping the last Indians would be his, had taken his team to Boston immediately after the loss to Detroit for the Play-Off Game.

What Boudreau found on his arrival was a city not interested in the possibility of defeat. The Braves had already won their first pennant since the Great Flood. And now the Red Sox were poised on the cusp of making it the first all-Boston Series. It was almost the duty of all good Bostonians everywhere to drink, drill, dress up and be dreadful on this day of all days as fire engines stood ready to blare sirens, churches ring bells, cars toot horns and people exude steam in celebration of what they viewed their just due. There was just one small rub: Those pieces de resistance called the Cleveland Indians.

As Boudreau sat in the visitors' locker room at Fenway Park going through his own private mental hells, his mind began to fill with daguerrotypes and darker plates of those who had had to face both that living explosion of hitting intimidation known as the Red Sox *and* that 37-foot left-field wall known as "The Green Monster." In order to reduce the frightening odds now facing him, Boudreau decided to load up his line-up with right-handed batters, all the better to draw a bead on that inviting wall, and penciled in the name Allie Clark at first instead of left handed Eddie Robinson.

Then, pencil still aflutter, Boudreau took an "I-say-it's-spinach-and-the-hell-with-it" approach to those who said you couldn't pitch a left hander in Fenway and marked in the name of his rookie left hander, Gene Bearden, as his starting pitcher. Writers, protecting the yellowing clips of their memories, couldn't believe that Boudreau would have the *chutzpah* to start a left hander in Fenway. After all, hadn't Lefty Gomez sat outside the stadium in a phone booth every time he was scheduled to pitch in order to acclimate himself to the unfriendly confines of Fenway? And hadn't manager Jimmy Dykes once told a rookie left hander then about to walk the gangplank for his first start in Fenway, "You're just like a mouse in a cage with nine large cats?" Hell, most managers would rather walk through a mine field than start a left hander in Fenway, which many of those same writers figured was much the same thing. But then again, they hadn't figured on Boudreau having the balls of a cat burglar.

Boudreau's opposite number, Boston manager "Marse" Joe McCarthy, also had a surprise up his sleeve, threadbare as it was. For in his final drive to the wire McCarthy had thrown everything he had, deck chairs and all, into the furnace to keep the Sox's pennant boat afloat. Having swept the Yankees in the final three games behind their big three—Joe Dobson, Jack Kramer and Mel Parnell—the Sox had closed the two-game deficit to make it to the wire by a nose, but without an arm. Now McCarthy had to look to his second line of pitchers to come up with a starting pitcher for the first American League Play-Off Game ever. The man McCarthy finally settled on to carry the Red Sox's hopes was a 36-year-old right hander with an 8-7 record named Denny Galehouse. It was a little bit optimistic, like doing the crossword puzzle in ink, but the last time Galehouse and faced the Indians he had held them to two hits in eight and two-thirds innings.

Indeed Galehouse picked up right where he had left off the last time he faced the Indians, getting lead-off batter Dale Mitchell and fill-in first baseman Allie Clark. That brought to bat Boudreau, who was thinking only of that sinful delusion out in left: The Wall. Galehouse went to two-and-one on Boudreau then came in with a pitch that was like catnip to a cat and Boudreau got around on it, catching it on the "sweet spot" on his bat and driving it into the screen atop the 37-foot "Monster." That made the score 1-0, Indians.

Rookie Gene Bearden, winner of the first Play-Off Game in American League history

GENE BEARDEN PRAISED BY MANAGER BOUDREAU

Ted Williams who only two days earlier had knocked the Yankees out of the race, went just 1-for-4 with all the chips on the line

Boston retaliated with one of their own in their half of the first. After Bearden had retired Dom DiMaggio, Boudreau, taking a page from his playbook, moved right fielder Bob Kennedy over toward the right-field line to defend against the ever-dangerous spray hitter Johnny Pesky. And sure enough, when Pesky drove the ball down the line, Kennedy was able to hold him to a double. That brought up the League's-leading hitter, Ted Williams. Boudreau, who two years before had devised the "Williams Shift" to keep Williams off the basepaths, now bethought to himself that Williams would just try to meet Bearden's knuckler and hit it back up the middle. Cheating ever so slightly over toward second, Boudreau and his unerring instincts robbed Williams of a drive up the middle for the second out. But the next man up, the League's second-leading run producer, Vern Stephens, hit the ball where even Boudreau couldn't defend for a single, driving in Pesky and knotting the score at one all.

And that's how the score stood when Boudreau came to bat for the second time, leading off the fourth. This time he drove a single into left, falling somewhat short of his target, The Monster. Joe Gordon followed with one of his own into the same area, putting men on first and second with none out and Ken Keltner coming to bat. Boudreau, having set up shop on second, now gave due consideration as to whether Keltner should sacrifice the two base runners into scoring position or swing away. Finally, he gave Keltner a la carte to hit away. And Keltner rewarded Boudreau with a towering shot that soared over the Green Monster for a three-run homer.

Galehouse, who had been a good pitcher as good pitchers go, was now gone—never again to win another Big League game in his career. McCarthy brought in Boston right hander Ellis Kinder. But the Indians hardly treated the stand-in pitcher any better than his predecessor, the first man Kinder faced, Larry Doby, rifling a shot off the left-center field wall for a double. Sacrificed over to third by Kennedy, Doby scored the Indians' fifth run on Hegan's ground-out to Stephens.

After Bearden had retired the BoSox in the bottom of the fourth, Boudreau came to bat in the Indians' fifth. Continuing his assault on the green citadel out in left, Boudreau, momentarily fooled by one of Kinder's breaking balls, pulled it over the Monster, following through with even more "ooomph" than the first time around to give the Tribe a 6-1 lead.

In the bottom of the sixth Bearden got the lead-off batter, Johnny Pesky. Then Williams lifted a towering fly back of second. Gordon, fighting the sun, got caught up in his fielding underwear

and, after circling around under the ball like a reeling drunk, had it drop out of his glove for an error. Unruffled, Bearden got the ever-dangerous Stephens. But then, making his only pitching mistake of the day, the young lefty came in with a fast ball to Bobby Doerr who sent it out as fast as it had come in, over the Monster for a two-run homer. The score now stood 6-3, Cleveland after six full innings.

But that was to be Boston's last gasp as Bearden, his arm still full of pitches even after having pitched a complete game only two days earlier, suffocated the Sox in knuckleballs the rest of the way. The Indians added another two runs, one each in the eighth and the ninth—the last one wrapped around Boudreau's fourth hit, a single—as they went on to win the game and the pennant in an unparalleled Play-Off Game.

Lou Boudreau had repaid his debt of gratitude to the Cleveland fans—and to Bill Veeck—with interest. And in the process had brought "The Green Monster" to its knees.

Playing manager Lou Boudreau, whose 4-for-4 sparked Cleveland's win

Indians Win American League Flag, Beating Red Sox in Play-Off, 8-3

Play-off Box Score

CLEVELAND INDIANS

	AB.	R.	H.	PO.	A.	E.
Mitchell, lf	5	0	1	1	0	0
Clark, 1b	2	0	0	5	0	0
Robinson, 1b	2	1	1	9	0	0
Boudreau, ss	4	3	4	3	5	0
Gordon, 2b	4	1	1	2	3	1
Keltner, 3b	5	1	3	0	6	0
Doby, cf	5	1	2	1	0	0
Kennedy, rf	2	0	0	0	0	0
Hegan, c	3	1	0	6	1	0
Bearden, p	3	0	1	0	2	0
Total	35	8	13	27	17	1

BOSTON RED SOX

	AB.	R.	H.	PO.	A.	E.
D. DiMaggio, cf	4	0	0	3	0	0
Pesky, 3b	4	1	1	3	4	0
Williams, lf	4	1	1	3	0	1
Stephens, ss	4	0	1	2	4	0
Doerr, 2b	4	1	1	5	2	0
Spence, rf	1	0	0	1	0	0
aHitchcock	0	0	0	0	0	0
bWright	0	0	0	0	0	0
Goodman, 1b	3	0	0	7	1	0
Tebbetts, c	4	0	1	3	1	0
Galehouse, p	0	0	0	0	1	0
Kinder, p	2	0	0	0	1	0
Total	30	3	5	27	14	1

Cleveland Pilot Modest About His Part In Playoff Victory Over Red Sox

32 Jackie Robinson's First Game

Brooklyn Dodgers vs. Boston Braves, April 15, 1947

BASEBALL HAS DISGRACED NO MAN. UNFORTUNATELY, A FEW have disgraced baseball. One of those was Adrian "Cap" Anson. And therein lies a tale of how baseball's Dark Ages and Non-Dark Ages merged one less-than-bright day back in June of 1884.

For on that day Adrian "Cap" Anson, whose legendary exploits as player-manager for the Chicago White Stockings had won for him the admiration of baseball fans everywhere and the appellation "The Superman of Baseball" by equally adoring pencil-pushers, led his team onto the field for an exhibition against the Toledo Mudhens of the rival American Association. As Anson cast an eye around the field—an eye that would cause a piece of toast to curl up around the edges—he chanced to come across the form of one Fleetwood Walker, the catcher for the Mudhens who, not incidental to our story, was black. In a moment that will never fully be explained, Anson's face suddenly turned red, his eyes flashed and his voice erupted, shouting—amongst other muttered maledictions—"Get that nigger off the field!"

Anson, a vainglorious man who strutted pouter-pigeon proud, was used to having his every whim served. Imposing his will now on the Toledo manager, Anson dropped the other shoe, threatening, ". . . or I will not allow my team on the field!" The Toledo manager, Charlie Morton, with a large crowd already on hand, gave in to Anson's demand, telling him that Walker—and his brother, outfielder Weldy Walker—would be fired the next day. And so Anson's charge against baseball's honor was honored.

But Anson's one-man campaign to preserve the game's so-called integrity was far from through. And when the very next year he heard that the New York Giants—of *his* league, for God's sake—were considering the purchase of black pitcher George Stovey from Newark of the Eastern League, he went into a demagogic rain dance of bigotry worthy of a giant pooh-bah of the exalted order of the pillowcase. Screaming something that sounded like, "There's a law against that," Anson cited the several private agreements currently in vogue to keep the sport lily-white. The Giants, too, gave in to Anson's bigoted temper tantrum.

His bugle call voice now a clarion call to team and teammate alike, Anson climaxed his vitriolic campaign with a personal appeal at the winter meetings in late 1887 attended by all Major League and minor league clubs. There Anson urged the adoption of a rule which would not only mandate against any club ever again signing a contract with a black, but also called for all those clubs with blacks on their roster—some 25 blacks then playing minor league ball—fire such unsavories forthwith. And although no formal agreement was adopted, something called a "Gentleman's Agreement" was put into effect by men who having now abrogated the United States Constitution shouldn't have been allowed to vote.

For Anson and all men of bad faith everywhere, the sun was now in its heaven and all was right with the baseball world. Now baseball had a chastity belt known as the "color line" to keep it racially pure, promulgated by men whose broad minds had changed places with their small waist lines. Never had such a hideous beanstalk grown from such a small seed.

Every now and then someone would come forward to challenge the "Gentleman's Agreement" as not being worth the paper it was written on. One such foolhearty was John J. McGraw, then manager of the Baltimore Orioles in the fledgling American League. Down in Hot Springs, Arkansas, to drown his troubles in the local baths, McGraw chanced to come across a light, copperskinned second baseman then showing his wares for a black team out of Chicago called the Columbia Giants. McGraw, knowing that the second baseman, Charlie Grant, would never pass the color line, decided to assist nature with a powder puff. Changing Grant's name to Tokahama, McGraw introduced him to the press as a "full-blooded Cherokee," complete with war paint and feathers. But when a band of local blacks adopted Grant as one of their own, presenting him with a huge floral display, the League saw through the ruse and sent McGraw a wire upholding their "Gentleman's Agreement" and demanding that McGraw adhere to their anti-Negro position, the "blacklisting" position of their patron saint, Cap Anson.

The legacy of Cap Anson was to continue for another four-and-a-half decades, abetted in no small way by Baseball Commissioner Kenesaw Mountain Landis. Landis, who had become Commissioner in 1920 after the infamous Black Sox scandal, ruled baseball with an iron hand from his headquarters on the 26th floor of Carew Tower in Chicago. Time and again he was tested for him humanistic ingredient, and it was always found conspicuously wanting by its absence.

When faced with the prospect of Philadelphia Phillies owner Gerry Nugent selling his club to Bill Veeck, whose plan to stock the team with Blacks was well-advertised, Landis, whose lightest wish was law, proved the one law he stood forthrightly, if not rightly, against was the law of nature by forcing Nugent to turn his club back to the National League rather than sell it to Veeck. And then, as if to prove himself, he and his henchman, National League president Ford Frick, both were overheard to boast that they had "saved the League from contamination." Another time, when the Pittsburgh Pirates offered "The Negro Babe Ruth," catcher Josh Gibson, a contract, Landis' mind rebelled at the thought, rejecting the contract in words which could be heard in the Netherlands Plaza Hotel adjacent to his offices, "The colored players have their own league. Let them stay there." Not only had Landis relegated blacks to the back of baseball's bus, he had effectively denied them entrance to the bus altogether.

But the times they were achanging. Sociological breadcrumbs had already begun to lead to the moment when baseball would overturn the vestiges of Jim Crow. First Joe Louis had beaten the cause of Aryan supremacy in 1938. Then blacks had fought and died in World War II so that America's way of life could survive. Many, like activist Paul Robeson, were openly questioning why if they could die they couldn't play professional baseball. Landis, with as straight a face as he could maintain with his tongue securely lodged in his upper cheek, airbrushed over such questions with an answer that came out "there was no rule on the books" prohibiting a black man from playing Major League ball. Others he dismissed with a "There's nothing further to discuss," further blackening baseball's name if not its ranks. But with Landis' death on the Saturday following Thanksgiving, 1944, the final bar to blacks playing Major League baseball had been removed. Although none knew it then.

The prime mover in removing the bar to the door marked "Closed to Blacks" was Wesley Branch Rickey, a color-blind man who now led the blind. With a reserve of inherited guile, Rickey had never paid full faith and credit to baseball's murky traditions, instead constantly trying his own wiles and ways. Always in the name of winning. Back in the '30s, Rickey had initiated the farm system, a chain of minor league clubs whose home-growns had made the Cardinals a winner. Now, while all others meekly accepted the "Gentleman's Agreement" as unalterable, Rickey knew that like all other great truths it was blasphemous. And determined to challenge it and put a black in the Dodger blue.

Before Jackie Robinson was even a glint in his eye, Rickey's first flirtation with the possibility of adding blacks to the Brooklyn roster had come before the '45 season, courtesy of the *Daily Worker*. With the Dodgers sojourning at the Bear Mountain Inn, a spring training spot dictated by strict wartime travel measures, Rickey had agreed to a demand by the Communist paper that he give a private look-see to two so-called "promising" black players. However, the *Daily Worker* had violated all pledges of secrecy, leaking the story of the try-out before it took place. In retaliation, Rickey opened the workout to the entire press, effectively killing their scoop. After seeing that the two players the paper had brought were, at best, mediocre, and that mediocrity is always at its best, Rickey excoriated the Communists and their stooges, accusing them of trying to force his hand. Then, at his thunderous Chattaqua Circuit best, he boomed, "This is a matter of evolution, not revolution," and he stalked off.

That evolution was already beginning to take form. With the War over, many now were anxious to look forward, not back, and get on to the business of living, with all the new plans, new hopes and new dreams that came with it. And with Landis now gone from the baseball scene, one of those who was anxious to get on with it was the new Commissioner of Baseball, Albert B. "Happy" Chandler, late of the Kentucky Chandlers and former United States Senator and Governor of the Blue Grass State. Chandler, a political animal who could talk in circles while standing foursquare, knew which way the wind was blowing. And talked the same way. When visited by Wendell Smith, a black columnist from the Pittsburgh *Courier,* Chandler came out foursquare for "The Four Freedoms," adding, "If a black boy can make it at Okinawa and go to Guadalcanal, he can make it in baseball." The bar was not only off the door, the door was now ajar for Rickey's move.

Throwing up, for want of a more delicate word in this scenario, a smokescreen, he formed something called the United States Baseball League, with the entry from Brooklyn to be called the Brown Dodgers. In August, he sent head scout Clyde Sukeforth out to Chicago to watch the Kansas City Monarchs play the Lincoln Giants, with special instructions to "Go up to that fellow Robinson, and introduce yourself."

That "fellow Robinson" was Jack Roosevelt Robinson, a four-letter athlete at UCLA before the War. During the War Robinson applied for admission to officer candidate school at Fort Riley, Kansas, where he won his commission as second lieutenant. He also won something else: A reputation. A fiercely proud man, Robinson fought against injustice in any form, coming away with

the reputation of being a trouble maker. And worse. Army Brass, unable to control either the pride or the iron will any more than ice can be welded or iron melted, first made him a morale officer and then gave him his honorable discharge in November of '44 so anxious were they to get rid of the "Uppity Nigger."

Mustered out, Robinson signed on the the Kansas City Monarchs as shortstop for the 1945 season at the going rate of $400 a month. At the time Sukeforth went "up to that fellow Robinson," the then-26-year-old was hitting .345 in forty-one games, and had been selected as the West's starting shortstop in the East-West Negro All-Star Game.

Sukeforth, still under the impression he was on a scouting mission for the Brown Dodgers, introduced himself and then asked Robinson to take infield practice in order "to see if that fellow has a shortstop's arm," as per Rickey's instructions. But Robinson had hurt his salary wing in a fall the previous evening and took batting practice for Sukeforth instead. Now operating on the rest of Rickey's marching orders, which were, "If you like his arm, bring him in," Sukeforth booked two berths on the train back to Brooklyn, one for himself and one for the shortstop, destination still unknown.

Ushering Robinson into Rickey's chambers on Montague Street, Sukeforth tried to interject with a "Mr. Rickey, I haven't seen this fellow throw." But it was useless. A monologist by nature, Rickey had already started like a clockwork toy, employing his usual sales patter that could sell anyone a watch and combination pocket knife with a free bottle of elixir thrown in for a dollar. Seated behind the walnut garbage chest he called his desk, Rickey began with a "You got a girl?" Without waiting to hear about Jackie's fiancee, Rachel, Rickey went on, "When we get through today you may want to call her up, because there are times a man needs a woman by his side."

Then, punctuating the air with his everpresent cigar, dropping ashes like a volcano all adown his shirt front and bow tie, Rickey got to the heart of the matter. "Jack, I've been looking for a great colored ballplayer, but I need more than a great player. I need a man who will accept insults, take abuse; in a word, carry the flag for his race." Without missing a beat, Rickey went on, his face now

The two men who were responsible for bringing Robinson up in 1947, Leo Durocher and Branch Rickey

looking like a new glove donned for the first time, the wrinkles forming a smile of sorts. "I want a man who has the courage not to fight, not to fight back." With this he launched into a laundry list of epithets impossible for a gentleman to brook or overlook. "If a guy slides into you at second base and calls you a 'black son-of-a-bitch,' I wouldn't blame you if you came up swinging. You'd be right. You'd be justified. But," and here he stopped to make his point, "you'd set the cause back twenty years. I want a man with courage enough not to fight back. Can you do that?" So saying Rickey leaned back in his big executive's chair, his gnarled hands holding his cigar as he stared at Robinson. Robinson thought for a few minutes and then finally said, "If you want to take this gamble, I promise you there'll be no incidents."

That did it. Branch Rickey had found his player, the man who would break the color line and have the courage to hold it.

Rickey, ever the Artful Dodger, had carefully sculpted Robinson's future. Trying his luck rather than merely risking it, he had decided not to bring him into the Majors immediately but to send him instead to Brooklyn's, if not organized baseball's, Northernmost outpost, Montreal. There, Rickey felt, Robinson would be a curio piece more than a hate object. And be inured to the pressures of having to make it in a city that saw things in black-and-white terms. Also Rickey thought that Robinson would benefit from being under the wing of one of his top managers, Clay Hopper, albeit Clay Hopper, was a prominent citizen of Greenwood, Mississippi.

Still on the Montreal roster, Spring Training, 1947

Those who had labored under the delusion that there was something different about "colored" players and that they were inferior—such as Joe Williams, who wrote, "Blacks have been kept out of big league ball because they are as a race very poor ballplayers."—didn't labor long. In his very first game, Robinson smashed a three-run homer and three singles, stole two bases and scored four runs as he led the Royals to a 14-1 victory over the Jersey City Giants. As the now-second baseman continued to make democracy work, he had to endure the slings and arrows of fans in several cities, most notably Baltimore. But answering the only way he could, he responded with his bat. By the end of the year he had responded enough with his bat to lead the International League in batting with a .349 average and in runs scored

with 113, winning the Most Valuable Player Award and leading his team to the 1946 Little World Series. At the finale of the final game, the proud *habitants* of Montreal ran to carry Robinson off the field, the first time in history, as one writer noted, that "a crowd had ever run to carry a black man off rather than hang him up."

There was still one more giant step—or Dodger step, if you will. But there was trouble lurking ahead. The 1947 Dodgers mirrored the overall make-up of the Majors, with almost sixty percent of their roster hailing from southern states. Here a Walker from Alabama, there a Casey from Georgia, a Bragan from Texas, a Reese from Kentucky, a Stanky from Alabama, a Higbe from South Carolina and everywhere it seemed a player with borderline anemia from one of the nearby states. With Robinson, still officially a member of the Montreal Royals, playing exhibition ball against the Dodgers in Havana, and hitting the ball at a lusty .625 pace, a petition began to circulate among members of the team, addressed to "Mr. Rickey" and calling for him to bar Robinson from playing for the Dodgers.

Rickey, who had hoped that the Dodgers—who had finished in a tie for first place the previous year—would see in Robinson a way to win and demand his services, was dismayed by the sudden turn of events. With eyebrows rising like storm clouds over the Gowanus and his cigar shooting from due east to due west with but a single movement of his lower lip, Rickey determined to have it out with those who had signed the petition, most notably the instigator, Dixie Walker. But even before he could get to Walker, or Walker to him—and Walker did, finally, sending him a letter asking "to be traded as soon as a deal can be arranged. . . . For reasons I don't care to go into I feel my decision is the best for all concerned."—something happened that was to take the heat off both Rickey and Robinson. And make the chore of bringing him up to the Dodgers easier.

By April 9th, just six days before the official opening of the '47 season, everything was in order for Robinson's elevation. The window-ledge stage had been passed. Montreal manager Clay Hopper had told Rickey that "Robinson is ready. . . . He can't prove any more on my team." The press were clamoring for Rickey "to end the phony suspense." And Dodger manager Leo Durocher was about to announce that Robinson was needed for the Dodgers' pennant drive.

But then, in a strangely worded and even more strangely reasoned-out pronounciamento, Baseball Commissioner Chandler suspended Durocher for "conduct detrimental to baseball." The convoluted rationale behind the decision by Chandler had to do with Durocher having consorted with undesirables, two of whom had been seen sitting in a box which belonged to Yankee owner Larry MacPhail at an exhibition game, and then writing about it in a ghost-written article. Whatever the rationale, it had effectively taken away Rickey's cover for the promotion of Robinson. Instead, Rickey now needed Robinson to cover up the noisome suspension of Durocher.

So, early the morning after the fiat hit the fan, Rickey routed Robinson from his bedstead and summoned him hurriedly down to his office to sign a Brooklyn contract. In a terse two-sentence release—which read, in toto, "The Brooklyn Dodgers today purchased the contract of Jackie Roosevelt Robinson from the Montreal Royals. He will report immediately."—issued during the sixth inning of the Montreal-Brooklyn exhibition game then going on down on the field, the Dodgers announced formally that baseball's color line, which had begun during an exhibition game some 63 years before, had finally come to an end in yet another exhibition game. But with all the hubbub swirling around the Dodgers and

Durocher, the signing of Robinson was, as writer Arthur Mann said, "A whisper in a whirlwind."

Tuesday morning April 15th broke bright and clear as the newest member of the Dodgers prepared to leave his home. Bob Considine, in a by-lined INS article, told it thusly: "He kissed his wife Rachel good-bye and said, 'Honey, if you come out to Ebbets Field today, you won't have any trouble recognizing me.' He then paused and said with a wry grin, 'My number is 42 . . .'"

Whether Considine, in the accepted style of journalists, was dealing more in apochrypha than fact makes little difference. For Jackie Robinson and 26,623 payees were all upbeat, witnessing a piece of baseball history that had started lo those 63 years ago with a "Get that nigger off the field." Now he was on the field. And in his first Major League game, batting against Johnny Sain and the Boston Braves.

He grounded out to third his first time up, the throw beating him by less than a step. Turning around to argue the call with umpire Al Barlick, he seemed to stop in mid-motion, almost as if he suddenly remembered Branch Rickey's admonition never to let himself be corrupted by human failings, and then turned back to the dugout and trotted in, his soon-to-be famous pigeon-toed steps taking him down into the bowels of the Dodger dugout, his new home. Twice more he came up, and twice more went down, once on what the *Times* called a "dazzling twin killing" started by Boston shortstop Dick Cutler, playing in on the grass, diving to stop his sure base hit and throwing to second baseman Connie Ryan while lying on the ground for the front part.

But then, in the seventh, Robinson gave promise of great things to come, his deft sacrifice bunt and speed forcing Boston first baseman Earl Torgeson to make a hurried throw which hit Robinson and caromed off his shoulder into right field. Robinson moved up to second, there to personally carry home the winning run on Pete Reiser's hit.

It was to be the first of many runs Jackie Robinson would go on to score in his illustrious 10-year career, a career that would ultimately carry him into the Baseball Hall of Fame, there to take his place next to other greats like Adrian "Cap" Anson.

Pete Reiser's Hit Brings In Robinson For 5-3 Dodger Win

BROOKLYN (N)	ab	r	h	o	a	e	rbi
Stanky 2b	3	1	0	3	0	0	0
Robinson 1b	3	0	0	11	0	0	0
Schultz 1b	0	0	0	1	0	0	0
Reiser cf	2	1	2	2	0	0	2
Walker rf	4	0	0	0	0	0	0
Tatum rf	0	0	0	0	0	0	0
cVaughan	1	0	0	0	0	0	0
Furillo rf	0	0	0	0	0	0	0
Hermanski lf	4	0	1	3	0	0	1
Edwards c	2	0	0	0	1	0	1
bRackley	0	0	0	3	0	0	0
Bragan c	1	0	0	0	0	0	0
Jorgenson 3b	3	0	0	0	1	0	0
Reese ss	3	0	1	3	2	0	0
Hatten p	2	0	1	1	1	0	0
aStevens	1	0	0	0	0	0	0
Gregg p	1	0	0	0	0	0	0
Casey p	0	0	0	0	0	0	0
Totals	29	5	6	27	10	1	5
BOSTON (N)	ab	r	h	o	a	e	rbi
Culler ss	3	0	0	0	2	0	0
eHolmes	1	0	0	0	0	0	0
Sisti ss	0	0	0	0	0	0	0
Hopp cf	5	0	1	2	0	0	1
McCormick rf	4	0	3	2	0	0	0
R. Elliott 3b	4	0	1	0	2	0	0
Litwhiler lf	3	1	0	1	0	0	0
Rowell lf	0	0	0	0	0	0	0
Torgeson 1b	4	1	0	10	1	1	0
Masi c	4	0	0	4	0	0	0
Ryan 2b	4	1	3	4	7	0	2
Sain p	1	0	0	0	1	0	0
Cooper p	0	0	0	1	0	0	0
dNeill	0	0	0	0	0	0	0
Lanfranconi p	0	0	0	0	0	0	0
Totals	31	3	8	24	13	1	3
Brooklyn				000	101	30x — 5	
Boston				000	012	000 — 3	

Robinson in his first Major League at-bat

Robinson in his first Major League game as a first baseman

33 Wamby's Unassisted Triple Play

Cleveland Indians vs. Brooklyn Robins, 5th Game, 1920 World Series, October 10, 1920

1920, TO COP A DICKENSENIAN LINE, WAS FOR BASEBALL THE best of times and the worst of times.

It was the year when the owners, in concert assembled, decided to make the homer a negotiable commodity with some alchemistic tinkering with the delicate lines and designs of the game. First they reduced the raised stitching on the ball and wrapped the yarn tighter, prompting one observer, the acid-tongued Westbrook Pegler, to observe, "When you hold the ball between your thumb and forefinger, you can hear a rabbit's pulsebeat." Then the owners enacted a protective barrier on pitching bunco artists, eliminating such pitches as the "spit" ball, the "emery" ball and the "shine" ball, and any other manner of ball which contained foreign matter, even if that matter was purchased in the good ol' U. S. of A. Almost immediately their attendance figures began to soar even higher than the parabolic clouts of Babe Ruth, the new apostle of the long ball, and take on the look of World War I body counts.

And it was also the year when two calamities struck baseball, both of which cast a pall over the game itself.

The first came during a game on August 16th at the Polo Grounds between the contending Indians and Yankees. With the Indians leading 3-0 after four innings, Cleveland shortstop Ray Chapman led off the fifth against Yankee submariner Carl Mays. The speedy Chapman had affected the most exaggerated crouch in the Majors, actually leaning over the plate, all the better to effectively get on base, whether by drag bunt, walk or getting hit by the pitch, all areas he was profficient in. Not incidentally, Mays was known as a brush-back pitcher with a heart full of bile, one who subscribed to the belief that "If you got to knock somebody down to win a ballgame, do it! It's your bread and butter." Chapman now set up shop against Mays, taking the first two offerings. With the count one-and-one, Mays let fly with a high, fast ball on the inside, designed to keep Chapman from bunting his way on. There was an audible "twack" as the ball hit batter with a report heard throughout the stadium and Mays, thinking the ball had hit the handle of Chapman's bat, picked up the ball dribbling out to the mound and threw to first. Only then did he turn back to the plate and see umpire Tom Connelly calling first to the Indians' dugout for help and then to the stands for a physician. Chapman staggered to his feet, helped by his Indian teammates, instinctively took two steps toward first and then, shaking like as aspen, dropped in a heap, his left eye hanging out of its socket. He was never to regain consciousness, dying the next morning—the only ballplayer ever to die in a Major League game.

Several of those who saw the tragedy, like Cleveland pitcher Ray Caldwell, thought that Chapman had actually "ducked his head into the path of the ball." Others, that Chapman, enchained in his own indecision, he had simply frozen at the plate, Indian player-manager Tris Speaker believing that "There was time for Chappie to duck when the ball was coming at him, but he never moved." Still, several of the Indians, and many in baseball, thought Mays to blame, Indian first baseman Doc Johnston even

going so far as to say, "Mays should be strung up."

The aftermath of Chapman's death sorely tried the soul of baseball. And tried the Indians even more so, off the field as well as on, their devine spark of fire gone and their pennant chances foundering. But when, in early September, they brought up little Joe Sewell to fill in at shortstop, they got their pennant express back on track and made a run at the defending champion White Sox.

And then, with two weeks left in the season, the second shoe dropped: Seven Chicago players, charged with complicity in a conspiracy with gamblers to rearrange the outcome of the previous autumn's World Series, were suspended from the Sox roster until a Cook County Grand Jury could investigate the charges. Baseball, which had heard the cries of "Fix" during the 1919 Series only too clearly, considered it sacrilegious even to take them into account and in I-say-its spinach-and-the-hell-with-it approach had held that the Series was on the up-and-up. But now the rumors had substance, and the gentle despoilers of the game's name were suspended.

With but a skeletal squad to finish out the season, the White Sox sputtered and the Indians, with the whip hand, crossed the final wire a bare two games in front of the limping Sox and three in front of the fast-closing Yankees led by Babe Ruth and his 59 homers.

Cleveland's first pennant winner *ever* had one great super-star—Tris Speaker, called "Spoke," a take-off on his last name and "The Gray Eagle," in tribute to his prematurely graying locks, who had spread-eagled the League's offensive categories, batting .388 to finish second in batting, and leading the league in doubles and finishing fourth in slugging average and total bases—and a deep pitching staff, led by Jim Bagby, a 31-game winner, the veteran Stan Coveleski, a 24-game winner, and Ray Caldwell, a 20-game winner.

Their opponents in the Series were the Brooklyn Robins, named, appropriately enough, after their manager, Wilbert Robinson. Robinson had a team about as glamorous as an unmade bed. Operating the Robins was, at best, a difficult task for Robinson, short-changed by his owner Charley Ebbets, who ran a pinch-penny operation. With no money to speak of, or to, the man called "Robbie" had collected a patchwork club at flea market prices. His infield consisted of Ed Konetchy, ex-Card, Pirate and Brave at first, Pete Kilduff, ex-Giant and Cub at second, Ivy Olson, ex-Indian and Red at short and Jimmy Johnston, ex-White Sox at third. His pitching staff was made up of Sherry Smith, ex-Pirate, Clarence Mitchell, ex-Red, Jeff Pfeffer, ex-Brownie, Burleigh Grimes, ex-Pirate and Rube Marquard, whom one paper described as having "pitched great ball for the Giants but on account of certain eccentricities, McGraw let go." In fact, one of the few home-grown talents on the team was Zack Wheat, who was part-Indian and all-hitter. Together, the Robins were the oldest club ever to play in the Series, and their very presence in the Series was a tribute to Robinson and his deep pitching staff.

Still, many thought that the Dodgers would win the World Series. And, indeed, for the first three games of the-then best-of-nine series, it appeared as if they were correct in their assessment as the Robins, after losing the first game to Coveleski, came back to take Games Two and Three behind Grimes and Smith for a 2-1 lead. Back in Cleveland for Game Four, Coveleski pitched a five-hitter and evened up the Series at Brooklyn, two, Coveleski, two. And set up one of the most memorable games in the history of baseball.

But even as Sunday, October 10th was adawning over Lake Erie, Fate had put her fickle finger into the pot and was stirring. Mightily. Her first visitation was to the Robins' hotel, where the Cleveland constabulary picked up Brooklyn pitcher Rube Marquard on charges of scalping eight box seat tickets for $400. Almost immediately Brooklyn owner Ebbets was heard to scream, "Marquard will never again wear a Brooklyn uniform." However, this event was merely a link in the natural chain of events as Fate now pointed her finger at old League Park, that vest-pocket park where Game Four would take place.

Game Four saw Robinson come back with Burleigh Grimes, the winner of Game Two. Grimes, who had been given a dispensation by the powers-that-be on his unsanitary habit of throwing the "spitter," had pitched a neat seven-hit shutout in that second game. But after the game Speaker had said to one newsman, "Grimes won't win another game in the Series." Speaker knew whereof he spoke. For what Speaker and all the Indians had espied was that Kilduff, playing second directly in the line of sight of the catcher's signals, had been tipping off the "spitter"—picking up sand before each and every time Grimes threw his "spit ball," so that he could get some of the "wet" off the ball and grip it better if it were hit to him. Convinced there was more to Grimes' delivery than met the eye, the Indians began looking out at second to watch Kilduff and his sand act. It was like taking cheese from a set mousetrap as the first three batters in Cleveland's half of the first all singled to load the bases to the plimsoll line. That brought up the Indian clean-up hitter, left-handed Elmer Smith who, true to his designation as "clean-up", cleared the bases with one mighty swing, taking one of Grimes' "spitters" downtown, thanks to Kilduff. That blast, which cleared out the place as surely as a three-alarmer in an excelsior factory, not only cleared out the bases, but was also the first grand slam homer in Series history.

The Indians weren't through with the pitcher with the "moistest on the ball" yet. In the fourth, after two Indians had reached base, Cleveland pitcher Jim Bagby tagged another of Grimes' wet ones into the center field stands, the first home run ever hit by a pitcher in Series play. That was nine hits and seven runs for the Indians off the man they had predicted would never win "another game in the Series." And more than enough for Brooklyn manager Robinson, who now brought in his other spitball pitcher, Clarence Mitchell.

Baseball has long counted amongst its number those who find it anti-intellectual to go to a ballgame to watch a pitcher bat. However, on this afternoon of afternoons, Mitchell made even the most sophisticated fan sit up and take notice as he hit into one of the most celebrated plays in baseball history.

With the Robins down 7-0, courtesy of the two homers by Smith and Bagby, they came to bat in the top of the fifth, needing something, anything, to piece back together their fast-crumbling hopes. And when the first two men, Kilduff and Miller, singled, it looked like that something was about to happen. Now it was Mitchell's turn at bat. Mitchell, a good hitter with a .266 lifetime average, was known as a pull hitter, and the Indian infield, knowing that the Robins needed a hit to keep their mini-rally going, was playing deep—especially second baseman Bill Wambsganss, who was playing back on the grass against the left-handed hitting Mitchell.

Mitchell, timing his swing, caught one of Bagby's fast balls,

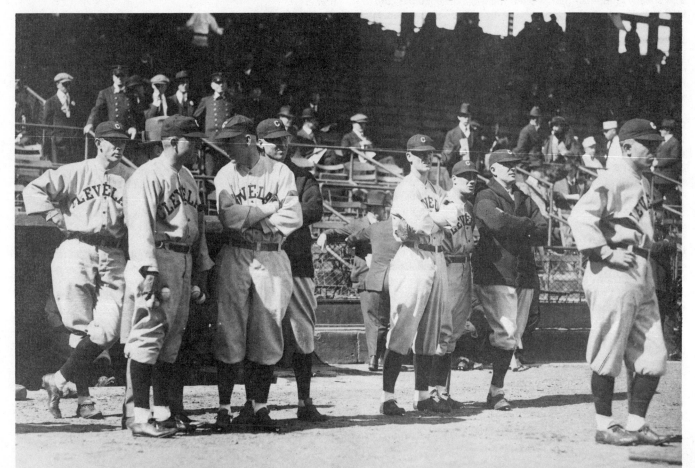

Elmer Smith, Cleveland outfielder, who hit first Series grand-slam homer in fifth game. (Note the black mourning band in memory of Ray Chapman)

driving it on a rising line toward center, a shade on the first base side of second. Wambsganss—whose name had been contracted to "Wamb'g'ss" by typesetters fighting for space and "Wamby" by merciful sportswriters who couldn't wrestle with his complete handle—with a divining rod sensitivity made an instinctive lunging stab at the ball, barely managed to catch it. One out. Looking like a marionette with one string broken, "Wamby" came down on unsteady legs, his momentum now carrying him in the direction of second. Seeing that Kilduff, unawares of the goings-on behind him, was still chugging his merry way toward third, Wamby kept right on toward the bag and regained his equilibrium just in time to touch it. Two outs. Then Wamby turned to find Otto Miller just a few feet away, standing stock-still in a manner patented by Lot's late wife. Taking but two more steps to his left, he touched the pillar of salt posing as a Brooklyn base runner on the shoulder. Three outs. And the first—and only—unassisted triple play in World Series play was over.

Fate had not only decreed that the three baserunners would be as foredoomed as Shadrach, Meshach and Abednego, but also that Brooklyn would be foredoomed from that point on as well, losing the last two games and the Series. Nevertheless, it would be the fifth game of the 1920 Series that would be remembered as one of the greatest games in baseball history, a game with footnotes and an entire glossary. And never-to-be-forgotten.

Smith Makes Home Run With Bases Full And Wambsganss An Unassisted Triple Play

Bill Wambsganss, the architect of the only unassisted triple play in World Series history

Score Of Fifth World's Series Game

CLEVELAND.	Ab.	R.	H.	O.	A.	E.	BROOKLYN.	Ab.	R.	H.	O.	A.	E.
Jamieson, lf..	4	1	2	2	1	0	Olson, ss.....	4	0	2	3	5	0
Graney. lf....	1	0	0	0	0	0	Sheehan, 3b..	3	0	1	1	1	1
Wamb'g'ss, 2b	5	1	1	7	2	0	Griffith, rf...	4	0	0	0	0	0
Speaker, cf..	3	2	1	1	0	0	Wheat, lf....	4	1	2	3	0	0
E. Smith, rf..	4	1	3	0	0	0	Myers, cf....	4	0	0	2	0	0
Gardner, 3b..	4	0	1	2	2	1	Konetchy, 1b.	4	0	2	9	2	0
W.Johnston,1b	3	1	2	9	1	0	Kilduff, 2b...	4	0	1	5	6	0
Sewell, ss....	3	0	0	2	4	0	Miller, c......	2	0	2	0	1	0
O'Neill, c....	2	1	0	3	1	1	Krueger, c...	2	0	1	2	1	0
Thomas, c....	0	0	0	1	0	0	Grimes, p....	1	0	0	0	1	0
Bagby, p.....	4	1	2	0	2	0	Mitchell, p...	2	0	0	1	0	0
	—	—	—	—	—	—		—	—	—	—	—	—
Totals	33	8	12	27	13	2	Totals	34	1	13	24	17	1

Brooklyn .... 0 0 0 0 0 0 0 0 1—1
Cleveland .... 4 0 0 3 1 0 0 0 x—8

Three-base hits—Konetchy, E. Smith. Home runs—E. Smith, Bagby. Sacrifices—Sheehan, W. Johnston. Double-plays—Olson to Kilduff to Konetchy; Jamieson to O'Neill; Gardner to Wambsganss to Johnston; Johnston to Sewell to Johnston. Triple play—Wambsganss (unassisted). Left on bases—Brooklyn, 7; Cleveland, 6. Base on balls—Off Grimes, 1; Mitchell, 3. Hits—Off Grimes, 9 in 3 1-3 innings; Mitchell, 3 in 4 2-3 innings. Struck out—By Bagby, 3; Mitchell, 1. Wild pitch—Bagby. Passed ball—Miller. Losing pitcher—Grimes. Umpires—Klem (at the plate); Connolly (at first); O'Day (at second); Dineen (at third). Time—One hour and 19 minutes.

(Facing page) Cleveland Indians being introduced before Game Five.

34 Babe Ruth's 60th Home Run

New York Yankees vs. Washington Senators, September 30, 1927

BABE RUTH. HIS VERY NAME BRINGS BACK MEMORIES TO that dwindling number of fans who saw this gargantuan figure on toothpick-thin legs boom parabolic shots into the stands time-after-time and then mince his way around the basepaths with cat-like steps. To the typical adult, he is a legendary figure who gave color to his age, much as John L. Sullivan gave color to his. And to the younger generation, he is merely a name, used only as a benchmark for modern ballplayers like Hank Aaron.

But Babe Ruth was more than a name. He was an institution, a deity. One prominent Methodist minister of the time even suggested, "If St. Paul were living today, he would know Babe Ruth's batting average." Legions of sportswriters followed his every move, chronicling his every word and deed for their daily two-cent journals, forming a cult of followers with high priests like Runyon, Lardner, Rice and Broun spreading the Ruthian gospel. To their readers he was The Sultan of Swat, the Wizard of Whack, the King of Clout, the Behemoth of Biff and, of course, the Bambino. In short, he held a sacred seat in the exclusive inner circle of celebrityness.

For the so-called "Roaring '20s" was an age given to celebrityness. And nobody made it roar like Ruth, a four-letter man who dedicated himself to the national pastime of "Making Whopee." Believing it was far better to be a good liver than to have one, Ruth was always to be found in the company of the choicest products of the grape, the silkworm and the protoplasm. And yet, almost as if he had another body hanging in his well-stocked closet, he could show up at the ballpark the next day, his camel's hair coat garnished with lipstick, and still tear the cover off the ball—a tribute to burning the candle at both ends.

Ruth had first burst on the scene as a 19-year-old left-handed pitcher for the Boston Red Sox back in 1914. But even as he was setting the baseball world on fire with his fastball, he was also sparking some pyrotechnics with his massive bat, leading the league in homers with 11 in the war-shortened year of 1918. By 1919 Boston management had seen enough and converted the young star into an outfielder, with a little pitching on the side. Many, like Tris Speaker, thought the conversion a mistake, Speaker saying: "Ruth made a grave mistake when he gave up pitching. Working once a week, he might have lasted a long time and become a great star."

But Ruth set to work to prove his detractors wrong. And, in his first year as an outfielder, he hit one homer in April, and two in May, and before long those remorseless type seekers known as writers noticed that Ruth was running up a new home run total, 29, in one season.

Suddenly, the home run, suffocated by the bunt-and-stolen base game made popular by the Orioles before the turn of the Century, broke out of its cocoon with a vengeance. The owners, sensing that a financial bonanza lay in the newly-discovered long ball made some immediate adjustments to insure the continuation, if not the exploitation, of the home run. First they tightened the construction of the ball itself, reducing the raised stitching and wrapping the yarn tighter. The effect, described by one writer, who held the ball between his thumb and forefinger, was like "hearing a rabbit's pulsebeat." Then, they outlawed the spitball, the emery ball, and every other "freak" pitch known to man. And, finally, two owners in concert assembled changed the entire course of the game when, on January 3, 1920, Harry Frazee of the Boston Red Sox and Tapioca City sold Ruth to Jacob Ruppert and the New York Yankees for $125,000 and other "considerations", including a personal loan and a first mortgage on Fenway Park. It was to be the biggest rape since the Dutch bought Manhattan Island for some $24 in trinkets.

Ruth and New York were made for each other, both bigger than life. To borrow the title of Irving Berlin's paean of praise, "Along Came Ruth," and with him the long ball. And the crowds. In 1920 the Babe "hit," "clouted," "swatted,"· and "whacked" a record 54 home runs, one of which caused a bleacherite to die of excitement as he witnessed one of Ruth's mighty swats land near his section high up in the Polo Grounds. Each day brought new accolades and exaggerated stories about the man who had become a legend in his own time, fashioned by the sportswriters who by now had made him a sports page myth. And with every move he made—real or imagined—his legendary status became enshrined in the lore of the 20s.

The year 1925 was a watershed year for Ruth. During his 11-season career, he had played on six pennant winners, three second-place teams, one third-place club and on only one second-division club, the 1919 Red Sox. During his last seven years, playing as a full-time outfielder, he had averaged almost 40 homers, 120 RBIs, batted at a .357 clip and had a .740 slugging average. He was a superstar, a monument in that city which adored its monuments.

But suddenly, in 1925, all that seemed behind him. For Ruth had gone to pot, literally. Once the proud possessor of a slyphlike figure, now Ruth bulged so generously in every direction possible that, when seen up close, he gave the impression of enormous size. And his nocturnal habits seemed finally to have caught up with him. Sent to Hot Springs in the spring of 1925 to take the waters by the Yankees, Ruth left the authorities huddled together nervously wondering if there'd be enough. And then, on the trip north from Spring training, Ruth collapsed from some unexplainable malady, causing him to be borne back to New York wrapped in poultices of wet towels for observation. Those romantics who fashioned myths out of such goings-on called it "The Great Bellyache," ascribing his pains to a massive overdose of hot dogs and soda pop. Others, influenza. And some even had the indelicacy to call it what it was: A social disease. But whatever it was, it laid the Babe low for the first few months of the '25 season and caused more than a few with knowing nods to write off his career, feeling that even if such a rare bird as Ruth could fly on one wing, even he could not fly on none.

But then again, Ruth was no ordinary mortal. And, as 1926 bloomed, so too did Ruth, regaining his touch on the field with a league-leading 47 homers, and off the field as well, where he followed those inalienable 1920's rights of life, liberty and the happiness of pursuit, surrounding himself with scotch and women, depending upon their vintage.

By 1927 Ruth had thoroughly captivated both fan and non-fan alike, brass bands and fireworks attending his every move. In a year given to fashioning heroes of the first magnitude—Lindbergh, Ederle and Dempsey—Ruth stood alone.

Playing on what many baseball experts call the "Greatest Team of All Time," the 1927 Yankees, Ruth recaptured, at the age of 32, the greatness that once was his, smashing home run-after-home run with titanic swings and spending his off-the-field hours in making profligate demands upon the science of cork pulling. From his very first 1927 home run on the afternoon of April 15th off Philadelphia's Howard Ehmke down through the end of August Ruth amassed a total of 43 homers—just 15 shy of his personal

The Greatest Player Ever: Babe Ruth

high and baseball's all-time record as well. However, his quest for the all-time record was only of passing notice to many sports fans, who were treated to what the press called a two-man "Marathon" between Ruth and teammate Lou Gehrig, who moved into a tie with Ruth on September 5th, each having hit 44 round-trippers. However, the two-man "Marathon" never really materialized as Gehrig began to tail off, finishing 47. Ruth, his sights set on the record, continued to assault his personal Everest. Finally, on September 29th against Washington, Ruth hit numbers 58 and 59 to tie the record with but two games left in the season.

There now seemed to be no doubt about Ruth's capacity to break the record. As sportswriter Paul Gallico wrote, "Once he had that 59, that number 60 was as sure as the setting sun. A more determined athlete than George Herman Ruth never lived. He is one of the few utterly dependable news stories in sports." And so it was that with one strike and one ball on Ruth in the eighth inning, Washington pitcher Tom Zachary laid a fastball down the middle of the plate and Ruth responded in kind, driving the ball into the upper reaches of the right field bleachers for his 60th home run of the year, a record of 17 for the month of September and a season's record every one of the 8,000 fans on hand thought would stand for the ages.

Ironically, in the very next inning, baseball history of yet another sort was made: Washington was to open their half of the ninth by sending up a pinch hitter for Zachary, Walter Johnson, who was making his last big-league appearance after 21 years with the Senators. Not only did Johnson's appearance go unheralded in most newspapers the next day, but even the final score went unreported—the only news being Ruth's 60th. For the press was caught up in the Babe Ruth storyline, all echoing John Kiernan's famous line: "From 'One Old Cat' to the last 'At Bat,' was there ever a guy like Ruth?"

RUTH WITH 60th HOMER MAKES 1927 BANNER YEAR

WASHINGTON (A)							NEW YORK (A.)						
	ab	r	h	po	a	e		ab	r	h	po	a	e
Rice, rf	3	0	1	2	0	0	Combs, cf	4	0	0	3	0	0
Harris, 2b	3	0	0	3	4	0	Koenig, ss	4	1	1	3	5	0
Genzel, cf	4	0	1	1	0	0	Ruth, rf	3	3	3	4	0	0
Gostin, lf	4	1	1	5	0	0	Gehrig, 1b	4	0	2	10	0	1
Judge, 1b	4	0	0	5	0	0	Meusel, lf	9	0	1	3	0	0
Ruel, c	2	1	1	2	0	0	Lazzeri, 2b	3	0	0	2	2	0
Riuege, 3b	3	0	1	1	4	0	Dugan, 3b	3	0	1	1	1	0
Gillis, ss	4	0	0	2	1	0	Benguogh, c	8	0	1	1	2	0
Zachary, p	2	0	0	0	1	0	Piperas, p	2	0	0	0	2	0
aJohnson	1	0	0	0	0	0	Pennock, p	1	0	0	0	1	0
Total	30	2	5	24	10	0	Total	30	4	0	25	13	1

a Batted for Zachary in nineth.

Washington	0 0 2 0 0 0 0 0 0	-2
New York	0 0 0 1 0 1 0 2	-4

Two-base hit – Rice. Tree-base hit – Koenig. Home run – Ruth. Stolen bases – Ruel. Bluerge, Rice. Sacrifices – Meusert. Double plays – Harris and Bruege. Gillis, Harris and Judge. Left on bases – New York 4, Washington 7. Bases on balls – Off Pipgras 4, Pennock, 1, Zachary 1. Struck out – By Zachary 1. Hits – Off Pipgras 4 in 6 innings. Pennock 1 in 3. Hit by pitcher – By Pipgras (Rice). Winning pitcher – Pennock. Umpires – Dinneen, Connolly and Owens. Time of game – 1:38.

Babe Ruth's 60th home run

35 Casey Stengel's Run for Home

New York Giants vs. New York Yankees, 1st Game, 1923 World Series, October 10, 1923

YANKEE STADIUM IS AT ONCE A PATCH OF GROUND AND A state of emotion. It wasn't always thus, and therein lies the tale at hand. Or, in this case, at foot.

By the dawning of the third decade of the 20th century, the most dominant personality in that portion of the baseball world known as the National League was John McGraw. There were many, in fact, who thought that McGraw *was* the National League. Which was only as it should be, the National League still three years shy of birthing when McGraw himself was born.

John Joseph McGraw had jumped out of the womb a born hustler. Playing his scams across the early face of baseball with all the breeze, bluff and buncombe of an early-day nostrum salesman, he had led a merry band of rough-and-tumble ballplayers, the 1890 Baltimore Orioles, in those days religious scholars would label B. C. Together, the Orioles had pioneered in developing a game which included such strategums as the hit-and-run, the squeeze bunt and the delayed steal, all part of a game which scorned the big hit, scratching out one and two runs and then holding on—literally, as they looped their fingers in baserunners' belts to prevent them from advancing, and introduced such other ploys as scuffing up the ball and running from first to third upon the happy occurrence of an umpire turning his back. The Orioles' style of play soon became known as "Inside Baseball," and was the prevailing game played back in those days before the so-called "Modern Era."

Over the next two decades, baseball was to wear McGraw's label. And the National League his yoke, as his New York Giants played baseball the way God and John McGraw intended it to be played—averaging 91 wins a season, winning the pennant six times and finishing second another eight times. But being second galled McGraw.

McGraw viewed those who played on his second-place teams as transitory, their presence subject to discontinuance without further notice. Or ado. And so, when his players grew long in the tooth, he replaced them with others. Like the axe which has had its head and handle replaced so many times that, while it no longer resembled the original, it was still thought to be the same old unit, the New York Giants may have had different names and faces, but they were still the same old team, the team of John McGraw. Playing the same old game of "Inside Baseball."

By the beginning of the 1920 season, Mathewson was gone. So too were the pitchers Rube Marquard, Red Ames, and Hooks Wiltse. Gone too were catcher Chief Meyers, infielders Fred Merkle, Art Devlin, and Al Bridwell. And outfielders Red Murray, Fred Snodgrass and Josh Devore. Their places taken by George Kelly, Dave Bancroft, Frankie Frisch, Ross Youngs, Art Nehf and Jesse Barnes.

But there was one other player who also came to the Polo Grounds in 1920, and his presence was to threaten McGraw's dominance: Babe Ruth.

Babe Ruth had come to the Yankees during the off-season, sold by Boston Red Sox owner Harry Frazee as part of a liquida-tion sale. Of sorts. Frazee was an incurable entrepreneur who dabbled in all manner of entertainment: Broadway shows, boxing bouts, even wrestling matches. If Frazee was anything, he was consistent: almost everything he touched, in a reverse Midas syndrome, turned to dung. As his investments took on the look of flour flowing down a chute, Frazee sought out an "angel," someone who could bail him out. He found that someone in Jacob Ruppert, owner of the Yankees. Ruppert made Frazee a personal loan of $350,000 to put back into his foundering shows. But there was a catch: Frazee had to give Ruppert a mortgage of Fenway Park as security. Then, on January 3, 1920, Ruppert called the first installment of his loan, buying the man he called "Baby Root" from the Red Sox and Frazee for $125,000. Babe Ruth and his big bat, "Black Betsy," had arrived in New York to play for the Yankees. And to threaten John McGraw's domination of baseball and New York. Baseball's Caesars, having seen the coming of the end of the "Dead Ball" era with 448 home runs hit in 1919—211 more than the previous year—including a record-breaking 29 by that new apostle of the long-ball, Babe Ruth, made some off-season adjustments to insure the continuation, if not the exploitation, of the home run. First, they tightened the construction of the ball itself, reducing the raised stitching and wrapping the yarn tighter. The effect, described by one writer who held the ball between his thumb and forefinger, was like "hearing a rabbit's pulsebeat." Then, they outlawed the spitball, the emery ball and all other "freak" pitches. Suddenly, McGraw's "Inside Baseball" was a thing of the past, replaced by Ruth's 54 homers in 1920.

But while the old guard may die, it never surrenders, and McGraw, making no unconditional surrender to undeniable facts, continued to field winning teams in 1921 and 1922, twice beating his by-now archenemies, the Yankees, in the World Series.

It was during that '22 season that McGraw, a conspirator from the cradle and a New York matinee idol by proclamation, had decided as a majority of one—which was all it took—that the Yankees had outstayed their welcome at the Polo Grounds. For ever since Frank Farrell, Ruppert's predecessor, had petitioned the Giants for leave to move his-then "Highlanders" into the Polo Grounds in 1913, the New York American League team had played at 155th and Eighth Avenue. The 38,000-seat stadium known as the Polo Grounds and hailed by *The Sporting News* as a "monument to baseball," had been more than adequate to fill the needs of the Highlanders, soon to be rechristened the New York Yankees. That is, until Babe Ruth and his home runs came along.

By 1922, the Yankees, like fish, had begun to take on the odor of those too long in residence. Especially to the nostrils of McGraw, whose salary was based in part on the Giants' attendance. From the very first day Ruth had appeared in Yankee flannels, Yankee attendance had doubled and now had exceeded that of the Giants. With a brooding malevolence, McGraw once approached a news-man who was now identified in his eyes as being from the "enemy" camp and who had just reported a crowd of only 3,500 at a Giant game, and demanded, "What was that? More American

141

League propaganda?"

With McGraw, the mastiff-at-the-gates, now salivating at the very name Ruth and snarling at mention of the word "Yankees," the Yankees knew they had worn out their welcome and sought a stadium of their own. They found it, ten acres just across the Harlem River from the Polo Grounds in the Bronx, formerly known as Jerome Park, owned by Leonard W. Jerome, the grandfather of Winston Churchill. Ruppert and his elegantly-named partner, Colonel Tillinghast L'Hommedieu Huston, hired the Osborn Engineering Company of Cleveland to design "the biggest stadium in baseball," a three-tiered edifice that would take 248 working days and $2,300,000 Harding dollars to build. Ruppert and Huston had intended it to be a lasting monument to themselves. Instead, it would become a monument to Babe Ruth, "The House that Ruth Built."

On April 19, 1923, a larger army converged on Yankee Stadium than Gallieni had led out of Paris to the first battle of the Marne—some 100,000 fans, believing that nature, like the Yankees, abhorred a vacuum. It was a classic case of demand far outstripping supply, as 74,200 fans, by official count fought their way in, with another 25,000 more, give or take a thousand, flattened against the gates that had long since closed, all there to see the new Yankee Stadium. And Babe Ruth. They got both for their money, with Ruth baptizing the new Stadium with a three-run homer—appropriately enough, the first ever in "The House that Ruth Built"—as the Yankees won 4-1.

It was to be but the first of Ruth's 41 homers for the year and the first of the Yankees' 98 wins as both went on to lead the League. The Yankees of 1923 were called "The Best Team Money Can Buy," courtesy of the aforementioned Mr. Frazee. In a gigantic rummage sale, Bring Cash!, Frazee repaid his loan to Ruppert, with interest, sending Everett Scott, Wally Schang, Sad Sam Jones, Herb Pennock, Bullet Joe Bush, Waite Hoyt, George Pipgras and Joe Dugan to join Babe Ruth as former Red Sox now playing for the Yankees. With the passing of their best players to the Yankees, Bostonians facetiously were able to say that the only Boston clubs ever to lose a World Series were the Yankees of 1921 and 1922.

Even while the Yankees were outdistancing their intraleague rivals by some 16 games and outdrawing their interleague rivals, the Giants, by some 200,000 in attendance, the Giants, smugly content with having the Polo Grounds to themselves, went on their merry way, believing themselves still to be the Kings of the New York Sports Mountain. Lightly brushing off the Yankees and the rental moneys they had lost in evicting their tenants, the Giants enlarged the seating capacity of their "Pleasure Palace" to 54,000 and added yet another fresh coat of paint to her outsides. Then the McGrawmen added their third consecutive pennant, setting up, like the watering of last year's crops, a third straight all-New York Series. If he couldn't put the Yankees in their place during the season, McGraw reasoned, he could recoup his loss in prestige with another win in the Series over the Yankees. No one had ever achieved three World Series victories in a row! No one ever had a shot at it, not Mack or Chance or Jennings or anyone else. Now McGraw had a chance to do what no one else ever had done.

But there was something else that motivated McGraw and stoked the fires that burned within: The Yankees. Here was the chance he had been waiting for, the chance to avenge himself against the team that had taken over the town he had ruled so long, capturing New York while his Giants were conquering the world.

McGraw hated the Yankees and all they stood for so much that he wouldn't even permit his team to dress at Yankee Stadium for Game One. Instead, they dressed for the game at the Polo Grounds and made the trip over to "that" Stadium in a fleet of taxis, using the visiting players' Clubhouse at Yankee Stadium only as the "Little Napoleon's" field headquarters. And to change their shirts.

The Series would be a battle between the two titanic forces of baseball, John McGraw versus Babe Ruth, mind versus matter, intelligence versus brute force, the old school versus the new, "Inside Baseball" versus the long ball.

Somehow the pre-Series prophets had overlooked an old vagabond, part suitcase and part gypsy, who went by the name Charles Dillon Stengel, or "Casey." The left-handed batting Stengel, who had been platooned by McGraw against right-handed pitchers, had played all of 57 games, batting .271. Stengel was viewed more as a curio piece than a player, an amiable whack known as a clown, a comedian, a comic. Mention the name Stengel and most would recall that once, upon his return to Ebbets Field, he had doffed his cap to the stands and let loose a bird. But little else. His bowed, spavined legs almost spelled the word "Ox," so warped were they. And his age was indeterminate. Some whispered "33", others said "33, going on 50." Whatever, Stengel was dismissed as a factor. This one was going to be McGraw versus Ruth, no others need apply.

While most so-called experts had expected the Giants to go with little Art Nehf and the Yankees to retaliate with a southpaw of their own, Herb Pennock, both teams changed their signals, the Giants sending up right-handed Mule Watson, a late-season acquisition who had won just eight games for McGraw, and the Yankees coming back with right-hander Waite Hoyt. That meant that Stengel would be playing.

The first out in the World Series play in Yankee Stadium, as fate would have it, was a fly-out to Babe Ruth in right field. After the Giants had been retired, the first run in World Series play in the Stadium was scored by Ruth, who came around on a double to center by Bob Meusel—but only after Stengel had raced to the spot where he saw it would land and gotten his glove on the ball before it struck the ground and twisted away from him.

After the Giants had gone down without incident in the top of the second—the only loud ball hit off Hoyt being Stengel's deep fly to Ruth in the right-field corner—the Yankees scored two more off Watson, who by this had shown why he wasn't used more during the season, having the proverbial "nothing" on the ball. Then, in the top of the third, the Giants filled the bases to the brim on two singles and a walk and then, on Groh's triple and Frisch's single, scored four times for a 4-3 lead after three.

The Giants' Old Man: Charles Dillon Stengel

In their two previous meetings, McGraw had ordered his pitchers to pitch carefully to Ruth, and they responded, walking him every chance they got and then some in the 1921 and '22 Series. Now pitching carefully to Ruth in the fifth, reliever Rosy Ryan left a curve on the outside part of the plate and Ruth caught it, driving it down the left-field line for a triple. The next batter up, Bob Meusel, blooped a fly into short right which Frisch, backing up quickly turned into a great catch and then turned as quickly as a swinging door to gun down Ruth out at the plate on a sensational throw.

Still behind 4-3 as they came to bat in the seventh, the Yankees suddenly smelled the coffee, and came alive. Or so it seemed. First pitcher Bush singled, and then, with one out, third baseman Dugan tripled into the right-field corner, scoring Bush and tying up the game. Now Ruth came to the plate with a chance to break the game open. With the bellows of the throng ringing in his ears, Ruth drove one of Ryan's fast balls somewhere to the left of first, on a line to the outfield. But first baseman George "Highpockets" Kelly, true to his nickname, extended his entire 6'4" frame to make a stabbing back-handed stop, and then, righting himself like a three-fold carpenter's rule being opened, threw out Dugan at the plate from a seemingly impossible angle. Now the game wound down, going into the ninth tied at four apiece. And with two outs, who should come to bat but one Charles Dillon Stengel? Back in the seventh Stengel had gotten the Giants' only hit off Bush since he came on in relief of Hoyt in the third, but that was hardly his reward, merely his workman's compensation. The chance for his reward would come now.

As Bush came in with his change-up, Casey's bat was already aswinging. Devouring the ball just as easily as an overstuffed banquet guest would devour a plate of rare roast beef, Stengel caught it with a resounding "thwack," driving it on a line out toward left field. The ball moved with an independence of its own, almost as if seeking the higher ground, as the two Yankee outfielders, Witt and Meusel, took off in pursuit of it. Casey was off as well, running as if he had gout in both feet and dreaded ever putting them down on the field. Witt and Meusel converged at the spot where the ball should have been, but the ball had bounded off in the direction of the center-field fence, almost as if possessed. And there was Casey, who now had turned second and almost lost his shoe in the process, chained to Morpheus' slow carriage. Trying mightily to run his home run home, Stengel got to third, his warped old legs giving him the look of a broken toy. Witt got to the ball about the time Casey got to third and threw it back toward the infield. Stengel, by now swimming upstream, kept coming, gills working up and down in anticipation, legs pumping. Meusel, the relay man, wheeled and fired in the direction of the plate with all his might. By now chugging almost as if his legs were calling out "K-C, K-C, K-C," in the manner of the Little Train that Could, Stengel drove and dove for the plate, landing atop it but one tick ahead of the throw for his inside-the-park home run.

As Stengel lay there, breathing hard, like a horse when one takes the saddle off, his teammates mobbed him. The improbable had happened, Casey Stengel had hit the first World Series homer ever hit in Yankee Stadium and won the first game of the 1923 Series.

Unfortunately, although Stengel was to repeat his heroics in Game Three and, in the things-that-aren't-supposed-to-happen category, also won that game on a solo homer for a 1-0 Giants' win, those were to be the only two games the Giants did win in the entire Series, losing to the Yankees, four games to Stengel's two. John McGraw had lost, too, to Babe Ruth and "modern baseball."

"Bullet" Joe Bush, the victim of Stengel's inside-the-park home run

Game 1 October 10 at Yankee Stadium

NY-N	0 0 4	0 0 0	0 0 1
NY-A	1 2 0	0 0 0	1 0 0

New York-N	Pos	AB	R	H	RBI	PO	A	E
Bancroft	ss	4	1	1	1	3	0	0
Groh	3b	4	1	2	2	1	3	0
Frisch	2b	4	0	1	1	2	2	0
Youngs	rf	3	0	0	0	1	0	0
I. Meusel	lf	4	0	0	0	6	0	0
Stengel	cf	3	1	2	1	2	0	0
Cunningham	cf	0	0	0	0	1	0	0
Kelly	1b	4	1	1	0	5	2	0
Gowdy	c	0	0	0	0	1	0	0
a Maguire		0	1	0	0	0	0	0
Snyder	c	2	0	0	0	4	1	0
Watson	p	0	0	0	0	0	1	0
b Bentley		1	0	1	0	0	0	0
c Gearin		0	0	0	0	0	0	0
Ryan	p	2	0	0	0	1	2	0
Totals		31	5	8	5	27	11	0

New York-A	Pos	AB	R	H	RBI	PO	A	E
Witt	cf	5	0	1	2	5	0	0
Dugan	3b	4	0	1	1	0	3	0
Ruth	rf	4	1	1	0	3	0	0
B. Meusel	lf	4	0	1	1	0	0	0
Pipp	1b	4	0	2	0	10	0	0
Ward	2b	4	1	2	0	6	3	0
Schang	c	3	1	2	0	2	2	1
E. Scott	ss	2	0	0	0	1	6	0
d Hendrick		1	0	0	0	0	0	0
Johnson	ss	0	0	0	0	0	1	0
Hoyt	p	1	0	0	0	0	0	0
Bush	p	3	1	2	0	0	2	0
Totals		35	4	12	4	27	17	1

Pitching	IP	H	R	ER	BB	SO
Giants						
Watson	2	4	3	3	1	1
Ryan (W)	7	8	1	1	1	2
Yankees						
Hoyt	2⅓	4	4	4	1	0
Bush (L)	6⅔	4	1	1	2	2

a Ran for Gowdy in 3rd.
b Singled for Watson in 3rd.
c Ran for Bentley in 3rd.
d Flied out for Scott in 8th.

Doubles—Bush, B. Meusel, Schang. Triples—Dugan, Groh, Ruth. Home Run—Stengel. Stolen Base—Bancroft. Sacrifice Hit—E. Scott. Double Plays—Scott to Ward to Pipp 2, Ryan to Groh to Frisch, Frisch to Snyder. Wild Pitch—Ryan. Left on Bases—Giants 2, Yankees 7. Umpires—Evans (A), O'Day (N), Nallin (A), Hart (N). Attendance—**55,307.** Time of Game—2:05.

36 Phils Beat Dodgers for Pennant

Philadelphia Phillies vs. Brooklyn Dodgers, October 1, 1950

TEARY-EYED SENTIMENTALISTS OF THE BROOKLYNUS AMERI-
canus stripe will tell you that between 1947 and 1953 their
Dodgers were always in the running, only two games separating
their heroes from winning six pennants in seven years. One of
those two that not only found them in the running but in there
running as well was the final game of the 1950 season, a game that
finished in such a memorable finish that sportswriter Warren
Brown was moved to write, "There hasn't been such a finish since
sporting officials carried Durando over the line in the 1908 Marathon."

The Dodgers' opponents that first Sunday in October were the
Philadelphia Phillies, the most woebegone franchise in the history
of baseball and the reason for Joe E. Lewis' immortal ine, "Show
me a Philadelphia team and I'll show you a loser." In a city where it
is rumored they never recognize a trend until it's a tradition,
Philadelphians long ago had come to recognize the sorrowful plight
of their Phillies, a team with talent so dreary and threadbare they
hadn't won anything since the year 19-and-15. Backsliding down
baseball's social scale ever since, they had finished in last place 18
times in the next 30 years.

But back in late 1943 something had happened that was to
serve as the seed from which the 1950 Phillies were to grow. That
was the year that Robert R. M. Carpenter bought the Phillies for
$400,000. The first thing old man Carpenter did was name his son,
Bob, as club president. Bob not only brought with him an enthusiasm heretofore unseen in what H. L. Mencken called "The most
pecksniffian of American cities" and a commodity heretofore
unknown in Philadelphia sports circles, money, he also initiated a
fan contest to rename the team. The name the shell-shocked
Philadelphia fans came up with was "Bluejays."

But that misnomer stayed with the Philadelphia National
League entry only one year. What stayed longer was Bob, who
began spreading his money around like fertilizer to enrich his
impoverished team. His first year at the till he added catcher Andy
Seminick. The next year it was shortstop Granny Hamner. Still
tilling, Carpenter added outfielder Del Ennis in 1946, pitcher Curt
Simmons and third baseman Willie "Puddin' Head" Jones in '47,
and a bumper crop in '48 that included outfielders Richie Ashburn
and Dick Sisler and pitchers Robin Roberts and Jim Konstanty. His
1949 harvest included first baseman Eddie Waitkus, second baseman Mike Goliat and pitcher Russ Meyer. And when, in 1950, he
added the last product of his financial pump-priming, Bubba
Church, Carpenter had finally gathered together a group of fuzzy-
faced home-growns and transplants which would collectively become known as "The Whiz Kids."

However, Carpenter didn't exactly reap the fruits of what he
had sown. Not immediately anyway. After sinking to their accustomed eighth-place position in the National League basement in
both 1944 and '45, the Phillies finally deserted their permanent
digs in 1946, rising to the rarefied atmosphere of fifth place. But
when they reverted to seventh in '47 and became mired in sixth in
'48, Carpenter decided to do without the services of manager Ben

Chapman and on July 26th brought in the manager of the Phillies'
Toronto farm club, Eddie Sawyer.

Sawyer's contributions were not readily discernible, his '48
edition finishing in the same sixth-place position he had inherited.
But in 1949, Sawyer took the team that had so long been treated
like leper colony outcasts and guided them to their highest finish
since 1917, third place. With all the optimism of a guy who marries
his secretary and thinks he'll continue to dictate to her, Sawyer
called a team meeting after the last game of the '49 season and
told his operatives "to come to camp in shape in the spring . . .
because we have a chance to win it all."

The team "with a chance to win it all" staggered out of the gate
with a six-and-six record for the month of April, falling two-and-a-
half games behind the front-running Dodgers. But then, in May,
forgetting their past performance charts, the Phils won 16 of 25
and moved into third place behind the Dodgers and Cards, only
one-and-a-half games off the pace. June saw them win 14 of 25
and close the gap to but a half game behind the Dodgers. And
then, wonder of wonders, when that magic day of July 4th came
around—the day when the team in first place is already conceded
the pennant according to those who read the standings through tea
leaves—who should be in first place but the Phillies?

However, the Phils' lofty position was subject to some of the
same doubts that assault those who are constantly touching the
paint to see if it is really wet. Some of those who were constantly
poking at the Phils to see if it was really them included the
Dodgers, the Braves and the Cards, all tightly bunched with the
Phils atop the National League mountain. How tightly bunched
were they?, you might ask. Well, consider that on July 17th,
Brooklyn, although in fourth place, was a scant one game out of
first. Or that the very next day the other three moved into a three-
way tie for first. But after the Cardinals had forced their way into
the lead by a nose on July 25th, the Phils recaptured the lead on
double shutout wins over the Cubbies by Bubba Church and
Robin Roberts in the first two games of a long home stand.

The Phils, with all the naive belief in themselves that only the
young without experience can muster, now came to confidently
accept their place atop the heap. Now at home, in first place, they
scrapped to stay there.

With almost every Phillie having the best of all possible worlds,
and years as well, the Phils not only had come home to roost, but
to roost atop the National League. Winning 10 of the first 14
games in the friendly environs of Shibe Park, they opened up a
three-game lead by August 1st and began pulling away. Now all
that stood between them and their most successful home stand in
35 years was a series with the pesky New York Giants.

It was during that last series that the team's biggest scrapper,
Andy Seminick, damned near wiped out the entire infield of the
Giants in one swell foop and became the center of the biggest
rhubarb of the year.

Seminick, the team's elder statesman, had almost become the
team's erstwhile elder statesman earlier in the year when the

Phillies had tried to trade him to the Pirates for catcher Clyde McCullough and infielder Pete Castiglione. But proving the line attributed to Branch Rickey, amongst others, that the "Best trades are those you never make," Philadelphia decided not to trade him to Rickey's Pirates and now Seminick, who had gone into the campaign with a .242 average for his first seven years in the Majors, was smiting the ball at a rate hovering in the neighborhood of .300. And smiting those around him with the same frequency.

Built like a brick Boulder Dam with legs, Seminick was possessed of a firmly set I-can-do-it granite jaw and a body that would make anyone who took a near sight of the mere size of him shudder. Both were to come into play on the afternoon of August 12th, a day that began with head umpire Lon Warneke politely requesting that Giant manager Leo Durocher that he make Giant second baseman Eddie Stanky cease and desist his previous day's distracting tactics of jumping up and down behind second like Rumplestiltskin and wig-wagging his hands every time Seminick came to bat. Leo just as politely had agreed to a truce.

But Seminick, like anyone his size, remembered such insults and made a point of entering them in his personal book for later repayment. That repayment was to come the first time Seminick got on base that afternoon when, on a close play at second, he barreled into Stanky with a crunching body block, depositing the Giant second baseman's remains somewhere south of centerfield. That was only the down payment on his debt. On the next pitch, a long outfield fly, Seminick, with a long memory and a longer ledger of accounts payable, tagged up and thundered off in the direction of third. Giant third baseman, Hank Thompson, stood at third eagerly awaiting the relay. The ball never got to Thompson. Unfortunately, Seminick did, turning Thompson every which way but loose and not only causing the poor third baseman to lose several of his teeth in the resulting impact, but causing him to be removed from the game on a stretcher.

Stanky declared an end to the agreed-upon moratorium and on Seminick's next time to the plate began his gyrations anew. This time umpire Lon Warneke had had enough of Stanky's antics and banished "The Brat" from the game. A few innings later Seminick came to the plate again. And sure enough, got on base again, this time to slide with considerable vigor into Giant shortstop Bill Rigney in a close play at second. Rigney, his valor getting the better of his discretion, threw a punch at Seminick and Seminick retaliated in kind, causing Rigney to be removed on a stretcher and inciting a general melee. Durocher, who couldn't help but note that three-quarters of his infield was now up for disability, gingerly approached the umpires and asked that the gentle despoiler of his team, now standing on third and apawing the ground like a wounded bear, be removed from the game. The umpires, taking pity on Durocher, less ordered than suggested that Seminick excuse himself from the game. Seminick did, later to be fined all of $25 in a League meeting that also disallowed the Giants' protest of the game based on Stanky's ejection, further ruling that such arm-waving gestures would be illegal from that time forth and forevermore.

Winners of 12 of those 16 home games and 20 of their 28 August games, the Phillies began pulling away from the pack, leading their now-nearest pursuer, the Dodgers, by six games on September 1st. By Monday, September 4th, Labor Day, that lead had grown to seven, and by September 19th had grown to a seven-and-a-half game lead over the Braves and a nine-game lead over the Dodgers.

However, there was trouble right there in Brotherly City. For even though their infield combination was performing like men of iron, with Waitkus, Goliat, Hamner and Jones missing but 19 games all season between them and the outfield combination of Ennis, Ashburn and Sisler almost matching their at-work ratio, the pitching staff was ashambles, their arms on the missing list. Pitcher Curt Simmons had been called up for active duty by the National Guard on September 10th, taking with him his good left arm and a 17-8 record; Bob Miller, who had won his first eight games, and hurt his back and was of little or no use; and rookie Bubba Church, after contributing eight wins to the Phils' cause, had been struck in the face by a line drive off the bat of mighty Ted Kluszewski on September 15th, rendering him *nolo pitchendre* from that point on. The Phils' thinning list of pitchers now numbered but two, Robin Roberts and Jim Konstanty, a twosome that rivaled Boston's Spahn and Sain in stature, if not verse.

All of a sudden the road to the pennant had become a marathon route as the wingless Whiz Kids, now approaching journey's end, began to falter, losing eight of their next 11 games while the onrushing Dodgers won 12 of their next 15. By September 29th, with but two games remaining in the season, the Phils' quickly-evaporating lead stood at just two games—two games to be played in head-to-head combat with the Dodgers. It was enough to make grown men gnash their teeth and kids wail. And to cause Red Smith to write, "They have neither won nor lost the championship, but they had qualified for off-season employment—substituting for the diving horse in Atlantic City."

And when, in the first game of the two-games series to decide the championship, the Dodgers and Erv Palica beat the Phillies 7 to 3, visions of what was and what might be merged in the heads of the Brooklyn faithful. Now only one game stood between their heroes and a play-off with the terminally flagging Phillies.

Even as the Flatbush fanatics gathered outside the gates of Ebbets Field minding their P's and queues and awaiting a chance to cheer for their "Burrs"—as in Burrs of Summer—a little melodrama was playing itself out down on the field. Seems that Andy Seminick, who only four days before had suffered a painful bone separation in his left ankle when Giant infielder Monte Irvin, in his best imitation of a billy goat, had crashed into him, was hobbling around the greensward looking for New York *Herald-Tribune* writer Harold Rosenthal. Seminick was incensed by the fact that after he had been given a watch by his grateful fans, the deathless line "Now all he needs is an arm to put it on," had appeared in New York papers. Unfortunately, Seminick had mistaken Rosenthal for the author of the phrase, Dick Young of the New York Daily *News,* and now sought out Rosenthal to pay his respects. Rosenthal, to his credit, had the good sense to remain safely esconced in the press box, there to mull over such things as mistaken identity and other verities of life.

Another who exhibited good sense was Phillies manager Eddie Sawyer. Feeling that the deficiencies of the day might not be supplied by the morrow, Sawyer selected his ace, Robin Roberts, to pitch what had suddenly become a one-game season. "With that easy delivery he had," Sawyer remembered later, "Roberts seldom got tired. He could work with two days' rest. He had pitched four games in eight days, and given the number of pitches he threw, it was the equivalent of two games." With that thought in mind, Sawyer gave the ball to Roberts, determining that if he went down he would go down with the best he had.

Roberts, who had failed six previous times in his quest to become the Phillies' first 20-game winner since 1917, hooked up with Brooklyn's ace, Don Newcombe—also seeking his 20th win—in a classic which gave the very words "Pitching Duel" a good name. With concentration in his every move, Roberts was pinpoint perfect, keeping the ball low and on the outside and inside two inches of the plate. For the first five innings he had put down the Dodgers on just two hits, both coming to naught. Newcombe, on the other glove, was experiencing some difficulties; however, his teammates time and again helped him out of his self-made jams.

But the Dodgers' gloves took an early vacation in the Phils' half of the sixth when, after two were out, Dick Sisler got on with his second single, just out of Gil Hodges' long reach. The next batter up, Del Ennis, hit a high fly to centerfield, a tall can of corn with tassels on. Duke Snider, playing deep in left center, couldn't race in fast enough, and second baseman Jackie Robinson, feeling it was Snider's ball, didn't race out fast enough with the result that the ball bounced between them leaving Sisler astanding on third and Ennis ahugging first. And when the next batter up, "Puddin' Head" Jones, caught Newcombe's first pitch and lined the ball through the infield, the Phillies had their first—and all-important—run.

In Brooklyn's half of the sixth, Dame Fortune, who heretofore had taken a rather apathetic view of the goings-on, now took up the Dodgers' cause, wrapping them softly in the folds of her skirts. And wrapping Pee Wee Reese's wrong-field fly ball softly in the folds of the mesh that stood atop the right-field scoreboard, the ball coming to rest on the ledge. As Reese thundered into third ahead of the anticipated throw, the umpires, aided by 35,073 voices all raised in larygeal maltreatment of the ear, shouted Reese home on a ground-rule homer of the Oriental persuasion. Now the faithful, assured that the seeing-eye home run was an omen, were convinced that fate had smiled on them.

But Lady Fate can hold her smile only so long. In this case she managed to hold it through the seventh and eighth innings. However, Roberts, his plain vanilla delivery picking the corners and picking up outs as well—with most Dodger balls being pounded into the ground, Waitkus having fifteen putouts and Roberts, six assists—continued to hold off both fate and the Dodgers.

Now the 1-1 game went into the ninth, an inning when fate came forward and offered the Dodgers a chance, with a string attached. The inning started with left fielder Cal Abrams going to a count of three-and-two on Roberts. Roberts then delivered a pitch low and inside which umpire Larry Goetz called a ball, putting Abrams on first. Reese stepped up, with no malice aforethought, but with the object in mind of bunting the winning run over to second. Twice Reese bunted and twice the ball went foul. Roberts came in with his best pitch, inside, to keep Reese from hitting behind the runner, and Reese hit a frozen rope to left field, moving Abrams over to second. That brought up Duke Snider and the moment that has been branded in the memories of Brooklyn fans everywhere from that time and forevermore.

Snider's obvious course of action would be to lay down a bunt and move the two baserunners over. However, that was not necessarily a highly negotiable piece of information, everybody else in the park thinking the same think. Everyone that is except Eddie Sawyer, who was trying to outthink all. "It was far from a certainty that Snider would bunt," went his reasoning, "because a good many times during the year he hadn't bunted in similar situations against Roberts and liked to hit against Robin." And so, playing it both ways, Sawyer had his men in to cut off the run that might cost them the pennant but still playing for a bunt—if that were possible.

Roberts, who had divorced himself from the distractions on the basepaths, all the better to concentrate on the only thing that

mattered, Snider, also believed the batter he now faced would bunt. Others too believed Snider had but one thought in mind, including catcher Stan Lopata, who had come in to run for the gimpy Seminick during a Phils' mini-rally in the top of the inning, and centerfielder Richie Ashburn, never inclined to be too severe on balls hit to him and who now had moved in to short center to back up the play at second. But one of those who didn't believe Snider was going to bunt was Snider himself who swung at Roberts' first offering, lining it just past second baseman Mike Goliat into center.

Roberts remembered turning around and thinking to himself that the ball was "a line drive to Goliat." Another who was similarly inclined was baserunner Cal Abrams, who at that magic moment was holding up at second, almost as if caught in monstrous quicksand, shifting its particles with his feet. Finally, after his little foot stammer, Abrams set sail for third, extending his feet alternately one after another with a resolution but unfortunately not a speed that would allow him to navigate home. Especially since Ashburn had already engulfed the ball on the first bounce much as a cat laps up cream and was even now releasing it from behind his right ear.

Third base coach Milt Stock, showing a profound contempt for Ashburn's throwing skills and feeling no risk was too great if the goal was ultimately to be won, was already waving to his own drummer, signaling with that unambiguous forth-and-back motion that meant "run." Abrams now set his course for home, running like a bird of prey ready for a take-off. Unfortunately, his plumage was soon to betray him, for as he rounded third, a mite on the wide side, and the stands erupted in a high and shrill shriek, Ashburn's throw came in to Lopata on a line, one-hopping into his glove. Suddenly the high and shrill shriek died in 35,073 throats, there to be replaced by another shriek that owed its particular cant

Philadelphia regulars joyously greet Sisler after game-winning homer.

as from a separate and individual agony. For there stood Lopata in a thou-shalt-not-pass fashion, holding the ball like a fox sitting in a coop, awaiting Abrams' ultimate arrival. Abrams, who read in Lopata's presence the silent accusation he had been found wanting, kept coming, lumbering now with the expectations and hopes of the faithful. Finally, after a here-I-come-ready-or-not half-slide, Lopata tagged Abrams out some three feet southwest of home plate. The faithful returned to their seats, a presentiment sweeping over them that all was over.

But the inning was still far from over. There were two Brooklyn baserunners still bivouacked on second and third, both having moved up on the throw. After a short mound consultation with Sawyer, Roberts passed Robinson intentionally to load the bases and then proceeded to retired Furillo and Hodges to get out of the inning. The moment of tension had passed unavailing. The score had held at 1-1 and the game now went into extra innings.

The Phillies were to be more availing in the tenth. After Roberts had opened the stanza with a single, Waitkus, after failing to bunt, singled into short center to put men on first and second. Ashburn

bunted into a force at third. But all of that was to serve as parsley on the platter for the main dish, the next batter up, Dick Sisler. Sisler, who already had three straight singles, raised his sights—and the ball as well—driving a Newcombe fastball that had gotten away from him in a high arc just 348 feet down the left-field line for a three-run homer. And Philadelphia's first National League pennant in 35 years—a helluva long time between drinks.

Three decades-plus later "The Run" still echoes down the corridors of time. And every time someone brings up Abrams' feat of feet, someone else will give him cauliflower ears bringing up the fact that there was a pick-off attempt at second, orchestrated by Granny Hamner, which had kept Abrams close. However, as they say in Brooklyn, any such *ex-post facto* rationalization is an attempt to make something out of nothing, a *tzimis*, one embroidered out of whole cloth. For if anyone should have known about a pick-off play, it was the pitcher, Robin Roberts. And Roberts could only say: "There was no pickoff on; that's all story. If there was a pickoff on I didn't know about it, and I had the ball." But it makes a good story anyway.

Dick Sisler Clouts Homer With Two Aboard In Tenth To Carry Phils Into Series

PHILADELPHIA	ab	r	h	o	a	e	rbi
Waitkus 1b	5	1	1	18	0	0	0
Ashburn cf	5	0	2	1	0	0	0
Sisler lf	5	2	4	0	0	0	3
Mayo lf	0	0	0	2	0	0	0
Ennis rf	5	0	1	0	0	0	1
Jones 3b	5	0	1	0	3	0	1
Hamner ss	4	0	1	1	2	0	0
Seminick c	4	0	0	5	0	0	0
a-Caballero	0	0	0	0	0	0	0
Lopata c	0	0	0	1	0	0	0
Goliat 2b	4	0	1	1	3	0	0
Roberts p	3	1	1	1	0	0	0
Totals	**39**	**4**	**11**	**30**	**10**	**0**	**4**
BROOKLYN	ab	r	h	o	a	e	rbi
Abrams lf	2	0	0	2	0	0	0
Reese ss	3	1	3	3	3	0	1
Snider cf	4	0	1	3	0	0	0
Robinson 2b	3	0	0	4	3	0	0
Furillo rf	4	0	0	2	0	0	0
Hodges 1b	4	0	0	9	3	0	0
Campanella c	4	0	1	2	4	0	0
Cox 3b	3	0	0	1	2	0	0
b-Russell	1	0	0	0	0	0	0
Newcombe p	3	0	0	3	2	0	0
c-Brown	1	0	0	0	0	0	0
Totals	**33**	**1**	**5**	**30**	**17**	**0**	**1**

```
Philadelphia    000 001 000 3—4
Brooklyn        000 001 000 0—1
```

2b. Reese; hr, Reese, Sisler; s, Roberts; dp, Reese, Robinson and Hodges, Roberts and Waitkus; left, Philadelphia 7, Brooklyn 5; bb, off Roberts 3, Newcombe 2; so, by Roberts 2, Newcombe 3; winner, Roberts (20-12); loser, Newcombe (19-11); u, Goetz, Dascoli, Jorda and Donatelli; t, 2:35; a, 35,073; A—Caballero ran for Seminick 9th; b—Russell struck out for Cox 10th; c—Brown fouled out for Newcombe 10th.

37 The "Black Sox" World Series

Cincinnati Reds vs. Chicago White Sox, 1st Game, 1919 World Series, October 1, 1919

WITH THE END OF WORLD WAR I, AMERICANS TURNED FROM the rigors of problem solving to the rituals of pleasure seeking. The world was an entirely different one from that which had gone marching off to war just two years earlier: Morals were down and skirts were up. And on January 16, 1919, the Prohibition amendment to the Constitution was ratified. Morals would suffer even more.

Disenchanted Americans, believing their privations and principles had failed to give them the promised peace they had fought for turned from the rigors of problem solving to the rituals of pleasure seeking. From a gigantic laundry list of available diversions, they almost universally settled on one form of escapism—sports. And among the sports they embraced most avidly in their freewheeling mood was the sport of baseball. But, by the end of 1919, America's love affair with baseball was to turn sour, yet another casualty in what was to become a losing battle against postwar immorality.

During the two war years there were serious doubts as to whether baseball would survive the war and, if it did, whether it would ever again rise to its exalted level of "National Pastime." But by 1919 the storm clouds had lifted and baseball, together with everything else, began to head back to what Warren Harding called "Normalcy." On January 10, the president of the New York Giants, Harry Hempstead, delivered a ringing speech in support of the game's future: "I truly believe the old game will thrive this year as it has not since the World War began in 1914." And then, four days later, believing his own campaign oratory, Hempstead took advantage of the optimism he had showered on baseball by unloading the controlling interest in the Giants to a syndicate headed up by Charles Stoneham for $1.3 million. It came as no surprise to the establishment that Stoneham, whose occupation was officially listed as "curb broker," was, in reality a racetrack owner and gambler. Such were baseball's strange bedfellows in 1919.

One of the first players Stoneham and his partner-hyphen-manager John McGraw acquired for the Giants was Hal Chase, a brilliant left-handed first baseman with few peers as a fielder, but who, it was suggested, also thought left-handed. Chase had jumped out of the womb a born hustler and had played his scam across the early face of baseball with all the breeze, bluff and buncombe of a claim jumper. His "corkscrew mind," it was hinted by many, was used to perfect the fine art of throwing games for fun and profit. Chase had played for the New York Yankees, nee Highlanders, for eight years, gaining a reputation for being the finest fielding first baseman in the American League, if not all of baseball. But it was during his tenure there that Joe Villa, writing in the New York *World* wrote in 1912: "In this city with no horse racing to command attention, baseball had become a medium for wagers large and small. Sporting men who never cared for the national game when the race tracks were open, now make their bets before going to the ball parks." When, in 1914, Chase jumped to the fledgling Federal League, he acquired a second reputation,

apparently well-earned, for skulduggery. And when the Federal League folded after two disastrous seasons, and Chase sought to re-enter baseball, no American League club would touch him. However, Chase found a taker in the Cincinnati Reds who bought his contract for the 1916 season and Chase immediately rewarded them by winning the National League batting championship. But even then there was talk that Chase's loyalty was to others than the Reds.

Those rumors came to a head late in 1918 when, just before he enlisted for overseas duty, Cincinnati manager Christy Mathewson formally charged Chase with throwing games. However, the ensuing National League investigation was hampered by Mathewson's absence. And despite the fact that National League president Heydler thought Chase guilty, he had "no proof that will stand up in a court of law," and on February 6, 1919, exonerated him of "any wrongdoing." Thirteen days later McGraw acquired Chase from the Reds in a trade and Chase withdrew his claims against Cincinnati and signed with the Giants. It was something that would come back to haunt baseball after the strange and sordid story of the 1919 World Series finally came to light.

The first postwar Series pitted the Chicago White Sox, winners of their second pennant in three years, against the Cincinnati Reds, winners of their first pennant in 50. The White Sox, called by many, including Boston Red Sox manager Ed Barrow, "one of the greatest teams of all time," were installed as a 7-5 favorite.

Almost from the day the season ended on September 29, rumors began circulating, all beginning and ending with the word "fix." But most dismissed them as exactly that, rumors. It seemed financially impossible, for the teams would be playing for the largest World Series pot in history. And even if financially possible, it seemed physically improbable; how could any one man affect the outcome of the games that much?

And yet, the rumors increased in crescendo, with substance being lent to the rumors by the shifting of the odds in Cincinnati's favor and by the invasion of Cincinnati by what was then politely known in society as "the sporting crowd."

The scene in Cincinnati that week of October 1st was pure carnival. Devotees, dilettantes and denizens of the netherworld all descended upon the Queen City—and the Metropole Hotel—ready for almost anything. Any "action." There the sports, wearing heavy gold watches called "turnips" on their watchchains along with other paraphernalia which could be safely carried, including gold knives, gold cigar cutters, gold toothpicks and gold ear-cleaners which doubled in brass for reaming out pipes and which all could be converted into cash in any pawnshop on a moment's notice, congregated, offering Cincinnati money. All had the conspiratorial appearance of men to whom life had appeared as a reversible coat, seamy on both sides: Sport Sullivan, betting commissioner for the likes of George M. Cohan, was there. So were former featherweight champion Abe Attell, Nicky Arnstein and "Sleepy" Bill Burns, former big league pitcher—all emissaries of Arnold Rothstein, the man who bankrolled the dice game held every night in a building next door to the Claridge Hotel on New York's West 44th Street, and who was rumored to be "bankrolling" Cincinnati in this Series. And so was the ubiquitous Hal Chase, recently given his release by the Giants under a cloud.

All were liberally equipped with one-way pockets and money that seemed to be crying out, "Bet me! Bet me!" And bet it they did, as the odds changed from 7-5, Chicago, to 6-5, Cincinnati. Something was going on. Later revelations would reveal exactly what that "something" was: The Series had indeed been fixed.

But who had gotten to whom? The answer was provided to those in the know on the second pitch of the first inning by Chicago White Sox pitcher Eddie Cicotte. Cicotte, one of baseball's great shineball pitchers—he carried transparent paraffin on his trousers and used it to make the ball slide off his fingers and break just as it reached the plate, something like a spitter—also had great control, hitting just two batters during the season and walking just 49 in 306 innings. But, on the second pitch to Morrie Rath, the Reds' lead-off batter, he hit him in the back, signaling that the "fix" was on.

Cicotte's "signal" was to become the first run of the Series. But Cicotte's real contribution was to come in the fourth inning when Cincinnati scored five runs. Cicotte, who later admitted he had thrown the game by "giving Cincinnati easy balls and putting them right over the plate . . . a baby could have hit them . . ." gave up, in succession, a single to Greasy Neale, a single to Ivy Wingo, a triple to opposing pitcher Dutch Ruether, a double to the same Morrie Rath who had been the hittee in the first inning and a single to Jake Daubert. In all, five runs and the game, the Reds winning 9-1.

Cicotte's form reversal impressed many observers; the odds jumped to 8-5 on the Reds and doubts in the minds of some became reality in the minds of others. Hughie Fullerton, the perspicacious columnist for the Chicago *Herald and Examiner,* was forced to admit, "I don't like what I saw out there today. There is something smelly. Cicotte doesn't usually pitch like that."

Others, too, were suspicious. The rumors had spread far and wide, even reaching the ears of Charles Comiskey, the president of

Eddie Cicotte, who was to say "I played a dishonest game," starting with his first pitch of Game One

Game 1 October 1 at Cincinnati								
Chicago	Pos	AB	R	H	RBI	PO	A	E
S. Collins	rf	4	0	1	0	0	0	0
E. Collins	2b	4	0	1	0	3	3	0
Weaver	3b	4	0	1	0	0	1	0
Jackson	lf	4	1	0	0	3	0	0
Felsch	cf	3	0	0	0	4	0	0
Gandil	1b	4	0	2	1	7	0	1
Risberg	ss	2	0	0	0	5	6	0
Schalk	c	3	0	0	0	2	2	0
Cicotte	p	1	0	0	0	0	2	0
Wilkinson	p	1	0	0	0	0	0	0
a McMullin		1	0	1	0	0	0	0
Lowdermilk	p	1	0	0	0	0	1	0
Totals		32	1	6	1	24	15	1

a Singled for Wilkinson in 8th.

Double—Rath. Triples—Daubert, Ruether 2. Stolen Base—Roush. Sacrifice Hits—Felsch, Groh, Rath, Roush, Wingo. Double Plays—Risberg to E. Collins, Risberg to E. Collins to Gandil. Hit by Pitchers—Rath (by Cicotte), Daubert (by Lowdermilk). Left on Bases—Chicago 5, Cincinnati 7. Umpires—Rigler (N), Evans (A), Nallin (N), Quigley (A). Attendance—30,511. Time of Game—1:42.

Chi.	0 1 0	0 0 0	0 0 0
Cin.	1 0 0	5 0 0	2 1 x

Cincinnati	Pos	AB	R	H	RBI	PO	A	E
Rath	2b	3	2	1	1	4	2	0
Daubert	1b	4	1	3	1	9	0	0
Groh	3b	3	1	1	2	0	3	0
Roush	cf	3	0	0	0	8	0	0
Duncan	lf	4	0	2	1	1	0	0
Kopf	ss	4	1	0	0	1	3	1
Neale	rf	4	2	3	0	3	0	0
Wingo	c	3	1	1	1	1	2	0
Ruether	p	3	1	3	3	0	2	0
Totals		31	9	14	9	27	12	1

Pitching	IP	H	R	ER	BB	SO
Chicago						
Cicotte (L)	3⅔	7	6	6	2	1
Wilkinson	3⅓	5	2	1	0	1
Lowdermilk	1	2	1	1	1	0
Cincinnati						
Ruether (W)	9	6	1	0	1	1

the Chicago White Sox himself. But Comiskey could not turn to American League president Ban Johnson because of an internecine feud he was having with him. Having shut himself off from the president of his own league, the "Old Roman," instead, turned to the other two members of the then-presiding National Commission, National League president John Heydler and Reds' president Garry Herrmann. Heydler heard out Comiskey and even though he believed his suspicions were nothing than those of a man whose team had lost to an underdog, agreed to serve as liaison, going to Johnson to convey Comiskey's misgivings. But Johnson was unmoved, and responded, "That's the yelp of a beaten cur!"

Cicotte would come back again to lose the fourth game and the Sox would lose the then nine-game Series, five games to three. Still many didn't believe—or want to believe—what they had seen happen. Al Spink of *The Sporting News* was one of those, writing, "The managing editor asked me what I thought of the rumors of crookedness. . . . I replied that the talk of the selling out of certain players was pure buncombe, that there was not enough money in all the world to buy up the contenders on either side in a world's championship baseball series."

But as revelations, which came to light just before the close of the 1920 season and took baseball amidships were to prove, there *was* enough money. And sadly enough, when everything had been said and done, the greatest spectacle in sports had been dishonestly played, especially by the eight men who had changed the color of their uniforms from White to Black: Eddie Cicotte, Lefty Williams, Chick Gandil, Joe Jackson, Swede Risberg, Buck Weaver, Hap Felsch and Fred McMullin, all of whom were to have their accomplishments written in sand and their venality in gravenstone.

In the final analysis, baseball had repeated its mistake because nobody had been listening the first time when Hal Chase was charged with dealing off the bottom of the pack, and now had to pay for its inattention. Nelson Algren, then a little boy living in Chicago, was later to express his disgust when he wrote: "Benedict Arnolds. Betrayers of American Boyhood, not to mention American Girlhood and American Womanhood and American Hoodhood."

Joe Jackson, the most natural hitter in the history of baseball and of the eight "Black Sox."

EIGHT WHITE SOX PLAYERS ARE INDICTED ON CHARGE OF FIXING 1919 WORLD SERIES; CICOTTE GOT $10,000 AND JACKSON $5,000

COMISKEY SUSPENDS THEM

Promises to Run Them Out of Baseball if Found Guilty

TWO OF PLAYERS CONFESS

Cicotte and Jackson Tell of Their Work in Throwing Games to Cincinnati.

BOTH ARE HELD IN CUSTODY

Prosecutor Says More Players Will Be Indicted and Gamblers Brought to Task.

38 Pete Rose's Record-Breaking Game

Cincinnati Reds. vs. San Diego Padres, September 11, 1985

JUST WHEN IT SEEMED THAT THE OLD-TIME VIRTUES OF IN-dustry and energy had disappeared completely from the base-ball landscape, along came a throwback to yesteryear named Pete Rose who spat on his hands, rolled up his sleeves and with workmanlike vigor brought the hardhat ethic back to baseball.

The legend of Pete Rose had its start during Spring Training, 1963. Normally, spring training is a paid vacation, a time during which players rarely let success go to their playing. With most players standing around to take their turns like numbers at a meat market and cruising on all batteries, their performances tend to serve as a substitute for sleeping potions. And so, when a 21-going-on-22-year-old rookie trying to make the Cincinnati Reds attacked spring training in an effort to dispose of the fair advantage most veterans had over him by hustling every which way, almost as if he were coming apart at the seams, he raised more than a few eyebrows. And a few voices. One of those belonged to Mickey Mantle, who, sitting on the bench during a Yankees-Reds spring training to-do and watching what looked to him like one of nature's irregularities almost running out of his uniform hustling down to first on a walk, said with all the breezy nonchalance of a cracker barrel hugger to teammate Whitey Ford, "Look at Charlie Hustle."

The remark, meant as a derogatory aside, was the most classic understatement since a Crow scout told Colonel Custer there might be some trouble along the Little Big Horn. For Rose, who took the comment as his Big Red Badge of Courage, continued to hustle, not only to first but into the Reds' line-up at second, where Cincinnati manager Freddie Hutchinson inserted the spunky new kid on the block in place of Don Blasingame. And then Rose hustled, from his very first Major League hit—a triple off Bob Friend that saw him belly-thomp into third—all the way to the National League's Rookie of the Year Award.

While there must be some argument against hustling, Rose was never swayed by it, so he continued on his merry way, playing with a manifesto gusto unseen in many a year, always giving one hundred fifty percent of himself. Putting whole timber and pallette into his every move, Rose soon became Public Energy Number One, dashing off to first, throwing himself at any base with a damn-the-torpedoes-full-speed-ahead belly-flop and bowling anyone in his way over like a tenpin.

Together with the excitement he created on the basepaths, the switch-hitting Rose could also step to the plate and make any dues-paying fan feel "Charlie Hustle" alone was well worth the price of admission. Stepping into the batter's box, his eyes holding his opponent's in his fixed stare, Rose went through a little ritual, be he batting from the right or left side: He would tap his spikes with his bat, shove his batting helmet back on his head with a vigorous thrust and then crouch down, his posterior approximately two furlongs behind him. But a ballplayer's record is as expressive as his stance, and by 1965, his hits from both sides of the plate had begun to come in heaping platefuls as he led the National League in base hits with 209—only the second time in history a switch-hitter had led the League in hits.

However, despite his growing list of accomplishments at the plate—including leading the League in batting in 1968 and 1969—Rose was still viewed by most as a "hustler," one who played with a ball's-out joy. Perhaps the memory most have of this gristmill imbued with animality was of Rose roaring like a train out of control into, and over, American League catcher Ray Fosse in the 1970 All-Star Game, leaving Fosse with a separated shoulder and the look of a man run over by a municipal tram.

But even as he was making a dent in Fosse with his shoulder, Rose was also making a dent with his bat in the all-time hit totals, recording his 1,000th hit on June 26, 1968, in only his sixth season. By 1970, as an integral cog in what was labeled "The Big Red Machine," Rose's bat began ringing to notes of victory as he contributed 205, 192 and 198 hits to the Reds' pennant drives in the next three years. And hustled his way to his 2,000th hit on June 19, 1973, in his 11th year.

At the conclusion of his first decade in the Majors, then but 78 hits shy of the 2,000-hit plateau, Rose had taken a look at his horizons, which seemed limitless. "My goal," he confessed that day back in '72, "is 3,000. If I can play 150 games for the next five years, I'll reach 3,000 on July 16, 1977 . . . no, make that 1978." Then, taking another look at the crystal ball, he added, "I'm the only active guy with a legitimate chance to get 4,000 hits. I'm proud of the fact that most of the name guys like Ty Cobb got most of their hits in their second 10 years. I got 1,922 in my first 10 years . . . and if you throw out my first two seasons when I got 170 and 139, I've averaged 202 hits the last eight years."

Now the man of whom writer Larry Merchant once noted, "Gets hits in the present and lives in the past," began to stake more claims than an Alaskan claim jumper, passing some of the greatest names in baseball history like signs on the way to Cooperstown. Clawing and scratching his way up the hit ladder, Rose passed Chuck Klein and Clyde Milan in 1973, Bill Terry and Joe DiMaggio in 1974, Edd Rousch and Mickey Mantle in 1975, Jimmie Foxx and Ted Williams in 1976 and Frankie Frisch as the all-time switch-hitter in 1977.

Even though the Bob Haldeman-style Brillo pad he had once worn on his head had given way to a mod haircut, his square torso filled out with more trunk space than a new model car and his granite jaw added a few more lines, Pete Rose still played like a man who had just discovered the joint secrets of perpetual motion and emotion. Here he could be seen belly-flopping in that preda-tor's headlong dive of his almost as if his stomach were getting chilly; there racing the basepaths in a manner that looked like he was answering his mother's last call to dinner; and everywhere playing the game with a defiant pride known only to youngsters—even if he were 36, "going on," as he said, "21."

Now the young prodigy who had continued being young long after he had stopped being a prodigy continued to prove his potency, becoming the lucky 13th man to pass the 3,000-hit mark on May 5, 1978. And during the rest of '78 not only hit in a National League Record-tying 44 consecutive games but raised his hit total to 3,164, passing Cap Anson and Paul Waner in the bargain.

But if Rose had made "hustling" a negotiable commodity, he sought to be duly rewarded for becoming its biggest carrier West of New York's 42nd Street. Declaring himself to be a "Free Agent," Rose went home to await offers at a time in life when most men would be happy to get a pipe and slippers for their efforts. Finally, after some financial maneuvering that took on the look of a corporate buy-out, the Philadelphia Phillies, their coffers bolstered by some extra advertising revenues from a soft drink distributor, offered Rose a multi-million dollar contract. And so the man-boy from Cincinnati was on the move, the moving van backing up to his house taking 3,164 hits, nine 200-hit seasons, three batting titles, two World Series rings and his .310 batting average to Philadelphia.

Ecstatic with the deal, Rose announced to the gaggle of newsmen gathered to witness the signing, "With the money I'm making, I should be playing two positions." And saying so, Rose, who throughout the first 16 years of his career had played three positions—second, outfield and third, in that order—now assumed a fourth position: First base. But it wasn't his position afield, but in the batter's box that brought the fans out to Veteran's Stadium in 1979 as Rose continued his one-man assault on the all-time hit record, recording his record 10th 200-hit season, batting .331, raising his hit total to 3,362.

Now only 819 hits—and a thinning list of players in the rarified atmosphere of the 3,000-hit club—separated Rose and the all-time leader, Ty Cobb. That meant at least five more seasons for the man who was now demonstrating admirable resistance to the erosion of time. But 1980 was to provide another retardant to the process of aging. The Phillies were not only in the pennant chase, they were the rabbit, leading the pack. And Rose, practicing his own style of regentrification, had another 185 hits, leading the Phillies to their first-ever World Series win and raising his total to 3,547, passing Eddie Collins, Honus Wagner and Tris Speaker. Now there were three ahead of him: Stan Musial, Hank Aaron and Ty Cobb.

Rose had a league-leading 140 hits in the strike-shortened '81 season, one of which was his 3,631st, breaking Stan Musial's National League record, and another 172 in 1982 to bring his total to 3,869. Only 322 hits stood between Rose and Ty Cobb, nothing else. Or so it seemed.

But 1983 almost saw the end of Rose's challenge. For even though the Phillies had renewed his contract for 1983—Phillies president Bill Giles giving him a new $1.3 million contract with a "Ty Cobb Clause" because, as Giles explained it, "We think you'll catch Cobb and we want you to do it here."—Rose was benched in August, his consecutive-game streak of 745 games halted and his status reduced to that of a pinch-hitter. And although he had amassed another 121 hits during the year, bringing his total to 3,990, it was apparent to all that the sand in Pete Rose's sturdy 42-year-old hourglass was beginning to flow down and that his days were numbered. Apparent to all, that is, except Rose himself, who constituted a majority of one who still thought he could do it; and that's all it took.

At the age of 43, when any self-respecting ballplayer would be well advised to stay home and feel his oats and corns at the same time, Pete Rose was still full of spit and vinegar, ready to pursue Cobb, now only 201 hits away. Unfortunately, that pursuit would not be in a Phillies uniform, the Phillies having put him out to pasture and wished him well to boot. But Rose determined he was not through, not on his immortality!, and within months had signed

a $700,000 one-year contract with the Montreal Expos for '84. But though Rose played 95 games for Montreal and got 72 hits, including his 4,000th on April 18th, by August 16th he was gone again. This time back to Cincinnati as player-manager.

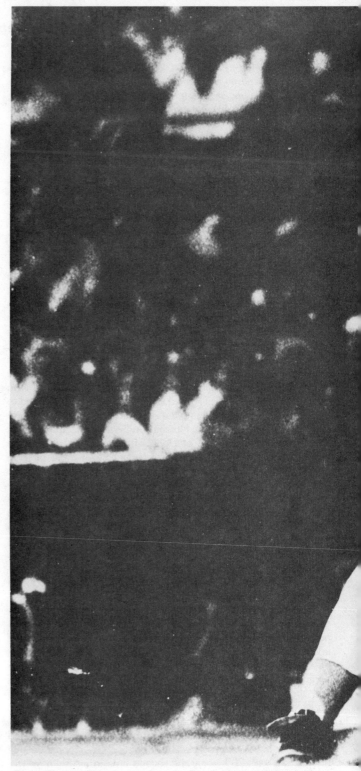

Pete Rose: the man who took a bat and dubbed himself the most prolific hitter of all time.

Rose inherited a fifth-place team. And he also inherited something else as well: The inevitable comparisons with Cobb. For both men had been driven by a devine spark of fire, their styles of play those of men caught in their own personal crucibles. Cobb, too,

had been a playing-manager, managing the Detroit Tigers for six years from 1921 through '26, a period that saw Cobb the player get 1044 hits for Cobb the manager. Rose, however, would be a full-time manager and part-time player, platooning himself at first with right-handed hitting Tony Perez. Then there were those few remaining graybeards who remembered Cobb and were protecting the yellowed clippings of their memories by pointing out that Rose had batted nearly 2,300 more times than Cobb—who had retired after the '28 season by saying, "I'm quitting while there are plenty of hits left in my bat." But such comparisons were odious to Rose who merely responded to them with a "That's tough . . . too bad!" And then, as if to prove himself and his point, Rose went on, like a priest asking a few friends in to hear confession, "I don't want to hear all that stuff that I had more at bats. I'll make it in one less year than he did. That proves I am more durable."

And for the last 42 games of the season, the new Cincinnati municipal monument let his bat do his talking for him, winding up the '84 season only 94 hits away from the once unassailable record of 4,191. 1985 would be the year, Rose's year.

With no deadline, no timetable, no nothing, Rose went about his dual chores, managing the surprising Reds, who were in second, and playing first against right-handed pitchers. The only real pressure on Rose came from Cincinnati fans and Reds owner Marge Schott who wanted Rose to get the tying and breaking hits in front of "his" fans.

As the final countdown continued throughout the '85 season, hits Number 4,188 and 4,189 came at Chicago's Wrigley Field on Friday, September 6th. And when Rose went 0-for-4 on Saturday, it began to look like "The Cincinnati Kid" would return to his hometown for his record-making twosome two days hence. Especially since the announced pitcher for the last away game with the Cubs on Sunday was left-hander Steve Trout. But here fate interfered with the best-laid plans of Rose and men, Trout falling off his bicycle the night before the game and injuring his shoulder. When Chicago manager Jim Frey found out about the injury an hour before game time, he erased Trout's name and penciled in the name of right-hander Reggie Patterson. Rose, so torn by the sense of civic responsibility resting on his shoulders he "didn't know whether to scratch my watch or wind my behind," finally decided to insert himself at first in place of Perez. And delivered, twice, with a single in the first off Patterson and another in the fifth. The count now stood at Cobb, 4,191, Rose, 4,191.

The day that had become inevitable with Rose's first Major League hit 22 years before finally came on Wednesday, September 11th. In front of a standing room only crowd of 47,237 at Cincinnati's Riverfront Stadium Rose came to bat in the first inning against San Diego's Eric Show. With a count of 2-and-1, Show delivered a slider, down and in. Rose set his granite, I-can-do-it jaw in position and caught the ball on the meat part of his bat, driving it like a shot from a howitzer out toward left field. As the ball bounced in front of Padres left fielder Carmelo Martinez, Pete Rose added the final note to his fabulous career by hustling all the way to first.

"Charlie Hustle" had finally done it. The longest "running" show in Major League baseball had taken a bat and dubbed himself the most prolific batsman of all time.

39 "Home Run" Baker Wins His Name

Philadelphia Athletics vs. New York Giants, 3rd Game, 1911 World Series, October 17, 1911

THE AMERICA OF THE EARLY 1900S WAS CONFIDENT AND cocksure, casting about for its own identity though already sure of its place in history. It found that identity in its heroes: Teddy Roosevelt in politics, Jack London in literature and Christy Mathewson in sports.

Baseball had other celebrities, to be sure, men like Napoleon Lajoie, Ed Delehanty, Honus Wagner and Ty Cobb, to name but a few. But in a day and age when baseball had a reputation for the rough-and-tumble, its ballplayers, as Jimmy Powers was to characterize them in later years, "tobacco-chewing, beer-guzzling bums," Christy Mathewson was a Frank Merriwell character, one who seemed to be made of sunshine, blood-red tissue and clear weather. In a field devoted to fashioning halos for its performers, "Matty" wore a special nimbus.

Under the blond grassplot he wore on his head, Matty's face was as clearly chiseled as a Roman emperor's on an old coin, giving him the overall look of a sun god. Six-feet-two, blond as a Viking, quiet as a deacon and dangerous as a six-shooter, the man they called "Big Six"—after the famed New York City fire engine of the same name—was treated with such reverence by fans that if they had but worn hats they would have doffed them at the very mention of his name.

Mathewson's reputation was built upon his famed "Fadeaway"—a reverse curve now given the somewhat less-fanciful name "Screwball"— and on his uncanny control. Elegantly moving the ball in and out, Matty would alternate his "Fadeaway," fast ball and curve, all the while picking his spots with all the precision of a barber shaving a mustachioed patron. Giving up but one-and-a-half walks per game, Matty's control prompted sportswriter Ring Lardner to rhapsodize, "Nobody else in the world can stick a ball as near where they want to stick it as he can."

The cornerstone of Mathewson's fame, however, did not lie merely in his control. Nor in his "Fadeaway." But in his three shutout wins over the Philadelphia Athletics in the 1905 World Series, three hills from which he now looked down on the baseball world.

Over the next half-a-decade, Mathewson's growing stature on the mound extended far beyond his 6' 2", made all-the-bigger by his list of achievements—not only did he average 27 wins a season for those five years, but in there somewhere twice led the League in complete games, strike outs, shutouts and ERA and three times in wins. His precision and concision were such that it was always a pleasure to watch him, even when his opposition was, at best, commonplace. Two teams in particular, the Cardinals and the Reds, with the easy repose of the Red Man at the stake, had lost to Mathewson 23 and 22 in a row, respectively and respectfully. It had almost gotten to the point where all Mathewson had to do was throw his glove on the mound to win, as one writer, Damon Runyon, noted, leading off his story: "Mathewson pitched against Cincinnati yesterday. Another way of putting it is that Cincinnati lost a game of baseball. The first statement means the same as the second."

Then, in 1911, the Giants once again finished atop the baseball world, winning the National League pennant by seven-and-a-half games over the defending champion Chicago Cubs. And Matty was back in the World Series. Again, against the Philadelphia Athletics.

The 1911 version of the defending World's Champion Philadelphia Athletics was a star-studded team, with so many stars their talents were available at a discount. Their infield of Stuffy McInnis, Eddie Collins, Jack Barry and Frank Baker was so renowned that it was labeled "The $100,000 Infield," high praise indeed when measured in terms of 1911 Taft dollars. And their pitching staff was made up of three of the more storied pitchers in baseballdom, Jack Coombs, Eddie Plank and Chief Bender, who, as a trio, had won 67 games between them as the A's won a total of 101 games and the American League pennant by 13½ games.

While the Giants of 1911 were hardly as talent-laden as the A's, they did have two of the best pitchers in all of baseball on their staff, Mathewson and Rube Marquard, performing as the two trace horses McGraw hitched his pennant wagon to. Marquard, later to become an important part of our story, was an interesting character, one who bears inspection of a brief nature at this point. Bought by the Giants for the then-unheard of price of $11,000, he came up the Giants in the fall of 1908. The newpapers promptly tagged him the "$11,000 Beauty" and demanded that fans get a look at him in action. Pressured by the papers and presented with a pressing need for pitching help of any kind as the days dwindled down to a precious few in that famous pennant race of 1908, McGraw conscripted Marquard to "Go in and pitch" the second game of a double header against Cincinnati. Marquard, worried that "McGraw had paid $11,000 for me and now they were going to find out whether he had gotten stuck, whether he had picked up a gold brick with the plating on it very thin," made his wary way to the mound. He promptly plunked the lead-off man, Johnny Kane, in the ribs and while he was worrying about him, Kane stole second, which worried him some more. The next man up, Hans Lobert, tripled and, as he reached third, hollered at Marquard, "You're identified, you're a busher!" Five innings, six hits and two walks later, to the cries of "Take him out!," Marquard was gone. The "$11,000 Beauty" had soured, turning instead into the "$11,000 Lemon."

For the next two years, instead of bringing Marquard along on a diet of teams carefully graded in significance, he was continually thrown to the wolves, his contributions progressively diminishing in importance. As the 1911 season dawned, his career record of 9-18 seemed to have earned him permanent possession of the "$11,000 Lemon" label. Then Giant manager John McGraw, who had a reputation for being able to make a player out of far less promising stock, wisely turned Marquard over to coach Wilbert Robinson. His stock soared in value almost immediately, the tense and nervous prospect turning into a finished performer. Paying testimony to Marquard's turn-around was Chicago shortstop Joe Tinker, who said, "When he throws his fast one, the only way you know it's past you is because you hear the ball hit the catcher's glove." Further testimony was his 24-7 record for the 1911 Giants.

Now, with both Marquard and Mathewson ready, willing and rested, McGraw hoped to be able to repeat his victory over the A's of 19-aught-five. The superstitious McGraw—who had indulged his belief in old wives' tales by actually adopting a mascot named Charley Faust for the 1911 season because it was believed he had the powers of a "jinx killer"—even went so far as to dress up the Giants in the same black broadcloth uniforms they had worn six years before. Not content with mere superstition, McGraw also tried psychological warfare on the A's, instructing his Giants, who had stolen 347 bases for the year, a new record in the base-stealing dodge, to greet the Athletics as they came onto the field for Game One with the spectacle of each and every one of them sharpening their spikes on the bench, all the better, it was figured, to eat them up alive.

But it wasn't the uniforms nor the sharpened spikes that won Game One. It was Mathewson. In a *redux* of the last time he had pitched in a Series lo those six years before, Matty once again was matched-up with Chief Bender. And, in what must have looked like a mirror image of their last pitching duel, Matty gave up the same number of hits, six, to the same number for Bender, five, as he again outpitched Bender, this time 2-1—the A's run by Frank Baker with two outs in the second inning breaking Matty's consecutive scoreless streak at 28⅔ innings. It was not to be the last time Mathewson, or the Giants, would hear Baker's name.

McGraw came back with Marquard in Game Two against Philadelphia's Eddie Plank. And for five innings the brilliant and brillantined Marquard more than held his own, giving up but two hits and one run, all in the first, and retiring the last 11 batters to face him. Still, he was no better than even with Plank, who had

Rube Marquard, the Giants' 24-game winner who served up a homer to Baker in Game Two

given up only three hits and one run to the Giants over the first five. Then, after Marquard had retired the first two A's in the sixth on outfield flies, Eddie Collins doubled down the left field line. That brought up Frank Baker, the A's third baseman. The left-handed Baker, known for his powerful wrists, arms and shoulders—and known to the world by the abbreviated name "Bake"—had led the American League in home runs that year and was considered, in those days of the "dead ball," one of the few long ball threats in the A's line-up. Sure enough, Baker caught one of Marquard's fastballs on the meat end of the bat and drove it, on a line, over the right-field wall, making the score 3-1. And ended all the scoring for the day.

Back in those prehistoric days of yore before radio or TV, the game itself was not defined by the four walls of the stadium nor the instantaneous communication of what had taken place within, but by what was reported in the next-day's papers. Newsmen, aware that many readers had learned to run when one of their grizzled veterans launched into a story that began "Once upon a time," or other such florid phrase, had now invented a new strategum for having the games reported to the breathless masses, something called "ghosted" articles. The strangers within the editorial gates were athletes who rented their by-lines to the papers for their supposedly insightful comments on the game—although truth to tell, dear reader, the articles were actually penned by dishonest ventriloquists called "ghosts" who wrote the article in the athlete's name.

The next morning after Baker had frescoed Marquard's fast ball, the New York *Herald* carried an article under Mathewson's by-line actually written by sportswriter Jack Wheeler, who had had the courtesy to consult Matty before committing the great pitcher to paper. The article took Marquard to task, and read, in part: "Marquard made a poor pitch to Frank Baker on the latter's sixth-

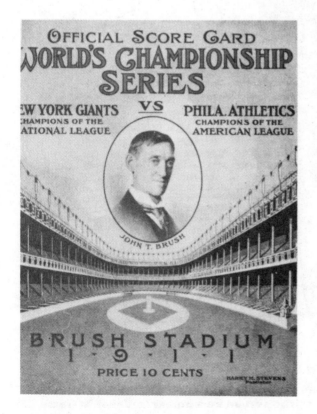

inning home run. There was no excuse for it. In a clubhouse talk with his players, Manager McGraw went over the entire Athletics' batting order, paying special attention to the left-handed hitter, Frank Baker. We had scouted Baker, knew what pitches were difficult for him to hit, and those he could hit for extra bases. Well, Rube threw him the kind of ball that Baker likes."

The public censure of Marquard by one of his teammates—especially when that teammate was Matty, the man Marquard called "a grand guy"—was enough to send reverberations throughout the sports world. But there was to be more to Baker's little one-act outrage. For the next day Mathewson the author was to become Mathewson the pitcher, and he would have a chance to show Marquard how to pitch to Baker.

Through the first eight innings, Mathewson had shut down the A's on five hits, and going into the ninth was just three outs away from a 1-0 victory. After retiring the first man up in the ninth, Mathewson found himself face-to-face with the subject in "his" article that very morning: Frank Baker. Mathewson figured he had Baker's number having faced him in the first game and, in the third with two men on, striking him out on three pitches. But if he was laboring under a delusion he would escape Marquard's plight, he was not to labor long.

Going through his own mental playbook, Mathewson "figured Baker could not hit a low curve over the outside corner," and prepared to feed him a steady diet of same. With a thoughtful exploration of Baker, Matty came in with two curves and ran the

Christy Mathewson, the Giants' 26-game winner who served up a homer to Baker in Game Three

count to one-and-one. Then, with all the precision he could muster, Matty threw Baker a curve aimed for the outside corner. But Baker, taught by his manager, Connie Mack, to regard altruistic advances with extreme suspicion, received the overture coldly and let it go. Umpire Brennan, who cared nothing for Mathewson's reputation for accuracy, called it a ball. Now behind two-and-one, Matty was forced to lay the next one somewhere over the plate or face the risk of falling too far behind Baker. Pitching with proprietary alacrity, Matty came right back with another curve, but it "cut the plate better than I intended." The next sound he heard was one not unlike that of the surf cracking the sands as the ball took off for parts unknown down the right-field line. As the ball entered the conveniently located stands nestled close at hand, and Baker

made his way around the bases, the Polo Ground crowd fell to a hushed silence. Had their faith in Gibraltar been misplaced? They had thought it sacrilegious to consider the possibility, and now it had happened, that repeating decimal Baker had also skewered the Great Matty.

The finale was anti-climatic, the A's pushing over two runs in the 11th to win. The winning run, appropriately enough, scored by Frank Baker, the man who had taken a bat and dubbed himself "Home Run" Baker on the basis of his two home runs, the last one coming off the man he now had replaced as baseball's idol.

FRANK BAKER CHAMPION BATSMAN OF 1911 WORLD'S SERIES BATTLES

Franklin Baker at the end of the swing that forever made him known as "Home Run" Baker

Game 3 October 17 at New York

| Phi. | 0 0 0 | 0 0 0 | 0 0 1 | 0 2 |
| N.Y. | 0 0 1 | 0 0 0 | 0 0 0 | 0 1 |

Philadelphia	Pos	AB	R	H	RBI	PO	A	E
Lord	lf	5	0	0	0	5	0	0
Oldring	cf	5	0	0	0	0	0	0
Collins	2b	5	1	2	0	5	4	2
Baker	3b	5	2	2	1	2	1	0
Murphy	rf	5	0	0	1	2	0	0
Davis	1b	5	0	2	1	10	0	0
Barry	ss	3	0	2	0	1	3	0
Lapp	c	4	0	1	0	8	6	0
Coombs	p	4	0	0	0	0	1	0
Totals		41	3	9	3	33	15	2

Pitching	IP	H	R	ER	BB	SO
Philadelphia						
Coombs (W)	11	3	2	1	4	7
New York						
Mathewson (L)	11	9	3	1	0	3

New York	Pos	AB	R	H	RBI	PO	A	E
Devore	lf	4	0	0	1	0	0	0
Doyle	2b	4	0	0	0	5	5	0
Snodgrass	cf	3	0	0	0	3	0	0
Murray	rf	2	0	0	0	2	1	0
Merkle	1b	3	0	0	0	11	1	0
Herzog	3b	3	1	1	0	4	3	3
Fletcher	ss	4	0	0	0	3	4	2
Meyers	c	4	1	1	0	4	4	0
Mathewson	p	3	0	1	0	1	4	0
a Becker		1	0	0	0	0	0	0
Totals		31	2	3	1	33	22	5

a Safe on error for Mathewson in 11th.

Doubles—Barry, Herzog. Home Run—Baker. Stolen Bases—Barry, Collins. Sacrifice Hits—Barry, Murray. Double Play—Doyle to Fletcher. Left on Bases—Philadelphia 6, New York 2. Umpires—Brennan, Connolly, Klem, Dinneen. Attendance—37,216. Time of Game—2:25.

4O Reggie Jackson's Three Home Runs

New York Yankees vs. Los Angeles Dodgers, 6th Game, 1977 World Series, October 18, 1977

SUFFICE IT TO SAY THERE ARE MORE GREAT PICTURES OF players than pictures of great players. But draw up a chair and we'll tell you the story of one that will remain forever pressed between the pages of time: The third of three homers hit by Reginald Martinez Jackson on the night of October 18, 1977.

Reginald Martinez Jackson. His very name is a strange and incongruous melange of a proper English handle, a melifluous Spanish appellation and a proud Black name. And, say some Jackson observers, he was almost as confused as his Baptismal name. One such observer, the great sportswriter Red Smith, once called him "Hamlet in double-knits." But, truth to tell, Jackson was more like the whole damn cast of Hamlet, with Rosenkrantz and Guildenstern thrown in for good measure.

Those double-knits referred to by Mr. Smith came with one singular identifying mark: A case of insecurity carefully hand-stitched to the sleeve and worn for all to see. Almost from the very moment Jackson strolled onto the baseball scene, stage left, back in 1967, it became evident to all that he possessed an obsession to slay dragons. And he did so with the only weapon at his disposal, his bat, driving the ball further and further away from the plate with each air-shattering swing, almost as if each swing was another blow at the demons which bewitched him. Add to his insecurity a case of gall—large enough to be divided into three parts, one for each of his names—and you have a case history that would keep clinical psychologists busy for weeks.

But even encumbered by all that emotional baggage, the man who became known to all as just plain old "Reggie" was the Richard Burton of modern day baseball, a man whose presence could fill a stadium the way the mere look of a great actor can fill a stage. When he hit a home run, he got cheers; and when he struck out, which was even more frequent, he got cheers, too. In short, if Reggie Jackson was the most enigmatic player of the '70s, he was the most charismatic as well.

Reggie's first full year in the Majors was put in with the A's in their first full-year ever at Oakland. There he gave the fans something to "Oh" and "Ah" about, his swing and follow-through alone worth the price of admission as he threw himself hook, line and sinker into every swing, and threw himself off-balance more often than not. The trouble with whirling around on your axis is that sometimes you are liable, if you're not an adagio dancer, to trip over your feet and fall on your axis—something Jackson did often, leading the League in fanning the air with 171 strike outs. But he also connected more than occasionally, driving 29 home runs out into the wild blue yonder. Both would serve as harbingers of things to come.

Jackson's second full year, 1969, saw him begin to acquit the label of "greatness" that had become attached to his name, hitting 49 homers—most of them before the All-Star Game, when news-paper writers hurried to their typewriters to exhume hackneyed phrases like "Ahead of Maris' pace" to describe his early-season barrage.

With 77 homers in two years-and-a-piece, Jackson now felt his worth to be more than the $20,000 he had been making, and asked for $60,000 for 1970. But owner Finley, to steal a line, threw nickles around like manhole covers, and countered with an offer of $40,000. The result was an eyeball-to-eyeball confrontation that led to a six-week holdout by Jackson before the two headstrongs came to a compromise of $47,000. The holdout took its toll, Jackson's home run total cut in half, along with his runs scored and runs batted in, and his batting average falling 38 points to .237. The only statistic which Jackson seemed to have no trouble sustaining from his previous efforts was strike outs, with his total of 135 leading the League for the third straight time.

1971 saw Jackson's stock treble in value along with his self-esteem as he began to mix his homers with verbal footwork, claiming, "I don't want to be a hero; I don't want to be a star. It just works out that way." And it did on July 13th, when in the 42nd All-Star Game, he sent an awesome cloud-buster that would have soared out of Tiger Stadium had it not bounced off the light towers high atop the right-field stands more than 100 feet above the ground, the longest home run ever in All-Star competition.

By now Jackson was commingling quote with smote, rewriting his legend with both pen and bat. After telling anyone who would listen, "When I strike out, a billion people in China don't care," he went out to make billions-upon-billions of those in the most populous country in the world ennuied by leading the League in strike outs for the fourth straight year, something even Babe Ruth couldn't manage. By the end of '71, his dual exploits had led teammate "Catfish" Hunter to comment, "The thing about Reggie is that you know he's going to produce. And if he doesn't, he's going to talk enough to make people think he's going to produce."

But produce he did, starting in 1972. With a swagger so pronounced he could almost strut sitting down, Reggie led the A's to three straight World Series triumphs and personally led the League in the glamour categories of home runs, runs scored, runs batted in and slugging average on his way to the Most Valuable Player Award in '73. Teammate Darold Knowles, taking note of Jackson's dual diet of bombast and blast, could only shake his head and mutter, "There's isn't enough mustard in the whole world to cover that hot dog."

After one more year under Finley, Jackson, ever the quote maven, followed the lead of Gertrude Stein—who had said of Oakland, "There's no there there"— by opting out, leaving no Reggie Jackson there either. Traded to the Baltimore Orioles before the '76 season, Jackson played one year there and then, as a free agent, moved on to New York, signing a multi-year contract with the Yankees for $2.6 million, making him the highest-paid player in baseball history.

Joining the Yankees, Jackson, me deep in conversation, told the gathered press, "I didn't come to New York to be a star. I brought my star with me." But he also brought something else, something he called his "straw"—as in "I'm the straw that stirs the drink."—and put it into the most combustible and noisome concoction this side of the Court of the Borgias, with slightly more intrigue. For the situation that confronted him in New York was one made up to two parts owner, George Steinbrenner, one part manager, Billy Martin, one part superstar, Reggie Jackson, and garnished with more than enough stars to shake a stick, or "straw," at. Which is exactly what Jackson did.

Almost from Day One Jackson put his finger into the pot and began stirring. Having finished a full 10½ games ahead of their Eastern Division rivals the previous year, none of the Yankees understood why they needed Jackson, especially at $2.6 million. None, that is, except owner George Steinbrenner, who was an advocate of the star system and had wooed Jackson with all the avidity of a love-struck teenager. Manager Billy Martin viewed Jackson's arrival with something akin to the love lavished on the invading Huns by their conquered subjects, believing him to be "George's Boy." And then there was the grumpy team captain, Thurman Munson, who had been promised the second-highest salary on the team after "Catfish" Hunter and felt betrayed by Steinbrenner. And when Jackson's "Straw that stirs the drink" quote appeared in *Sport* Magazine, along with the remainder of it—"Munson thinks he can be the straw that stirs the drink, but he can only stir in bad"—Munson found he had no use for the "Straw." Others found the "straw" to be a "strawman," and directed their hate of Steinbrenner at the new kid on the block, Steinbrenner's kid.

The boiling pot gathered momentum and finally came to an overboil on the afternoon of June 18th at Fenway Park. There, in front of a full house and another five-or-so million on national TV, Jackson nonchalanted a ball, his lack of charge rivaling the uphill ascent at San Juan so hotly disputed at the time by the Spaniards and later by the Democrats. Billy Martin, who might have excused Jackson's play for the same reason as Jack the Ripper on the basis of his being human, instead saw Jackson as less than human and removed him forthwith from the game. As Jackson approached the dugout, he read in Martin's move a silent accusation that he had been found wanting, and not prone to hold his guns, went at Martin. Martin, never one to ignore a glove thrown down in the name of challenge, wheeled around like a Water Pik out of control,

Home Run #2

and began referring to Jackson's immediate family and parentage in an inquiring manner, speaking in two languages, English and profanity, and ended his monologue with a "Kiss my Dago ass . . ." With both men going at it, hot and heavy, burning the candle with their verbal blow torches, it took the intervention of several sturdy Yankees to break up the utterly dependable scenario.

For the remainder of the season, the Yankee clubhouse took on the look of an armed camp under a white flag of truce. With a large amount of weeping and gnashing of teeth, the Yankees went back to the task at hand, winning the Eastern Division race once again by 2½ games. Jackson, his greatness compromised by his tortured soul and corrupted by human failings, was now hearing boos from the fans for the first time, his contributions short of a home run met with Bronx cheers, especially by those who had sided with Martin and Munson. Still, he was able to contribute 32 homers and 110 RBI's to the Yankees' cause, all the time bemoaning his fate: "It makes me cry the way they treat me on this team. The Yankee pinstripes are Ruth and Gehrig and DiMaggio and Mantle. I'm just a big black man with a IQ of 160 making $700,000 a year, and they treat me like dirt . . ."

The Yankees went on to beat the Kansas City Royals in the Championship Series, three games-to-two. But Jackson, who only had one hit in 15 at-bats through the first four games, was benched in Game Five, even though he was to pinch-hit in the eighth inning and drive in an all-important run. There was now some question whether he would start at all in the Series against the Yankees' old cross-city, now cross-country, rivals, the Dodgers.

Martin, announcing Jackson's inclusion in the starting line-up for Game One of the Series, threw a barbed insult Jackson's way. Fuming, Jackson responded, "I know what I can do. If he did, we might be a lot better off." In the first game, against the offerings of Los Angeles' Don Sutton, Jackson tried to show he knew what to do, blooping a single to center in his first plate appearance. But that was all, and for the first two games of the '77 Series—the first won by the Yankees, 4-3, and the second by the Dodgers, 6-1—all Jackson had to show for his nine plate appearances was that one bloop single.

In Game Three, Jackson began to show he knew what to do a little more, rocketing a single to left in the first inning and scoring twice in the Yankees 5-3 win. Then, in Game Four, even if he didn't know what to do, his bat did with instincts all its own, as he doubled inside the third-base line off left-handed Doug Rau and homered into the left-field pavilion off right-hander Rick Rhoden in leading the Yankees to a 4-2 win and a three-games-to-one lead in the Series. Game Five saw him continue on his hot streak, singling in the seventh and homering in the eighth off the right-field foul pole in a losing cause as the Dodgers won behind Don Sutton, 10-4.

Now it was back to New York for Game Six with the Yankees ahead in the Series three-games-to-two and Jackson leading the charge with six hits in 17 at-bats, four in his last eight appearances. Mr. October now knew what he could do. But nobody else could believe just how well he could do it. Yet.

For on that night of October 18th, 1977, Reggie Jackson, with an element of hyperbole in his style, was to make baseball history. And he was to do it on the stage that Babe Ruth had made famous, Yankee Stadium, appropriately enough called "The House that Ruth Built."

Coming to bat for the first time that night with Los Angeles ahead 2-0 on Steve Garvey's first inning triple, Jackson watched four pitches by Dodger pitcher Burt Hooten sail by and took first unmolested, there to be driven in by Chris Chambliss' homer, tying the game at two apiece. Los Angeles countered with a run of their own in the third, giving Hooten a 3-2 lead to take into the bottom of the fourth. Now it was Jackson's turn. With Munson stationed on first, Jackson hammered Hooten's first pitch deep into the right-field stands on a line to make the score 4-3, Yankees. By the time Jackson stepped into the batter's box again, the Yankees had added yet another run and Hooten had been replaced on the mound by Elias Sosa. Proving he could hit any pitcher worth his resin bag, Jackson swung at Sosa's first offering, and with an economy of effort and an efficiency of results drove the pitch into the right-field stands, deeper than before, for another two-run homer. The score was now 7-3, Yankees.

But the score was unimportant now. All that mattered to the fans was "REG-GIE ! REG-GIE ! REG-GIE !," the fans reducing everything to essentials as they canonized the man they had once cannonaded. And, as Jackson stepped in to take his turn at bat in the eighth inning, the fans stood on their feet, crying out in a high and shrill pitch their litany to the myth-in-the-making down on the field. The pitcher he stepped in to face was Charlie Hough, who had struck out Jackson on a knuckler the only time he had faced him before, back in Game Three. However, Game Three was then. What was now was a Hough knuckler coming up to the plate as pretty as a $20 streak with mushrooms on the side. Believing anything worth doing was worth doing quickly, Jackson came to life like a clockwork toy, swinging that magnificent swing of his. THWACK! Ball met bat and took off for destinations unknown, straightaway toward the centerfield bleachers, 450 feet away, a megablast that dwarfed his other two by comparison. As the tiny speck disappeared from sight and with no need to go into a home run trot, Jackson stood at the plate admiring his handiwork and drinking in the roars erupting from the crowd which had finally come to accept him as a *persona grata*. It made a perfect picture of a picture-perfect home run.

Down at first, Steve Garvey watching the flight of the lethal drive, later admitted that "When I was sure nobody was looking, I applauded in my glove." Others did too, a film forming over their eyes at witnessing Jackson's legendary three-homers-in-three-swings feat—four if anyone was counting, his last homer in Game Five coming on his last swing.

In what losing manager Tommy Lasorda was to call "The greatest single performance I've ever seen," Jackson had not only tied Babe Ruth's Series record of three homers in one game—first done in 1926 and repeated in '28, albeit not in consecutive at-bats—but also established Jacksonian records for most home runs in one Series with five, most runs with ten and most total bases with 25.

Just as autumn follows summer, so too did Mr. October follow the end of the regular season. And although there were still a few Yankees who were to say, "I don't like the guy, but I have to admire what he did . . . He's a great performer," he had finally gotten the admiration he had sought for so long. One of those who couldn't help but admire Reggie was baseball's resident whacko, Red Sox pitcher Bill Lee, who gave Jackson the ultimate in back-handed compliments: "I think there are going to be a lot of Reggies born in this town."

Home Run #3

Game 6 October at New York							
Los Angeles	Pos	AB	R	H	RBI	PO	A	E
Lopes	2b	4	0	1	0	0	4	0
Russell	ss	3	0	0	0	1	4	0
Smith	rf	4	2	1	1	1	0	0
Cey	3b	3	1	1	0	0	1	0
Garvey	1b	4	1	2	2	13	0	0
Baker	lf	4	0	1	0	2	0	0
Monday	cf	4	0	1	0	3	0	0
Yeager	c	3	0	1	0	4	2	0
b Davalillo		1	0	1	1	0	0	0
Hooten	p	2	0	0	0	0	0	0
Sosa	p	0	0	0	0	0	0	0
Rau	p	0	0	0	0	0	0	0
a Goodson		1	0	0	0	0	0	0
Hough	p	0	0	0	0	0	0	0
c Lacy		1	0	0	0	0	0	0
Totals		34	4	9	4	24	11	0

Pitching	IP	H	R	ER	BB	SO
Los Angeles						
Hooten (L)	*3	3	4	4	1	1
Sosa	1⅓	3	3	3	1	0
Rau	1⅓	0	0	0	0	1
Hough	2	2	1	1	0	3
New York						
Torrez (W)	9	9	4	2	2	6

*Pitched to three batters in 4th.

L.A.	2 0 1	0 0 0	0 0 1				
N.Y.	0 2 0	3 2 0	0 1 x				

New York	Pos	AB	R	H	RBI	PO	A	E
Rivers	cf	4	0	2	0	1	0	0
Randolph	2b	4	1	0	0	2	3	0
Munson	c	4	1	1	0	6	0	0
Jackson	rf	3	4	3	5	5	0	0
Chambliss	1b	4	2	2	2	9	1	0
Nettles	3b	4	0	0	0	0	0	0
Piniella	lf	3	0	0	1	2	1	0
Dent	ss	2	0	0	0	1	4	1
Torrez	p	3	0	0	0	1	2	0
Totals		31	8	8	8	27	11	1

a Struck out for Rau in 7th.
b Beat out a bunt for Yeager in 9th.
c Popped out for Hough in 9th.

Double—Chambliss. Triple—Garvey. Home Runs—Chambliss, Jackson 3, Smith. Sacrifice Fly—Piniella. Double Plays—Dent to Randolph to Chambliss, Chambliss to Dent to Chambliss. Passed Ball—Munron. Left on Bases—Los Angeles 5, New York 2. Umpires—McSherry, Chylak, Sudol, McCoy, Dale, Evans. Attendance—56,407. Time of Game—2:18.

41 The Wild Horse of Osage Runs Wild

St. Louis Cardinals vs. Philadelphia Athletics, 5th Game, 1931 World Series, October 7, 1931

ON OCTOBER 24, 1929, THE STOCK MARKET FELL WITH A resounding Crash! The feverish Twenties had exploded, to be replaced by the troubled Thirties; and the word "unemployed," once a seldom-used adjective, now became an oft-used and ominous noun as every fourth worker lost his job. The American Dream had become a nightmare. And, as it did, bread lines and bonus armies took the place of the boom and bust atmosphere of the '20s. People who couldn't fill their bellies with food looked for heroes to fill their souls with hope.

Baseball, which had given them Babe Ruth in the Era of Excess, would now provide them with a tonic for their sagging spirit in the Thirties, allowing them to live vicariously through their hero's daring exploits.

If, as has been suggested by numerous writers, baseball is merely a microcosm of life itself, then it was no coincidence that the hero of the World Series of 1931—the bleakest year in our economic history—would be a dirty-faced, underpaid, hungry-looking outfielder from the Oklahoma Osages, who had entered baseball on the rods of a freight train: Johnny Leonard Roosevelt Martin, a player whose nickname was almost as picturesque as his exploits, "Pepper."

"Pepper" Martin's exploits are accorded no special place of prominence in *The MacMillan Baseball Encyclopedia*. His 16 lines are sandwiched somewhere between the records of Jerry Martin, a National League outfielder some 40 years later, and Stu Martin, a Cardinal teammate. But no player so captured the fancy of the public, fan and nonfan alike, as the perpetual motion machine who literally stole the 1931 World Series from the heavily-favored Philadelphia A's.

The Philadelphia A's of 1931 were one of baseball's all-time great teams. Their roster contained no less than four bonafide great stars in Jimmie Foxx, Al Simmons, Mickey Cochrane and Lefty Grove and several lesser novas in the personages of Max Bishop, Jimmy Dykes, Bing Miller, George Earnshaw and Rube Walberg. For the third straight year they had won more than 100 games, finishing with a .704 won-lost average, the fifth best in modern baseball history—and finished no less than 13½ games in front of the talent-laden New York Yankees. "Bucketfoot" Al Simmons, who worked himself into a self-induced rage before every at-bat and could take off the head of an unwary third baseman with one shot, again led the American League in batting with .390, and catcher Mickey Cochrane had finished fourth with .349, the then-highest average ever for a catcher. On the mound, the A's possessed one of the greatest staffs in history, led by Lefty Grove who led the league in strikeouts, ERA and wins, 31, 16 of those coming in a row, and Earnshaw and Walberg each winning 20. In short, based on past performance charts, the A's looked like a cinch to win the World Series, repeating over the team they had beaten the previous year, the St. Louis Cardinals.

But everyone had tended to discount the Cardinals. Not only did they possess the league's Most Valuable Player in Frankie Frisch, but also had the league's batting champion, Chick Hafey

and three on the top four pitchers in winning percentage—Paul Derringer, Bill Hallahan and the crusty old Burleigh Grimes, who, behind his two-day growth of stubble, looked like he should be arrested for assault and battery every time he took the mound.

The mastermind behind these Cardinals was Wesley Branch Rickey, a man who could sell a Phi Beta Kappa key to anyone wearing a three-piece suit. Rickey had determined on one course of action for building a winner: a farm system. And through his victory garden had harvested almost the entire team, including Jim Bottomley, Charlie Gelbert, Hafey, Derringer and a youngster brought up from Rochester just the previous year, "Pepper" Martin.

Martin had labored in the anonymity of baseball's vineyards and backyards for the previous eight years, traveling down highways and byways of America that not even Mssrs. Rand and McNally had identified. Starting in 1923 with the Ardmore, Oklahoma, team, this stocky 5'8" son of the Sooner State had then hied himself to Greenville, South Carolina, in 1924 and 1925 where he played second base and the outfield with varying success, his batting and fielding averages almost achieving parity. It was there that Charley Barrett, a scout for the Cardinals, signed the man then called Johnny Martin for Mr. Rickey's growing system of chain-store franchises and sent him to Fort Smith of the Western Association. It was while he was performing as a shortstop for the Fort Smith franchise that someone hung the handle "Pepper" on him in tribute to his style of play. Of such things are legends made.

But the name "Pepper" tended to obscure an appreciation for the skills of Martin. For, in those days when the home run had tended to devalue the stolen base, a sort of the Gresham Law of Baseball, Martin had become a one-man burglary squad. In his first full year of organized ball, Martin stole a total of 55 bases, eschewing the classic Coast League slide but instead employing his own ball's-out belly flop—one made all the more remarkable because of his failure to wear any sort of protective cup!

After compiling a .315 average over his first four years in professional ball, Martin was brought North by the 1928 version of the Cardinals. However, he exhausted the seat of his pants more than played during the '28 season, coming to bat just 13 times. Sent back to Houston in '29 for some more grafting on of skills, they apparently took as he hit .298 for Houston and then .363 for Rochester in 1930, leading the Red Wings to the International League pennant and a win in the Little World Series.

At this point, entire Judge Kenesaw Mountain Landis, front and center. Landis, brought into the game as Baseball Commissioner in 1920 after the Black Sox scandal, had taken it upon himself to run every facet of the game, including the minor leagues. Landis, who was never a supporter of Rickey's, would gleefully find any loophole (legalese for excuse) to undermine his farm system. And so it was that after the 1930 season, Landis communicated his misgivings about "monopolizing" talent to Rickey, ordering him either to bring Martin up to the Majors or trade him, his protected status in the lower leagues now having tried the Commissioner's patience. Rickey chose to bring up Martin rather than cross swords with the Commissioner, something no one had been able to do and come away unscathed.

After spending the first few weeks of the '31 season sitting in his accustomed place, the bench, Martin burst into Rickey's office and demanded, "If you can't play me, Mr. Rickey, trade me . . .," lacing his comments with more than a few "John Browns," the closest he ever came to an expletive deleted. Rickey, his cheeks burning with the imputation of parsimony that the saving of $10,000 in salaries implied, promptly traded Taylor Douthit, who had hit .303 for the 1930 pennant winners, to the Cincinnati Reds and gave Martin and his $4,500 salary a chance. Almost immediately Pepper proved that he was no also-ran who also ran, but one who could hit as well. Approaching even the most ordinary games with out-of-the-ordinary performances, ones which would make any dues-paying fan feel good, Martin proved that he could earn his keep. But the wide-shouldered, hawk-nosed Martin also earned something else as well: A second nickname. For while some players are thought so nondescript as never to merit even one, the Salty Pepper was now thought to be worthy of two, his perpetual motion and emotion earning him the name "The Wild Horse of the Osage," hung on him by the team's trainer.

The Wild Horse of the Osage: John "Pepper" Martin

With a friendly confidence beaming on his smiling face, Martin played every game with the look of a truant schoolboy out on a romp. And he cavorted the same way off the field, too. Once, asked by his manager why he looked so disheveled and out of sorts, Martin replied, "I fell down in a foot race and still beat the other guy." When asked why he even bothered, Martin beamed

and answered triumphantly, "To win a bet . . . two gallons of ice cream!" Another time, during a dressing down of the team by the exasperated manager, Martin held up his hand and called out, "Can I ask a question?" "What?," snapped the already snappish manager. "I wonder," said Martin, his face pensive, a film coming down over his eyes, "If I oughta paint my midget auto red with white wheels, or white with red wheels . . ." As the meeting dissolved into laughter, the manager couldn't help but join in. That was Pepper Martin, a man with the yeasty feeling of good-will towards his fellow specie.

But one specie that good will didn't quite extend to were the Philadelphia A's. Nor to catcher Mickey Cochrane. For in the 1931 World Series, Martin showed the stuff that not even heroes are lucky enough to be made of, his achievements for the season merely serving as a throat clearing for his heroics in the Series.

In the first game of the Series, all Martin did was get two singles and a double off Grove and a stolen base off Cochrane in a losing effort. Game Two saw Martin, hurling himself through the air like a man trying to get through closing subway doors, stretch an ordinary bloop hit into a double in the second, then steal third ahead of Cochrane's throw with a beautiful belly slide and score on a sacrifice fly, then open up the seventh with a single, steal second and, after being moved to third on a fielder's choice, come home on a squeeze bunt. The final score was Martin 2, A's 0. Game Three witnessed more of Martin's heroics, this time against the same Lefty Grove who now had a 32-4 record for the year, counting his win in the first game. Martin singled in the second and scored the second Cardinal run, and doubled in the fourth, his drive hitting scant inches from the top of the wall and then scoring the fourth run, as St. Louis beat the A's 5-2. Game Four was more of the same, with Martin getting two hits and stealing one base as Earnshaw shut down the Cards on two hits, both Martin's.

By now the A's had seen enough of Martin to last a lifetime, his totals for the first four games reading: Nine hits in 14 at-bats with four runs scored and four bases stolen. His go-as-you-please wildcatting attitude on the basepaths had even driven George Earnshaw with muttered malediction to plead with Connie Mack to replace catcher Mickey Cochrane, feeling that Martin had picked him clean, taking everything but his wallet.

Mickey Cochrane, who had everything but his wallet stolen in the Series

Lefty Grove, off whom Martin had five of his twelve Series hits.

But the first four games were merely to act as a table setting for Martin in Game Five of the Series, one of the greatest one-man performances in the history of the October Classic. Cardinal manager Gabby Street, perhaps because he was in Philadelphia where they never recognize a trend until it becomes a tradition, finally moved Martin up in the batting order from his accustomed sixth position to clean-up hitter. And Martin, riding his particular hobbyhorse to his heart's content, responded with three hits in four at bats, including one homer—the only time the A's retired him was on a long fly to Simmons who caught the ball a step in front of the wall, and even that brought in a run—and drove in four of the Cardinals' five runs as they beat the A's 5-1, and took a 3-2 lead in the Series.

Now the toast of the country, Martin unabashedly announced to one and all, "I can hit any pitcher that ever lived." At the Broad Street Station, as the team pushed its way through throngs to catch the train that would carry them back to St. Louis, one man, Judge Landis, now as caught up in the drama as any ordinary fan, sought out the greatest baseball hero since Babe Ruth and proclaimed, "Young man, I'd like to be in your place tonight . . ." Pepper, letting the remark set in, wryly grinned and retorted, "Well, Judge, I'll tell you what . . . I'll swap places, and salaries . . . My $4,500 for your $65,000," proving that he, too, knew that ballplayers back in those Depression days were born and not paid.

In the final two games, as the A's watched their performance close on the road, Martin was reduced to a mere mortal, already having staked more claims to records than an Alaskan claim jumper. Still, he was able to steal one more base in the seventh and final game, his fifth off Cochrane, who by now was shell-shocked, the gilt of his greatness peeling off for all to see, and on the very next batter, dropped a third strike, allowing the Cardinals to score the go-ahead run. It was only fitting that the final out of the Series was a line drive which Max Bishop hit sharply to left center and which, appropriately enough, was outrun by Johnny Leonard Roosevelt "Pepper" Martin, the human litter bearer, who had personally carried away and buried the A's in the greatest one-man performance in Series history.

SIX RECORDS MAY GO TO MARTIN

A'S RELY ON BIG RIGHT-HANDER IN LAST-DITCH STAND IN SERIES; ADMIRING CROWD MOBS MARTIN

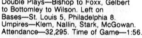

Game 5 October 7 at Philadelphia								St L.	1 0 0	0 0 2	0 1 1				
								Phi.	0 0 0	0 0 0	1 0 0				
St. Louis	Pos	AB	R	H	RBI	PO	A	E	Philadelphia	Pos	AB	R	H	RBI	PO	A	E
Adams	3b	1	0	1	0	0	0	0	Bishop	2b	2	0	0	0	3	2	0
a High	3b	4	1	0	0	2	3	0	b McNair	2b	2	0	0	0	1	1	0
Watkins	rf	3	1	0	0	3	0	0	Haas	cf	2	0	0	0	2	0	0
Frisch	2b	4	1	2	0	6	1	0	c Moore	lf	2	0	1	0	1	0	0
Martin	cf	4	1	3	4	0	0	0	Cochrane	c	4	0	1	0	3	2	0
Hafey	lf	4	0	1	0	1	0	0	Simmons	lf-cf	4	1	3	0	5	0	0
Bottomley	1b	4	1	2	0	7	1	0	Foxx	1b	3	0	2	0	8	1	0
Wilson	c	4	0	2	0	7	0	0	Miller	rf	4	0	0	1	2	0	0
Gelbert	ss	4	0	1	1	1	2	0	Dykes	3b	4	0	1	0	0	1	0
Hallahan	p	4	0	0	0	0	0	0	Williams	ss	4	0	1	0	2	5	0
Totals		36	5	12	5	27	7	0	Hoyt	p	2	0	0	0	0	0	0
Pitching	IP	H	R	ER	BB	SO			Walberg	p	0	0	0	0	0	0	0
St. Louis									d Heving		1	0	0	0	0	0	0
Hallahan (W)	9	9	1	1	1	4			Rommel	p	0	0	0	0	0	0	0
Philadelphia									e Boley		1	0	0	0	0	0	0
Hoyt (L)	6	7	3	3	0	1			Totals		35	1	9	1	27	12	0
Walberg	2	2	1	1	1	2											
Rommel	1	3	1	1	0	0											

a Ran for Adams in 1st.
b Fouled out for Bishop in 6th.
c Flied out for Haas in 6th.
d Flied out for Walberg in 8th.
e Struck out for Rommel in 9th.

Doubles—Frisch, Simmons. Home Run—Martin. Stolen Base—Watkins. Double Plays—Bishop to Foxx, Gelbert to Bottomley to Wilson. Left on Bases—St. Louis 5, Philadelphia 8. Umpires—Klem, Nallin, Stark, McGowan. Attendance—32,295. Time of Game—1:56.

Martin displays his go-as-you-please wildcatting attitude on the basepaths.

42 Zim Chases Home Collins

Chicago White Sox vs. New York Giants, 6th Game, 1917 World Series, October 15, 1917

THE NEW YORK GIANTS WERE, BY 1917, "THE BEST KNOWN team in baseball," according to *Baseball Magazine*. And, according to the records, the best team in all of baseball, as well. No team had won more pennants, more games or had a higher winning percentage in the history of baseball than the Giants.

The Giants traced their proud ancestry back to 1880, when Jim "Smiling James" Mutrie, a former player, and John B. Day, a businessman whose interests included tobacco and liquor, sat next to each other at a game between the Brooklyn Atlantics and the New York Mutuals. Finding that their interests in sponsoring a club were as mutual as the team on the field, they formed the Metropolitan Exhibition Company on the spot. Their first venture was the New York Mets, an independent team. In 1882 they joined the American Association, and, hedging their bets, the following year took over the moribund Troy (New York) Haymaker franchise and entered a team in the old National League, forming the first baseball "syndicate." The National League team, which played its games at the old Polo Grounds at 110th and Fifth Avenue, became known as the Giants in 1888 when the stovepipe-hatted Mutrie, by then the manager of the team, remarked that his tall, broad-shouldered troops were "giants in action as well as stature."

And "Giants" they became, a proud nickname for a proud team. Led by future Hall of Famers Tim Keefe and Mickey Welch on the mound and Buck Ewing and Roger Conner afield, they won two National League pennants in 1888 and 1889 and capped off both seasons by winning what was then the world's series (small "w," small "s"), defeating the second-place club in the league both years. However, the Brotherhood War, which broke out in 1890, turned the club from a prosperous venture into a losing proposition, all but wiping out Day and Mutrie.

By 1892 Day was done, finally losing control of the club to a syndicate of baseball knights who rescued the floundering franchise. Three years later, they sold 51 percent to Andrew Freedman, a prominent Tammany politician. However, after seven lean years of what New York papers called "Freedmanism"—with the Giants finishing ninth, seventh, third, seventh, tenth, eighth and seventh—the remainder of the syndicate (read: John T. Brush, owner of the Cincinnati ballclub) exerted their influence to prop up their investment. And, not incidentally, to protect their franchise against raids then being made on a regular basis by the new kid of the baseball block: the fledgling American League.

Brush went for the jugular, going after one of the American League's most famous names—and with him an entire franchise. The man was Baltimore manager John J. McGraw; the franchise was the Orioles. In a deal as complicated to understand as a three-card monte game, Brush had McGraw ostensibly resign and sell his stock in the club back to the president of the Orioles and sign a four-year contract with the Giants. His comrade-in-arms, longtime friend and teammate Wilbert Robinson, also supposedly sold his interest back to the Orioles for the announced purpose of "securing enough money to buy out McGraw's interest in the saloon on North Howard Street."

However, what Brush, who had too much intelligence to be honest, had done was to set up a corporate raid that would have brought tears of joy to the eyes of John D. Rockefeller. Without wasting precious breath on the corporate shenanigans one thing soon became certain: McGraw would go to the National League. And the New York Giants.

What McGraw found was a ballclub in name only. Years later, almost tearful indignation and not even bothering to embroider, feeling that truth would make all things plain, McGraw would complain, "When I took charge of the Giants the club was in last place by fourteen games—a good safe margin. The attendance was almost nothing (and) when I first walked on the field to see my team I found Christy Matthewson playing first base."

That, in the argot of the day, "tore it." Approaching Freedman, McGraw extracted a list of the 23 players assigned to him and crossed out nine of the names with one stroke of the pencil, telling the flabbergasted owner, "You can begin by releasing these." Freedman could only fuffump, "But you can't do that, those players cost me nearly $14,000." McGraw was unmoved, telling the owner, "The club wouldn't be any worse without them. And their salaries for the rest of the season would amount to more than that. You would be saving money." Now sure of his ground, he continued, "I'm going to get Kid Elberfeld, Fielder Jones, Ed Delehanty, George Davis . . ." "Stop right there!," hollered the by-now overwhelmed Freedman. "I won't have George Davis on my club . . . I don't like him . . . and that's final." McGraw, without so much as batting an eye said, "I'm going to have him, Mr. Freedman. I *am* the manager, you know."

Freedman threw up his hands. And opened his purse. He knew then, as all of baseball would know soon, that McGraw was indeed "*the* manager."

McGraw did sign Elberfeld, Jones and Delehanty. However, a subsequent agreement between the two leagues prevented him from playing them. Still, McGraw's ambitious stockpiling plan soon took shape: Here a Mike Donlin, there a Bill Dahlen, and everywhere an ex-Oriole—Dan McGann, Roger Bresnahan, Billy Gilbert and Joe McGinnity. But Freedman was a man of limited means, by all means. And an even more limited imagination. And when McGraw once again approached him with Davis' contract, it was the straw that broke Freedman's back. That was it for Freedman. He sold his interest in the Giants to Brush at the end of the season and retired from baseball, thus ending the Giants' most futile era and signaling the start of their most fertile one—the reign of John J. McGraw and John T. Brush.

With Brush's backing ("He was the heart and soul with me in my plan to build up a club. He didn't care what players I bought or what I paid for them as long as my judgment dictated their purchase."), McGraw built a proud and mighty franchise. His all-new team finished second in 1903, first in 1904 and 1905, second in 1907, second in 1908, third in 1909, second in 1910 and first again in 1911 and 1912. When Brush died in the winter of 1912, his son-in-law, Harry Hempstead, took over control of the team and left McGraw to his own devices. And McGraw's devices were winning, winning and more winning. He finished first again in 1913, then second in 1914, eighth in 1915 (but only 3½ games out of the first division), fourth in 1916. And 1917 was to be another year for winning.

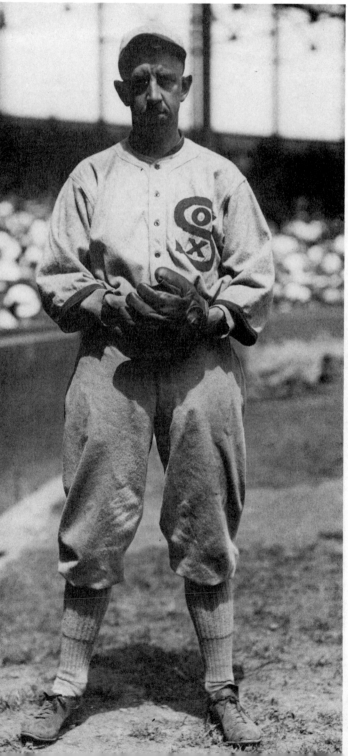

The 1917 team that McGraw had built differed mightily from his previous editions. The pitching staff—which only two years before had been ridiculed by writer Heywood Broun for the constant use of pitchers Ferdie Schupp and Rube Schauer as one where, "It never Schauers, but it Schupps"—was now well balanced. With little Ferdie Schupp winning 21 in all and Slim Sallee putting together a personal winning streak of ten in a row on his way to 18 wins overall and Rube Benton throwing in another 15, the Giants' staff carried the club to the front. At bat they had two of the league's six .300 hitters in Benny Kauff and George Burns, the majors' co-leader in homers in Davy Robertson, and the leader in RBI's in Heinie Zimmerman. They were to lead the league in home runs, stolen bases, fielding, ERA and saves; and the league in standings for all but two weeks of the season on their way to the pennant.

McGraw's opponents in the 1917 Series were the Chicago White Sox, making their first appearance since 1906. But one thing that made its first appearance in that Series was patriotic fervor, the world being at war. Thousands of fans jammed into Comiskey Park, there to become part of the red, white and blue bunting that festooned the stands and to scream for the heroes and at the hated McGraw, calling him, amongst other things, "Muggsy", a name that caused the object of its derision to cast an eye in the general direction of the taunt with a look that could curl up and crackle anyone within its gaze, much like a burnt piece of toast.

But no matter how much McGraw glowered and screamed like a frustrated sargeant major who enjoyed barking out orders, Eddie Cicotte and his shineball captured the first game in what *Spalding's Official Baseball Record* called "one of the best—if not the best—world series game that has been played since this series was inaugurated." The second game also went to the White Sox, who treated Schupp rather inhospitably and took a 2-0 lead in games back to New York for Game Three.

New York took on a new life back in the friendly confines of the Polo Grounds, winning the third game on Davy Robertson's triple and the fourth on Benny Kauff's two homers—one of which was irretrievably lost in a Polo Grounds rosebush—sending the Series back to Chicago tied at two games apiece.

Game Five, back in Chicago, picked up right where Games Three and Four left off with the Giants jumping on starter Reb Russell, who faced three men and was unable to retire any of the three. Chicago manager Pants Rowland, instead of lighting votive candles for his team's chances, brought in Cicotte, who brought the game back under control. In the seventh, with the score 5-2, New York, the Giants began to come apart, with Robertson letting a ball fall in front of him for a double, Buck Herzog—whom McGraw would later claim, "Sold me out"—dropping a relay throw and the Sox scoring three runs to tie the score. In the eighth, Zimmerman made a bad throw and the Sox got four more hits and three more runs to win for relief pitcher Red Faber, who had held the Giants hitless in their last two at-bats to preserve the win.

The sixth game—and, as it turned out, the last—saw Faber going back to the mound for the Sox. This time the Sox won without any of their four runs being earned. The first run, and one of the most famous in World Series history, came in the fourth inning. Eddie Collins led off by grounding to Zimmerman, who made a wild throw to first, allowing Collins to trot unmolested down to second. Joe Jackson then lifted an easy fly ball to Robertson who dropped the ball, Collins advancing after the error. The next hitter, Hap Felsch, tapped the ball back to pitcher Rube Benton. Benton fielded the ball cleanly and ran to the third base line, turning Collins back to third. He then threw the ball to

Eddie Collins, the man who turned a run-down into a runaway in Game Six

Zimmerman, who was covering the bag. As Benton made his throw to third, Giants catcher Bill Rariden advanced up the line. Whether Rariden was curious about the play or merely communing with nature was unclear. What was clear was that he had left home plate unprotected, with no one to back him up. Collins seeing that Zimmerman had the ball and the bag both, turned back toward the plate, and finding the rest of the Giants doing their imitation of Lot's wife, took off. Zimmerman, suddenly finding no one to throw the ball to, took off after Collins, chasing the man who had speed enough to steal 743 bases in his career across the plate for the first run. The White Sox were to score two more runs in the fourth and another in the ninth to win the game and the Series 4-2, with Faber getting his third win.

Despite Chicago's four victories, Faber's three wins and Kauff's two homers, the one moment that will always be remembered is the one when Heinie Zimmerman chased Collins across home plate. Crucified by the fans, villified in the press—one reporter, Hughie Fullerton, even went so far as to paraphrase Kipling's Gunga Din, ending his poem, "I'm a faster man than you are, Heinie Zim!"—Zimmerman claimed nobody was covering the plate, and so the can which had been tied to his tail didn't belong to him. "Who was I supposed to throw the ball to? Klem?" he asked. When told of Zimmerman's comment, plate umpire Bill Klem could only answer, "I was afraid he would."

However, as in most incidents, there are two versions to every story. Competing with the one told by Zimmerman was one added after the game by Clarence "Pants" Rowland, Chicago manager and coach at third during the famous incident. Not holding with Zimmerman's version, Rowland offered his own: "I was racing alongside Collins all the way from the coaching box to the plate. I know Zimmerman could have made a play at the plate, because Rariden called for the ball. But Zimmerman shouted, 'Get out of the way . . . I'll get this monkey myself.'" Of such stuff are controversies and great moments made.

Heinie Zimmerman, who finished in the place position behind Collins in the run for home

1917

Game 6 October 15 at New York

| | | | Chi. | 000 300 001 |
| | | | N.Y. | 000 020 000 |

Chicago	Pos	AB	R	H	RBI	PO	A	E
S. Collins	rf	3	0	0	0	1	0	0
b Leibold	rf	2	0	1	1	1	0	0
McMullin	3b	5	0	0	0	0	1	0
E. Collins	2b	4	1	1	0	1	8	0
Jackson	lf	4	1	1	0	1	0	0
Felsch	cf	3	1	0	0	3	0	0
Gandil	1b	4	0	2	2	14	0	0
Weaver	ss	4	1	1	0	2	2	0
Schalk	c	3	0	1	0	4	1	1
Faber	p	2	0	0	0	0	0	0
Totals		34	4	7	3	27	12	1

Pitching	IP	H	R	ER	BB	SO
Chicago						
Faber (W)	9	6	2	1	2	4
New York						
Benton (L)	5	4	3	0	1	3
Perritt	4	3	1	1	2	3

New York	Pos	AB	R	H	RBI	PO	A	E
Burns	lf	4	1	0	0	2	0	0
Herzog	2b	4	0	2	2	2	5	0
Kauff	cf	4	0	0	0	2	0	1
Zimmerman	3b	4	0	0	0	1	2	1
Fletcher	ss	4	0	1	0	1	2	0
Robertson	rf	3	0	1	0	0	1	1
Holke	1b	4	0	1	0	12	0	0
Rariden	c	3	1	0	0	7	1	0
Benton	p	1	0	0	0	0	0	0
a Wilhoit		0	0	0	0	0	0	0
Perritt	p	1	0	1	0	0	1	0
c McCarty		1	0	0	0	0	0	0
Totals		33	2	6	2	27	12	3

a Walked for Benton in 5th.
b Popped out for S. Collins in 7th.
c Grounded out for Perritt in 9th.

Double—Holke. Triple—Herzog. Sacrifice Hit—Faber. Hit by Pitcher—Robertson (by Faber). Passed Ball—Schalk. Left on Bases—Chicago 7, New York 7. Umpires—Klem, O'Loughlin, Evans, Rigler. Attendance—33,969. Time of Game—2:18.

43 The Addie Joss – Ed Walsh Pitching Duel

Cleveland Naps vs. Chicago White Sox, October 2, 1908

FOR THAT RARE BASEBALL FAN WITH AN EYE FOR PITCHING delicacies, we respectfully refer you back to that time when men were men and women were damned glad of it: October 2, 1908. For on that fateful date two of the greatest pitchers in the long history of the sport pitched what may arguably be called the greatest pitching duel in baseball, their feat forming an institution.

Throughout the long and storied annals of baseball there have been but a few match-ups which could be affixed with the label "great": Walter Johnson versus "Smokey" Joe Wood back in 19-aught-12; Carl Hubbell versus Tex Carlton in 1933; Bob Feller against Bob Cain in 1952; and Sandy Koufax versus Bob Hendley in 1965. Then, throw in a few of the great pitching duels, such as the ones between Christy Mathewson and Mordecai "Three-Fingered" Brown, and in later years Feller and Hal Newhouser, and you have almost exhausted all of those pitching battles which could inhabit that sparsely populated island marked "great."

But if there were an investiture, the one that would be crowned "greatest" took place on October 2, 1908, between Addie Joss and Ed Walsh—not incidentally, a duel between the two pitchers with the lowest lifetime ERA's and one with the pennant at stake.

Those with their values plucked from the prevailing winds had handicapped the 1908 American League race as a two-team chase between the defending champion Detroit Tigers and the Cleveland Naps. The Tigers, with Ty Cobb leading them at bat and on the basepaths and Sam Crawford providing the fire power, were viewed by the smart money as the favorite to repeat. But the Naps, named for their leader, Napoleon Lajoie, were the sentimental favorite. Two years before the Naps had led the League in batting and it was felt by many observers that if the heart of Cleveland's batting order—Lajoie, Bradley, Turner, Stovall, Clarke and Bemis, who had collectively fallen off their 1906 pace by 47 percentage points, from a .296 average to a .249 average in 1907—could only recapture their 1906 form, then Cleveland would be a factor.

But not even the long-shot bettors had handicapped the White Sox as a factor. For even though the 1906 World's Champions had started the 1907 campaign with the same team intact, their pitching staff had turned sour on them, with Altrock, Owen and Patterson all disappointments. What they hadn't considered was the emergence of Big Ed Walsh in 1908.

But the emergence of Walsh in 1908 was the story of the American League pennant race. For never before, or since, has a pennant contender been carried on the strong back of one pitcher as much as the '08 White Sox.

Walsh was one of a new breed, a "spitball" pitcher. Coming up to the White Sox in 1904, Walsh had roomed with a 30-year-old rolling stone named Elmer Stricklett, who had just come up from the West Coast for a "look-see" by the Sox. While at Sacramento, Stricklett, nursing a sore arm, had been tutored in the fine art of the "spitter" by one George Hildebrand, who had learned the secret by watching a teammate warming up after a heavy rain had left the grass wet. Experimenting, Hildebrand found that by expectorating on the ball, it could be made to take peculiar dips and

doodles. Stricklett, while staying in Chicago for exactly one game and a cup of java, passed on the pitch, like a family heirloom to Walsh.

Walsh, who possessed a strapping body which repaid inspection, being as well-knit as his uniform, carried his label as a "spitball" pitcher in full view for all to see. With his cap worn far down on his face, Walsh would open his mouth to apply the juices from his cud of slippery elm to the ball, causing an ever so imperceptible muscular tightening of the jaw, announcing to all that his "spitter" was on the way. Then, after a thoughtful exploration of the batter, he would rear back and fire, the ball flashing to the plate in a spray that framed his face—doing justice to a fountain statue of Neptune spewing water in the air. As the ball neared the plate, heavy with saliva, it still moved with a lightness, like a moth toward a candle, veering down quickly. And proving all but impossible to hit. Whereas those describing fellow spitball pitcher Dick Rudolph's spitter were hardly rhapsodic, saying, "About the best you can say for Dick's spitter was that it was wet," Walsh's spitball was described by Sam Crawford as "disintegrating on the way to the plate. I swear, when it went past the plate it was just the spit went by . . . and the catcher put it back together again."

But Walsh brought something else to the mound as well, a confidence that bordered on bravado. It was said by some that he could strut sitting down. As Walsh continued to strut his stuff, both on the field and off, one writer, Ring Lardner, found an entertaining quality in the big pitcher and patterned his character "Elmer the Great" after him. However, Walsh wasn't amused and one day approached Lardner at his desk in the Chicago *Tribune* offices to render a complaint. Lardner, then busy writing one of his "In the Wake of the News" columns, looked up to see a familiar figure standing over him. "I don't like the way you write about me in 'Elmer' ", Walsh said.

Rather than give Walsh his famous "Shut up, he explained" line, Lardner pointed out the chronicler's right and that "Elmer the Great" was a fictional character. "Your name isn't even used," Lardner said.

"That's the trouble," the unhappy pitcher responded. "Nobody will know it's me." But everybody knew who Walsh was.

Pitching with pomp and pompadour, Walsh took his turn on the mound every third day. And when he was not starting, the pitcher who was posing as the proverbial one-armed paper hanger, doing all he could to carry the team, was filling in as a reliever. By the time Walsh had passed his 30th win, the White Sox were very much in the pennant race—a pennant race that was a race in fact as well as name, all four western division teams contending.

Now, with less than a week to go, one-and-a-half games were all that separated the three top teams, Detroit, Cleveland, and Chicago, with surprising St. Louis only another three games back in the pack. And, as fate would have it, on that second day of October, Cleveland was hosting Chicago and Detroit was playing host to St. Louis.

With everything on the line, Chicago manager Fielder Jones

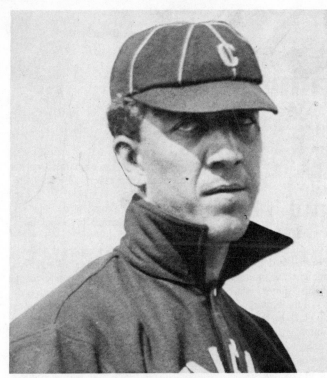

Addie Joss, the "perfect" pitcher

It was Chicago versus Cleveland, Walsh versus Joss, "spitter" versus "jump ball." A classic match-up by any standard. And for two-and-a-half innings, Walsh's pitches rolled over Cleveland batters like a tidal wave while Joss' danced in gyrations unseen anywhere since Little Egypt delivered hers at the 1893 World's Fair.

Then, in Cleveland's half of the third, Nap center fielder Joe Birmingham led off with a single, one of only four balls to be hit out of the infield all day. Walsh, who under the tutelage of fellow pitcher Nick Altrock—who had once picked off seven straight men back in 1901—had been practicing his pick-off move, made his move to first. It was perfect, Birmingham, leaning the other way, was caught napping. But as Birmingham sought salvation in the only way possible, second base, Sox first baseman Frank Isbell, throwing the ball to second for the put out, hit Birmingham in the head and, as the ball bounded into the outfield, Birmingham went to third. Walsh then loaded up the next ball, and as it bore in on batter Bill Bradley, a prankish flurry carried it past the outstretched reach of Sox catcher Ossie Schreckengost, Birmingham scoring—Walsh by his own pitch undone.

Although they didn't know it then, that run was to be the only run either team scored all day. For Joss, now throwing his whole timber and pallette into every effort, was painting a masterpiece, laying layer-after-layer down with each pitch. His jangling medley of arms, elbows, legs and knees all harmonizing beautifully as batter-after-batter held their bat out to catch the ball, which usually arrived from some direction other than from the one they were expecting.

Back in Chicago, White Sox owner Charles Comiskey was watching the results of the game on a huge electronic scoreboard set up by the Chicago Tribune. Now and then muttering a remark, more to himself than to his entourage, Comiskey was heard to utter, "Walsh is pitching a great game. But we can't get a man to first. We can hardly hit out of the infield."

Walsh, for his part, was throwing a masterpiece of his own, throwing what the papers called his "freak" pitch with "startling and crazy shoots" past Cleveland batter-after-Cleveland batter. Over the first eight innings he struck out right fielder Goode four times, catcher Clarke twice, and Lajoie twice, and a total of 15 Naps in all. Then, with Joss at bat in the bottom of the eighth, Walsh let loose with another spitter, one which snapped off like an electric light. Catcher Schreckengost—called "Schreck" for short, but not for long—reached for it. But even "Schreck," who had been catching for 11 years had "never seen anything break that way," and, letting out a cry not unlike that of an elephant removing his foot forcibly out of a bamboo trap in a Burmese teak forest, fell to the ground holding his throwing hand. For, depending upon which yellowing newsclip one reads, the ball either had broken his finger or ruptured the tendons on his meat hand, either way rendering him *hors de combat*. It was one of the small collateral liabilities of those who played with Walsh and his spitter.

Now it was the top of the ninth. Chicago's last chance to get a man on base, let alone score. Trying a new form of persuasion, Sox manager Fielder Jones sent up three pinch-hitters to try to reach Joss. But the first one, pitcher Doc White, was retired easily by Joss. Pitching carefully to the second pinch-hitter, Jiggs Donohue, Joss struck him out. Now he faced the 27th batter, John Anderson, a .262 hitter. With no economies of motion, Joss came at him with a ball from what seemed to be coming out of nowhere and Anderson, protecting the plate, hit it in the general direction of third base. Nap third baseman Birmingham scooped it up and threw it over to first. And almost over first, the throw one better

sent Walsh to the mound, despite the fact that just three days before he had pitched and won two games in a doubleheader against Boston, giving up but one run. How he was back in circulation after only two days rest defied explanation, but nevertheless, he was back and Chicago had him. Cleveland manager Lajoie countered with his best, Addie Joss.

Addie Joss was every bit the pitcher Walsh was, and there were those, especially those in Cleveland, who thought he was better. Over the past three years, Joss had won 68 games and finished 93 of the 101 games he started. And he had already added his fourth 20-game season in succession only the previous week. Like Walsh, Joss also had a delivery that had acquired no small measure of fame, a corkscrew windup motion, like an early-day Luis Tiant, which found him turning away from the batter before pitching, delivering the ball everywhere save through his legs. As the long-legged, slatternly pitcher-turned-electric-fan wheeled around on his unsuspecting opponent in the batter's box, he did so with something of the air of a conjurer who, to amuse children, produces two rabbits and a grand old flag from somewhere inside a borrowed top hat.

Only it wasn't two rabbits and a grand old flag he produced, but something called the "Jump ball." The jump ball did not depend on spin, but instead on a false rise. Thrown overhanded, it aimed at the level of the batter's knees and then, unexplainably, rose. The total effect, as one bemused batter tried to describe it, was: "The ball, coming downward with great speed, packs air below it. Just when the ball begins to lose speed, the elastic air cushion for a fraction of a second, has equal power with the attraction of gravity and carries the ball horizontally for a few feet until the further loss of motion brings it to the ground." But however explained, the effect was a misdirection worthy of a master magician, and before the batter could figure out the brand of misdirection, the ball was as beyond him as sleight-of-hand has been for generations.

suited for basketball than baseman. Fortunately, first baseman George Stovall was able to stretch to the full limits of his 74 inches and barely catch it. The game was over! And only the second no-hit, no-run, no-man-reached-first game in modern baseball history had been pitched.

Back in Chicago, all the crestfallen owner of the team could say, after sitting for five minutes in abstracted silence, was: "That game must have broken Walsh's heart. If I were a betting man, I'd have bet anything he could win."

As there is with every good story, there must be a postscript. There is. For that very afternoon, the Detroit Tigers beat the St. Louis Browns on a disputed play, a play the Chicago papers called "phony." Down 6-5 going into their half of the ninth, the Tigers had scored once on a double by Crawford to tie the score. Then, with Cobb on base, Detroit first baseman Claude Rossman hit a ball down the left-field line and into the spectators crowded onto the field. As the umpires and the players argued whether the ball was "fair" or "foul," Cobb turned third and started to home, but stopped, almost as if to watch the argument. Tiger manager Hughie Jennings raced out of his coaching box to almost carry Cobb home and put his feet on the plate, while behind him the umpires were deciding that the hit was "fair" and that the ground rules established before the game covered only hits to right field and not left.

And so, with Chicago's loss and Detroit's win, the season came down to the final day. And a game between Chicago and Detroit. Cleveland, which had already finished its season because of the capriciousness of the weather—and owing to the fact that the-then rules had mustard spread between them, its rained-out games never to be made up—was already officially eliminated, their record at 90-64. The winner of the game between Detroit, which stood at 89-63, and Chicago, at 88-63, to be the winner of the pennant by one-half game over the Naps.

Chicago again went with Walsh, by now the winner of 40 games, the league's leading pitcher in games and innings pitched, strikeouts and wins. But whereas Walsh had once run on high octane, his gas tank was now empty, and the Tigers triumphed 7-0, winning the pennant by one-half game over the Indians, with Chicago third, one-and-a-half games back.

And so ended the closest pennant race in Major League history, one which featured the greatest pitching battle ever to be seen.

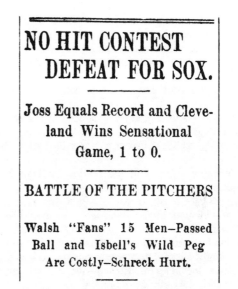

NO HIT CONTEST DEFEAT FOR SOX.

Joss Equals Record and Cleveland Wins Sensational Game, 1 to 0.

BATTLE OF THE PITCHERS

Walsh "Fans" 15 Men—Passed Ball and Isbell's Wild Peg Are Costly—Schreck Hurt.

Big Ed Walsh, king of the "Spitballers"

SCORE OF SOX-NAPS GAME.

CHICAGO.	AB	R	BH	TB	BB	SH	SB	PO	A	E		CLEVELAND.	AB	R	BH	TB	BB	SH	SB	PO	A	E
Hahn, rf........	3	0	0	0	0	0	0	1	0	0		Goode, rf........	4	0	0	0	0	0	0	1	0	0
Jones, cf........	3	0	0	0	0	0	0	0	0	0		Bradley, 3b.....	4	0	0	0	0	0	0	1	0	0
Isbell, 1b.......	3	0	0	0	0	0	0	1	1	1		Hinchman, lf...	3	0	0	0	0	0	0	3	0	0
Dougherty, lf...	3	0	0	0	0	0	0	0	0	0		Lajoie, 2b......	3	0	1	1	0	0	1	3	5	0
Davis, 2b.......	3	0	0	0	0	0	0	0	0	0		Stovall, 1b......	3	0	0	0	0	0	0	16	0	0
Parent, ss.......	3	0	0	0	0	0	0	1	3	0		Clarke, c........	3	0	0	0	0	0	0	4	1	0
Schreck, c......	2	0	0	0	0	0	0	13	0	0		Birmingham, cf.	3	1	2	2	0	0	0	0	0	0
Shaw, c.........	0	0	0	0	0	0	0	3	0	0		Perring, ss......	3	0	1	1	1	0	0	1	1	0
*White	1	0	0	0	0	0	0	0	0	0		Joss, p..........	3	0	0	0	0	0	0	0	5	0
Tannehill, 3b...	3	0	0	0	0	0	0	0	0	0												
**Donohue	1	0	0	0	0	0	0	0	0	0												
Walsh, p........	2	0	0	0	0	0	0	1	3	0												
***Anderson ...	1	0	0	0	0	0	0	0	0	0												
Totals......27		0	0	0	0	0	0	24	7	1		Totals......28		1	4	4	1	0	1	27	16	0

*Batted for Shaw in ninth. **Batted for Tannehill in ninth. ***Batted for Walsh in ninth.

CHICAGO...... .... 0 0 0 0 0 0 0 0 0—0
CLEVELAND...... .... 0 0 1 0 0 0 0 0 *—1

Struck out—By Walsh, Goode (4), Lajoie (2), Clarke (3), Joss (3), Bradley, Hinchman, Birmingham; by Joss, Dougherty, Jones, Donohue. Passed balls—Schreck (2). Time of game—1:33. Umpires—Connolly and O'Loughlin.

44 Hank Greenberg's Last Game Grand Slam

Detroit Tigers vs. St. Louis Browns, September 30, 1945

WHEN THE DECADE OF THE 1940'S STARTED, THE WINDS OF war were beginning to gust over the country and everyone, athletes included, was to get caught up in the ensuing draft. But one man who didn't wait for the Day of Infamy was Hank Greenberg, the massive Detroit first baseman-hyphen-outfielder, who volunteered a full seven months before that fateful day in December of 1941.

The four years Greenberg was to lose in the service of his country were his vintage years, those which promised to be the most rewarding of his long career, a career that had started back in 1930.

Greenberg was raised in the shadow of Yankee Stadium, playing ball at nearby James Madison High. And the Yankees, ever on the lookout for talent, dispatched Paul Krichell, their veteran scout, to give the youngster a "look-see." The man called "Krich," who had signed Lou Gehrig to a Yankee contract after watching the Iron Man-to-be swat a ball completely out of Columbia's Baker Field up onto the steps of the library—and would later sign several other Yankees, including Phil Rizzuto—was dutifully impressed by the big awkward youth who bore a resemblance to George "Highpockets" Kelly, the old New York Giants' first baseman, and offered young "Hank" a contract. But Greenberg and family, doing battle with the facts decided that the Yankees offered him little opportunity. With Gehrig giving every promise of being "there forever," Greenberg decided instead to sign with Detroit Tiger scout Jean Dubuc.

The door of opportunity rarely gets its lock picked, but instead must be opened with the correct combination. Greenberg had it, almost from the beginning. Sent out to Hartford in the Eastern League and then to Raleigh for the 1930 season—with one cup of coffee of the instant variety in Detroit—the 19-year-old hit .303 spread over the three clubs with 21 homers. His second season, 1931, saw him with Evansville in the Three-I League where his .318 average with 15 homers earned him a late-season elevation to the Beaumont team in the Texas League. By 1932, Greenberg began, like the contortionist, to come into his own, leading the league in homers, RBI's and runs and his team, the Beaumont Exporters, to the Texas League championship.

Detroit, then in the rebuilding stage, was dutifully impressed with the way its young hope was feeding on the offerings of opposing pitchers in the Texas League and brought him up in 1933 along with "Flea" Clifton, "Schoolboy" Rowe and "Hot Potato" Hamlin from Del Baker's championship Beaumont team to flesh out their young team. Greenberg repaid the Tigers' faith in him almost from the beginning, taking over the first base chores from Harry Davis and then, in one of the early-season games, driving one of Earl Whitehill's offerings into the near-horizon, the ball clearing the scoreboard in deep left-center field. His .301 average and 12 homers were to serve only as an appetizer.

1934 was to be a different story. Entirely. In those days before TV, the world in a golden airship wafted on two wings, print and dreams. And new manager Mickey Cochrane, employing the print

media to indulge in his dreams, boldly predicted at the start of spring training that the Tigers "would win the 1934 pennant." Owner Frank Navin had scoffed at the comment, saying, "In no other sport does form run as true as it does in baseball. We finished fifth last year and the year before. With Cochrane catching and Goslin supplying added batting punch, we should be a bit stronger this year, and, with luck, finish fourth. Forget this talk about winning a pennant." Navin was wrong on two counts: Detroit *did* win the pennant and it was Greenberg not Goslin who supplied the added punch, batting .339, hitting 26 home runs, and driving in 139 runs, including the tying or winning run in 40 of Detroit's 101 wins. The World Series program that year ran the following thumbnail biography under its picture of Greenberg: "Henry Greenberg is playing his first full season in the major leagues but he has established himself as one of the great sluggers in baseball. He will cover near averaging two bases per hit. An awkward fielder when he made his debut last season, he has developed into one of the best fielding first basemen in the big leagues. He is a competitor of the finest type, adding a flaming spirit to his physical assets such as height, reach, wrist, forearm and shoulder power. He is still improving and will, within a few years, be rated as one of the best of all time."

In 1935 Greenberg took a giant step toward becoming "one of the best of all time," leading the Tigers to yet another pennant and in the process leading the league in homers and runs batted in—driving in 51 more than the runner-up, Lou Gehrig, the man he couldn't displace some six years earlier. For his efforts, Greenberg was rewarded by being named the League's Most Valuable Player.

1936 broke bright and hopeful for the Tigers, picked by all to repeat as World's champions. And for Hank Greenberg, now on the threshhold of greatness. But then, after playing only 12 games, something else broke: Greenberg's wrist, putting him out of action for the rest of the season. However, 1937 saw him once again begin his quest for greatness as he came back, hitting .337 with 40 homers and a league-leading 183 runs-batted-in.

However, the year that secured Hank's right to be officially called "one of the best of all time" was 1938. For that was the year Greenberg took aim at Babe Ruth's supposedly unassailable 60 home run record, a record that stood like Everest for all to measure their accomplishments against. And when, on September 27th, he hit two tremendous drives off St. Louis Browns' pitcher Bill Cox for his fifty-seventh and fifty-eighth homers of the season with five games left to play, it seemed that the record was well within reach. However, those last two homers were never to be. Still Greenberg had tied the all-time record for most home runs ever by a right-handed batter and established the record for hitting two or more homers in a single game during a season with 11, records which would propel him more than half-way to Cooperstown on their own.

Two years and 74 home runs later, Greenberg, having heard only too clearly the sound of hob-nailed Nazi jack boots overrunning Europe, enlisted in the U. S. Army, the first major leaguer to

volunteer his services. His final game before he stepped forward was May 6, 1941, against the Yankees in Detroit. As Greenberg remembered the moment, and related it to sportswriter Arthur Daley, "In my first at bat I leaned against one and darned if I didn't hit a homer. The next time up I hit another, both off Tiny Bonham. You know what they say about ball players—that all of them have their batting averages practically written on their cuffs and that they can rattle off every statistic at any moment. Well, I was standing in the outfield and I started to do a little figuring. I told myself that I hold some sort of record for hitting two home runs a game over the course of a season. Yet I never once was able to punch out three. I suddenly realized that I'd just walloped the 248th and 249th of my major league career and I thought what a wonderful flourish it would be to wind up with three homers for the first time—the third also being my 250th."

Greenberg recalled becoming "intensely interested in hammering one into the stands. That's the funny thing about baseball. In my first two trips to the plate I'd never even given it a thought, just taking my cut without consciously trying for that home run, yet connected both times. As I stepped up to bat in the last of the eighth, we had the game won and everybody was pulling for me to finish with a homer—myself included. Atley Donald was pitching and the bases were full. What a perfect spot! Donald didn't have a thing, but he was wild enough to toss up three balls. I didn't want to walk and I was both surprised and amused that even Yankee catcher Bill Dickey was rooting for me. The next pitch came in as large as a balloon. I missed it. I swung at the next pitch and missed again. Then came the final pitch, the pay-off for my home-run ambitions. I really took a belt at that one. A home run? No, I fanned magnificently."

For Greenberg, it would be his last swing in almost four long years. Number 250 would have to wait. For the next morning, May 7, 1941, Greenberg went down to the induction facility in downtown Detroit and enlisted. Ironically, he was to be mustered out on December 5, 1941, under a law releasing all men over 28 years of age. But two days later America was at war, and Greenberg re-enlisted, this time for the duration.

For the next four years Major League baseball stocked its rosters with men who would have done Emma Lazarus proud. Attempting to masquerade skim milk as cream, the Caesars of Baseball stocked their rosters with the wrong, the short and the tall; in short, the 4Fers. In fact, everybody but the Singer Midgets had been conscripted for what had been the National Pastime before World War II supplanted it. And there were even rumors that four or five teams were attempting to sign even *them* to contracts. Scouts were combing the country signing babes in swaddling clothes and throwing mosquito nets over anybody this side of the undertaker. Baseball, like all of war-torn Europe, had a missing generation between the too-young and the too-old.

And then, on May 8, 1945, the war in Europe was over. And Johnny came marching home—along with Ted, Bobby and even Hank, who was mustered out on June 14, 1945. And four years and fifty-days after his last game, on the afternoon of July 1, 1945, Hank Greenberg picked up right where he had left off, hitting homer number 250 in his very first game back.

Hank Greenberg, the first Major Leaguer to enlist for WW II, comes back from the service to win the pennant for the Tigers with a dramatic grand-slam home run on the last day of the '45 season.

That home run propelled Detroit into first place in the standings. But even though they were to hold on to the lead for the rest of the year, they had to fight off the valiant challenge of the Washington Senators, who, led by their four knuckle ball pitchers, had climbed from the depths of the cellar the year before to challenge for the lead. Going into the final day of the season Detroit had won 87 games and lost 65; Washington, which had finished its season a week before, had 87 victories and 67 defeats. The previous day's game against the improbable defending American League pennant winners, the St. Louis Browns, had been postponed due to rain, and was now part of a scheduled doubleheader on the last day of the season.

One win would give the Tigers the pennant. But if St. Louis won both, it would force a play-off for the pennant for the first time in Major League history. In preparation for such an eventuality, the Senators had already sent their team to Detroit for the next day's Play-Off game.

But a rain from no particular source almost mitigated against the game being played at all. In fact, play had been held up for an hour before it was decided to attempt to get the game in; and then on a field so muddy that the players had difficulty wading around. For eight innings, the Tigers fought the constant rain and Nelson Potter's screwball as the Browns' premier pitcher held them to seven hits and just two runs. On the other side of the ledger, the Browns had gotten to Tiger starter Virgil Trucks—discharged only three days earlier and making his first mound appearance in two years—and reliever Hal Newhouser for eight hits and three runs. As the ninth started, the Tiger situation rivaled that of the heavens: gloomy. But Hub Walker, pinch-hitting for Newhouser, delivered his only pinch hit of the season to open the ninth. Skeeter Webb, Detroit shortstop, then laid down a bunt toward first, and both runners were safe when the throw to second was not in time to get Walker. Eddie Mayo then sacrificed the runners over to second and third. Brownie manager Luke Sewell, gingerly skirting the puddles between the dugout and the pitcher's mound, came out to consult with Potter, and decided to walk the next man up, Tiger center fielder Doc Cramer, to load the bases and set up a double play. The only problem with this strategy was: the next batter was Hank Greenberg.

Greenberg came to the plate, vigorously rubbing his bat with a hunk of bone he carried with him. Throwing the bone away, he shivered a little and turned his back to the mist and, looking out at the bases, which, in the premature darkness were now pimpled with hulks of merchandise on every base. Taking his place at the plate, Greenberg watched one of Potter's screwballs come over for a called "Ball." He then stepped out again. Finally, sensing that beyond the possibility of a slight nip of frost there was no formidable evil to be looked for, he stepped back in. Potter came down with yet another screwball. Only this time the ball never quite reached the catcher for the umpire to call it anything. For Greenberg, taking aim, took the ball downtown as well, driving it just inside the left-field foul line into the upper reaches of the Sportsman's Park bleachers for a grand slam homer.

As Greenberg made his way slowly around the basepaths, his aching muscles rebelling violently to the run, his teammates flocked to the plate where they jumped up and down, both to register their emotions at having won the pennant and to restore their circulation. Finally the author of the grand-slam homer crossed the plate. The 1945 season had ended in one of the most dramatic moments in baseball history: a moment in which the rain and the darkness had been parted by Hank Greenberg and his bright rainbow of fame.

GREENBERG HAILED BY JOYOUS TIGERS

Hank Acclaimed at Home Plate After Winning Hit and in Clubhouse Celebration

TIGERS ANNEX FLAG ON FOUR-RUN HOMER

Greenberg's Blow With Bases Filled in 9th Tops Browns, 6-3, to Clinch Pennant

NEWHOUSER WINS NO. 25

Relieves Trucks and Receives Credit for Victory—Second Contest Is Washed Out

DETROIT (A.)							ST. LOUIS (A.)						
	ah	r	h	po	a	e		ah	r	h	po	a	e
Webb, ss	2	1	1	3	3	0	Gutte'ge, 2b	3	1	1	6	3	0
Mayo, 2b	4	0	1	3	3	0	Finney, lf	3	0	2	1	0	0
Cramer, cf	5	1	1	2	0	0	By'r, cf	2	0	0	2	0	0
Greenb'g, lf	5	1	2	1	1	0	cChristman	1	0	0	0	0	0
Cullen'e, rf	4	1	1	0	0	0	Gray, c	1	1	0	2	0	0
York, 1b	5	0	0	6	1	0	McQui'n, 1b	4	0	1	5	2	0
Outlaw, 3b	2	0	1	1	1	0	Moore, rf	4	1	1	0	0	0
Richards, c	4	0	1	10	1	0	Stephens, ss	4	0	2	2	2	0
Trucks, p	2	1	0	1	1	0	Mancuso, c	4	0	0	5	0	0
Newhou'r, p	0	0	0	0	0	0	Schultz, 3b	4	0	0	3	4	0
aWalker	1	0	1	0	0	0	Potter, p	2	0	1	1	0	0
bBorom	0	1	0	0	0	0							
Benton, p	0	0	0	0	0	0							
Total	35	6	9	27	11	0	Total	32	3	8	27	11	0

aBatted for Newhouser in ninth.
bRan for Walker in ninth.
cBatted for Byrnes in sixth.

Detroit .... 0 0 0 0 1 1 0 0 4—6
St. Louis .... 1 0 0 0 0 0 1 1 0—3

Runs batted in—Finney, Mayo, Richards, Stephens, McQuinn, Greenberg (4). Two-base hits—Gutteridge, Potter, McQuinn, Moore. Home run—Greenberg. Sacrifice hits—Webb, Mayo. Double plays—Richards and Mayo; Outlaw, Mayo and York. Left on bases—St. Louis 5, Detroit 9. Bases on balls—Off Trucks 2, Potter 5, Newhouser 1. Struck out—By Trucks 3, Potter 4, Newhouser 5. Hits—Off Trucks 3 in 5 1-3 innings, Newhouser 1 in 2 2-3, Benton, 1 in 1. Winning pitcher—Newhouser. Umpires—Pipgras, Berry, Rue and Hubbard. Time of game—2:23. Attendance—5,582.

45 Babe Ruth's Last Hurrah

Pittsburgh Pirates vs. Boston Braves, May 25, 1935

BASEBALL IS AN ORDERLY SPORT, SPROUTING, APPROPRI-ately enough, in the spring, blooming full-grown in the summer, and fading in the first autumnal chill. It is a game of continuity as well, with an historical methods of double-entry bookkeeping which allows for the tying of every player, date, and record into one another.

But the tying in of ballplayers and dates goes even farther, forming a continuous succession of events, none of which can be distinguished from neighboring parts. It was just such a string that baseball played out on the dates of May 24th and May 25th, 1935, as the torch was passed from the world that once was to the world that would be in baseball's version of the changing of the guard. For on the night of May 24, 1935, the lights went on at Crosley Field in Cincinnati for the first night baseball game in Major League history. And less than 24 hours later, Babe Ruth, the sand now visibly pouring out of his hour glass, hit three home runs in one of the last games he ever was to play.

By 1934 the legend called Babe Ruth was but a flickering image of what once was. Where his home runs had at one time been repeating decimals, almost redundant, his receding skills now allowed only occasional bursts of the light that had made him glow just a few short years before. And his swing, once almost instinctive, even after an all-night affair, now took all his conscious efforts and coordination, his abilities ceasing to function. One of those who watched the tired, discouraged and totally unconvincing national monument-turned-embarrassment as he waddled through the motions was Ben Chapman, who played center field alongside Ruth. Believing that the truth made all things plain, Chapman chose not to embroider, saying to Ruth, "If I were as old as you, and as rich as you are, I wouldn't risk my health by playing any more."

But still Ruth played on, the gilt of his greatness now peeling off for all to see. Although he had lost none of his hitting power, it looked like he had lost just about everything else, including his will to play. Fading in all the worst placed, Ruth no longer carried the sylphlike figure of his youth, but instead, like a tree, had added a circumferential ring each year around his middle to go with his every World Series ring. His upper body was now so vast that his legs could no longer carry the weight of his maturity, moving Ruth to express grave concern for the condition of his legs as early as spring training '34. He had not played one full month into the season before they gave unmistakable evidence of deterioration, three times buckling under the overload. Proving that tradition still carried a heavy whallop, Ruth managed to hit 22 home runs and bat in 84 runs in 1934. But it was apparent to all that he was merely a memory of his greatness now.

If Yankee Stadium was known as "The House that Ruth Built," a shrine to his once-greatness, it was a shrine with a mortgage as well, his continued presence. He couldn't just be discarded like some broken toy onto the used player pile, lest some of those ancient and honorable romantics who were Yankee fans second

and Ruth fans first would turn against the team. In effect, the star was dragging the wagon.

Yankee owner Jacob Ruppert and General Manager Ed Barrow now sought ways to somehow, someway, somewhere rid themselves of the legend-cum-albatross. It was long past the time when he should have been presented with a gold watch and put out to pasture. Other strategems had to be employed. The tried to trade him, getting nibbles from teams like the Detroit Tigers, who were interested in Ruth as their field manager. But Ruth stood up Tiger owner Frank Navin in favor of a trip to the Orient and the Tigers traded for Mickey Cochrane, making him their player-manager. Next the Yankees offered Ruth the position of manager of their Newark farm club. Ruth, whose heart was set on managing the Yankees first and in the Majors second, thought Newark was a step downward, and declined. And then, just when it seemed that the Yankees would have to bite the bullet, Boston made an offer they couldn't refuse.

For years the Boston Braves had been one of baseball's poorer relations, both on the field and in the front office. A fifth-rate power, the Braves had only a winking acquaintance with the first division, finishing in the top four teams only six times in their previous 34 years. Their lack of success on the field had now engulfed the front office where the red ink couldn't be parted by Moses. And so it was that Judge Emil Fuchs, owner of the Braves, spurred on by Massachusetts Governor James Curley, sought out Ruppert to find out if Ruth was available.

With the interest in Ruth now matching the interest rate carried by municipal bonds—which during the Depression was about minus seven on the Richter scale—Ruppert and Barrow jumped at the chance to unload Ruth on Judge Fuchs and the Braves. Together the three worked out a "deal" which had Ruth going to Boston to become, in no particular order: a player; an assistant manager; an executive without portfolio, and an investor with a portfolio that included worthless Braves' stock. The Yankees, for their part, received no compensation. But they had something more important, they had rid themselves of Ruth and oppressive legend. It was, as Jim Murray was to write years later, "An act which won the Yankees the John Wilkes Booth award by acclamation."

But no matter the inducements Judge Fuchs had waved in front of Ruth, it was clear from the very beginning that his only reason for being was as a gate attraction. His job as "assistant manager" was nothing more than that of a glorified coach, the current manager of the Braves, Bill McKechnie, having no intention of either moving over or out. And his so-called option to buy stock in the Braves was second in the realm of sound financial investments only to buying a piece of the Brooklyn Bridge.

And so Ruth, forty, fat, flush and feeling foolish, was trotted out like the queen's jewels on ceremonial occasions, all the better it was hoped to draw the crowds the Braves needed to shore up their tottering franchise.

The crowds flocked to see the burned-out hollow shell who

Babe Ruth signs autographs for some of his many fans

had once been baseball's greatest player, now reduced to a well-nourished corporeity looking as if he had been stuffed by a good taxidermist. Still, the hollow shell gave a murmur when it was held to the ear, and on opening day 1935, in front of 25,000-plus fans in Braves Field, Ruth had a single and a home run in four times at bat against Carl Hubbell and figured in all four runs as the Braves beat the Giants, 4-2.

RUTH BEGINS NEW CAREER IN BLAZE OF GLORY

Responsible For All Of Braves' Counters In 4-2 Victory Over Giants

But even though the fans continued to show up, Ruth seldom did, even when he was in uniform, his efforts insults to the noble Ruth of fast-fading memory. Pitchers who were years shy of birth when Ruth first broke in showed no reverence for a baseball hero, honing in on the jugular by throwing heaping plates of fastballs by him that had once been Ruth's meat-and-potatoes. Yet the fans showed up in record numbers, based no doubt on a theory related to some strange hypothesis of the watched pot, hoping against

hope to see the scales fall from his eyes and another Ruthian homer.

Between battling his annual spring cold which had developed into an infection, asking the Braves to put him on the "voluntarily retired" list and then, begrudgingly, acceding to Judge Fuchs' impassioned pleas to "play one more game . . . one more series . . . one more western swing . . ." etc., Ruth limped through the month of April and almost through May. "I'm all washed up," he would bemoan, and his on-the-field statistics did nothing to belie his feelings.

Finally, after a swing through the west that began in St. Louis, the Braves alit in Pittsburgh for a three-game series the third week of May, 1935. Ruth's first order of business was to attend a testimonial honoring his teammate and fellow elder statesplayer, Rabbit Maranville, who had started in Boston two years before Ruth and whose long career had included a stopover in Pittsburgh during the early '20s. Now finishing his career in Boston, Maranville would play in 23 games, five less than Ruth, during the '35 season. Still he was a beloved baseball character and, like Ruth, loved a good party. And so it was that during the tribute to the old warhorse, that another, Ruth, got up and having taken more than one cup of kindness yet for auld lang syne, gave one last lament for lost youth, mumbling something that sounded like, "I've known Rabbit for a long time and I love him . . ." Then Ruth put his ample arm around the man he called "Rab" and the two Merry Andrews went out on their diocesan rounds to treat the similarly sick and afflicted.

With more than three fingers of truth serum under his belt and more than three sheets to the wind, Ruth staggered in sometime after breakfast. In days of olde, Ruth's having been out on the town the entire night before a game would have spelled trouble with a capital "T" for any pitcher throwing up balls to the plate that looked like aspirins. But now, slowed down more than a step by age and other symptoms, it took the Babe two days, his first day-after producing only a single and a long fly to Paul Waner against the wall.

It was the day-after-the-day-after that Ruth's aging body finally made the readjustment he used to make in only one quick morning. But whether it was one day or two, the result was the same: Babe Ruth, almost as if drugged by the scent of his reconstituted past, once again built sand castles in the air with his bat.

Some 10,000-plus fans had come to Forbes Field more to relive their own senses than anything else on the off-chance they would catch a glimpse of the Ruth of old. The Ruth of 1935 did not disappoint. In the first inning, against starting Pirate pitcher Red Lucas, Ruth, practicing his own style of gentrification, drove a two-run homer into the stand. This one far beyond the reaches of Waner—his fourth of the year and 712th lifetime.

Baseball always seems to be one huge repertory theatre, with the same actors constantly entering and exiting to given lines. Now, as Ruth came to bat in the third, he found Lucas gone and in his place Guy Bush, his old bench-jockeying nemesis from the '32

Babe Ruth talks things over with his former manager, Bill Terry, before the game.

World Series. The last time the two had been on stage together, Ruth had given the finger to Bush in the "Called" shot game and Bush, in the very first time Ruth came to bat against him in the fourth game, had retaliated with a pitch striking Ruth on the arm. This time around there were no fingers nor brushback pitches, only a fast ball thrown down the pipe which Ruth promptly deposited into the right-field stands, just inside the foul line and barely over the fence—Number 713.

The Pirates kept pecking away, and by the time Ruth came up to face Bush again in the fifth, the score was tied, four each. This time Bush got away luckier, giving up only a run-producing single to Ruth, breaking the tie. However, the Pirates came back with three more in the bottom half of the fifth to go ahead 7-5. And, in the seventh, up again came Ruth.

Bush was determined not to let Ruth have another hit, let alone another homer. The third inning homer had angered Bush who said to himself, "Is that the kind of home runs he's been getting?" Coming out of the dugout to assume his position on the mound for the seventh, Bush decided "I'm going to throw three fast balls right by that guy and get my laugh."

Bush remembered the confrontation a full one score later and was to tell baseball historian Marshall Smelser, "I got the first pitch in there for a strike and Ruth just watched it go by just as pretty, like he was looking at a softball. And I didn't say a word. I got a signal for another fast ball and I come through with one . . . I mean, with everything I had on it. I hit the plate, maybe an inch or two inches off the plate, about halfway between his knees and his waist. Just where he could get that fat part of the bat on it."

The next instance saw Ruth leave the present and reemerge in the past, wielding his bat once again as if it were a toothpick. Then there was the sharp, crisp sound of bat meeting ball, and the ball, with a lightning-rod sensitivity, took off for the highest spot in Forbes Field. As the ball sailed into the wild blue yonder, soon to clear the top of the right-field roof where no ball had ever gone before, Guy Bush could only think to himself that it was "The longest cockeyed ball I ever saw in my life."

Ruth, who had always lived for the din of brass bands, the raucous cheers and almost obscure approval of the fans, now lumbered his way around the bases, drinking in the Niagara of roars that followed him. Guy Bush's eyes were following him too, but now they saw something different: "That poor fellow, he'd gotten to where he could hardly hobble along. I ain't mad no more then. So, when he rounds third, I just look over there at him and he

kinda looked at me, I tipped my cap just to say, 'I've seen everything now, Babe.' He just looked up at me and kind of saluted and smiled . . ."

Ruth was to remove himself abruptly in the middle of the seventh with four hits in four times at bat, six of the Braves' seven RBI's and three homers—the first time a player had hit three homers in a game in both leagues, his American League trio coming five years before. Unfortunately, while it would be properly fitting to note that the Braves won the game, the opposite is true, the Braves losing 11-7, one of their 115 losses as they established a record-in-reverse as one of the all-time worst teams in baseball history. And, even more unfortunate, while the home run was Ruth's valedictory, his last homer and last hit of any kind, it was not to be his last game.

While cinematic claptrap like "The Babe Ruth Story" would have us believe Ruth had gone out with a Bang!, such hardly was the case. For by now the Braves were a traveling nostrum show, using Ruth as their come-on to drum the unsuspecting rubes into the tent-cum-stadium. Here a "Babe Ruth Day," there a "Babe Ruth Day" and everywhere Ruth first appeared on the Braves' first road trip a "Babe Ruth Day." And while Ruth had considered quitting while on top, Judge Fuchs—the man Ruth now fondly referred to as "that son-of-a-bitch"—would have none of it and prevailed upon the once-mighty Ruth to play out the string of "Babe Ruth Days."

So it was that Ruth found himself in Cincinnati on May 26th, not incidentally "Babe Ruth Day," where he struck out three times. The next day, May 28th, he walked in his only time up as a pinch-hitter. Then, on May 28th, he went hitless in two times at bat and injured his leg running up the Crosley Field incline for a batted ball. Limping into Philadelphia for a Decoration Day double-header that also was designated "Babe Ruth Day" by those who trotted out the fatted calves in his benefit, Ruth came up to in the first against pitcher Jim Bivin and ground out weakly to Phillies' first baseman Dolph Camilli. In the second, Ruth retired from the game. Four days later he made it official, retiring from the game forever. Sitting in the Braves' lockerroom, his old age showing without the cover of his charitable woolens, Ruth could only say, "I'm quitting" in a voice so soft reporters who had gathered in knots around is locker had to cup their ears to hear him.

Thus the legend of Ruth ended with a whimper, not with the bang! it was worthy of.

Ruth Hits 3 Homers but Braves Lose, 11-7; Gets an Ovation From Fans in Pittsburgh

```
     BOSTON (N).            PITTSBURGH (N).
            ab.r.h.po.a.e            ab.r.h.po.a.e
Urbanski, ss.3 1 0 1 1 0  L. Waner, cf.5 2 3 3 0 0
Mallon, 2b..4 2 1 4 4 1   Jensen, lf..4 1 2 1 0 0
Mowry, rf..1 0 1 0 0 0    P. Waner,rf.4 2 2 5 0 0
Ruth, rf...4 3 4 3 0 0    Vaughan, ss.4 2 2 1 2 0
Berger, cf..5 1 3 4 0 0   Young, 2b...3 1 1 3 3 0
Moore, 1b...4 0 2 6 0 0   Suhr, 1b....3 2 2 11 0 0
Lee lf......5 0 0 3 1 0   Thevenow,3b 4 1 2 0 4 0
Coscarart,3b 4 0 2 0 3 0  Grace, c.....4 0 0 2 0 0
Spohrer, c..4 0 0 3 0 0   Lucas, p.....0 0 0 0 0 0
Betts, p....2 0 0 0 1 0   Bush, p.....3 0 0 3 0
Cantwell, p.1 0 0 0 1 0   Hoyt, p......1 0 0 0 1 0
aWhitney ..1 0 0 0 0 0
Benton, p...0 0 0 0 0 0    Total..35 11 14 27 18 0

 Total..38 7 13 24 11 1
aBatted for Cantwell in eighth.
Boston ................2 0 3 0 1 0 2 0 0—7
Pittsburgh ............0 0 0 4 3 0 3 1.—11
  Runs batted in—Ruth 6, Suhr, Thevenow 5,
Young 2, Grace, Lee, Vaughan.
  Two-base hits—Mallon, Thevenow. Three-base
hits—Thevenow, Suhr, L. Waner. Home runs—
Ruth 3, Young. Sacrifices—Mallon, Young, Jensen.
Double plays—Vaughan, Young and Suhr; Urbanski,
Mallon and Moore. Left on bases—Boston 8,
Pittsburgh 5. Bases on balls—Off Lucas 1, Betts
1, Bush 2, Cantwell 2. Struck out—By Betts 1,
Hoyt 1. Hits—Off Lucas 3 in 1-3 inning, Betts
9 in 4-2-3, Hoyt 2 in 2 2-3, Bush 8 in 6, Cant-
well 3 in 2 1-3, Benton 2 in 1. Winning pitcher—
Hoyt. Losing pitcher—Cantwell. Umpires—Rear-
don, Magerkurth and Moran. Time of game—2:14.
```

46 The 26-Inning Marathon

Boston Braves vs. Brooklyn Robins, May 1, 1920

AS SURE AS UNCLE WIGGLEY'S RHEUMATISM SERVED AS AN omen for the coming of a storm, the coming of the Brooklyn team onto the field signaled the coming of something out of the ordinary. May 1, 1920, was to be no different.

Regardless of what name they subscribed to—be it Trolley Dodgers, Superbas, Bridgegrooms, Robins or plain ol' Dodgers—the National League's Brooklyn entry seemed to be forever foisting some little one-act outrage on the sacred name of baseball. And on the record books as well.

Take the game played on August 13, 1910, for example, when Brooklyn played Pittsburg—then spelled without an "H" to hiss in—in the most evenly-played game in baseball history. When the game was finally called "On account of darkness" after nine innings, the score stood at 8-8. It was symmetrical in other ways as well, with each side having mirror-like statistics: 38 at bats, 13 hits, 12 assists, two errors, five strikeouts, three walks, one hit batsman and one passed ball. With every player trying to get into the act, the game began to take on the looks of a "Twelve Lords Aleaping" game, with each side having two pitchers, each giving up 13 hits, one hit batsman and three walks and having five strikeouts; each catcher, one passed ball, six put-outs, one assist, four at-bats, one hit and no runs; each shortstop two singles and no runs, etc., etc., etc., ad nauseum. It was a game like no other in baseball history. But then again, it was Brooklyn, which helps to explain it all.

We now beg you to join us ten years later. The year is 1920, the date May 1st, and the team called the Robins—named for their manager Wilbert Robinson—are playing in Boston. It is almost as if a trunk were opened and the odor of past exploits had filled their nostrils, for on that Saturday afternoon Brooklyn would become history again. This time the occasion will be the longest game ever played in Major League history, one which will stand even after fiction has been exhausted and newspaper items manufactured.

Robinson, a pug-nosed, chubby-cheeked expanse of a man who now resembled less a baseball figure than a father figure, fading in all the worst places, his belly that of an older man and with barely enough hair to fill a paint brush, has a team which, unbeknownst to him, will go on to capture the 1920 National League pennant. However, for the moment, he is trying mightily to cope with the matter at hand. And the matter at hand includes a game with the Boston Braves.

With a multi-faceted pitching staff which includes the likes of spitballers Burleigh Grimes and Clarence Mitchell, left-handers Rube Marquard and Sherry Smith and right-handers Jeff Pfeffer, Al Mamaux and Leon Cadore, Robinson has selected the last-named, Cadore, to start against the Braves. A big 6'1" curve-balling right-hander, Cadore won 14 games the previous year for the fifth-place Robins, and will go on to win another 15 in 1920. His opponent is Joe Oescheger, a right-handed rolling stone who played for three teams in 1919, two over the union limit. However, he now seemed to have solidified his place on the Braves' mound staff with his exploding fastball, one which will take him to 15 wins in 1920, the same number as Cadore. But on this afternoon of afternoons, neither Cadore nor Oescheger is destined to add to their win total, even as they take their place in history.

For the first four innings, the bill rendered for excitement was under the wire for show and place, but hardly a winner as Brooklyn scratched out hits in the first, second and fourth and Boston, for its part, had single hits in the second, third and fourth. Then, in the fifth, the Robins scored a run. Leading off, catcher Ernie Krueger worked Oescheger for a walk, only one of three times that Oescheger would offend the purist in this manner. The next batter, Cadore, tapped what masqueraded as a double-play ball back at his opposite number. But Oescheger, overly anxious, was barely able to get Cadore at first, Krueger going down to second on the fielder's choice. The next batter up, Brooklyn lead-off man Ivy Olson, thwacked the ball on a line over the head of Brave shortstop Rabbit Maranville for a single, scoring Krueger with Brooklyn's first run. Little did they realize at the time it would exhaust their total supply for the afternoon.

The Braves, for their part, came back in the sixth session to tie the score, when, with one out, outfielder Walt Cruise drove one of Cadore's off-speed pitches against the Braves Field scoreboard for a triple. Then, after first baseman Walter Holke flied out to Zack Wheat in short left, third baseman Tony Boeckel singled up the middle to drive in Cruise. However, the Braves werern't through with Cadore yet. For the next batter up, the effervescent Rabbit, followed Boeckel's single with a double of his own to center. But Boeckel, perhaps having seen the shape of things to come, tried for the Robins' second run and was gunned down on a throw from center fielder Wally Hood to Krueger, with more than a little help from Cadore, who took the relay and passed it along.

The little cause for celebration occasioned by the one-run outbursts in the fifth and sixth innings was to go a long way; as for the next three innings, while both Cadore and Oescheger doled out crumbs of comfort here and there, they were never to lead home.

Then, in the ninth, for the second—and, as it turned out, last—time, the Braves clustered more than one hit off Cadore, loading the bases with only one out. But Boston second baseman Charlie Pick picked that moment to hit a ground ball in the direction of Brooklyn's shortstop Ivy Olson who, after tagging Brave outfielder Ray Powell, doing his best impersonation of Lot's wife, threw over to first to double-up Pick.

The game now stood at 1-1 after the prescribed number of innings and went into overtime. Every now and when a minor disturbance would take place, but to no avail. Such as the time when Oescheger caught one of Cadore's curves on the meat part of his bat and sent it out toward the fence in left, a drive Oescheger later described as "a terrific belt which should have gone for a triple anyway . . . But Wheat, playing left for the Robins, somehow leaped up right at the fence and caught the ball." That would have given the Braves a run in extra innings and ended what was now becoming a marathon. But it was not to be. Other times someone or other would get on base, only to set like ice on the basepaths, almost as if they had said, "Here I am, and here I stay!"

For the next seven innings the batters approached the plate as docilely as lambs led to slaughter. And with the same result, as both Cadore and Oescheger mowed down batter-after-batter, their bats so unused they could be rented out for advertising space.

In the seventeenth, the Robins momentarily awakened from their self-induced slumber to threaten, filling the bases with one out on two safeties and a walk. But somehow they were denied, almost as if there were a force field around home plate. For Oescheger forced reserve catcher Rowdy Elliott, who had replaced Krueger, to hit back to the mound. Oescheger went home with the ball, forcing Wheat at the plate. But then reserve catcher Hank Gowdy, who had come in in the tenth for starting catcher Mickey O'Neil, threw the ball low to Robin first baseman Ed Konetchy in his haste to double up Elliott. For his part, Konetchy compounded the felony, fumbling it away. Now, as Brave first baseman Holke thundered his way around third vaguely trying to set a tentative and aspiring foot on that forbidden territory of home plate, Konetchy collected both himself and the ball and hurriedly threw back to Gowdy. His glove worn thin with use, Gowdy took Konetchy's throw to the side of the plate in his bare hand. Then, blindly throwing himself in the direction of the plate his bare hand holding the ball, he caught both Holke and his upraised spikes at the same time for the third out.

That for all intents and purposes, was the last offensive gasp, or burp, of the game. With the passage of the 22nd and nary a run in sight, those in the know amongst the curious and ennuied who hadn't ordered hot dogs to go were aware they were watching baseball history-in-the-making, as the two teams locked in mortal combat broke the National League record for longevity set back in 1917 by the same Brooklyn Robins against the Pirates. Two innings more and the Major League record of 24 innings, set back in 1906, sailed by, much as a passing boat on the nearby Charles River, sailing by in semi-darkness, six P.M. sunset having been long since accomplished.

The marathon contest dragged on. But now it was a marathon merely to get to first, no hint of a hit in sight as batter-after-batter merely flailed at the ball, any ball, as meek and undesirous of accomplishing anything as a cat with cream on its whiskers—their ebbing strength and ambition attested to by the fact that of the 185 total appearances at the plate by both teams, only eight batters had the patience, and strength, to wait out the pitchers for a walk, the others first-ball hitting.

And still, after 24 innings, those two fugitives from the law of averages, Cadore and Oescheger, were out on the mound, their arms full of pitches. However, where once they threw up heaping platefuls of curves and fastballs, now they were forging their pitches from within the smithies of their souls, throwing just as hard even if the pitches weren't getting there as quickly.

Never had a game consumed so much energy and so few men. Watching the exhausted athletes on the field go through their motions without any accompanying emotions, several of the unused players on the Robins' bench—which accounted for the majority of the two teams, only 22 men, 11 a team, being employed all afternoon in the radically weeded-out line-ups—began agitating the man they called "Uncle Robbie" to let them into the game. One of them, pitcher Burleigh Grimes, noting that Oescheger was merely laying them in at "just my speed", was particularly vocal in his desire to play. Anywhere, even in the outfield. But Robbie was having none of that, his strategy of the plain vanilla type, going with his filibusterers in uniform. And with the arm he rode in on.

The 25th, the record-setting inning, flashed by in just six batters, Cadore and Oescheger skewering every one in sight. There were still no signs of let up as the two promised to be the greatest carriers until the advent of Mother Dionne. Now it was the 26th, and again, six-up-six-down.

The next-scheduled order of business was the 27th. But there would be none. For as the two teams were in the process of changing the guard to take up their positions for the 27th, moving more like institutions than players—which in a sense they now were—somewhere out of the darkness that had been engulfing the field for the past several innings stepped plate umpire Barry McCormick. As hungry for the conclusion of the game as a chorus girl at one A. M., McCormick called time after three hours and fifty minutes of play. Or what passed for same.

While most, if they had it to do all over again wouldn't, there were still those who masochistically wanted to continue the mid-summer madness having robbed the proprietors of their senses. One of those, Brooklyn shortstop Ivy Olson, now came running in to McCormick. "Just one more inning," pleaded Olson. "Why?," asked the incredulous umpire-in-chief. "Just so we can say we played the equivalent of three full games in one afternoon," answered Olson, sounding like the hours of playing had finally french-fried the last of his small gray cells and they were hallucinating.

But one more inning would not a record make. It was already made, 26 innings, the longest game in the history of baseball.

For Brooklyn, it was an utterly dependable scenario one more in their merry history of out-of-the-ordinary games—the next day they would go 13 innings against the Phillies in a loss and the day after that another 19 against the Braves in another loss, 58 innings without a win in three days. But for Cadore and Oescheger, it would so intertwine their names that they would forever be known in tandem, giving baseball a twosome that would forever take its place with Cain and Abel in the Bible, Damon and Pythias in mythology, Dow and Jones in finance, Gilbert and Sullivan in music and Franklin and Roosevelt in politics.

LONG TIE IN HUB SETS NEW RECORD

BROOKLYN (N.)						BOSTON (N.)					
	AbRBPoA						AbRBPoA				
Olson,ss	10 0 1 6 0					Powell,cf	7 0 1 3 0				
Neis,rf	10 0 1 9 0					Pick,2b	11 0 0 6 10				
Johnston,3b	10 0 2 3 1					Mann,lf	10 0 2 6 0				
Wheat,lf	9 0 2 3 0					Cruise,rf	9 1 1 4 0				
Myers,cf	2 0 1 2 0					Holke,1b	10 0 2 32 1				
Hood,cf	6 0 1 3 1					Boeckel,3b	11 0 3 1 7				
Konety,1b	9 0 1 30 1					Maran'le,ss	10 0 3 1 9				
Ward,ss	10 0 0 5 10					O'Neil,c	3 0 0 4 1				
Krueger,c	2 1 0 4 3					aChristen'y	1 0 1 0 0				
Elliott,c	7 0 0 1 2					Gowdy,c	6 0 1 6 1				
Cadore,p	10 0 0 1 13					Oescheger,p	8 0 1 11 0				
Total....36 1 9 78 34						Total....35 1 15 78 42					

a Batted for O'Neil in ninth inning.
Errors—Pick (3), Olson, Krueger.

Brooklyn	0 0 0	0 1 0	0 0 0		
	0 0 0	0 0 0	0 0 0	0 0	0—1
Boston	0 0 0	0 0 1	0 0 0		
	0 0 0	0 0 0	0 0 0	0 0	0—1

Called darkness.
Two-base hits—Maranville, Oescheger. Three-base hit—Cruise. Stolen base—Myers. Sacrifice hits—Hood, Oescheger, Powell, O'Neil, Holke, Cruise. Double play—Olson and Konetchy. Bases on balls—Off Cadore 5, Oescheger 3. Struck out—By Cadore 5, Oescheger 4. Wild pitch—Oescheger. Umpires—Messrs. McCormick and Hart.

26-INNING GAME ENDS IN TIE, 1-1

Oeschger and Cadore Both Go the Entire Distance in Spectacular Fashion

No Run Scored in the Last 20 Innings — Both Pitchers Have Great Support

Leon Cadore,
Brooklyn's Marathon Man

47 Cobb's "Strike" Game

Philadelphia Athletics vs. Detroit Tigers, May 18, 1912

NO PLAYER EVER CAME FREIGHTED WITH MORE PSYCHOLOG-ical baggage than Ty Cobb had to carry with him on his road to greatness. A man possessed, he played with all the ferocity of an alley cat in its ninth life, one who would gladly gnaw off its own leg in an effort to escape and get at its tormentor. Some said it was a throwback to his youth, when, in what was delicately termed an "accident", his mother shot his father, mistaking him, she said, for an intruder. Others merely ascribed it to his orneryness and cussedness. Whatever it was, as a hate-monger, Cobb never batted below .400.

Oh, sure, there was some Southern gentility in the man known as "The Georgia Peach." If one of the opposing number ever inadvertently got a foot under one of his descending spikes, Cobb, ever the Southern gentleman, with unimpeachable courtesy would hospitably allow it to remain there. And, as a thank-you-m'aam gesture, land atop it with full force, all the better, he figured, to teach him some baseball manners. And if an infielder were to receive the ball before Cobb arrived at a base and hold it as if to make a tag on the advancing whirlwind known as Cobb, Cobb would merely come flying in, sharpened spikes first, as if to l'arn him a lesson in good breeding, almost as if someone had entered a door before the woman they were holding it for.

For nothing hurt Cobb worse than not to be first at everything he did—in life as well as batting. He simply had to be first, period. The story is told of how Cobb, as a rookie, roomed with a fellow southerner who had come up as a pitcher with the Tigers the same year as Cobb. Despite their supposed equality in status, Cobb had demanded, and received, certain rights he felt were due him, one of which was the right to bathe first after the game back in those days when ballparks offered no such accommodations for the visiting troops. One afternoon so the story goes, Cobb returned to the room only to find his roommate, who had been knocked out of the box in an early inning, soaking away his troubles in the tub. Infuriated that his roommate had even dared to have the nerve to enter the sanctum sudsorium first, Cobb, his eyes black with congested rage, promptly pulled him from the tub and belabored him, with both his words and his fists as well.

Cobb, who would oftimes work off his choler on the first innocent bystander he came across, took them took them all on, teammates and opponents alike. Twice he challenged Tiger catcher Boss Schmidt, one of the toughest men ever to lace on spikes. Schmidt, it was rumored, could drive nails into boards with his bare hands. Despite the fact that Cobb's stare could cause strong men to curl up like snails whose tails had been assaulted with salt, Schmidt both times made short work of Cobb the pugilist.

But such momentary setbacks never deterred Cobb the pugnacious. His on-the-field demeanor was that of man who possessed the fevered desire of one who wanted to delve into his opponent's interior and remove its contents.

Pretty soon Cobb had acquired the reputation around the league of someone who was so unrelenting that after he passed on to that great Umpire in the Sky, he would have his ashes thrown in his face. And the league became polarized into two factions: the pro and anti-Cobb legions. Nothing would give those in the anti-Cobb faction greater pleasure than to read his name in headlines on the obituary page.

By the year 1910, Cobb's sixth in the Majors, those in the anti-Cobb faction came out of their closets, determined to do him out of his fourth batting title. That was the year that the Chalmers Motor Car Company offered its most expensive touring car to the batting champion of the Major Leagues. With but one month remaining in the season, only one thing was certain: That the car would go to the American League champion, its two leaders, Cobb and Nap Lajoie hitting more than fifty points higher than those in the National League.

With but two weeks to go, Lajoie led Cobb by a mere four points, .375 to .371. Cobb was riding the bench because of an inflammation of his eye when Lajoie went on a hitting spree, collecting 23 hits in 10 games to push his average up to .380. Returning to the lineup, Cobb went 7 for 13 against second-place New York. Before his eye flared up again, forcing him to sit out the last two games of the year, he had built his average up to .385. With two games remaining for him to take the Chalmers away from Cobb, Lajoie went into St. Louis for a season-ending double-header against the hapless last-place Browns. There the hate Cobb bloc did their best to deny him the batting championship—and with it the Chalmers. On orders from their manager, Jack O'Con-nor, the Browns played back on the edge of the infield, allowing Lajoie to beat out a total of six infield bunts during the course of both games. Throughout the afternoon a steady procession of interested fans paraded up to the press box to look over the official scorer's shoulder and find out how he scored each and every bunt. However, once in the second game, they came away less than pleased, the time he scored one of Lajoie's bunts as a sacrifice instead of a base hit. This brought forward an outpouring of displeasure, even prompting one anonymous fan to send a note to the scorer which read: "If you can see where Lajoie gets a base hit instead of a sacrifice, I will give you an order for a forty-dollar suit of clothes."

However, despite the rooting interest of the anti-Cobb contin-gent, both on the field and off, the president of the American League, Ban Johnson, ruled that Cobb had won the batting title by less than one decimal point, .385 to .384, and suspended Browns' manager Jack O'Connor and pitcher Harry Howell for their con-nivance in the scheme to deprive him of same.

But even though Johnson had awarded the batting title—and the car—to Cobb, it did nothing to still the hatred of him through-out the league, his name a hissing byword to all right-thinking men everywhere. His every appearance in Philadelphia, where he had spiked third baseman Frank Baker during the 1909 pennant race, was greeted with catcalls and cries categorizing him as the illegiti-mate offspring to end all illegitimate offsprings. Cobb fared little better in New York where well-wishers, in words that would cause a Billingsgate fisherman to blush, called out their hope that he would contract bubonic plague and other unprintable diseases of the flesh.

But no matter how much Cobb tried to ignore the ignoble comments hurled in his direction, the man with a low brawling point was always one step away from going off. Finally, on May 15, 1912, the fit hit the shan—and vice versa. On that bright Wednesday afternoon, playing before a sparse Highland Park crowd, Cobb was subjected for three innings to a string of vile epithets which would be better addressed to fit on asbestos paper from a party seated behind the Detroit dugout. One man in particular,

later identified as Claude Lueker, secretary to former sheriff Tom Foley, was especially unrelenting in his treatment of the Detroit outfielder. Finally, Lueker, full of the coward rage which dares to burn but not blaze, hurled out the one fighting word which one never dared to utter to Cobb: "Half-nigger." Now, there was one string in Cobb's heart that was best not to vibrate. And this was it! It was an eruption that would have left the casual observer with the impression that his boiler had just erupted as Cobb vaulted into the stands and laid hands on Lueker. For a brief second the sight was one of Cobb and Lueker tumbling over each other much like

Ty Cobb, the man who didn't come to play, May 18, 1912

clothes in a dryer, bobbing to the surface with Cobb always on top, doing a neat two-step on Lueker's head. Cobb's fellow Tigers, many of whom were on less than speaking terms with their volatile teammate, all rushed to the grandstand, there to watch with polite amusement, much as Mrs. Potter's class visiting a school for juvenile delinquents. But none interferred, feeling, as did Manager Hughie Jennings, that "it would be useless to restrain Ty, as he would have got his tormentor sooner or later. When Ty's Southern blood is aroused he is a bad man to handle." Finally, after Cobb had administered what one newspaper called "a good thrashing," the players and the private police intervened. Lueker immediately called upon the private graycoats to arrest Cobb; instead they escorted Lueker from the ballpark, forthwith. Nevertheless, umpire Silk O'Loughlin, who had been watching the goings-on from a comfortable distance, took the occasion to order Cobb out of the game, and American League president Johnson, who had been in attendance, suspended him for "conduct unbecoming."

To a man the Tigers rallied behind their teammate, sending a telegram to Johnson demanding that Cobb be reinstated. Or else. The "else" was that they would not play their next scheduled game in Philadelphia on Saturday, May 18th. Johnson, never one to give in to threats, refused to lift the suspension. And the Tigers, as obdurant as Balsaam's ass, dug in their feet and carried out their threat by not suiting up for the game.

Faced with the possible forfeit of the game and, a $5,000 fine, manager Jennings sent out a distress signal to any and all interested parties to fill in for his striking stars. Offering $50 and a chance to be a big leaguer for a day, Jennings rounded up a group of miscasts from St. Joseph's College and the local sandlots—all of whom could have had their pictures sent to the local constabulary for identification on suspicion of impersonating a ballplayer. He then added to this group of raw recruits three old-timers, inserting himself and his two coaches, Joe Sugden and Deacon Jim McGuire into the line-up. Together these three men who could

SHORT-LIVED REVOLT

 NEW YORK, N. Y., May 16.—Tyrus Raymond Cobb, of the Detroit Americans, hails from Georgia, and is conceded to be the greatest ball player of all time, appeared in a new role on the Hilltop yesterday, while the Highlanders were losing the final game of the series to the visitors by a score of 8 to 4. Just as the Detroits were preparing to go to bat in the fourth inning Cobb leaped into the grand stand and chastised a fan who had called him names. Tyrus was followed by the entire Detroit squad, but no one interfered until Cobb had handed the fan a good thrashing. Some of President Farrell's private graycoats finally broke up the scrap. The beaten fan requested the park police to arrest Cobb, but they refused, and he was led out of the stand by Thomas Davis, secretary of the New York Club. When Cobb returned to the bench his face was distorted with anger. He was immediately put out of the game by Umpire O'Loughlin. After the incident Hugh Jennings, the Detroit manager, went over to the press stand and explained that the fan had called Ty Cobb "a half-nigger." Jennings said no Southerner would stand such an insult. "I heard the remark," said Jennings, "but I knew it would be useless to restrain Ty, as he would have got his tormenter sooner or later. When Ty's Southern blood is aroused he is a bad man to handle." According to the "American," the man whom Cobb assaulted, is Claude Lueker, secretary for Tom Foley, formerly sheriff. He is a pressman by trade, but lost one hand and most of the other a little more than a year ago while working on a morning newspaper. Lueker is quoted by the "American" as saying that he did not know why Cobb singled him out for attack, and that after Cobb knocked him down he (Cobb) kicked Lueker and spiked him in the side.

TIGERS QUIT FIELD WHEN TOLD COBB'S SUSPENSION STOOD

Johnson and Navin Hasten Here to Confer on Strike

President of League Stands Pat---Players May Be Suspended for Season

Realizing that they were inviting the severest punishment by defying the stringent regulations governing the conduct of the players of the American League, the entire Detroit team went on a strike yesterday with the declaration that not a man composing it would play again under the colors of their club until Ty Cobb was reinstated.

As they had announced on Friday, every one of the players, including such well-known ball tossers as Sam Crawford, Jim Delehanty, George Mullin and Ownie Bush, refused to meet the Athletics at Shibe Park during the afternoon, when they learned that President Ban Johnson, of the American League, had not revoked his suspension of Cobb for striking a spectator at the New York Highlanders' grounds on last Wednesday.

STRIKING TIGERS FINED $100 EACH---JOHNSON DOES NOT REINSTATE TY COBB

charitably be called "veterans" averaged 43-plus years of age, had more than 68 years of service and had started playing baseball back in The Paleolithic Age—they were so ancient that baseball writer Bugs Baer wrote that "they could sleep in a swamp without mosquito netting." Putting this rag-tag group in uniforms did not produce Major Leaguers any more than baking kittens in the oven produces biscuits.

The game was, in fact, no game at all, the Athletics taking turns laughing and scoring on their way to a 24-2 romp, with every one of their eight regulars having at least one hit and one run and with more than a few, like second baseman Eddie Collins, having a brace of both.

The next day the strike was over, Ty Cobb intervening with his teammates. The man who had once been as lonesome as Robinson Crusoe's goat was touched by their solidarity in his behalf and now, telling them that he had "appreciated what they had done for him," implored them to go back to work or face being expelled by the American League.

But even as the regular Tigers took the field, eight of those who bobbed to baseball's surface as Tigers-for-a-day had had a chance to be part of one of baseball's most memorable moments—only two of those who filled in ever seeing their names in the boxscore again, Jennings and the third baseman Maharg, and then only for one more game apiece. Ironically, the one player who got the short end of the bat was the man who had taken Cobb's place in centerfield. His full name, Leinhauser, was too long for the typesetters and it came out in one of those bulky mattresses of printed stuff known as the Sunday papers as "L'n'h's'r," so nobody reading the boxscore the next morning would know for certain whether his full moniker was Lichtenheiser, Lagenhassinger, Loopenhauser or what, or so one writer opined. But whatever it was, it sure wasn't Cobb. There was only one of him.

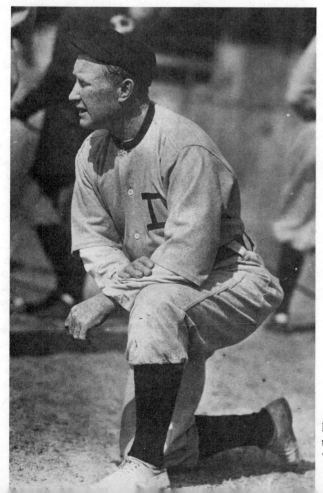

Detroit manager Hughie Jennings, who came off the base lines to pinch-hit in the famous "strike" game

STRIKEBREAKERS RUDELY TREATED

Game Was Howling Farce, But Mackmen Profited Greatly Their Individual Averages

BY JIM NASIUM

In the absence of the regular employes of the Detroit baseball machine, who have revolted against the mailed fist of plutocracy by laying down their tools and walking out of the shop just before the whistle blew, our Athletics yesterday met the Detroit "strikezreakers" inside the stockade of the works and wallowed them around in the mire of defeat to the merry tune of 24 to 2, while outside the mob howled and across the moor a little bird sang to its mate "cuckoo! cuckoo!"

The strikers themselves sat in the upper pavilion and piped off the guys who were trying to nab their jobs, but no attempt was made to picket the works and there was no rioting or use of violence in order to prevent the strike breakers from going to work. There wasn't a brick thrown by the strikers during the whole afternoon. There wasn't anything shown by the strikebreakers that necessitated such severe measures by the men who had walked out, but the fact that the spectators restrained themselves only goes to show what a long suffering assemblage it was.

It would be a libel on the national frolic to dip into the details of the course of events and attempt to give any idea of how the runs spattered over the pan, and the show was such a travesty on the popular pastime that fully one-third of the fifteen thousand persons who had gathered at Shibe Park just to see what would come off started for the gate to get their money back before four innings had been floundered through. When they failed in this they returned, however, and took the whole thing as a huge joke. Now it's up to somebody to show us who the joke is on.

* * *

ATHLETICS	ab.	r.	bh.	th.	sh.	sb.	po.	a.	e.
Maggert, lf	6	2	3	6	0	0	0	0	0
Strunk, cf	6	3	1	7	0	0	0	0	0
Collins, 2b	6	4	5	5	0	0	1	1	0
Baker, 3b	5	3	2	4	0	1	0	1	0
Murphy, rf	5	4	2	4	0	2	1	0	0
McInnis, 1b	6	2	4	6	0	2	7	1	0
Barry, ss	4	2	2	2	0	3	1	1	0
Lapp, c	4	1	2	1	1	0	16	1	1
Coombs, p	1	0	0	0	0	0	0	0	0
Brown, p	3	2	2	4	0	0	0	2	0
Pennock, p	1	1	1	2	0	0	0	0	0
Totals	43	24	26	42	2	10	27	8	1

DETROIT	ab.	r.	bh.	th.	sh.	sb.	po.	a.	e.
McGarr, 2b	4	0	0	0	0	0	1	3	1
Maharg, 3b	1	0	0	0	0	0	0	2	0
Irwin, 3b c	3	0	2	6	0	0	0	1	0
Travers, p	3	0	0	0	0	0	0	7	1
McGarvey, lf	3	0	0	0	0	1	1	0	1
Leinhauser, cf	4	0	0	0	0	0	1	1	0
Sugden, 1b	4	1	1	1	0	0	13	3	1
McGuire, c	2	1	1	1	0	0	4	3	2
Coffee, 3b	0	0	0	0	0	0	2	2	1
Meany, ss	2	0	0	0	0	0	0	3	0
Ward, rf	2	0	0	0	0	0	2	0	0
xJennings	1	0	0	0	0	0	0	0	0
Totals	29	2	4	8	0	1	24	24	7

xBatted for Travers in ninth.

Athletics—
Runs .... 3 0 3 0 8 4 4 2 x—24
Base hits ...... 3 1 3 2 7 4 3 3 x—26
Detroit—
Runs .... 0 0 0 0 2 0 0 0 0—2
Base hits ...... 0 0 0 1 2 0 0 0 1—4

Hits—Off Coombs, 0 in 3 innings, 8 at bat; hits off Brown, 3 in 3 innings, 12 at bat; hits off Pennock, 1 in 3 innings, 9 at bat. Runs Earned—Athletics, 14. Two-base hits—Strunk, Maggert, Pennock, Barry. Three-base hits—McInnis, Murphy, Brown, Strunk, Maggert, Baker Irwin, 2. Left on bases—Athletics, 4; Detroit, 4. Struck out—By Coombs, 3; Brown, 5; Pennock, 7; Travers, 1. Double plays—Meany to Coffee. First base on error—Athletics, 2. First base on called balls—Off Coombs, 2; Pennock, 1; Travers, 7. Hit by pitched ball—By Brown, 1; (Meany); by Pennock, 1, (Coffee). Missed grounders and fumbles—McGarvey, Sugden. Wild throws—Lapp, 1; McGuire, 2; Irwin, 1. Dropped thrown balls—McGarr, Meany. Umpires—Dineen and Perrine. Time, 1.45.

48 Ed Rommel's 17-Inning Relief Appearance

Philadelphia Athletics vs. Cleveland Indians, July 10, 1932

THOSE FEW BASEBALL AFFICIANADOS WHO REMEMBER THE name Eddie Rommel can undoubtedly be entered on the head of a pin with more than enough room left over for a choir of angels. But Eddie Rommel was one of baseball's best pitchers in that very short period of time between the formal leave-taking of Walter Johnson and the full-fledged entry of Lefty Grove. Generally credited with bringing the knuckleball into baseball, Rommel toiled diligently for an aggregation that could only aspire to the term "team," the Philadelphia Athletics of the 1920s.

The Philadelphia Athletics were a reflection of one man: Connie Mack, the rail-thin former catcher christened Cornelius McGillicuddy who took on the appearance of a scarecrow done up in ministerial clothing. Managing his team from the bench, his scorecard always at the ready to wave a fielder in or out and crossing and uncrossing his legs to signal the hit-and-run, Mack had put together the most successful franchise in the first decade-and-a-half of the American League's existence. He numbered amongst his charges such future Hall of Famers as Eddie Plank, Rube Waddell, Home Run Baker, Eddie Collins, Chief Bender, and Herb Pennock, together with other near-greats in the form of Jack Coombs, Stuffy McInnis, "Bullet" Joe Bush, Jack Barry and Harry Davis. Together, they won six pennants, three World Series and 1222 games, for a winning percentage of .605. In short, they were a dynasty on their way to happening.

But then a funny thing happened to the dynasty-to-be: in 1914 they met the upstart Boston Braves. Called the "Miracle Team" for their unprecedented stretch drive which took them from eighth place on July 4th to the pennant, the Braves won going away at the wire by 10½ games. And, in what was called the greatest upset in sports history, the A's lost in four straight to the Braves for the first "sweep" in World Series history.

Whether it was the humiliation of the stunning loss to the Braves, as some suggested, the imminent bidding war with the fledgling Federal League, as others claimed, the precarious condition of Mack's finances—made all the more so by the growing payroll and additions to Shibe Park—as many hinted, or baseball's uncertain future in the face of the impending World War that impelled Mack to break up the team is not known. But what is known is that Mack indeed broke up the A's, into more pieces than even Humpty Dumpty experienced. And with more disastrous results, if that were possible.

For the 1915 A's made baseball history by becoming the only pennant winner to plummet from the penthouse to the cellar in one short year. Playing without the services of stars like Eddie Collins, Eddie Plank, Chief Bender, Home Run Baker, Jack Coombs and Jack Barry, the A's went from a record of 99 and 53 to one of 43 and 109, a turnaround of 56 games as measured in baseball mathematics. Made up of culls and castoffs, the A's were so decimated that the only thing missing was a note from their mothers attempting to explain their emotional absence.

The 1916 edition was even worse; in fact, they may well have been the worst team of all time. Together, this desolate flotsam

trapped in players' uniforms won but 36 of their 153 games (a pathetic .235 won-lost percentage, lowest in modern Major League history), led the league in no less than eight negative categories, and two of its pitchers compiled the combined woeful figure of 2-36. It was a team with no presence and even less future.

The years 1917, 1918 and 1919 were no kinder to Connie as the Mackmen continued to hold an exclusive lease on the American League cellar. However, 1920 was the year in which Mack, instead of backing and filling his roster with baseball's vagabonds, went back out into the marketplace and began buying players. And one of the first was a tall and muscular pitcher named Eddie Rommel. Rommel, who had pitched two years in the International League winning a total of 34 games, had all the qualities Mack liked in a pitcher. But instead of being a power pitcher, he depended upon a pitch that danced its way up to the plate, causing batters to skip around like small girls jumping under a skip rope. The pitch would become known as the "knuckler," and Rommel would become known as its prime purveyor.

But even Rommel and his knuckler were not enough for the A's to vacate their permanent possession, last place, as he won seven of the team's 48 games. In 1921 Rommel raised his number of wins to 16, but lost a league-leading 23 as the A's finished in eighth place for the seventh straight year. In 1923 both Rommel and the A's improved. Rommel won a league-leading 27 games— only one of two times a pitcher has led the league in losses one year and come back to lead in wins the next—and the A's finally relinquished their stranglehold on last place.

Suddenly, Rommel's was a stock that had trebled in value as over the next three years he and his knuckler averaged 19 wins a year. And the infusion of Rommel's arm, both in starting roles and in relief, began to take effect on the A's as well—as they began to rise slowly in the standings like a balloon half-filled with gas, from eighth in 1921 to 7th in 1922 to 6th in 1923 to 5th in 1924. But 1925 was to be Rommel's last big year. For even though his knuckler put less strain on his arm than other pitches, he had been a one-man pitching staff for the A's during their lean years, averaging over 280 innings a year. And 1925 was the year when the A's made some of the greatest acquisitions in the history of baseball, adding to their roster the names of Jimmie Foxx, Mickey Cochrane, and pitchers Lefty Grove and Rube Walberg.

Now faced with a surfeit of good pitching and the realization that Rommel's pitching wing had begun to feel the burden of single-handedly carrying the A's for six years, Mack moved Rommel to the bullpen where he became, at best, a spot pitcher. It was a move which not only prolonged Rommel's career, but also gave him a chance to become part of one of baseball's great games.

The date of the game was Sunday, July 10, 1932, and Philadelphia, with no Sunday baseball in Pennsylvania because of the then-existing Blue Laws, had scheduled a one-game series in Cleveland. Mack, his investments wiped out by the Depression, was once again in a financial pinch despite the fact that the A's had just won three straight pennants and two World Series. And so, to

Philadelphia A's manager and owner, Connie Mack, the Grand Old Man of Baseball, and the champion pinchpenny as well

keep costs down, Mack took a skeleton crew to Cleveland, using the train as his traveling hotel. It was worse than a blunder; it was a crime—especially for the dozen or so Athletics who had to endure one of the longest games in the history of baseball. And, not incidental to our story, dear readers, one of the strangest games in baseball history as well.

The game, played in that little bandbox of a park known as League Park—baseball's answer to fallen arches—was played on a day so hot that everything that was supposed to stick together came apart and everything that was supposed to stay apart stuck together. With but two pitchers to call on, Rommel drew the short straw as Mack decided to use the younger one, Lew Krause, holding Rommel in reserve. It was akin to losing an election bet, as Rommel would soon discover.

Reserve came quicker than anticipated as the Indians greeted Krause with four hits and three runs in the first inning and Mack, going to the only other egg left in his basket, went to Rommel. As Krause went to take over the Lifebuoy concession in the showers, Rommel and what was left of his knuckler came in to pick up his fallen, sputtering torch. Forced by necessity and fate to stand and deliver, Rommel came in in the second to hold the Indians. But instead of holding the Indians, they held him, making him feel like General Custer at Little Big Horn. Without bothering to embroider, feeling that truth makes all things plain, let it be known that the Indians scored three runs off Rommel in the third, one each in the

fifth and sixth, six in the seventh and one in the ninth, the official scorer getting writer's cramp trying to keep track of the hits and runs—now both high up in the paint cards. One batter in particular, Cleveland shortstop Johnny Burnett, had become a repeating decimal and a nuisance to both the official scorer and to Rommel. All Burnett had done that hot July day was to get seven singles and two doubles in 11 at bats for nine hits, a Major League record.

Incredibly, Cleveland's 15 runs weren't enough! The A's also had participated whole-heartedly in the little recreations being played with the pieces of ash called bats—especially Jimmie Foxx, who had six hits and three home runs for a total of 15 total bases—and center fielder Mule Haas had made three unbelievable shoe-string catches to "hold" the Indians to 15 runs, the same number the A's had after nine innings. The game would go into extra innings.

And so, Rommel, his arm tired, his pitches more so, continued to pitch, his heart now worn visibly on his sleeve. And while the Indian batters continued to play on him as a stringed instrument, plunking him for a hit here and a hit there, they were now as tired as Rommel, having also passed through the furnace of what was a boiling July day, and the score remained at 15-all through the 15th. In the 16th the A's scored two runs off the third Indian pitcher, Wes Ferrell. But Rommel, his arm all but draped in black crepe, couldn't hold the lead and surrender two of his own. The game went on into the 17th and the 18th in front of just a few ennuied and vaguely curious fans.

Cleveland Shortstop Johnny Burnett, who set a record of nine hits in the 18-inning game.

And then, in the 18th, Jimmie Foxx drove home the A's 18th run with his sixth hit and Rommel, his eyes full of the hopeless tricky defiance that can be found in a cur cornered by his tormentors, went back out to the mound one more time. It was to be the last time. This time, reverting back to a form he had shown 13 years before when the A's first brought him up, he threw his knuckler almost as if he were pulling rabbits out of the hat with a flick of his wrist. And the Indians, knowing what he was throwing even if its nature puzzled them, went down docilely.

Finally, four hours and five minutes after the game had started, it was over. The carnage included 58 hits by the two teams, nine by one player and 29 given up by one pitcher, Ed Rommel—all records. And it was to be Rommel's last major league win and last major league performance, a victor by victory undone.

Knuckleballer Ed Rommel who went far beyond the union limit in relief, 17 innings.

Records Flop As Athletics Take Indians

CLEVELAND, July 10 (AP).— Cleveland and Philadelphia battled wildly and stubbornly today for eighteen innings—two full regulation games—before Jimmy Foxx crossed the plate with the run that gave the Athletics a hard-earned 18-to-17 victory.

Fifty-eight base-hits rattled off the offerings of five pitchers in today's baseball marathon, three of them home runs by Foxx and one a home run by Earl Averill.

Three New Records.

Two new all-time records and one modern record were established during the course of the long affair. Between 'em, the two clubs made a total of fifty-eight hits, as compared with an all-time record of fifty-one made by the Phillies (26) and the Cubs (25) on Aug. 25, 1922. Today the Athletics made twenty-five hits and the Indians thirty-three.

Nine of the Indians' hits were made by Shortstop Johnny Burnett in eleven times at bat. The previous record was seven hits in seven times at bat made by Wilbert Robinson, former Dodger manager, while playing for Baltimore against St. Louis, June 10, 1892.

Cleveland's thirty-three hits established a new modern record for hits by one club in one game, surpassing the thirty-one made by the Giants against Cincinnati, June 9, 1901. The all-time record is thirty-six, made by the Philadelphia Nationals against Louisville, Aug. 17, 1894.

A Giddy Thing.

In the ninth inning, Ed Morgan, Cleveland first sacker, allowed Dykes' easy roller to go between his legs. The error snatched victory from the Tribe, which was leading, 14 to 13, with two men out. As it was, Simmons walked and the irrepressible Foxx then singled to score both runners and keep the A's in the running.

Foxx hit homers Nos. 31, 32 and 33, batting in eight runs, scored the winning run and played hobb generally with the Indians.

PHILADELPHIA					at	CLEVELAND				
	ab	r	h	e			ab	r	h	e
Haas rf	9	3	2	0		Porter rf	10	3	3	0
Cramer cf	8	2	2	0		Burn't ss	11	4	9	1
Dkes 3b	10	2	3	0		Aver'l cf	9	3	5	0
Sim's lf	9	4	5	0		Vos'ik lf	10	2	2	0
Foxx 1b	9	4	6	0		Mor'n 1b	11	1	5	1
McN'r ss	10	0	2	0		Myatt c	7	2	1	0
Heving c	4	0	1	0		Cissell 2b	9	1	4	2
Madt'k c	5	0	0	0		Kamm 3b	7	1	2	0
Willi's 2b	8	1	2	0		Brown p	4	0	2	1
Krause p	1	0	0	0		Hudlin p	0	0	0	0
Rommel p	7	2	3	1		Ferrell p	5	0	0	0
Totals	80	18	25	1		Totals	84	17	33	5

Phila .. 201 201 702 000 000 201—18
Cleveland 303 011 601 000 000 200—17

49 Three Men on a Base

Brooklyn Robins vs. Boston Braves, August 15, 1926

THE BROOKLYN OF THE MID-1920S WAS A WONDEROUS PLACE to behold. It was then a borough filled with every conceivable classical incubus of architecture: Victorian mansions decorated with cupolas; fanciful gingerbread designs with curlicues; and houses festooned with Gothic lacework. All of these wedding-cake structures decorated tree-lined neighborhoods with august names, tenanted by working-class families, many of whom were second- and third-generation Americans. Brooklyn also was the proud home of the Brooklyn Bridge—that crowning masterpiece of Victorianism—Coney Island, and the borough's most important monument, Ebbets Field.

Built back in 1912 by the-then president of the Dodgers, not incidentally named Charles Ebbets, Ebbets Field was surrounded by Montgomery Street, Sullivan Place, McKeever Place and Bedford Avenue, all of which came after the fact. Soon the streets began to run crazy, breaking themselves up into small strips, making sharp angles and curves, all the better to accomodate the crow's feet of trolley tracks laid down to bring the fans to where the games were. Instantly Ebbets Field became the center of a huzzaing concourse of humanity.

No matter the names of the four streets which bordered the stadium, its real location was in the hearts and minds of loyal Brooklyn rooters who packed it every afternoon in an early version of group therapy. There swarms of adenoidal lummoxes, their lightest whisper like that of someone calling cattle home across the sands of time, whistled, hooted, stamped, cheered and communicated their advice at the tops of their lungs with all the gusto of a tub-thumping revival meeting. Any alienist in the land who, having listened to those brassy yells reminiscent of a steam calliope and the hopeful violence in their voices for their darlings, would have sprung at them and held them down with one hand all the while gleefully signing the necessary certificates of lunacy transferring them from the world's largest psychiatric chamber to a smaller, more restful one.

It was, therefore, poetic justice that those inmates running the asylum known as Ebbets Field should get one of their own down on the field: Floyd Caves Herman, better knwon as "Babe." It was to be the perfect fusion of souls.

Babe Herman was like nothing which had traveled down the baseball pike before or since. Looking like an altar boy in search of a service, Herman combined palm-leaf ears with a wide-open face which looked as if he had just seem something he couldn't believe. His size was less large than spacious, a tall, angular 6′4″, which was seriously deminimized by a perpetual slouch which gave him the appearance of someone who had left the hanger in his shirt.

However, Herman was far from a slouch in the batter's box. Called by Rogers Hornsby "The perfect free swinger," the left-handed hitting Herman coupled a well-timed swing with tremendous power in his right forearm. Even today, half a century after he last played with any regularity, Babe Herman still is the all-time Dodger leader in slugging percentage with .557 and has the highest batting average ever for a Dodger, .393 in 1930.

But Herman's fame rests not on his hitting, but on his other skills. Or lack thereof. For in that double-entry bookkeeping that entraps all baseball statisticians, where the debits and credits attributed to players are almost as precise as accountants' ledgers, Babe Herman's deficiencies in the field and on the basepaths leave his account deeply in the red.

Herman began his professional career in 1921, playing for Edmonton of the Western Canadian League where he hit .330. Over the first five years of his career he was to play for 12 teams and 18 different managers, always hitting with power and fielding with a prayer. Most of those who had Herman around feared for their young outfielder's life and their own sanity, letting him go rather than risk the chance of Herman becoming a fatality afield. Playing for Omaha in 1922, Herman was hitting .416 after 92 games when a pop fly hit him on the head. The owner demanded that Herman be fired, telling the manager, "I don't care if he's hitting 4,000, I am not going to have players who field the ball with their skulls!" And so it went, Herman going from road stop to road stop, carrying a big stick at the plate and on the field playing as if he were carrying his glove for a friend, his managers suffering from illness and fatigue—they were sick and tired of him.

After three more years of masquerading as a part-time hitter and a full-time rolling stone, Herman finally came to rest in Brooklyn in 1926. And then he almost kept rolling as Brooklyn,

Ebbets Field, home of the Brooklyn Dodgers

after having purchased his contract from Minneapolis for $15,000, tried mightily to give him back to the Millers for a no-name named Johnny Butler. But the Millers, having seen enough of Herman and undoubtedly fearing their casualty policy would be revoked, turned a deaf ear to Brooklyn's plea.

Back in the mid-1920s, when the decade was known as "The Era of Wonderful Nonsense," none were more wonderful than the boys from Brooklyn, then called the Robins after their field manager Wilbert Robinson and "The Daffiness Boys" after their exploits—on the field and off. And no one was to give that group of life's losing stuntment more coloration than Floyd Caves "Babe" Herman.

Herman quickly became a Brooklyn favorite, revered for his shortcomings, which were many. Teammate Dazzy Vance, after having watched Herman treat a ball in the outfield with all the deference of a leper and then throw to the wrong base only said, "The Babe is a hard guy to outthink; because how can you outthink a guy who doesn't think?" Other times, his base running left something to be desired, like direction. Again Vance filled in the blank, calling Herman "The Headless Horseman of Ebbets Field."

Whether the Babe was communicating with the fans or communing with nature, his head always seemed to be somewhere else. Those tireless old gentlemen who recount tales worth telling and retelling tell of how one day Herman was sitting in the dugout alongside manager Robinson when one of the opposing team's batsmen hit a ball down the left-field line. Robinson jumped up, trying to gauge whether the ball had gone fair or foul. Unable to see, he turned to Herman. "What happened out there, Babe?," he asked. The Babe, involved at that point with a newspaper, looked up sheepishly and could only say, "I don't know, Robbie, I was reading the paper."

Herman's reputation as a fielder—or non-fielder, creating respect at the plate and disrespect in the outfield—was so widespread that when second baseman Fresco Thompson joined the early "Toys 'R' Us" franshise, Herman greeted him with "It's a hell of a note to dress with a .250 hitter," and Thompson, without batting an eye or a hit, replied, "How do you think I feel dressing with a .250 fielder?"

And then there was his fielding. Or what passed for it. One writer, John Lardner, once penned, "Floyd Caves Herman did not always catch flyballs on the top of his head, but he could do it in a pinch." Others were less kind, calling his glove a lethal weapon, his head a target.

One day, Herman feeling hurt at what he considered the personal and unkind criticism of his fielding, approached one of the columnists. "You make me look like a clown all the time . . . Look, I'm a ballplayer. I make a living playing ball, like you make yours writing. And I got a wife and kids to support. If you keep on making fun of me, it's going to hurt me." The writer, feeling pity for the big guy slouched in front of him, said he understood. "I never thought of it that way, Babe. From now on," he promised, "I'll stop poking fun at you." Herman patted him on the back, pleased that their little talk had proven fruitful and that he had given a lie to the slander. Then he proceeded to fumble in his pocket and pull out what looked to be the butt of a slightly-used cigar and jammed it in his mouth. As the writer made as if to get his matches to light the stub, Herman waved him off, saying only, "Never mind, it's lit," and then puffed a few times as if to prove his point. The writer, only a few seconds before feeling contrite about having made fun of Herman, couldn't believe his eyes. "It's all off," he roared. "Nobody who carries lit cigars in his pocket can tell me he isn't a clown!"

Floyd Caves Herman, a mere "Babe" in the woods, and on the basepaths

However, it wasn't his fielding which was to win Babe Herman timeless allure, but instead his base running, something he had gotten down to a science, even if it wasn't a science known to mankind. Take the year 1930, for instance, the year Herman was to hit .393, and a year when Herman always seemed to be on base, there to commit blunders, crimes and other absurdities. On May 30th, when Robin first baseman Del Bissonette hit a home run, and on September 15th, when Brooklyn shortstop Glenn Wright performed the same trick, Herman, unartful Dodger-hy-phen-Robin, was standing somewhere around the basepaths. And both times, more intent on following the flight of the ball than the flow of the play, he was passed on the basepaths by the two baserunners, thus setting an unofficial record for being passed on the basepaths twice in a single season.

Then there was August 15, 1926, when in an affair of no great moment—the first game of a Sunday double-header between the Robins and the Boston Braves— Herman made his name for all time in one of the most memorable plays in all of baseball history. Because of his base running.

We pick up the game in progress. Boston is ahead 1-0 going into the bottom of the seventh. As Brooklyn prepares to take its turn at bat, reserve catcher Mickey O'Neil, sitting on the bench next to manager Robinson, begins to bitch and moan to Robbie that he "Never gets out of the dugout," and looking for something, anything to do, offers to fill in at third for coach Otto Miller in the seventh. It's an offer Robinson would have been well advised to refuse, but instead, having heard enough grousing from O'Neil, directs him to take Miller's place in the third-base coaching box for the inning. It's an inning neither O'Neil nor baseball will ever forget.

Dazzy Vance, another of Brooklyn's "Daffiness Boys" and original possessor of third base.

With O'Neil down at third looking like he knows what he's about, the lead-off batter, Johnny Butler, steps into the batter's box to do battle with Boston pitcher Johnny Wertz. Butler promptly singles and seconds later scores the tying run on catcher Hank DeBerry's double with coach O'Neil showing the way. Pitcher Dazzy Vance then singles with DeBerry, held up by O'Neil, stopping at third. Then, after Wertz hits Chick Fewster to load the bases full of Brooklyn, Boston manager Davey Bancroft lifts Wertz and brings on lefty George Mogridge in relief. Mogridge gets the first batter to face him, right fielder Merwin Jacobson, on a pop up.

All of which, of course, only serves to introduce our hero, Babe Herman, who now comes to the plate with the bases loaded, the score tied and one man out. Mogridge comes in with his speciality, a curve, but it hangs up around the letters and the Babe frescoes it, driving it high off the right-field wall in the direction of Bedford Avenue. DeBerry scampers across with the go-ahead run, but Vance at second, aided and abetted by the unsure O'Neil, hesitates, thinking the ball might be caught by Braves' right fielder Jimmy Welsh, then lumbers off in the direction of third. Meanwhile, Fewster on first, figuring there's no way in hell anyone short of the man Jack met at the top of the beanstalk would catch the ball, has started to tear around the bases at full speed. Ditto for the man right behind him, Babe Herman, running with his head down as if he were looking to check if his fly were open.

About this time in our scenario the viciously-hit ball has caromed off the wall back toward second baseman Doc Gautreau. As Herman comes sliding into second, someone calls out to Gautreau to "Throw home," which he does. Meanwhile, back at third, Dazzy Vance, who has once rounded it, now stops half way up the line, called to a halt by O'Neil, and retreats to the safety of third, followed by Boston catcher Al Siemer, menacingly waving the ball at Vance. During the goings-on, Chick Fewster, who had started this Marx Brothers' stateroom routine, at first, has continued on his merry, and is now on his way toward third under a head of steam. But so too is Herman, who upon hearing the call to Gautreau to "Throw home" had figured the throw was meant for Fewster, not Vance. Seeing the small commotion taking place down the third base line Herman bethought to himself that Fewster was caught in a run-down, and what better place to watch than from third?

Fewster, bearing down on third, now notices that the "Occupied" sign has been hung out and tries to stop. Unfortunately, just at the moment he is disengaging gears, along comes Herman, now running with blinkers on, and, as one writer put it, "Passing Fewster like the Limited passing a whistle stop," comes sliding into third from the other side of the bag.

With third base taking on the look of a suddenly crowded subway stop, Braves third baseman Eddie Taylor hollers down to Siemer for the ball. Time being all too brief for a course in etiquette, he starts tagging everyone in good standing in the belief that someone is redundant. Herman, who was out for having passed Fewster on the basepaths, is now standing on the bag grinning with embarrassment and disbelief. But to make sure of the out, Taylor tags him; although some think tagging was too good for Herman. Next Taylor tags Vance, but the pitcher, after regarding everything around him as inconsequential, determines that the bag rightfully belongs to him and he's not budging.

One who is budging is Fewster, who after watching the confusion taking place on third decides there must be a more relaxing place around somewhere else. Figuring it's a bad bargain that can't run both ways, he starts to run back to second. Now Gautreau shouts down to Taylor for the ball, a shout which can barely be heard above the din of the crowd, a din that would all but drown out a 21-gun salute. Fewster, with Gautreau in pursuit, races past second on his way to right field, where Gautreau finally tags him on the head for the third out.

In the dugout, manager Wilbert Robinson, after witnessing the indigestible sight before him, is choking on expletives deleted. Finally, after overcoming the moment, he screams in the direction of Fewster, "They shoulda tagged him with a blackjack."

It was that kind of day and that kind of play. One which put the scorekeepers up for disability after they had recorded the passage of the ball; which was an utterly dependable scenario for Babe Herman and "The Daffiness Boys"; and which will go down in history as one of the most memorable plays of all time. And, oh yes, the run driven in by Herman won the game for Brooklyn if anyone cares.

But despite rumors to the contrary, Babe Herman did not triple into a triple play. The Babe merely doubled into a double play. Or, as sportswriter Jim Murray put it, "Herman doubled to load the base." And for years after, whenever anyone was to say "Brooklyn has three men on base," the answer he was sure to get in return was, "Yeah, which base?"

50 Bill Veeck's Midget

St. Louis Browns vs. Detroit Tigers, August 18, 1951

WHEN, ON THE MORNING OF JULY 5, 1951, BASEBALL'S PREmier promoter and professional gadfly, Bill Veeck, announced that he had purchased the St. Louis Browns, John Lardner was moved to write, "Many critics were surprised to know that the Browns could be bought; because they didn't know that the Browns were owned."

Indeed there were many who would have been surprised to know that the Browns even existed, including their fans who had shown their appreciation for their team's lack of success by failing to show up in record numbers. For most of their fifty-year existence the Browns had held what amounted to a permanent lease on the second division, finishing in the bottom four 38 times and in the cellar eight times. For years the chore of a Brownie fan had been relatively simple: All he had to do was look at the bottom of the standings in his morning paper and there they were. July 5, 1951, was no different—the Browns were two full games out of seventh. And driving.

Proclaiming that "The Browns are unable to beat their way out of a paper bag with a crowbar," the tieless and tireless Veeck rolled up his mental sleeves and went to work trying mightily to improve his team's sorry state—both on the field, where they were leading the league only in highest ERA, and in the stands, where the previous year they had finished dead last in attendance, not only for the Majors, but for all Triple A clubs as well. (Things had gotten so bad that when one prospective ticket buyer called the Browns switchboard the day after he had taken up residency to ask, "What time does the game start?" Veeck had answered, "What time can you get here?")

Immediately setting to work, Veeck dug into his bag of surefire tricks and hired Max Patkin as coach-hyphen-contortionist and signed up Satchel Paige, the ageless wonder who just three years earlier had helped Veeck's Cleveland Indians to the American League pennant, installing him in a rocking chair in the bullpen. He added new wrinkles, including Grandstand Manager's Day, calling upon the crowd to give signals in response to signs asking questions such as "Shall We Move the Infield Back?" and was rewarded for his efforts by beating the Philadelphia A's. And he capitalized on St. Louis' rich baseball tradition—if not that of the Browns—by hiring former Cardinal heroes Marty Marion and Harry Breecheen as coaches and Dizzy Dean as an announcer.

But despite Veeck's time-honored schemes for levying contributions from the public, the Browns continued to play in a cathedral hush to private parties. By now even Veeck was beginning to get the idea that the Browns would cause a limburger cheese factory to remain undiscovered on a hot day in August.

And so Veeck determined on one big promotion; something that would put both the St. Louis Browns on the baseball map and fans in the stands. Believing that all promotional gimmicks are transferable—"You just change the gag line"—Veeck resurrected the core of a short story by James Thurber in which a midget named Duke du Monville came to the plate, garnished it with his remembrance of John McGraw's hunchbacked mascot, Eddie

Bennett, mixed them all up with a birthday party for his radio sponsor, and *voila!*, he had a promotion worthy of the name Bill Veeck: Eddie Gaedel.

A number of preliminary steps were necessary to set up the promotional gag so that it would work. First there was the problem of getting some semblance of a crowd into Sportsman's Park for the game—always a challenge. Obviously the Browns, a team of men forgotten but not gone, couldn't do it on their own. There had to be another attraction. Then it came to Veeck: This was not only the American League's 50th Anniversary, but also Falstaff, the beer stuck with the sponsorship of those God-awful Brownies, was celebrating some birthday or other. Veeck decided to combine the two and went to the owners of the brewery, claiming that he had "something terrific" lined up for a doubleheader a couple of Sundays hence. The brewery bought it and put its salesmen to work pushing tickets, something almost as difficult as pushing its malt uphill.

Next Veeck called a theatrical booking agent in Chicago for one midget, standard size. The midget, one Eddie Gaedel, was smuggled into town unnoticed, and signed to a contract calling for the standard equity salary of $100 a day. Veeck borrowed a uniform bearing the number 1/8 from the small son of vice president Bill DeWitt, had the programs imprinted with the fractional number and ordered a large birthday cake for the occasion, properly decorated. Now all was in readiness for the big day!

Sunday, August 19, 1951, broke bright and clear. True to form, the Browns lost the first game of the doubleheader to the visiting Tigers. But nothing could dampen the spirit nor the enthusiasm of the Browns' staff as they bustled about the Veeck office-cum-apartment high atop Sportsman's Park, making sure all was in readiness for the second game. The cake, the programs and the little elf's shoes had all arrived. The Falstaff birthday party was about to begin.

After more than a few old cars and two couples in Gay Nineties dress had paraded around the field and Satchel Paige and the wandering troubadors had serenaded the 18,369 fans—the largest Brownie crowd at Sportsman's Park in many a year—a seven-foot cake was wheeled onto the field. When the cake was opened and a midget popped out, the Falstaff execs failed to see the humor. "A goddam midget . . . what's so goddam 'special' about that?" bellowed one, who had been promised "something special" for the company's birthday. But Veeck, sitting next to them in his rooftop aerie, merely gave them his old Mona Lisa smile.

The second game started while the Falstaff contingent fiddled in its seats, unsure of what they had seen or of what was so "special" about it. Stricken by the strange sickness that often afflicted visiting clubs in Sportsman's Park, the Tigers went down in order in the top of the first.

The public address announcer intoned those breathless words, "Now batting, Numberrrrrrrr one-eighth, Gay-dell, batting for Sauc-ier . . ." and the three-foot, seven-inch elfin Gaedel strutted up to home plate carrying a toy bat, even the Falstaff executives

191

began to get the idea. When Saucier, the displaced batter, looked up at Veeck's box and shook his fist, Veeck waved back and so did all the Falstaff executives, now sure of what Veeck had meant when he promised "something special."

As Gaedel took his one-eighth of a place in the batter's box, plate Umpire Ed Hurley called time. Enough was enough. The between-the-games promotion was now leaking into the game itself. "Get him out of here," he hollered at St. Louis manager Zack Taylor. But Taylor had been well-prepped and ran out of the dugout waving a legitimate American League contract. Hurley, seldom at a loss for words, was stricken speechless and waved for Detroit pitcher Bob Cain to get on with the game.

As Tiger catcher Bob Swift shifted out of his normal position and got down on both knees, Cain stared incredulously at the batter, looking for something—anything—resembling a strike zone. It was there, somewhere, about one-third the size of an ordinary one. While cameras clicked gleefully away, he threw in a high hard one. Ball one. And then another. Ball two. The strike zone seemed to be getting even smaller. And then a third ball came as Cain gave up the ghost. Gaedel now stared up at Veeck's box, where Veeck sat staring frostily back, having threatened the new Brownie that if he so much as tried swinging at any of the pitches,

"he would be shot." Gaedel stared back at Cain, who merely went through the motions without any emotions and threw him ball four. As the ball sailed over Gaedel's head, he threw away his miniature bat and strutted to first. When Jim Delsing came out to run for him, Gaedel patted him avuncularly on the rump and then, instead of leaving the field, strolled around the infield waving his cap to the collective cheers of the 18,369 delighted fans.

It was a moment to be remembered by all. By Eddie Gaedel, who after the game was told by Bob Broeg of the St. Louis *Post Dispatch,* "You're what I always wanted to be . . . an ex-big leaguer." By Bill Veeck, the master promoter, who often said he wanted to be remembered as "The Man Who Helped the Little Man." And by the Lords of Baseball, those stout-hearted and headed men, whose idea of fun was to wear brown shoes and to whom the very name Bill Veeck was an anathema. The very next day they ruled that the further use of midgets was inimical to the "best interests of the game" and sought to expunge from the record books the one at-bat of the smallest man ever to play in the Majors, without even an asterisk. But it was a moment that will live in baseball forever, a giant achievement in the cloak of a promotion.

Eddie Gaedel at bat, small man in a big league.